# Midnight Secretary

Story & Art by Tomu Ohmi

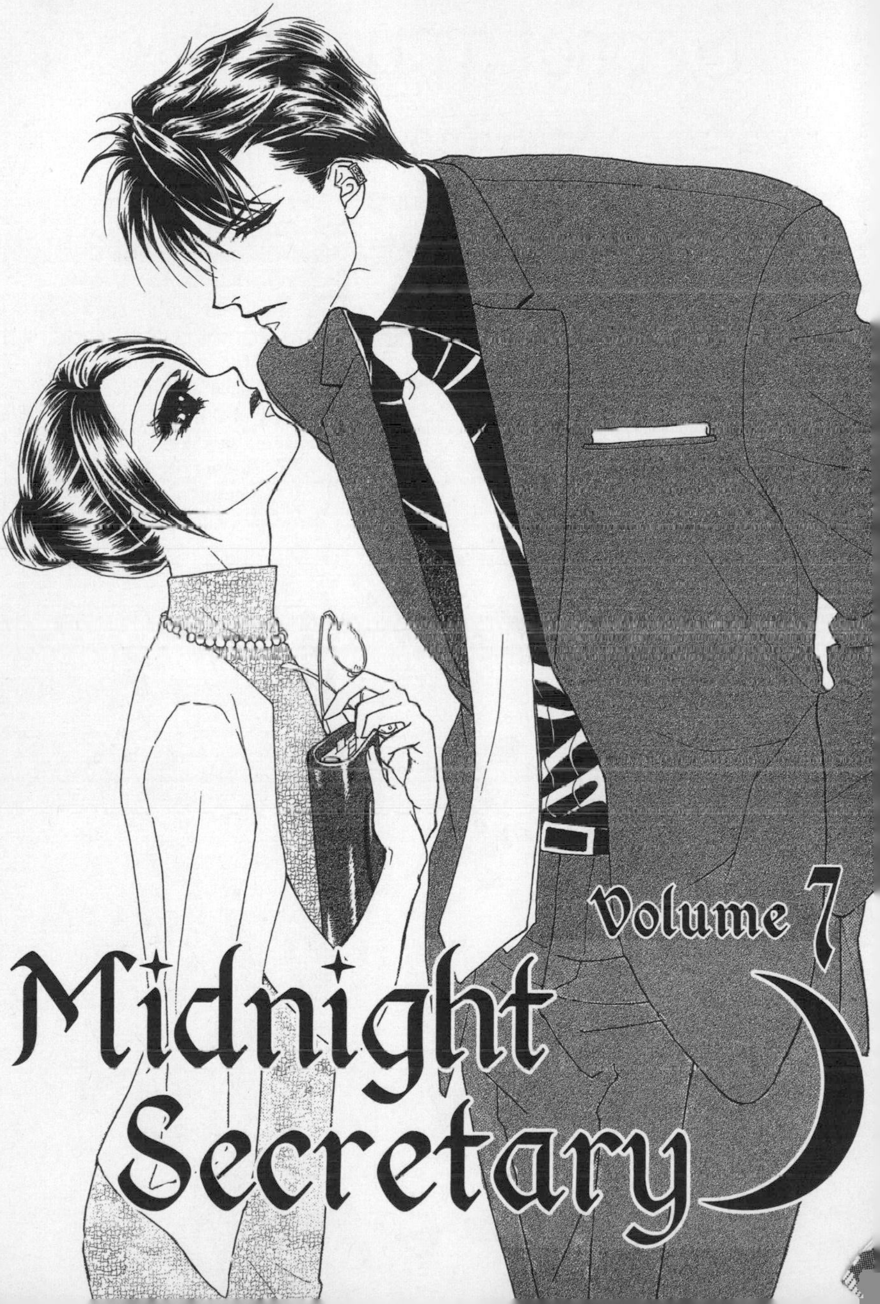

Volume 7

# Midnight Secretary

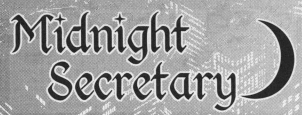

# Midnight Secretary Volume 7

## –Character–

**Kaya Satozuka (23)**
Although she was temporarily transferred to Erde, a subsidiary of Tohma Corp., Kaya resigned from her position when Kyohei established his own company. She's currently displaying her outstanding efficiency as Kyohei's executive secretary. She's uptight, serious and has a complex about her baby face. She's in love with Kyohei, despite the difficulties presented by the vampire clan.

**Kyohei Tohma (27)**
Former managing director of the major tableware manufacturer Tohma Corp. He's currently the president of the investment firm LVC (Lakes Venture Capital). Kyohei is good at his job, but he's demanding and arrogant. He is also a vampire, although he is in love with Kaya and only accepts her blood.

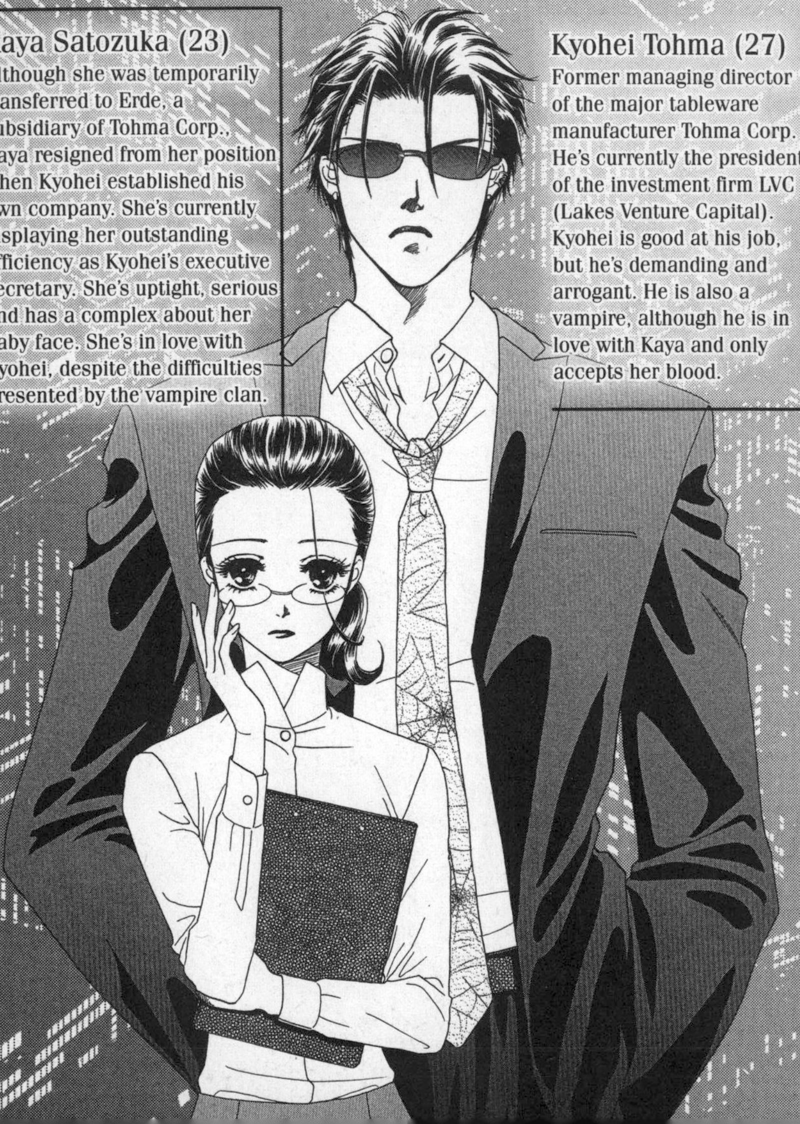

# —Story—

Kaya has been working for a vampire as his secretary, and has even been willing to give up some blood in the line of duty. When she realized that her enjoyment of his attention was getting unprofessional, she asked for a transfer from his office and ended up leaving Tohma Corp. altogether.

Meanwhile, Kyohei has refused to hire a new secretary and is working himself into exhaustion. Kaya's concern for him drives her to him, and she agrees to have sex with him in order to make her blood more fragrant with her ecstasy and quench his terrible thirst.

Kaya becomes a full-time secretary at LVC, the company Kyohei recently started, and despite incidents that painfully remind Kaya of the obstacle of Kyohei's vampire heritage, the two continue to grow closer. Kyohei declares that he loves Kaya and will feed only from her, which makes the vampire clan determined to interfere with their relationship. Rather than give in to pressure, Kyohei pushes back until he's finally banished from the clan...!

# Midnight

# Secretary

## Volume 7

### Contents

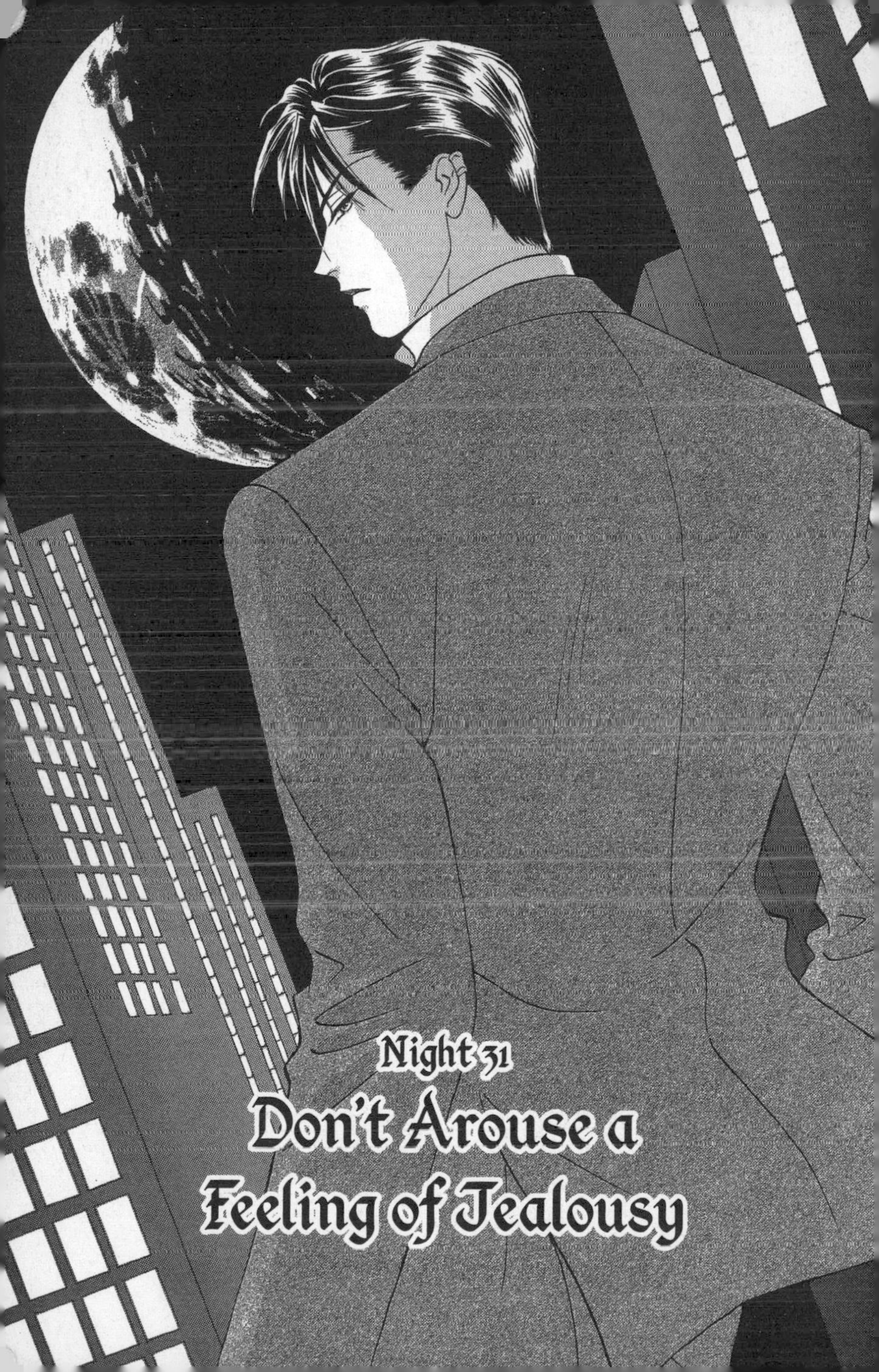
Night 31
Don't Arouse a Feeling of Jealousy

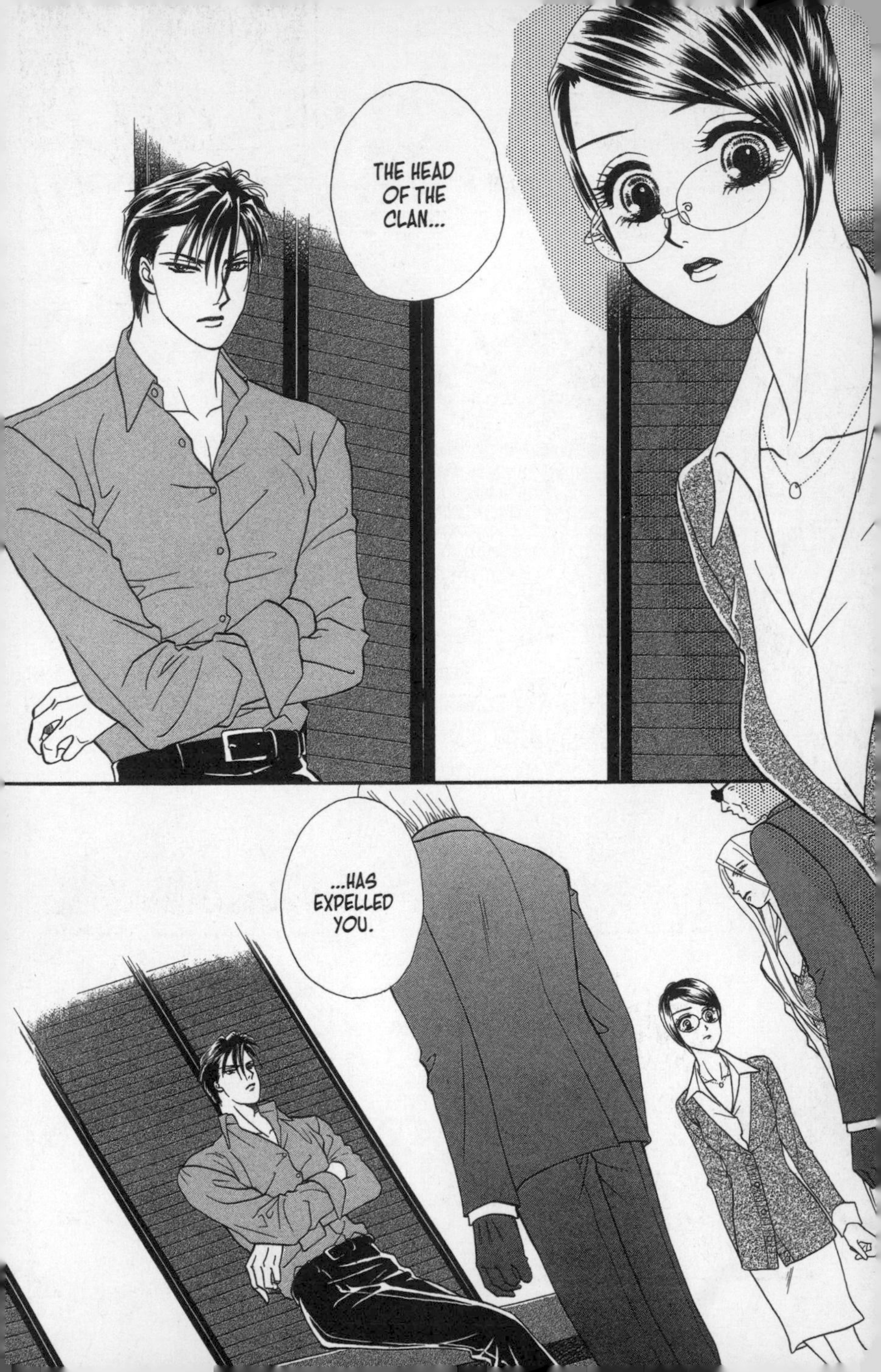
THE HEAD OF THE CLAN...
...HAS EXPELLED YOU.

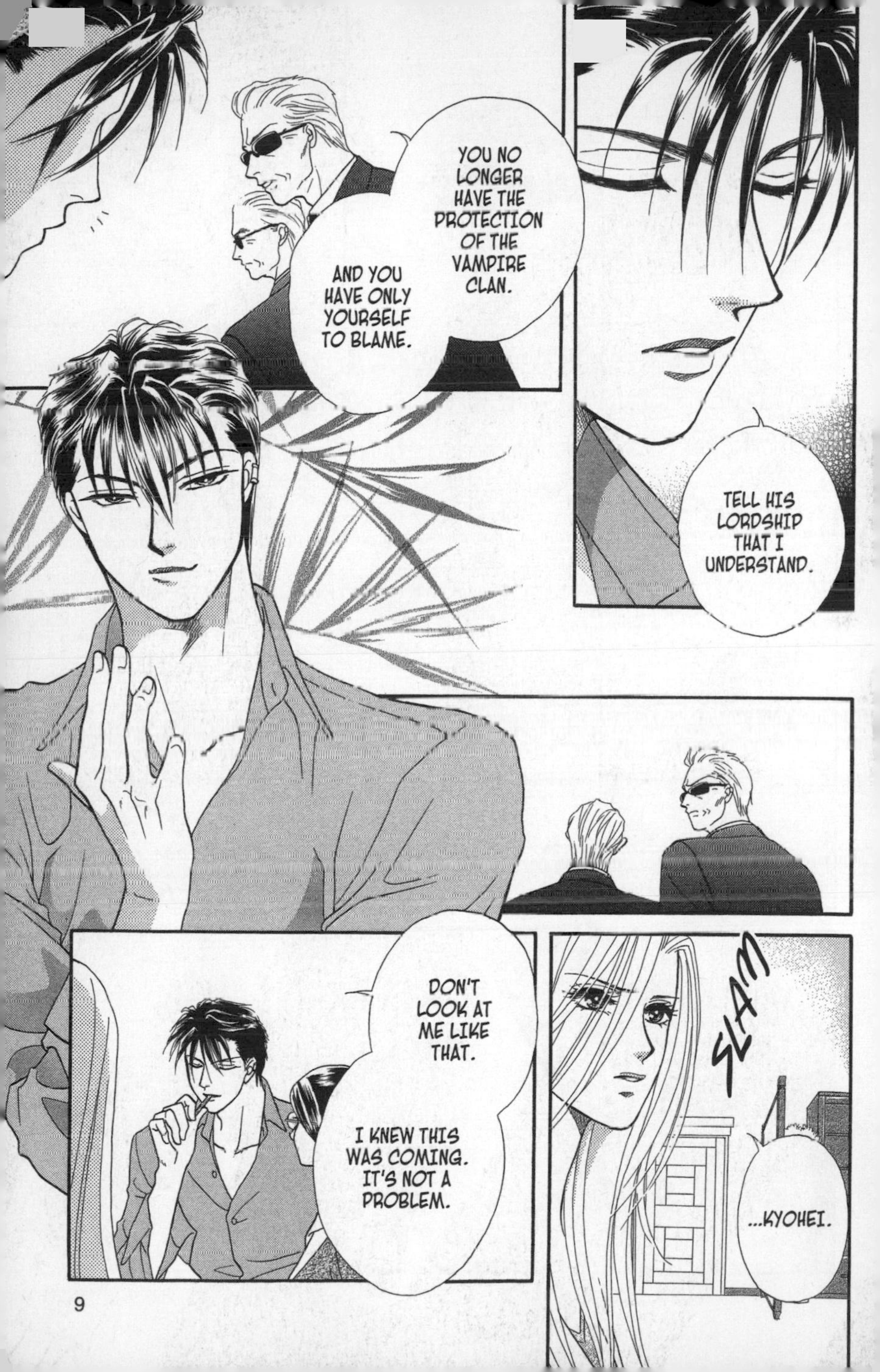
YOU NO LONGER HAVE THE PROTECTION OF THE VAMPIRE CLAN.
AND YOU HAVE ONLY YOURSELF TO BLAME.
TELL HIS LORDSHIP THAT I UNDERSTAND.
SLAM
...KYOHEI.
DON'T LOOK AT ME LIKE THAT.
I KNEW THIS WAS COMING. IT'S NOT A PROBLEM.

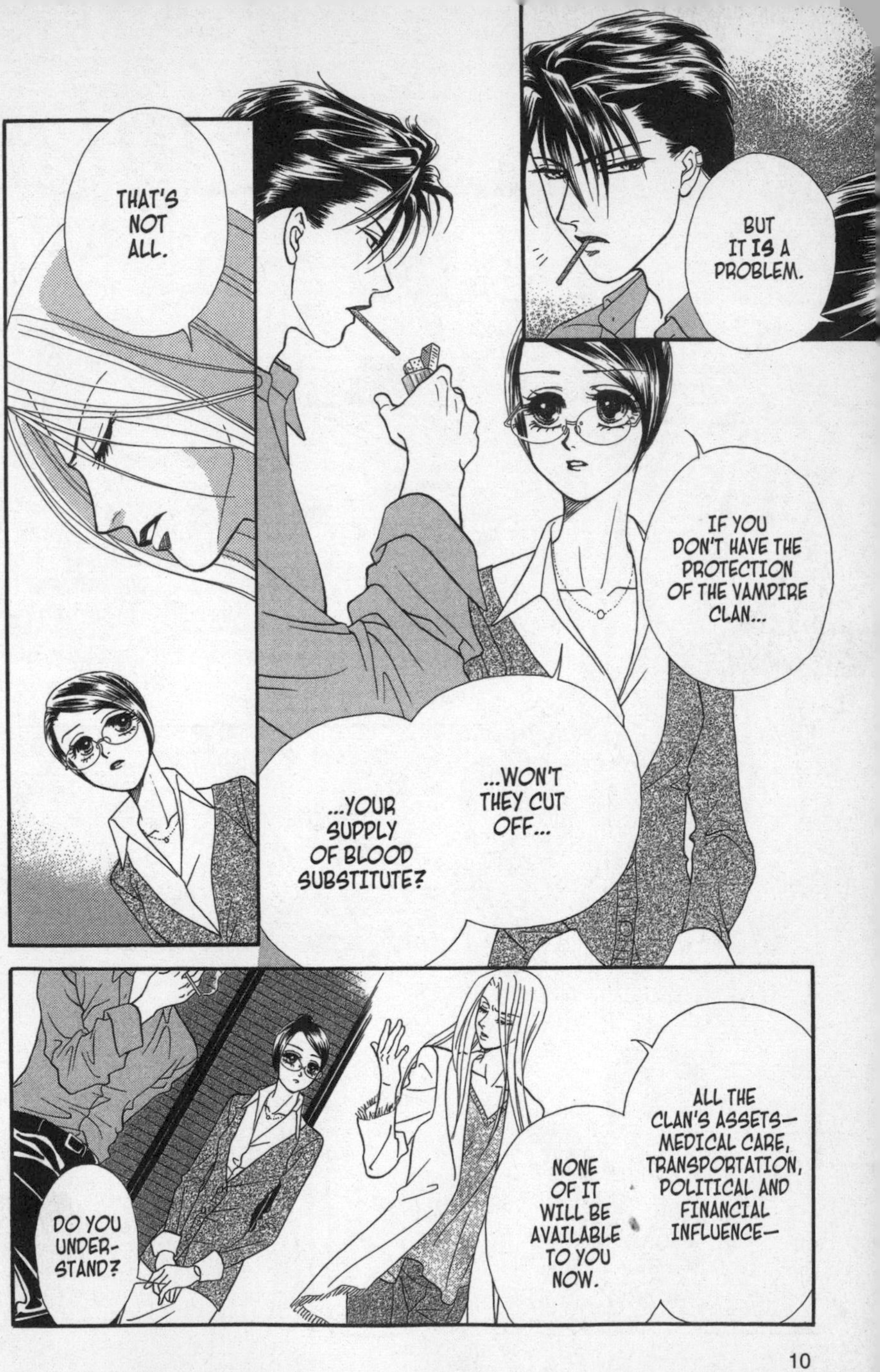
BUT IT IS A PROBLEM.
IF YOU DON'T HAVE THE PROTECTION OF THE VAMPIRE CLAN...
...WON'T THEY CUT OFF...
...YOUR SUPPLY OF BLOOD SUBSTITUTE?
THAT'S NOT ALL.
ALL THE CLAN'S ASSETS— MEDICAL CARE, TRANSPORTATION, POLITICAL AND FINANCIAL INFLUENCE—
NONE OF IT WILL BE AVAILABLE TO YOU NOW.
DO YOU UNDER-STAND?

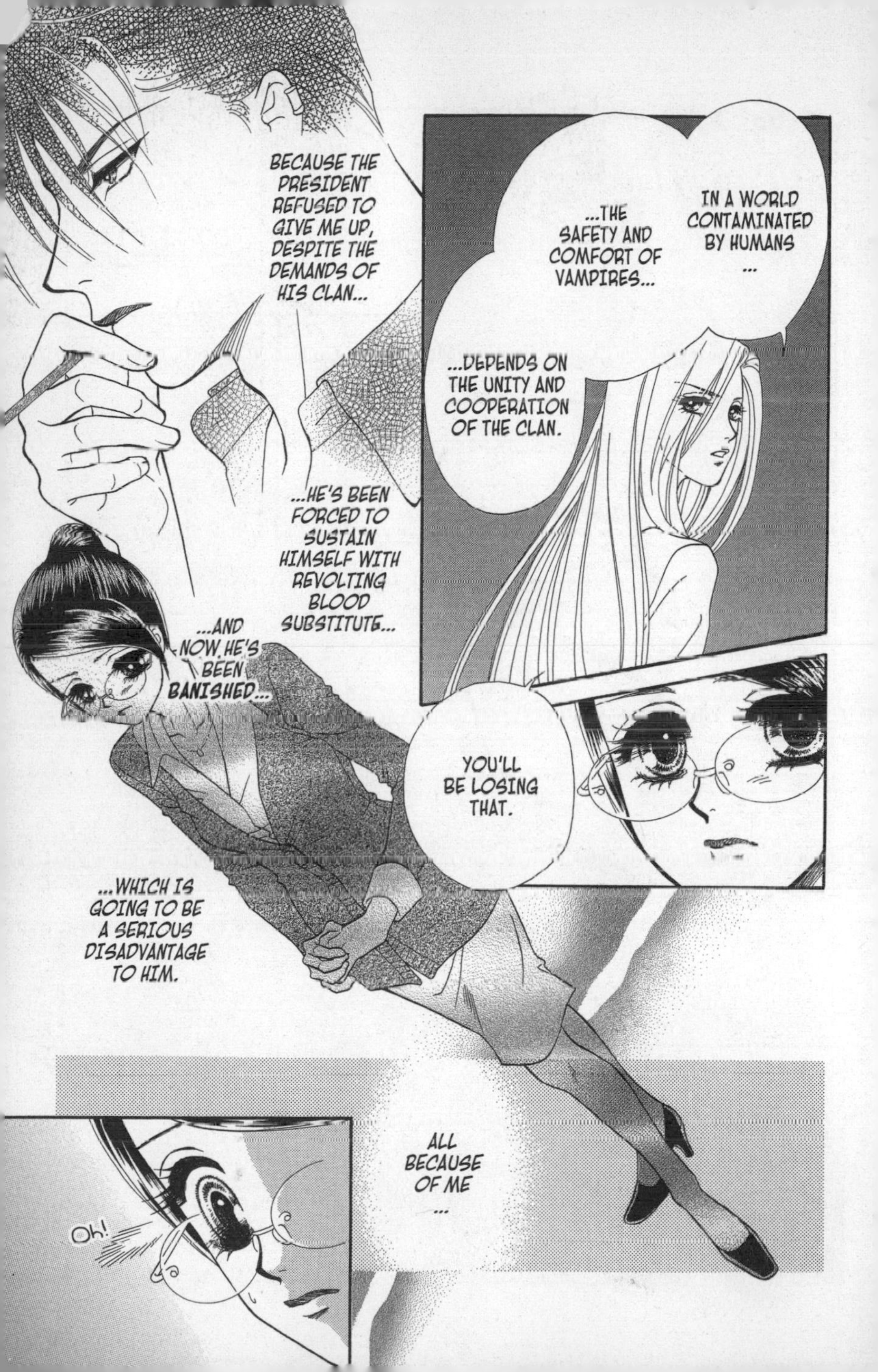
IN A WORLD CONTAMINATED BY HUMANS ...
...THE SAFETY AND COMFORT OF VAMPIRES...
...DEPENDS ON THE UNITY AND COOPERATION OF THE CLAN.
YOU'LL BE LOSING THAT.
BECAUSE THE PRESIDENT REFUSED TO GIVE ME UP, DESPITE THE DEMANDS OF HIS CLAN...
...HE'S BEEN FORCED TO SUSTAIN HIMSELF WITH REVOLTING BLOOD SUBSTITUTE...
...AND NOW HE'S BEEN BANISHED...
...WHICH IS GOING TO BE A SERIOUS DISADVANTAGE TO HIM.
ALL BECAUSE OF ME ...
Oh!

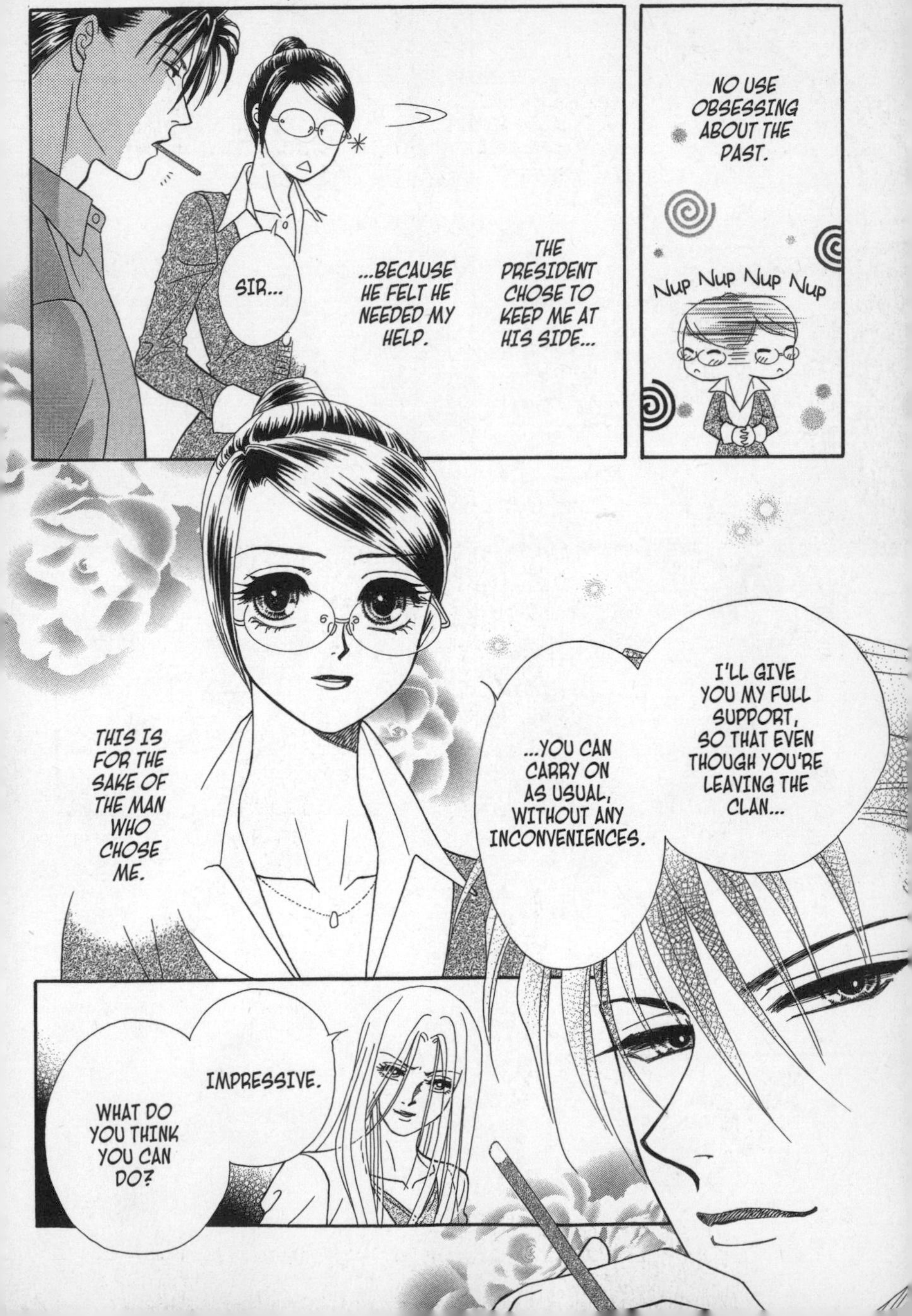
NO USE OBSESSING ABOUT THE PAST.
Nup Nup Nup Nup
THE PRESIDENT CHOSE TO KEEP ME AT HIS SIDE...
...BECAUSE HE FELT HE NEEDED MY HELP.
SIR...
I'LL GIVE YOU MY FULL SUPPORT, SO THAT EVEN THOUGH YOU'RE LEAVING THE CLAN...
...YOU CAN CARRY ON AS USUAL, WITHOUT ANY INCONVENIENCES.
THIS IS FOR THE SAKE OF THE MAN WHO CHOSE ME.
IMPRESSIVE.
WHAT DO YOU THINK YOU CAN DO?

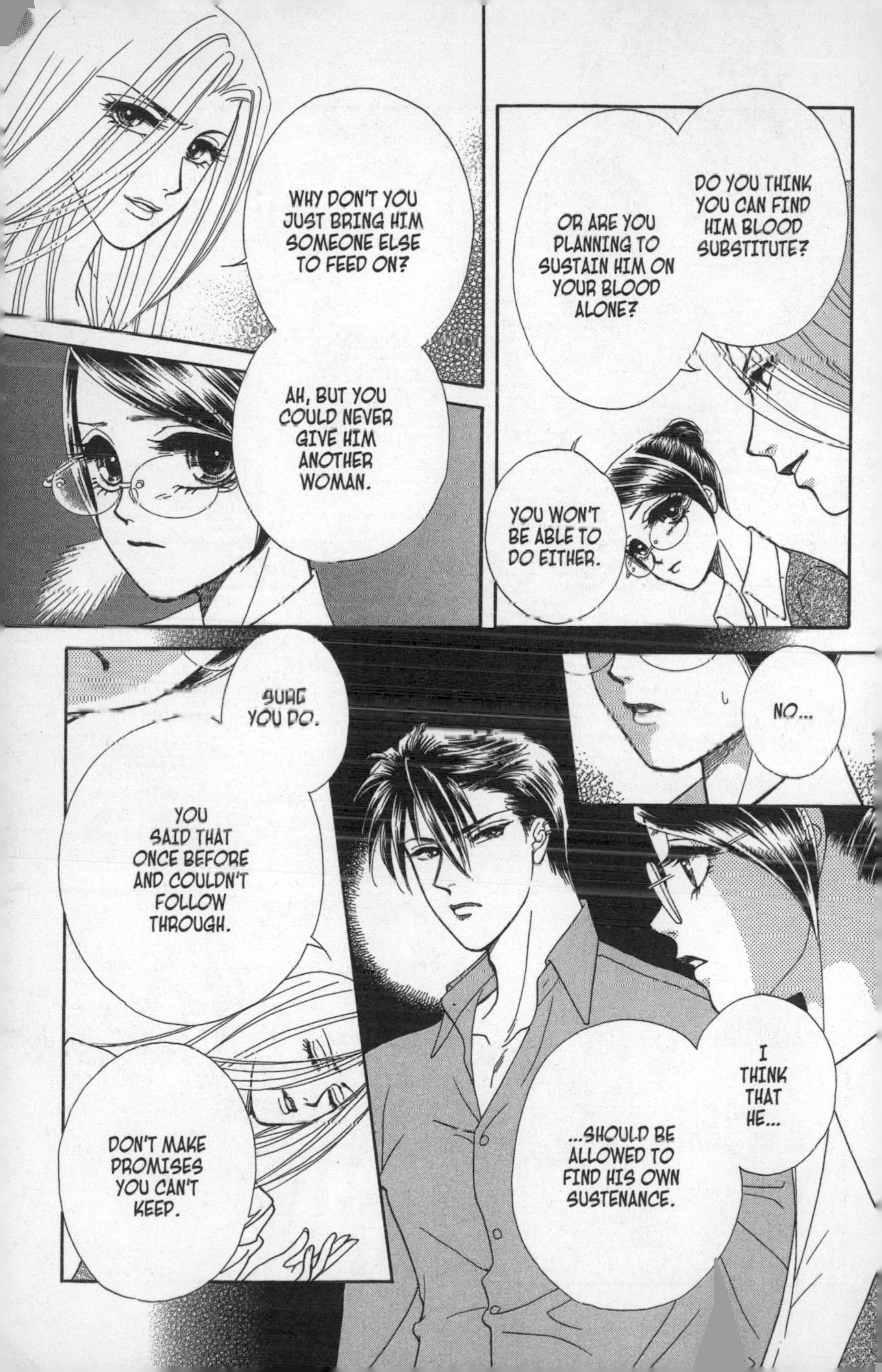
DO YOU THINK YOU CAN FIND HIM BLOOD SUBSTITUTE?
OR ARE YOU PLANNING TO SUSTAIN HIM ON YOUR BLOOD ALONE?
YOU WON'T BE ABLE TO DO EITHER.
WHY DON'T YOU JUST BRING HIM SOMEONE ELSE TO FEED ON?
AH, BUT YOU COULD NEVER GIVE HIM ANOTHER WOMAN.
NO...
I THINK THAT HE...
...SHOULD BE ALLOWED TO FIND HIS OWN SUSTENANCE.
SURE YOU DO.
YOU SAID THAT ONCE BEFORE AND COULDN'T FOLLOW THROUGH.
DON'T MAKE PROMISES YOU CAN'T KEEP.

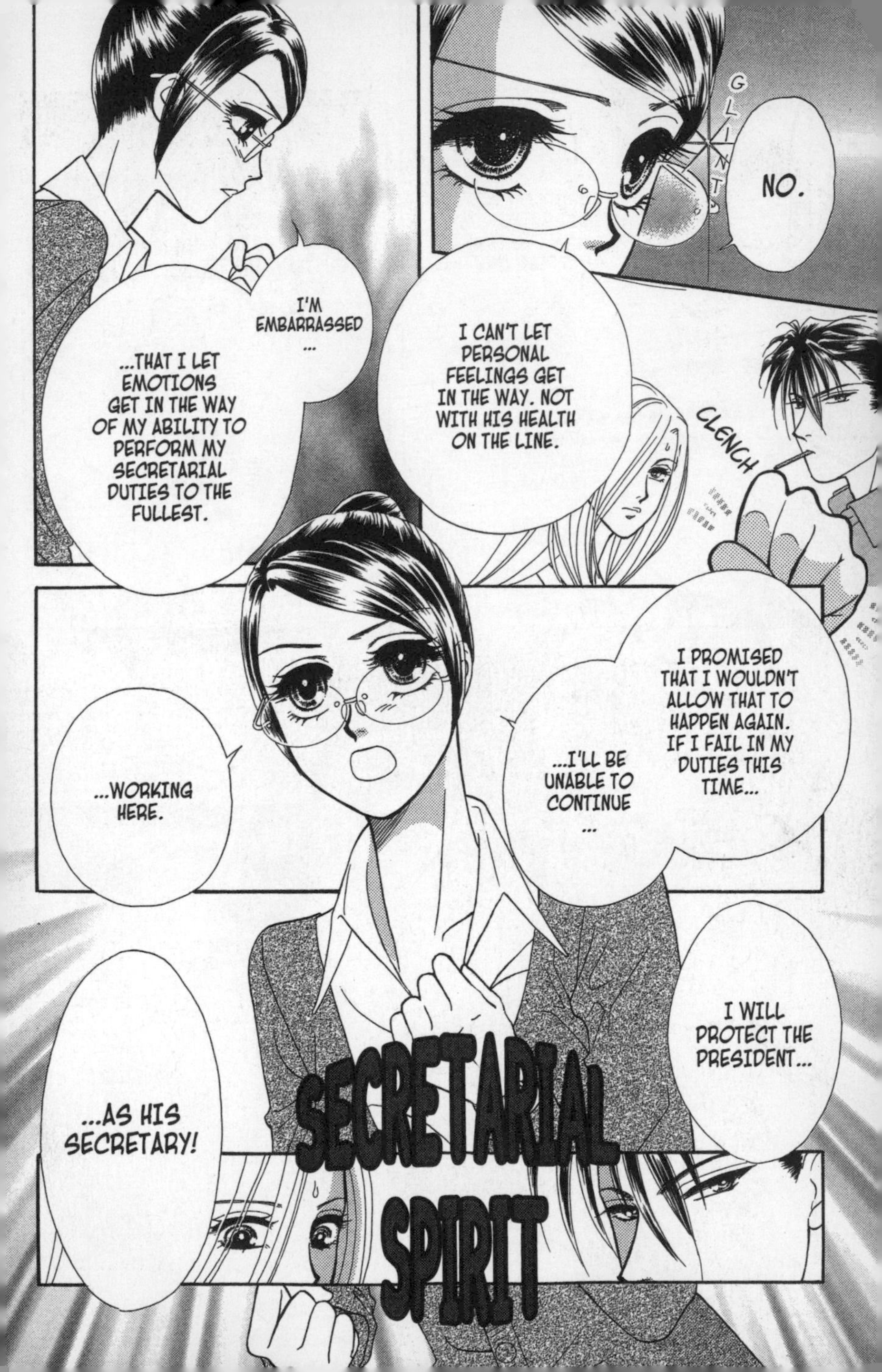
GLINT
NO.
I'M EMBARRASSED...
...THAT I LET EMOTIONS GET IN THE WAY OF MY ABILITY TO PERFORM MY SECRETARIAL DUTIES TO THE FULLEST.
I CAN'T LET PERSONAL FEELINGS GET IN THE WAY. NOT WITH HIS HEALTH ON THE LINE.
CLENCH
I PROMISED THAT I WOULDN'T ALLOW THAT TO HAPPEN AGAIN. IF I FAIL IN MY DUTIES THIS TIME...
...I'LL BE UNABLE TO CONTINUE...
...WORKING HERE.
I WILL PROTECT THE PRESIDENT...
...AS HIS SECRETARY!
SECRETARIAL SPIRIT

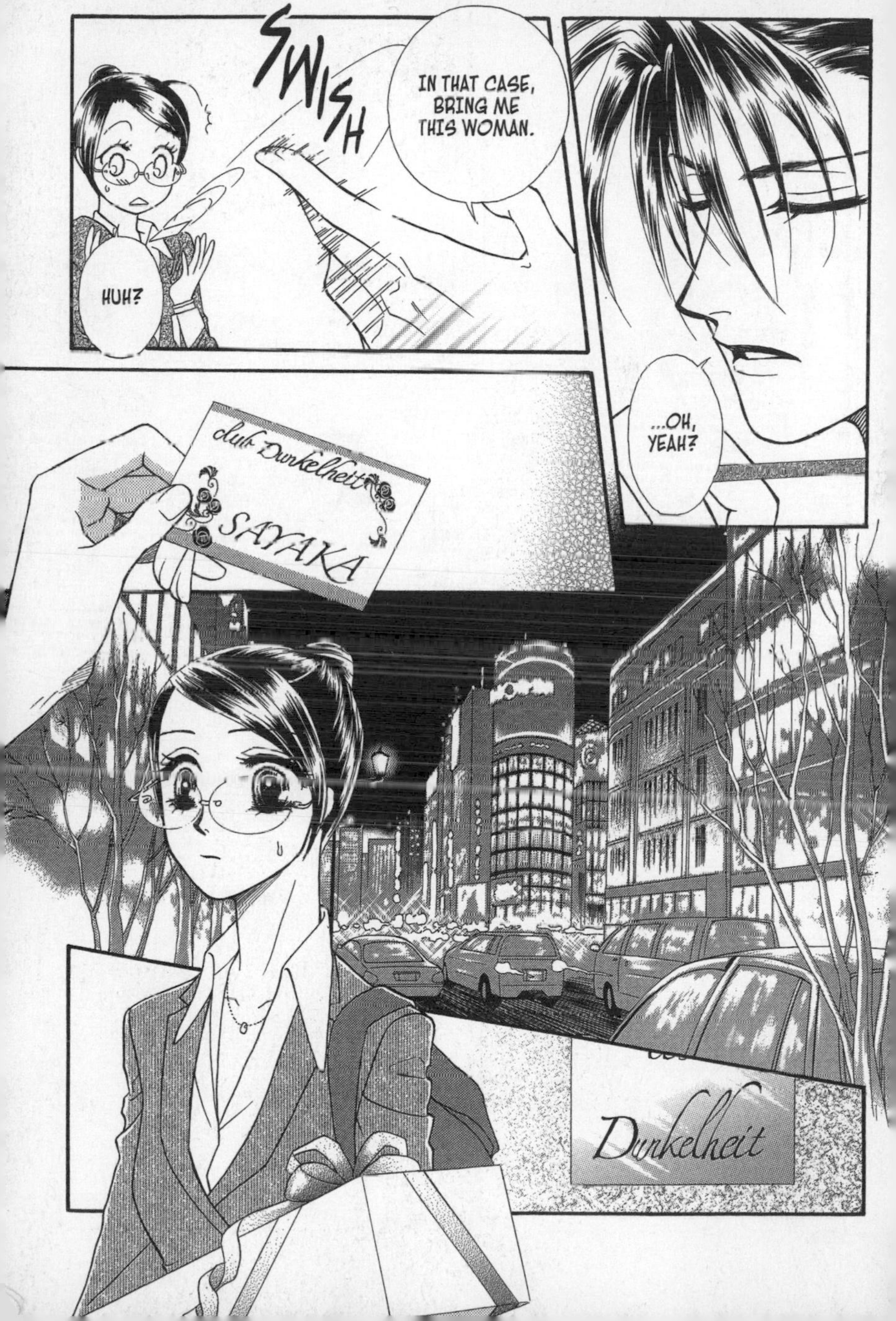
...OH, YEAH?
IN THAT CASE, BRING ME THIS WOMAN.
SWISH
HUH?
club Durkelheit
SAYAKA
Durkelheit

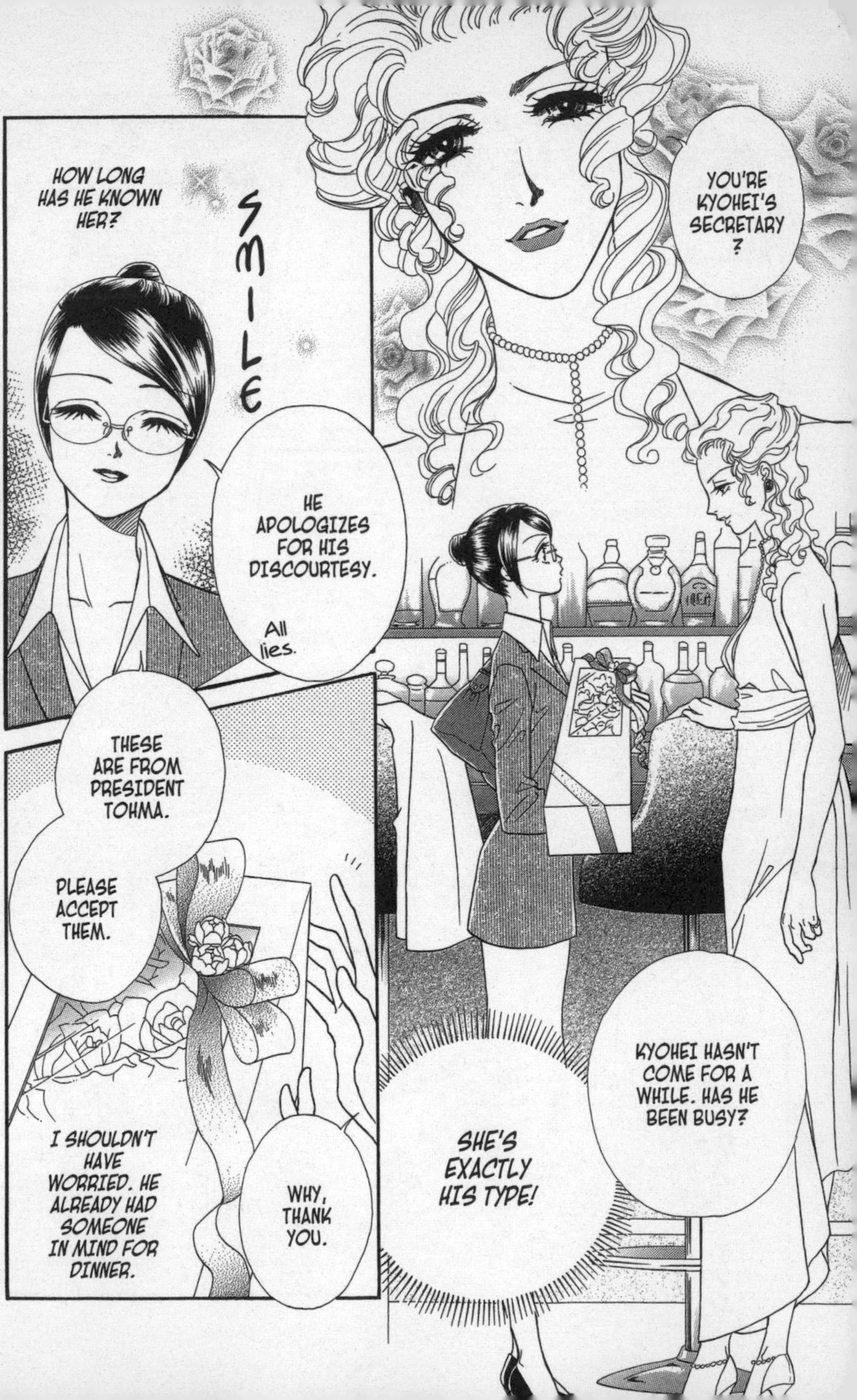
YOU'RE KYOHEI'S SECRETARY?
KYOHEI HASN'T COME FOR A WHILE. HAS HE BEEN BUSY?
SHE'S EXACTLY HIS TYPE!
HOW LONG HAS HE KNOWN HER?
SMILE
HE APOLOGIZES FOR HIS DISCOURTESY.
All lies.
THESE ARE FROM PRESIDENT TOHMA.
PLEASE ACCEPT THEM.
WHY, THANK YOU.
I SHOULDN'T HAVE WORRIED. HE ALREADY HAD SOMEONE IN MIND FOR DINNER.

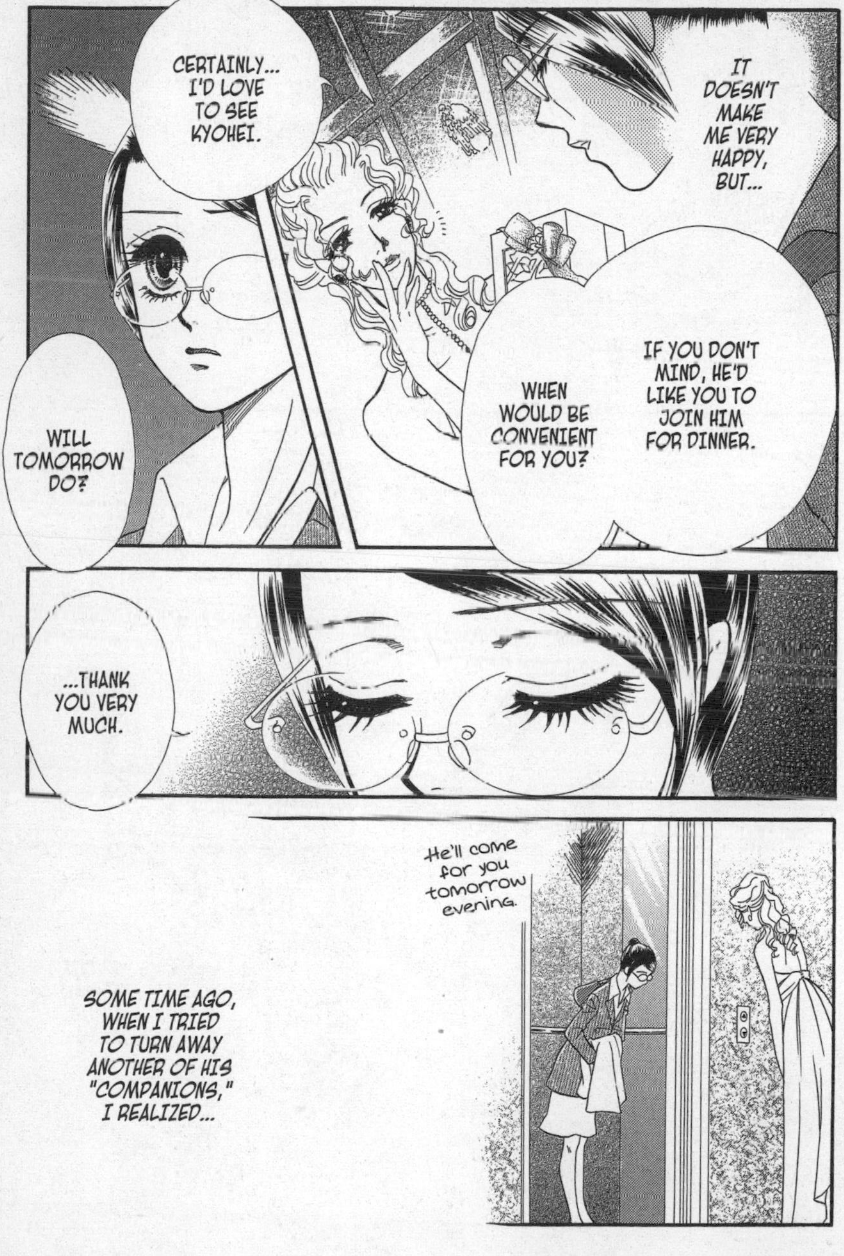
IT DOESN'T MAKE ME VERY HAPPY, BUT...
IF YOU DON'T MIND, HE'D LIKE YOU TO JOIN HIM FOR DINNER.
WHEN WOULD BE CONVENIENT FOR YOU?
CERTAINLY... I'D LOVE TO SEE KYOHEI.
WILL TOMORROW DO?
...THANK YOU VERY MUCH.
He'll come for you tomorrow evening.
SOME TIME AGO, WHEN I TRIED TO TURN AWAY ANOTHER OF HIS "COMPANIONS," I REALIZED...

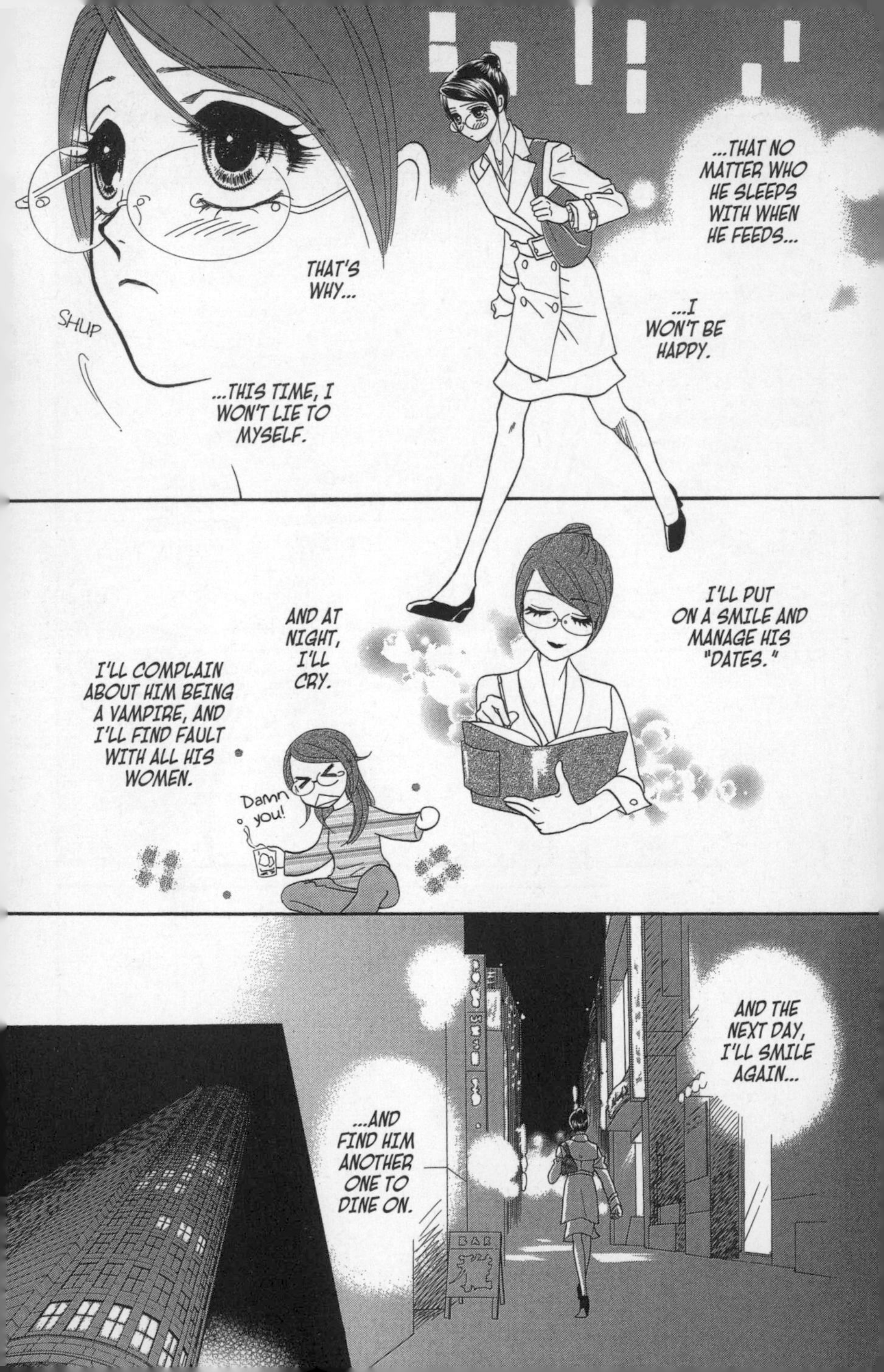
...THAT NO MATTER WHO HE SLEEPS WITH WHEN HE FEEDS...
...I WON'T BE HAPPY.
THAT'S WHY...
SHUP
...THIS TIME, I WON'T LIE TO MYSELF.
I'LL PUT ON A SMILE AND MANAGE HIS "DATES."
AND AT NIGHT, I'LL CRY.
I'LL COMPLAIN ABOUT HIM BEING A VAMPIRE, AND I'LL FIND FAULT WITH ALL HIS WOMEN.
Damn you!
AND THE NEXT DAY, I'LL SMILE AGAIN...
...AND FIND HIM ANOTHER ONE TO DINE ON.
BAR

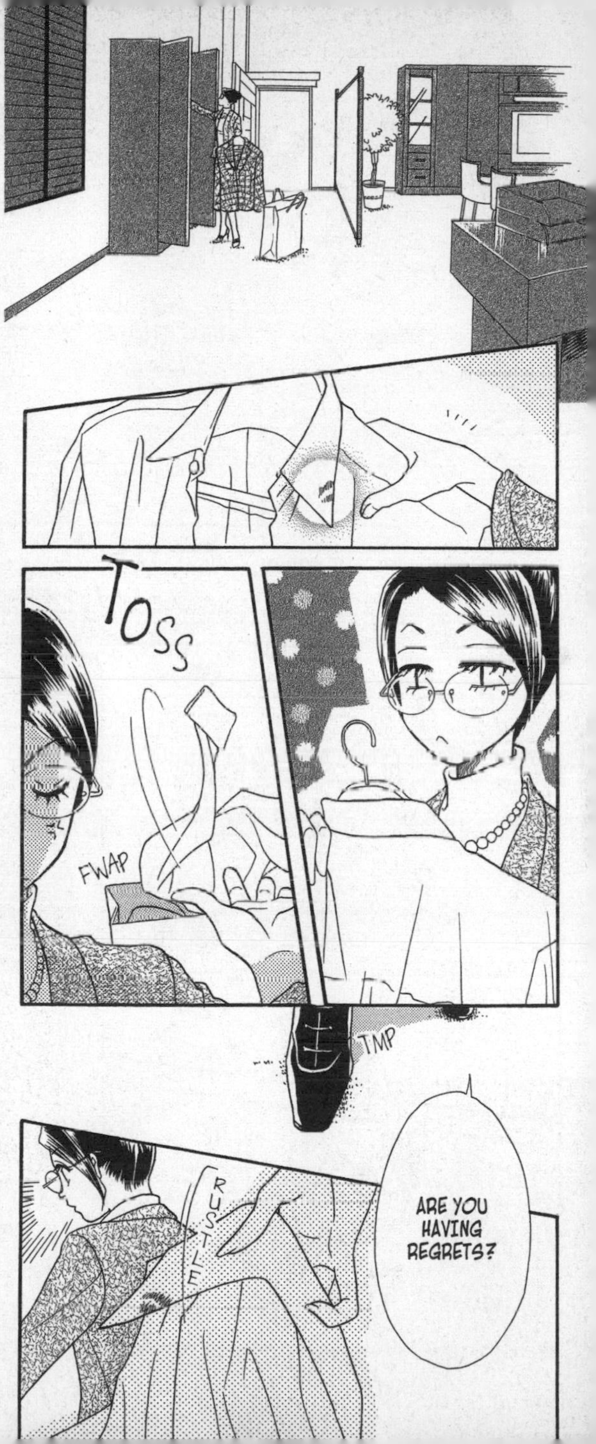
TOSS
FWAP
TMP
ARE YOU HAVING REGRETS?
RUSTLE

– Don't Arouse a Feeling of Jealousy –

Kyohei has fun with Kaya's secretarial spirit in this chapter. (smile)

Kaya's insistence on being the ultimate secretary often irritates Kyohei, but as his affection for her has grown, he seems to be able to have some fun at her expense.

...Can he now spare some time for love?! Kyohei is getting cocky. (smile)

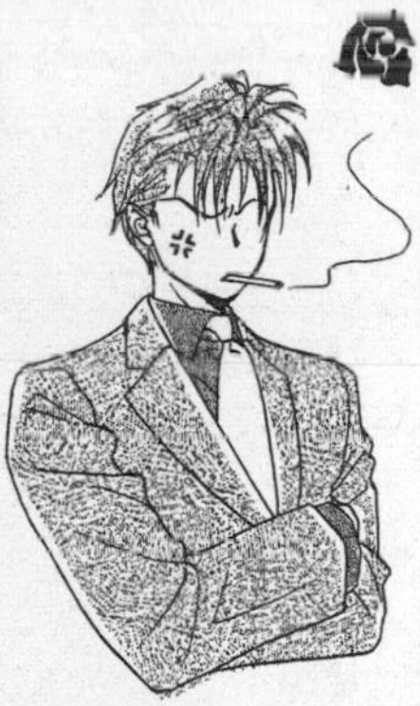

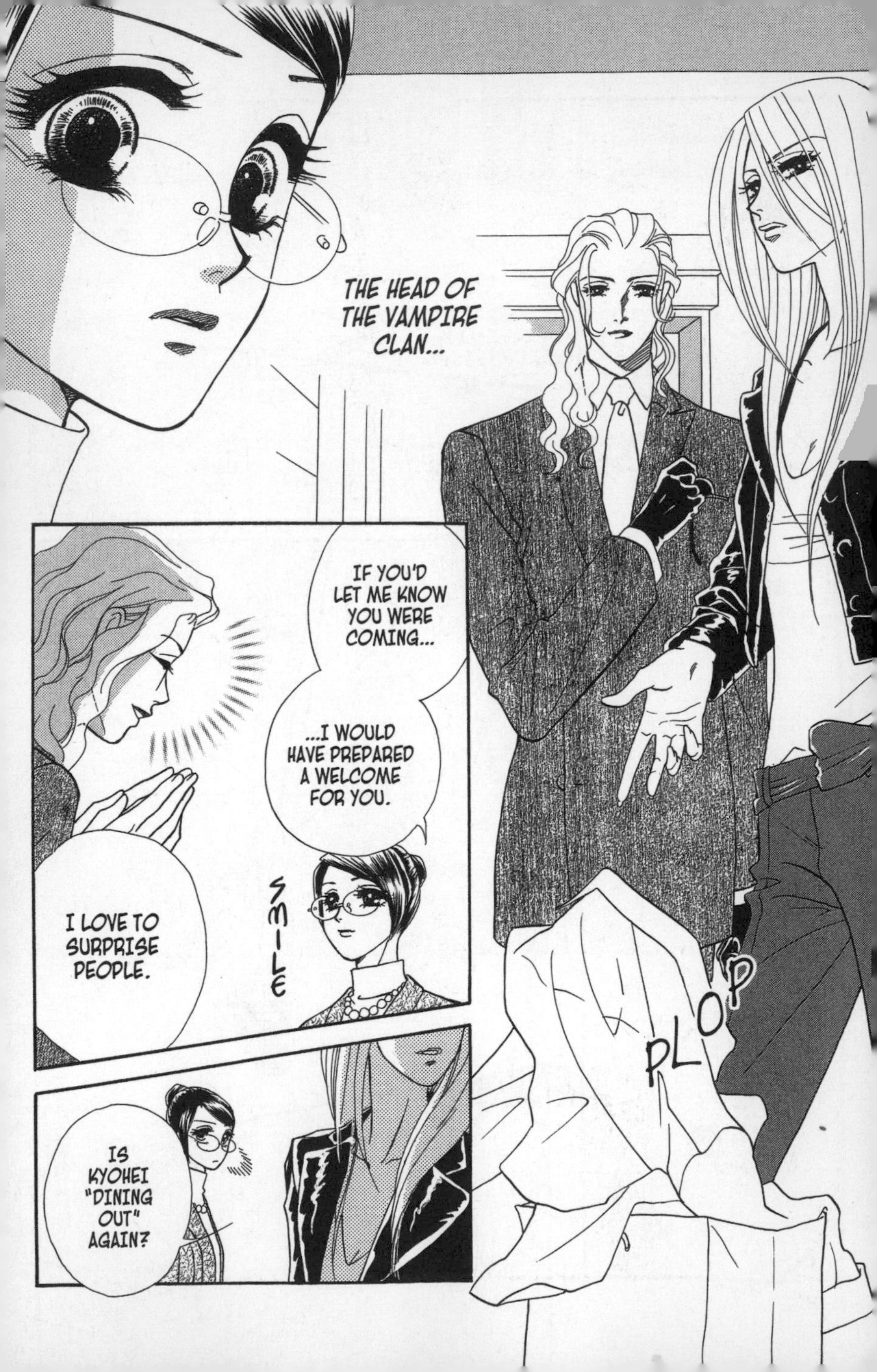
THE HEAD OF THE VAMPIRE CLAN...
PLOP
IF YOU'D LET ME KNOW YOU WERE COMING...
...I WOULD HAVE PREPARED A WELCOME FOR YOU.
SMILE
I LOVE TO SURPRISE PEOPLE.
IS KYOHEI "DINING OUT" AGAIN?

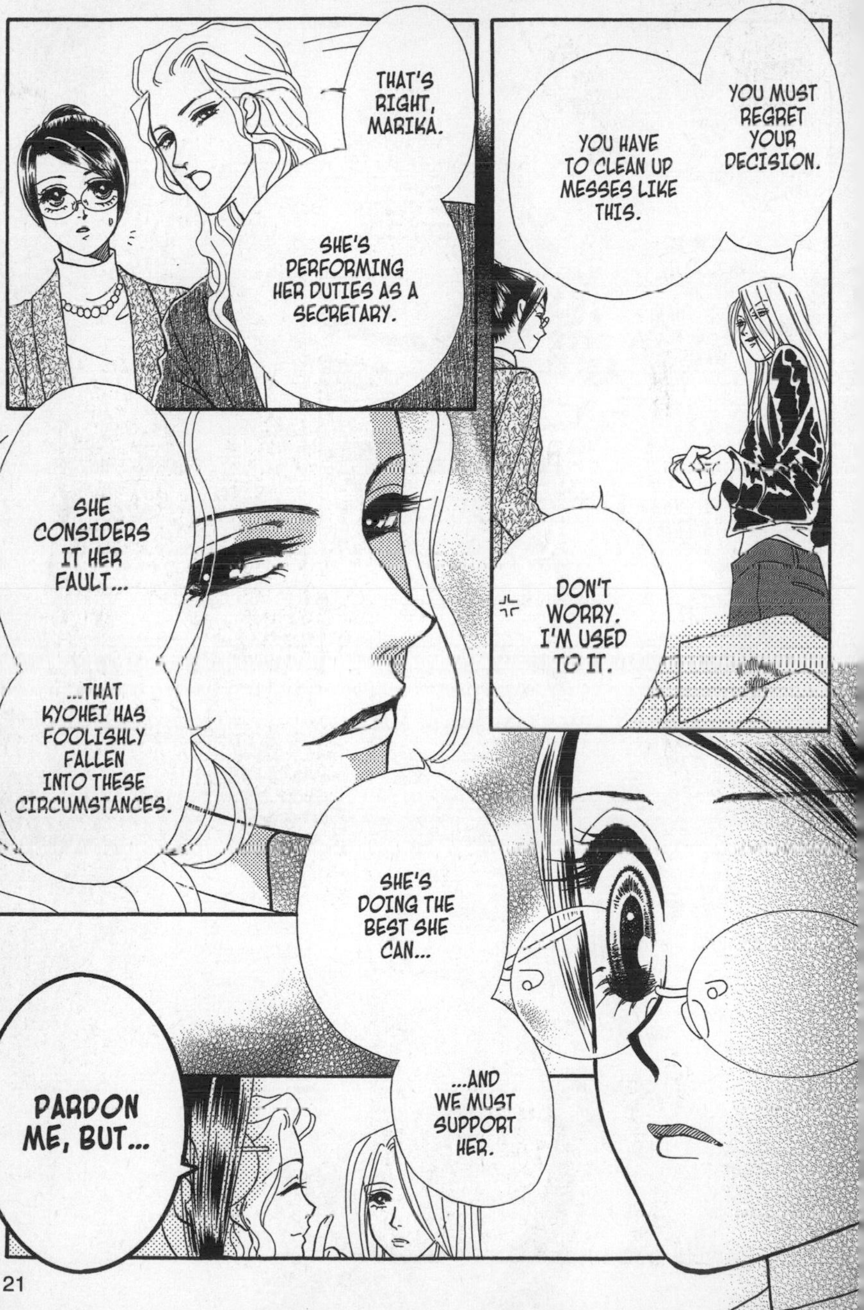
YOU MUST REGRET YOUR DECISION.
YOU HAVE TO CLEAN UP MESSES LIKE THIS.
DON'T WORRY. I'M USED TO IT.
THAT'S RIGHT, MARIKA.
SHE'S PERFORMING HER DUTIES AS A SECRETARY.
SHE CONSIDERS IT HER FAULT...
...THAT KYOHEI HAS FOOLISHLY FALLEN INTO THESE CIRCUMSTANCES.
SHE'S DOING THE BEST SHE CAN...
...AND WE MUST SUPPORT HER.
PARDON ME, BUT...

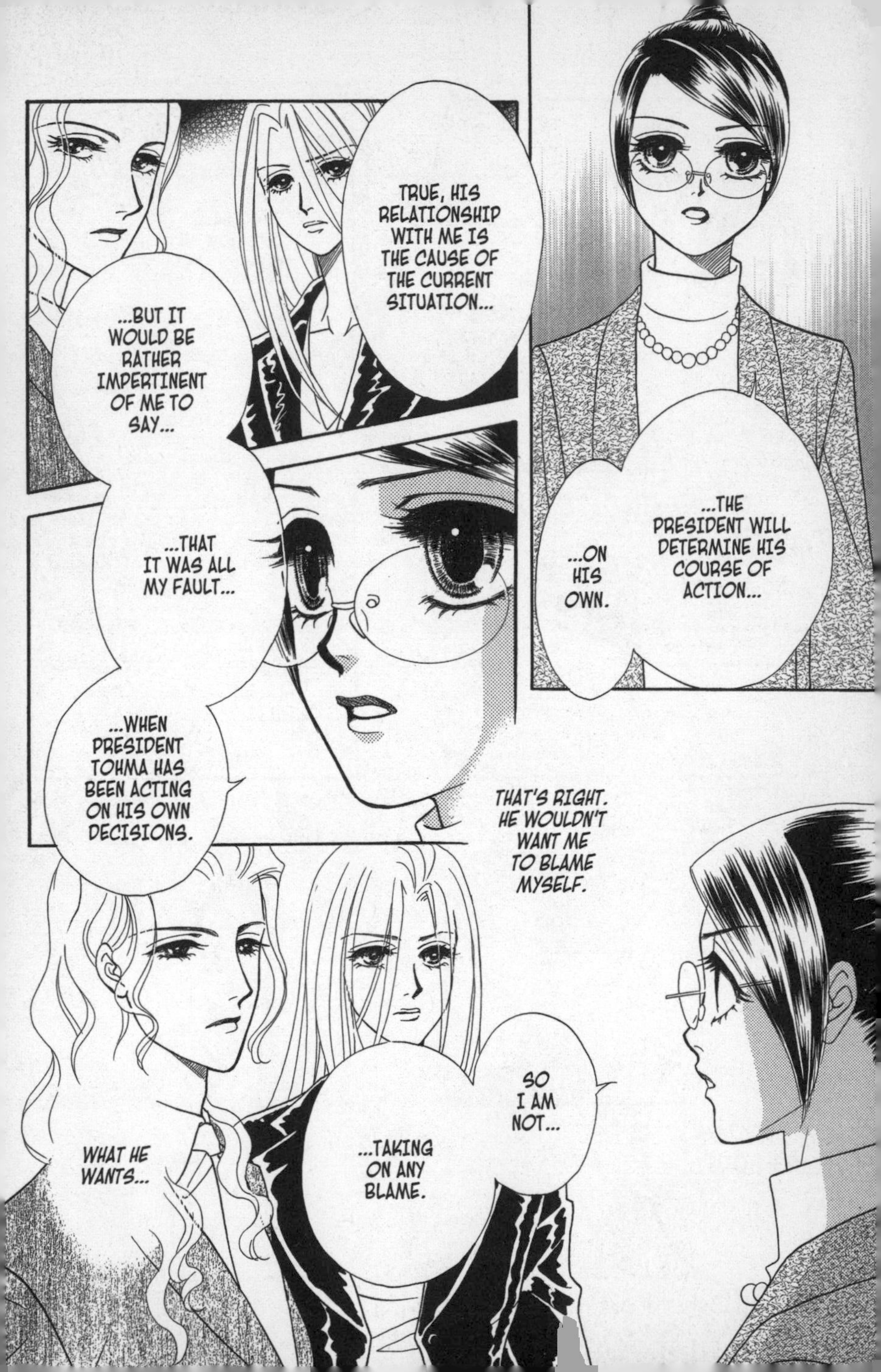
...THE PRESIDENT WILL DETERMINE HIS COURSE OF ACTION...
...ON HIS OWN.
TRUE, HIS RELATIONSHIP WITH ME IS THE CAUSE OF THE CURRENT SITUATION...
...BUT IT WOULD BE RATHER IMPERTINENT OF ME TO SAY...
...THAT IT WAS ALL MY FAULT...
...WHEN PRESIDENT TOHMA HAS BEEN ACTING ON HIS OWN DECISIONS.
THAT'S RIGHT. HE WOULDN'T WANT ME TO BLAME MYSELF.
SO I AM NOT...
...TAKING ON ANY BLAME.
WHAT HE WANTS...

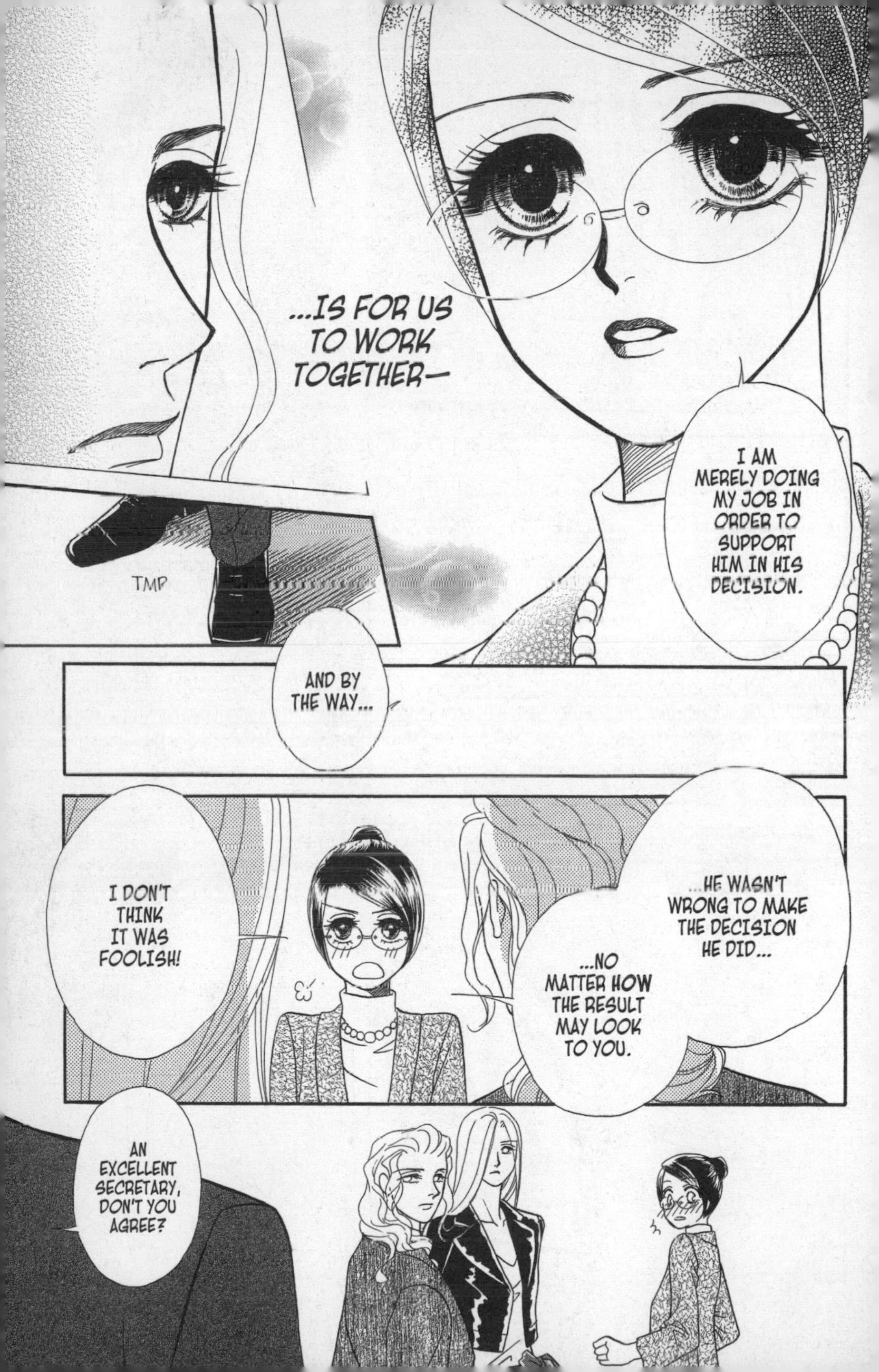
...IS FOR US TO WORK TOGETHER—
I AM MERELY DOING MY JOB IN ORDER TO SUPPORT HIM IN HIS DECISION.
TMP
AND BY THE WAY...
...HE WASN'T WRONG TO MAKE THE DECISION HE DID...
...NO MATTER HOW THE RESULT MAY LOOK TO YOU.
I DON'T THINK IT WAS FOOLISH!
AN EXCELLENT SECRETARY, DON'T YOU AGREE?

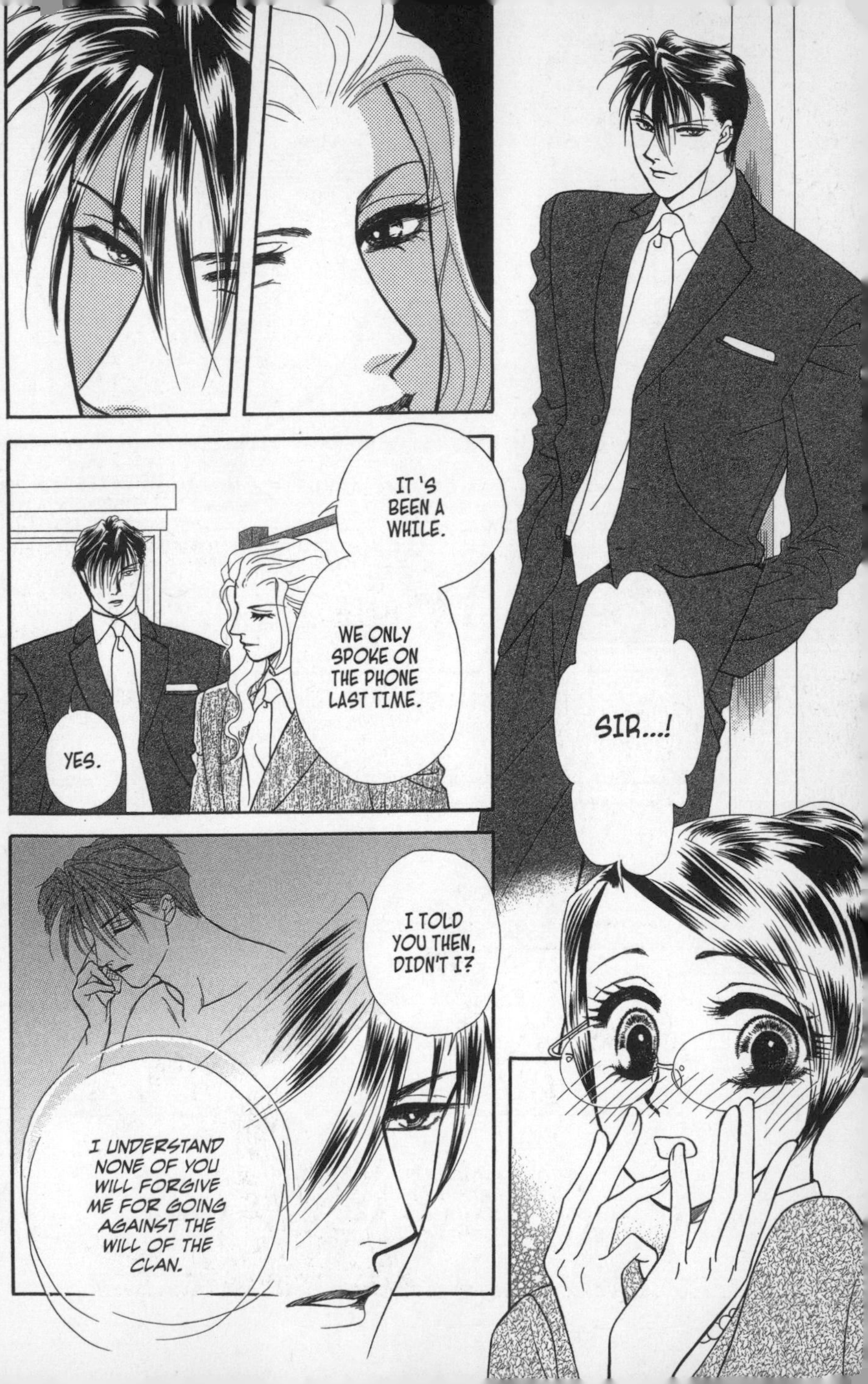
SIR...!
IT'S BEEN A WHILE.
WE ONLY SPOKE ON THE PHONE LAST TIME.
YES.
I TOLD YOU THEN, DIDN'T I?
I UNDERSTAND NONE OF YOU WILL FORGIVE ME FOR GOING AGAINST THE WILL OF THE CLAN.

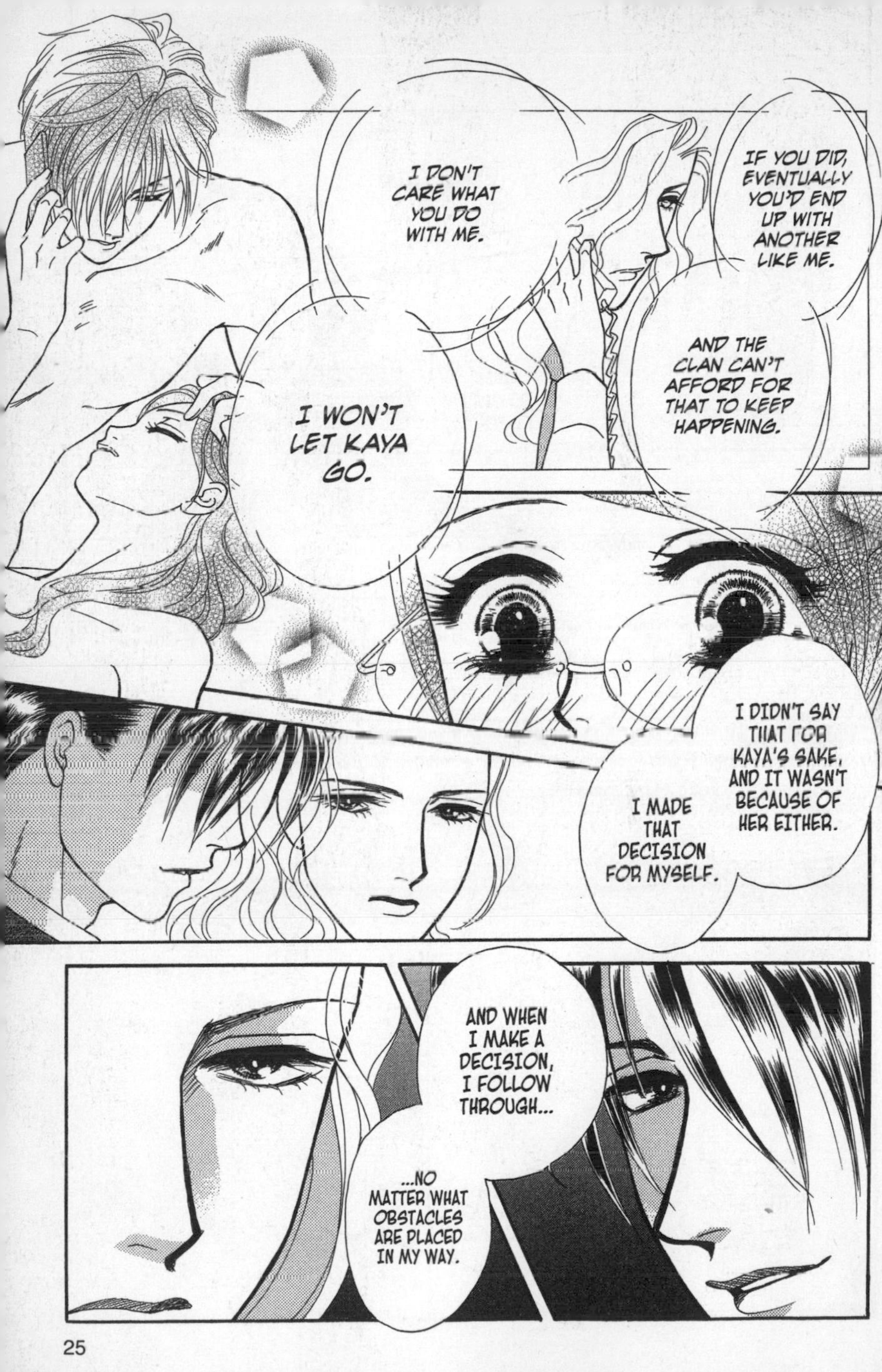
I DON'T CARE WHAT YOU DO WITH ME.
IF YOU DID, EVENTUALLY YOU'D END UP WITH ANOTHER LIKE ME.
AND THE CLAN CAN'T AFFORD FOR THAT TO KEEP HAPPENING.
I WON'T LET KAYA GO.
I DIDN'T SAY THAT FOR KAYA'S SAKE, AND IT WASN'T BECAUSE OF HER EITHER.
I MADE THAT DECISION FOR MYSELF.
AND WHEN I MAKE A DECISION, I FOLLOW THROUGH...
...NO MATTER WHAT OBSTACLES ARE PLACED IN MY WAY.

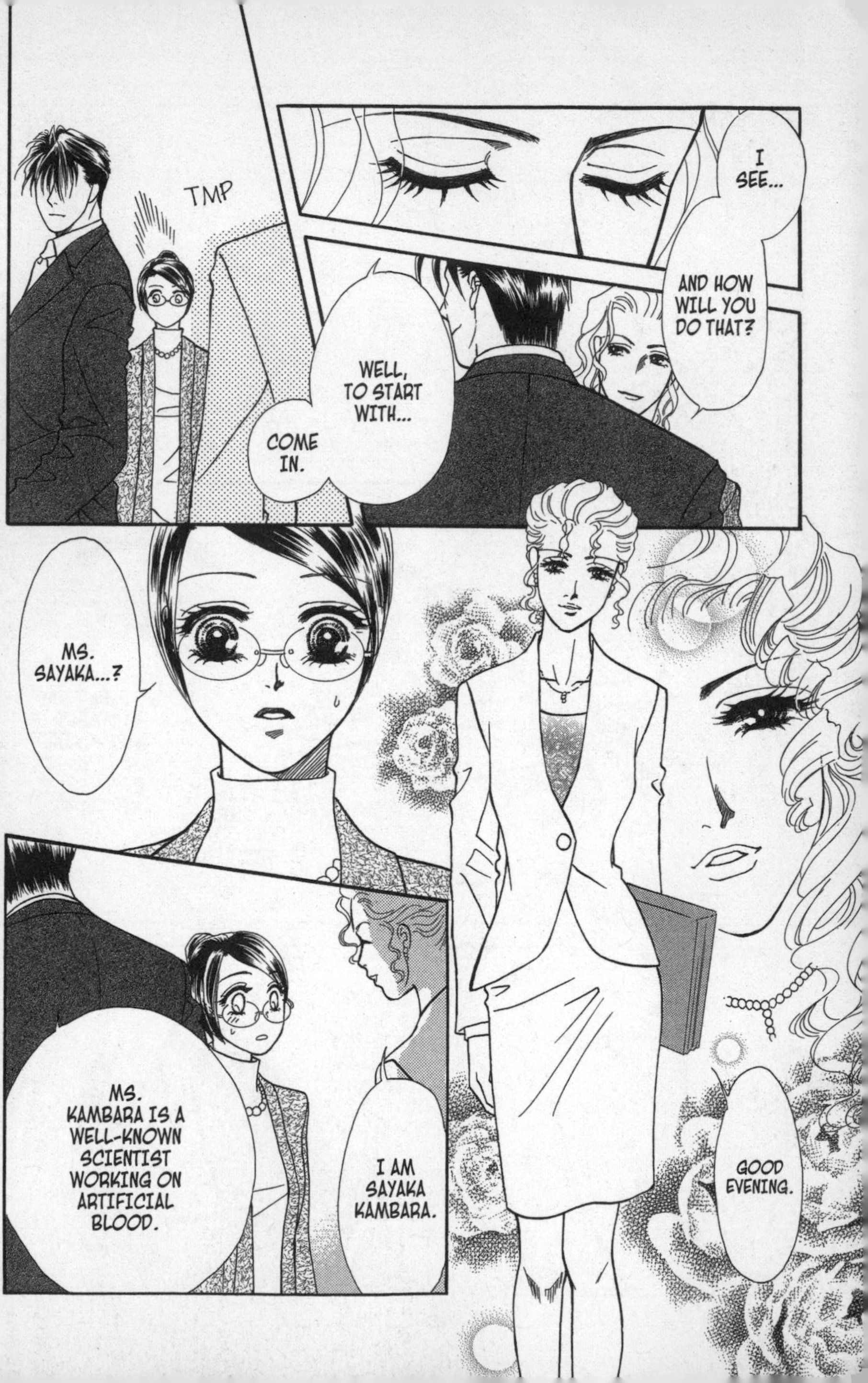
I SEE...
AND HOW WILL YOU DO THAT?
WELL, TO START WITH...
COME IN.
TMP
GOOD EVENING.
MS. SAYAKA...?
I AM SAYAKA KAMBARA.
MS. KAMBARA IS A WELL-KNOWN SCIENTIST WORKING ON ARTIFICIAL BLOOD.

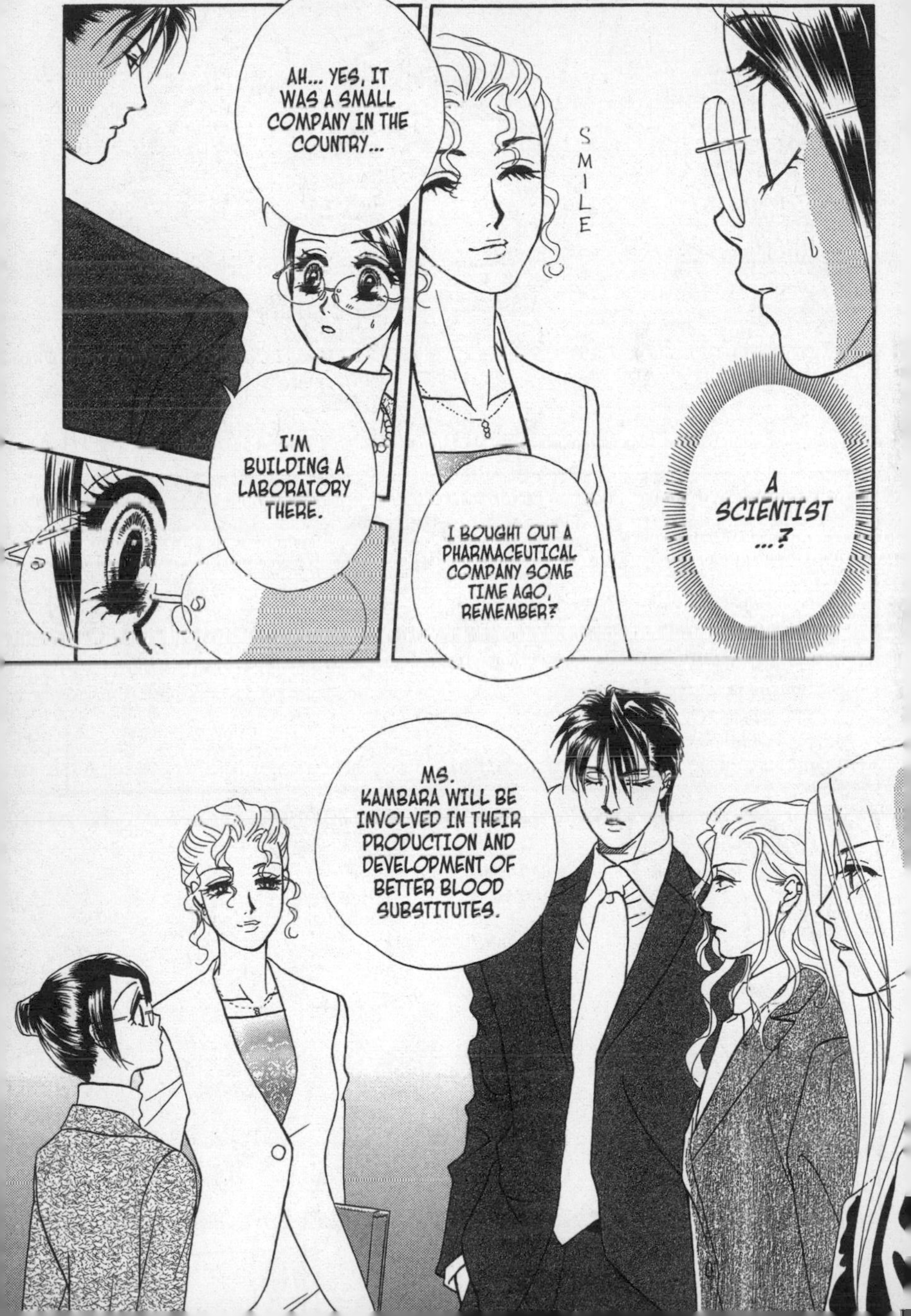
SMILE
A SCIENTIST ...?
I BOUGHT OUT A PHARMACEUTICAL COMPANY SOME TIME AGO, REMEMBER?
AH... YES, IT WAS A SMALL COMPANY IN THE COUNTRY...
I'M BUILDING A LABORATORY THERE.
MS. KAMBARA WILL BE INVOLVED IN THEIR PRODUCTION AND DEVELOPMENT OF BETTER BLOOD SUBSTITUTES.

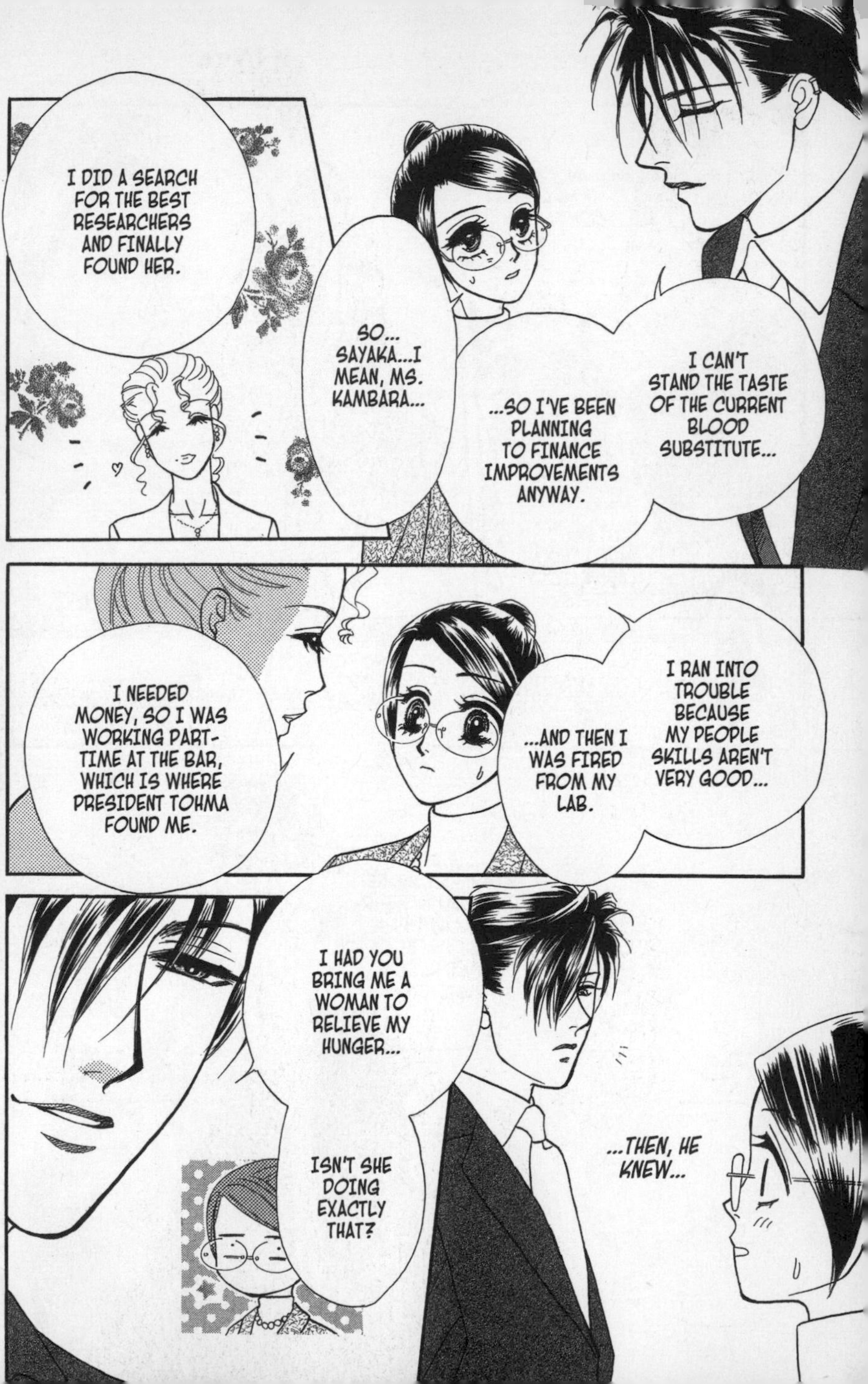
I CAN'T STAND THE TASTE OF THE CURRENT BLOOD SUBSTITUTE...
...SO I'VE BEEN PLANNING TO FINANCE IMPROVEMENTS ANYWAY.
SO... SAYAKA...I MEAN, MS. KAMBARA...
I DID A SEARCH FOR THE BEST RESEARCHERS AND FINALLY FOUND HER.
I RAN INTO TROUBLE BECAUSE MY PEOPLE SKILLS AREN'T VERY GOOD...
...AND THEN I WAS FIRED FROM MY LAB.
I NEEDED MONEY, SO I WAS WORKING PART-TIME AT THE BAR, WHICH IS WHERE PRESIDENT TOHMA FOUND ME.
I HAD YOU BRING ME A WOMAN TO RELIEVE MY HUNGER...
ISN'T SHE DOING EXACTLY THAT?
...THEN, HE KNEW...

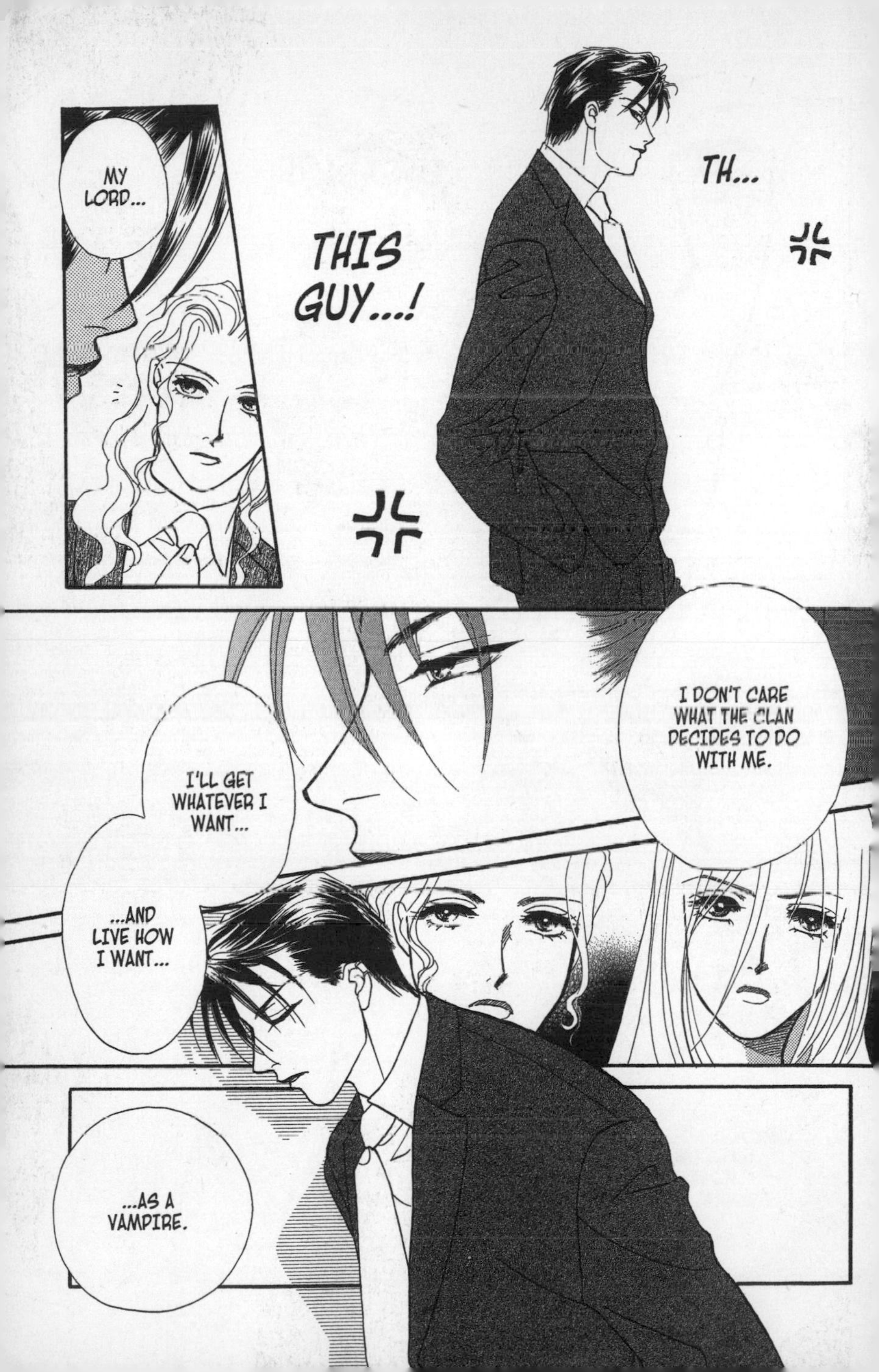
TH...
THIS GUY...!
MY LORD...
I DON'T CARE WHAT THE CLAN DECIDES TO DO WITH ME.
I'LL GET WHATEVER I WANT...
...AND LIVE HOW I WANT...
...AS A VAMPIRE.

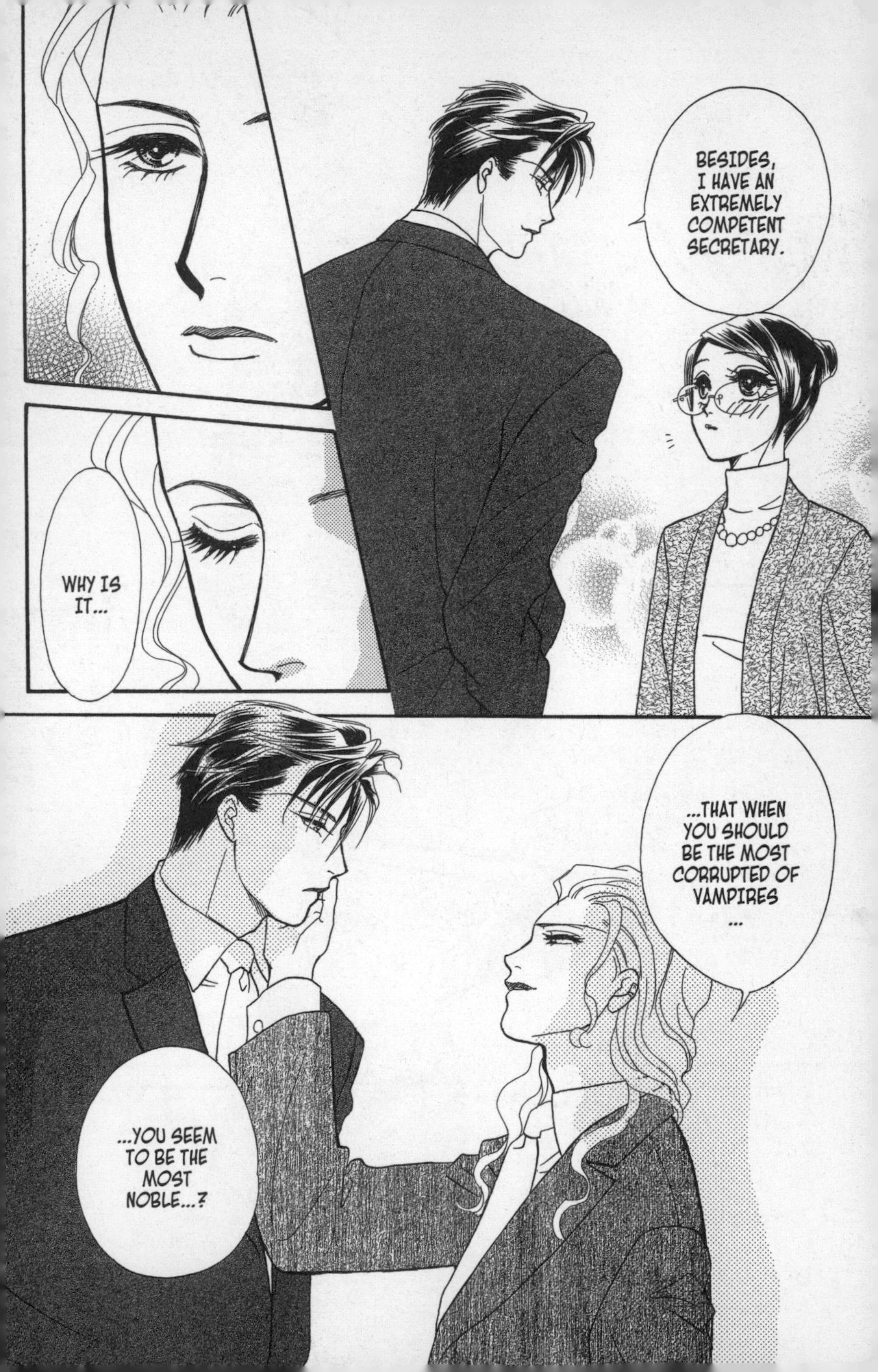
BESIDES, I HAVE AN EXTREMELY COMPETENT SECRETARY.
WHY IS IT...
...THAT WHEN YOU SHOULD BE THE MOST CORRUPTED OF VAMPIRES ...
...YOU SEEM TO BE THE MOST NOBLE...?

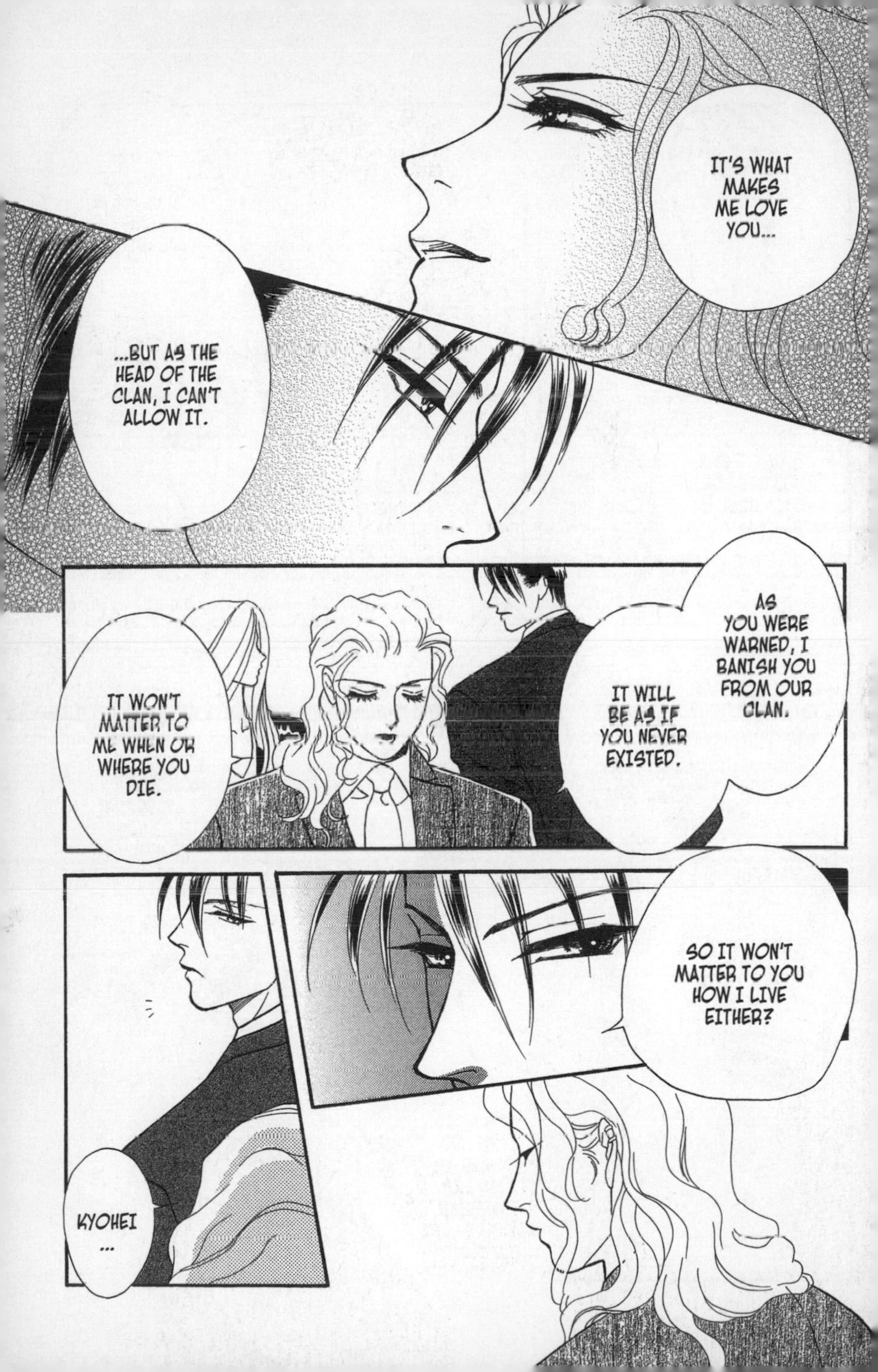
IT'S WHAT MAKES ME LOVE YOU...
...BUT AS THE HEAD OF THE CLAN, I CAN'T ALLOW IT.
AS YOU WERE WARNED, I BANISH YOU FROM OUR CLAN.
IT WILL BE AS IF YOU NEVER EXISTED.
IT WON'T MATTER TO ME WHEN OR WHERE YOU DIE.
SO IT WON'T MATTER TO YOU HOW I LIVE EITHER?
KYOHEI ...

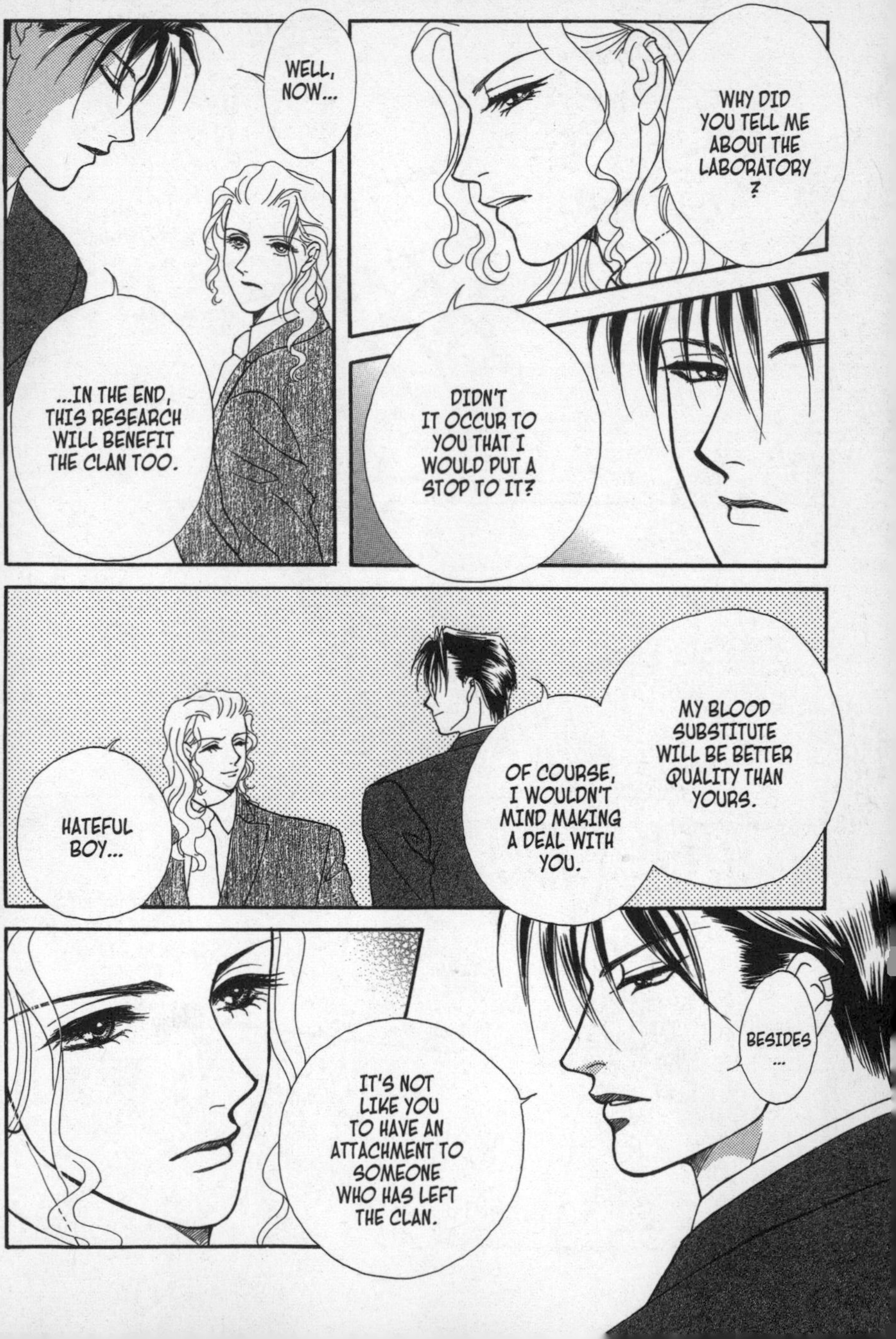
WHY DID YOU TELL ME ABOUT THE LABORATORY?
DIDN'T IT OCCUR TO YOU THAT I WOULD PUT A STOP TO IT?
WELL, NOW...
...IN THE END, THIS RESEARCH WILL BENEFIT THE CLAN TOO.
MY BLOOD SUBSTITUTE WILL BE BETTER QUALITY THAN YOURS.
OF COURSE, I WOULDN'T MIND MAKING A DEAL WITH YOU.
HATEFUL BOY...
BESIDES...
IT'S NOT LIKE YOU TO HAVE AN ATTACHMENT TO SOMEONE WHO HAS LEFT THE CLAN.

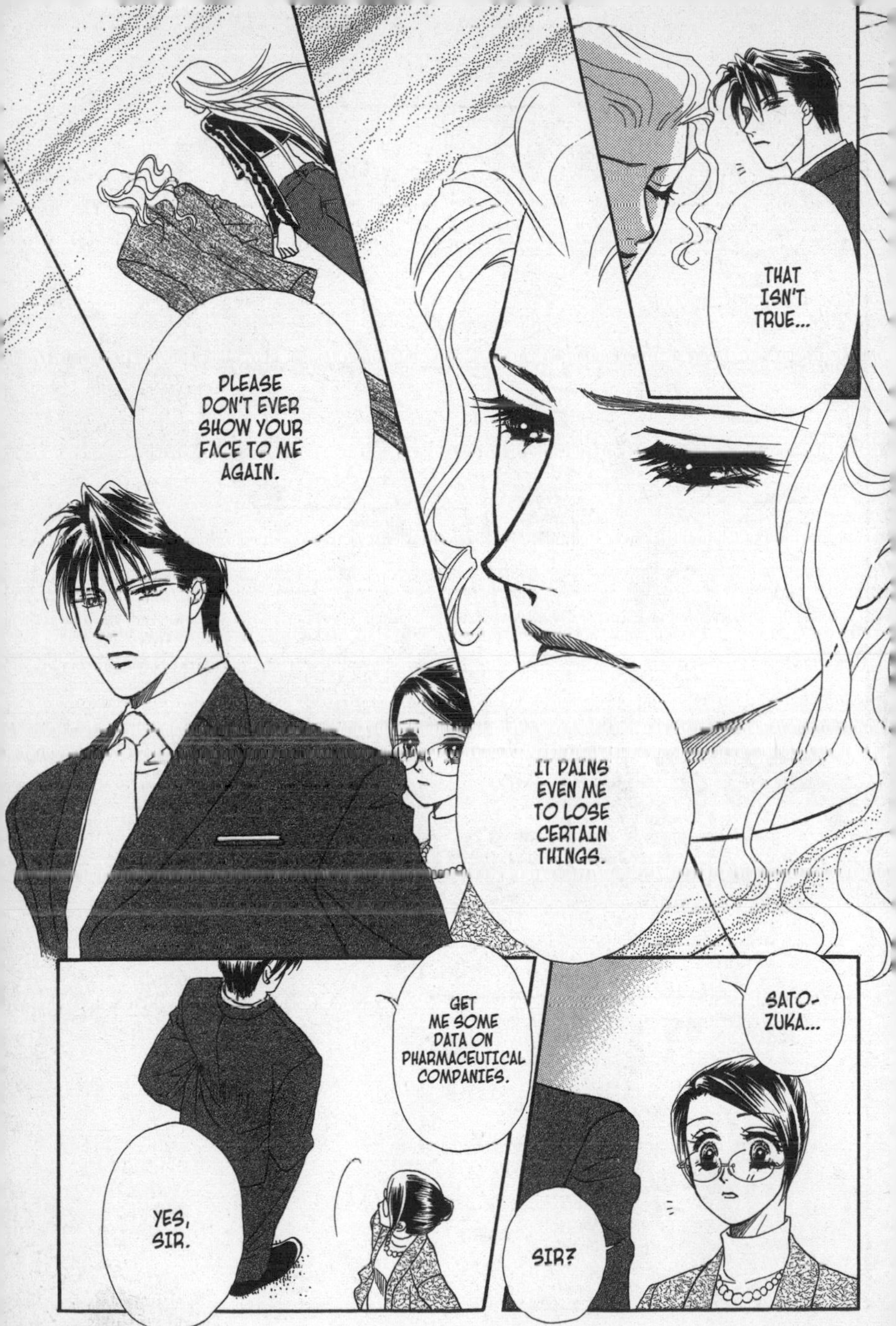
THAT ISN'T TRUE...
IT PAINS EVEN ME TO LOSE CERTAIN THINGS.
PLEASE DON'T EVER SHOW YOUR FACE TO ME AGAIN.
SATO-ZUKA...
SIR?
GET ME SOME DATA ON PHARMACEUTICAL COMPANIES.
YES, SIR.

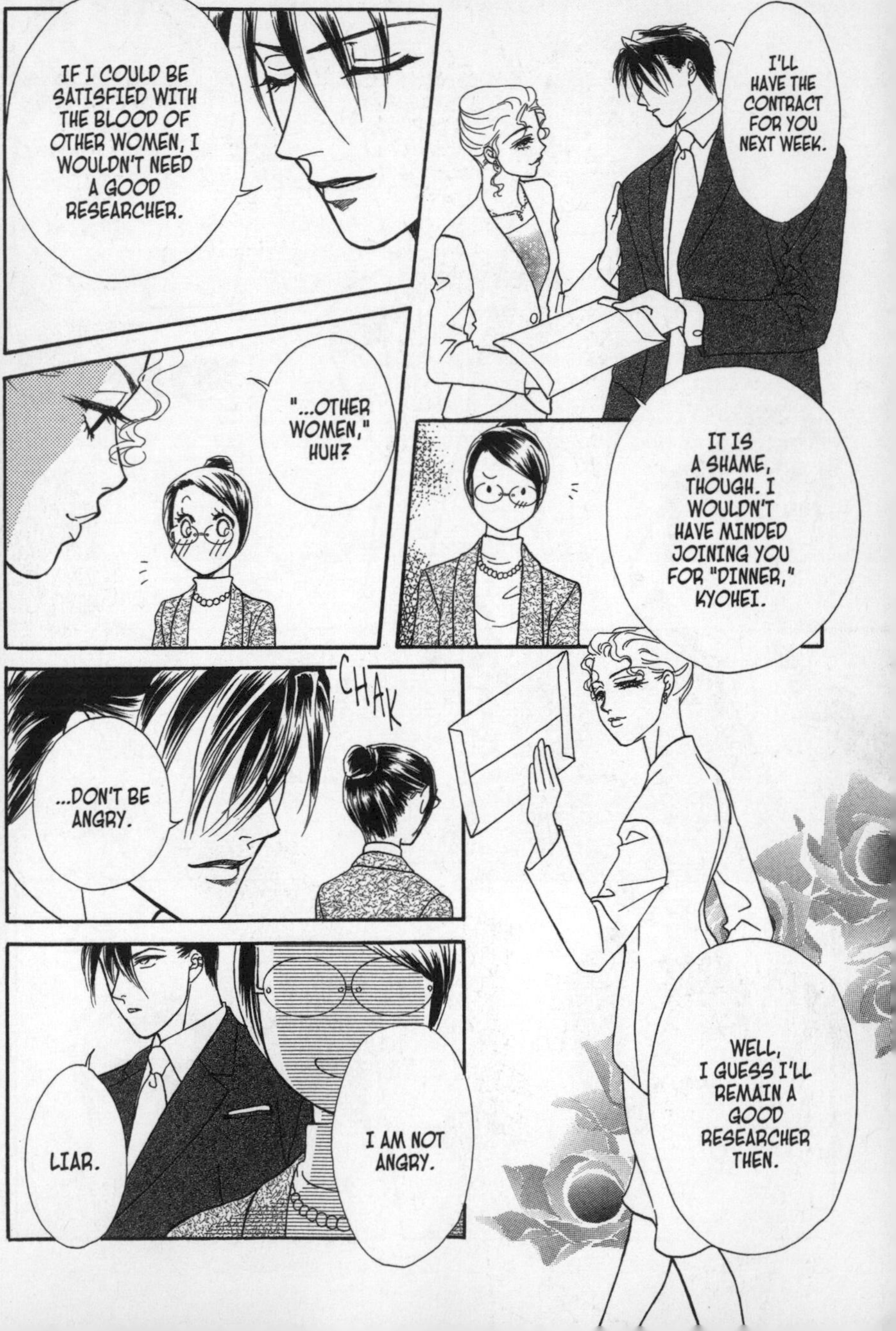
I'LL HAVE THE CONTRACT FOR YOU NEXT WEEK.
IF I COULD BE SATISFIED WITH THE BLOOD OF OTHER WOMEN, I WOULDN'T NEED A GOOD RESEARCHER.
IT IS A SHAME, THOUGH. I WOULDN'T HAVE MINDED JOINING YOU FOR "DINNER," KYOHEI.
"...OTHER WOMEN," HUH?
WELL, I GUESS I'LL REMAIN A GOOD RESEARCHER THEN.
CHAK
...DON'T BE ANGRY.
I AM NOT ANGRY.
LIAR.

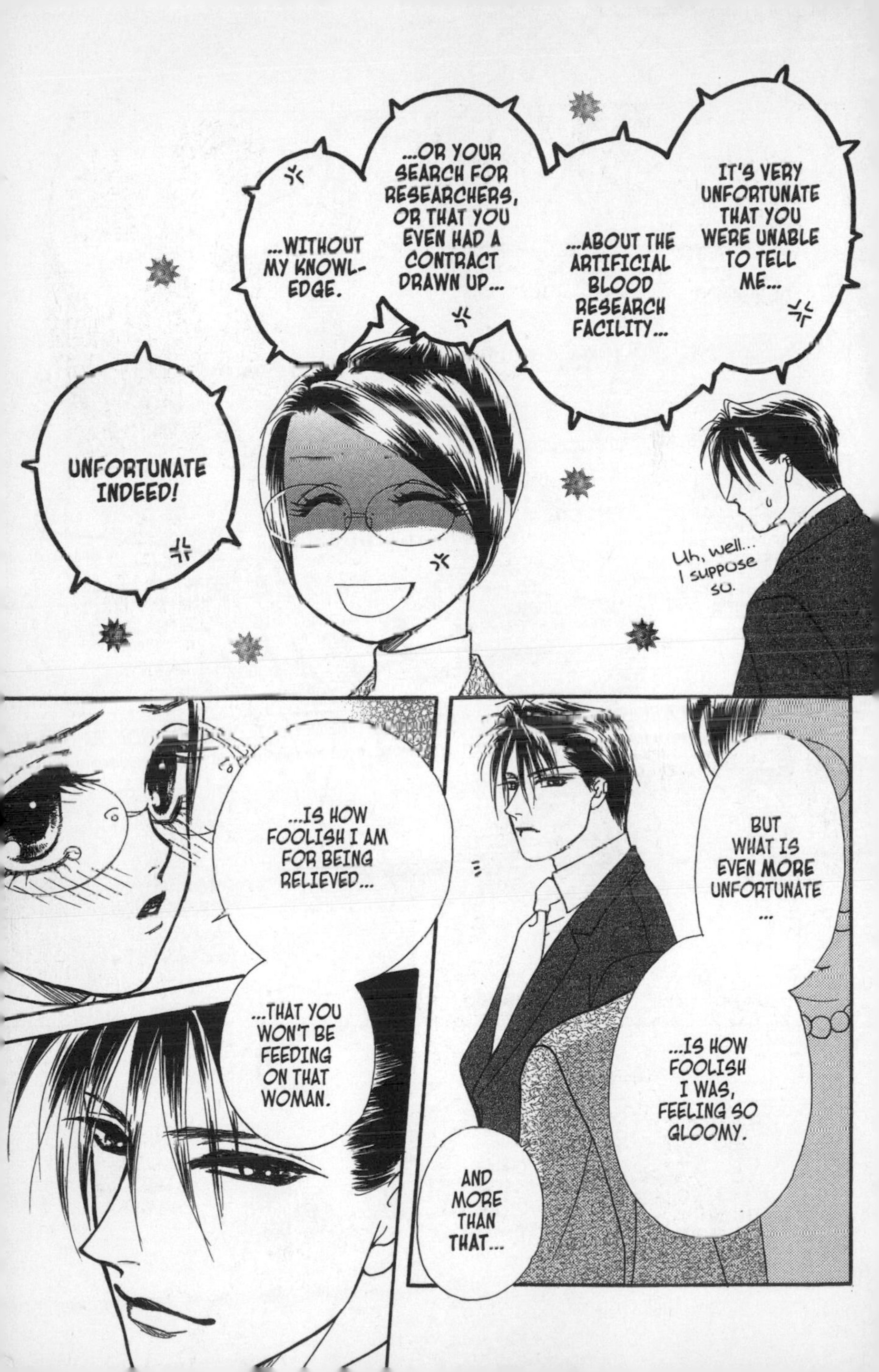
IT'S VERY UNFORTUNATE THAT YOU WERE UNABLE TO TELL ME...
...ABOUT THE ARTIFICIAL BLOOD RESEARCH FACILITY...
...OR YOUR SEARCH FOR RESEARCHERS, OR THAT YOU EVEN HAD A CONTRACT DRAWN UP...
...WITHOUT MY KNOWL-EDGE.
Uh, well... I suppose so.
UNFORTUNATE INDEED!
BUT WHAT IS EVEN MORE UNFORTUNATE...
...IS HOW FOOLISH I WAS, FEELING SO GLOOMY.
AND MORE THAN THAT...
...IS HOW FOOLISH I AM FOR BEING RELIEVED...
...THAT YOU WON'T BE FEEDING ON THAT WOMAN.

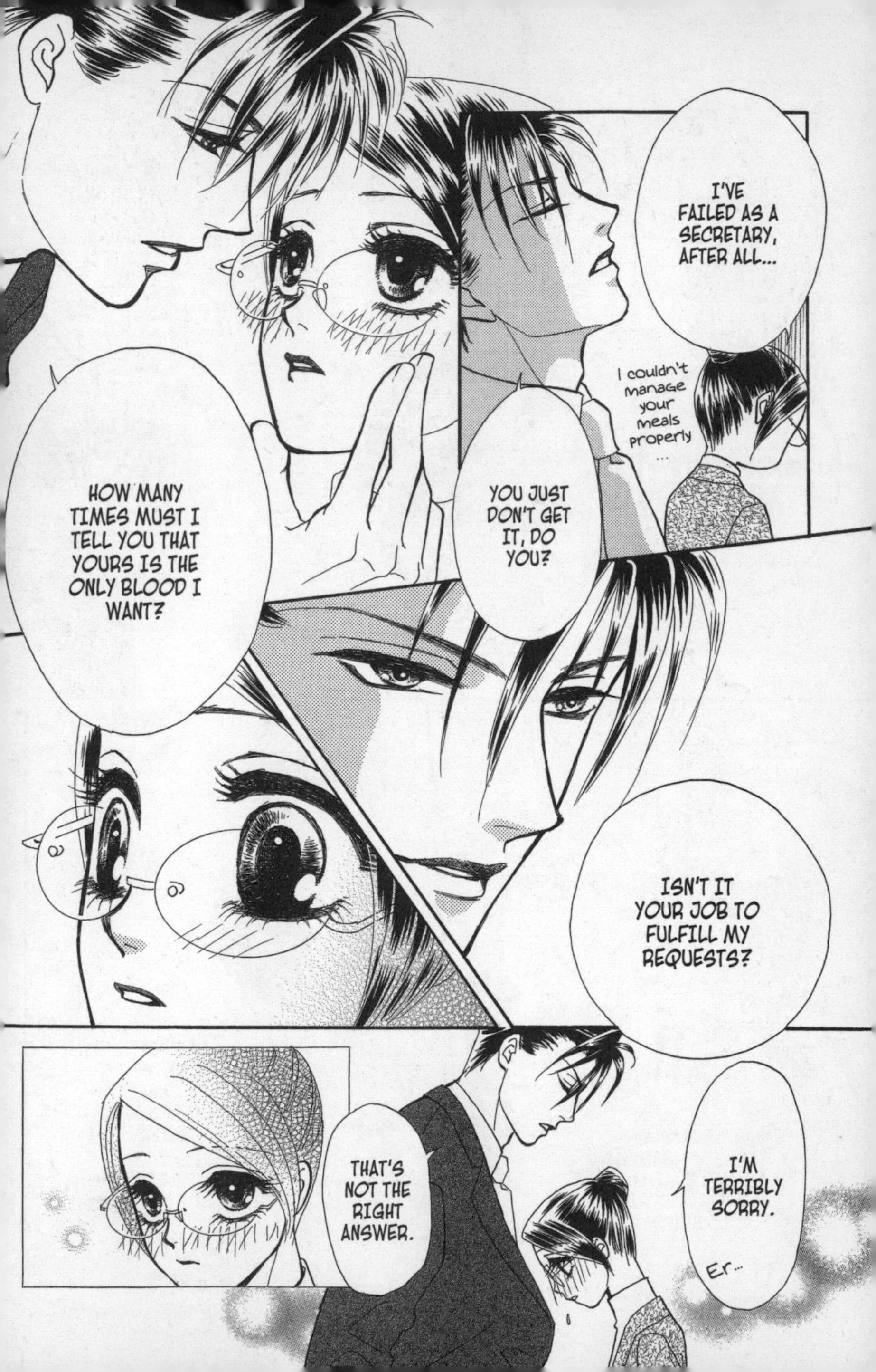
I'VE FAILED AS A SECRETARY, AFTER ALL...
I couldn't manage your meals properly ...
YOU JUST DON'T GET IT, DO YOU?
HOW MANY TIMES MUST I TELL YOU THAT YOURS IS THE ONLY BLOOD I WANT?
ISN'T IT YOUR JOB TO FULFILL MY REQUESTS?
I'M TERRIBLY SORRY.
Er...
THAT'S NOT THE RIGHT ANSWER.

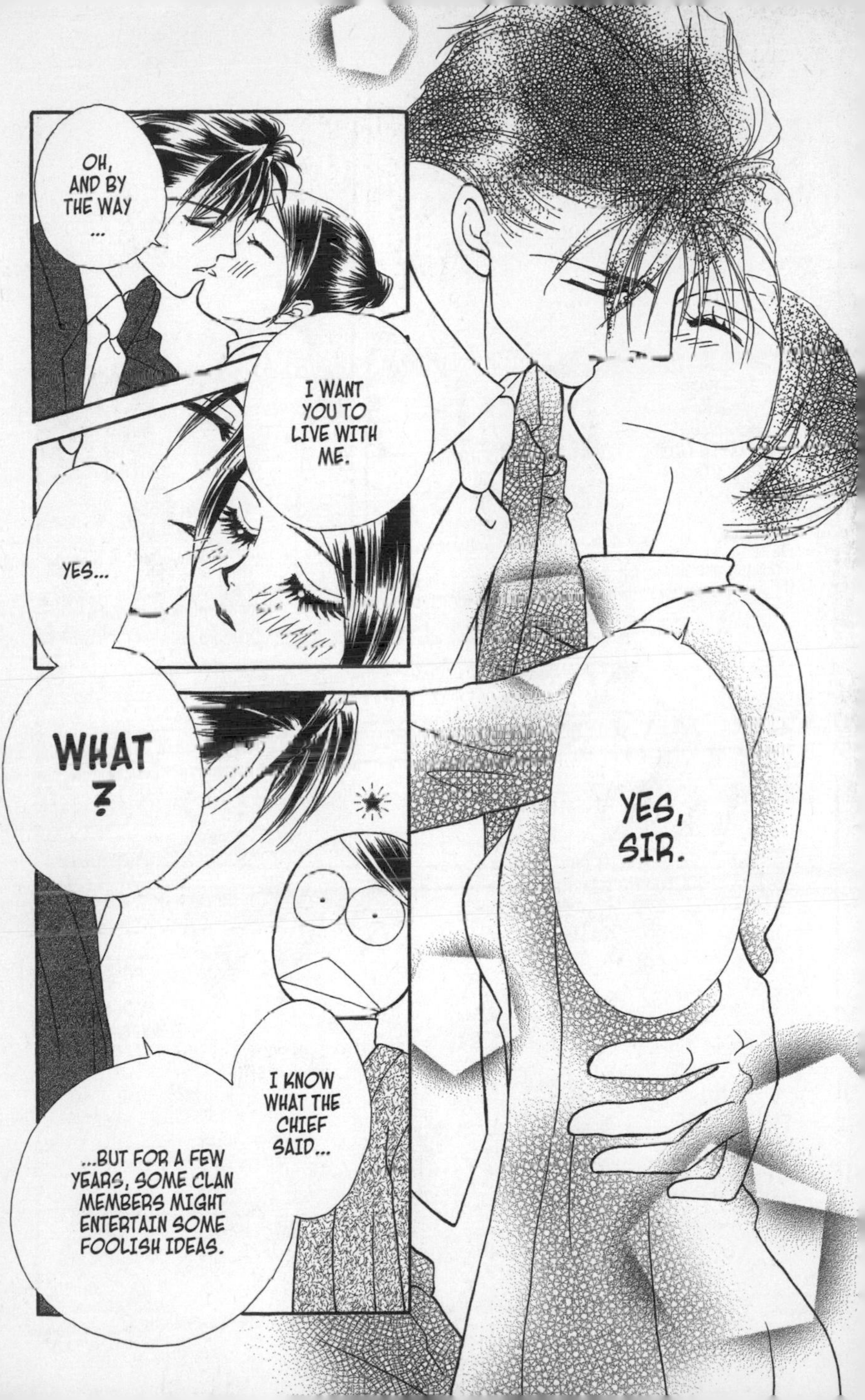
OH, AND BY THE WAY ...
I WANT YOU TO LIVE WITH ME.
YES...
WHAT ?
YES, SIR.
I KNOW WHAT THE CHIEF SAID...
...BUT FOR A FEW YEARS, SOME CLAN MEMBERS MIGHT ENTERTAIN SOME FOOLISH IDEAS.

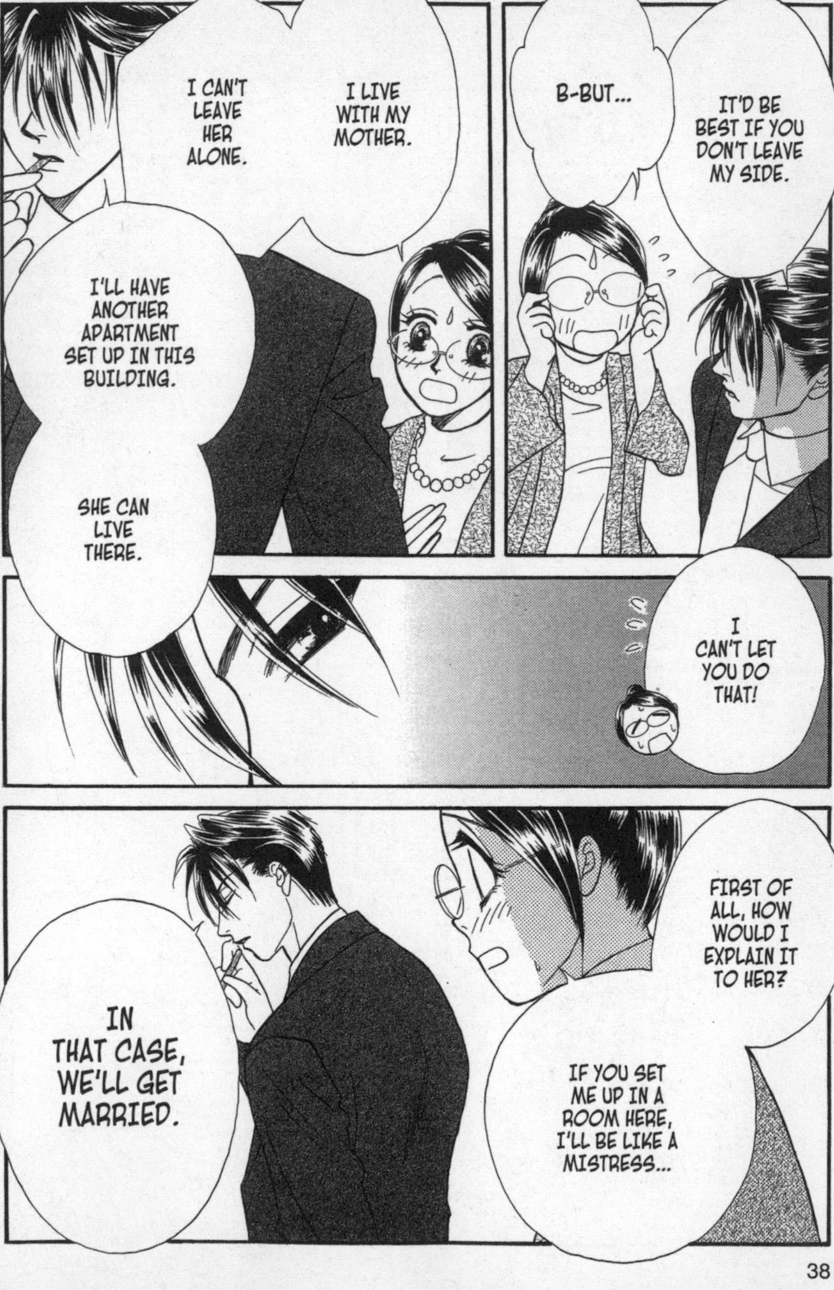
IT'D BE BEST IF YOU DON'T LEAVE MY SIDE.
B-BUT...
I LIVE WITH MY MOTHER.
I CAN'T LEAVE HER ALONE.
I'LL HAVE ANOTHER APARTMENT SET UP IN THIS BUILDING.
SHE CAN LIVE THERE.
I CAN'T LET YOU DO THAT!
FIRST OF ALL, HOW WOULD I EXPLAIN IT TO HER?
IF YOU SET ME UP IN A ROOM HERE, I'LL BE LIKE A MISTRESS...
IN THAT CASE, WE'LL GET MARRIED.

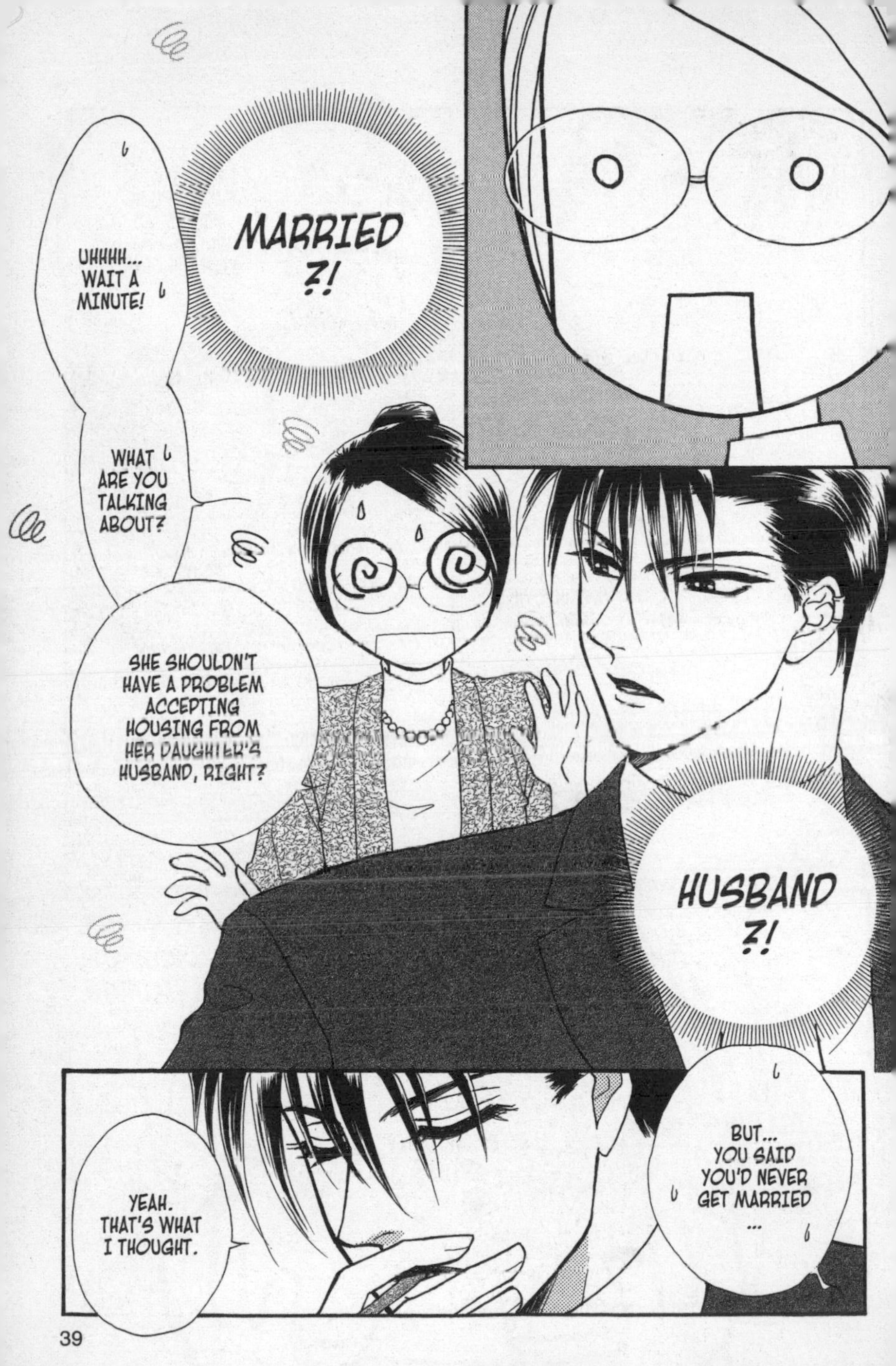
MARRIED ?!
UHHHH... WAIT A MINUTE!
WHAT ARE YOU TALKING ABOUT?
SHE SHOULDN'T HAVE A PROBLEM ACCEPTING HOUSING FROM HER DAUGHTER'S HUSBAND, RIGHT?
HUSBAND ?!
BUT... YOU SAID YOU'D NEVER GET MARRIED ...
YEAH. THAT'S WHAT I THOUGHT.

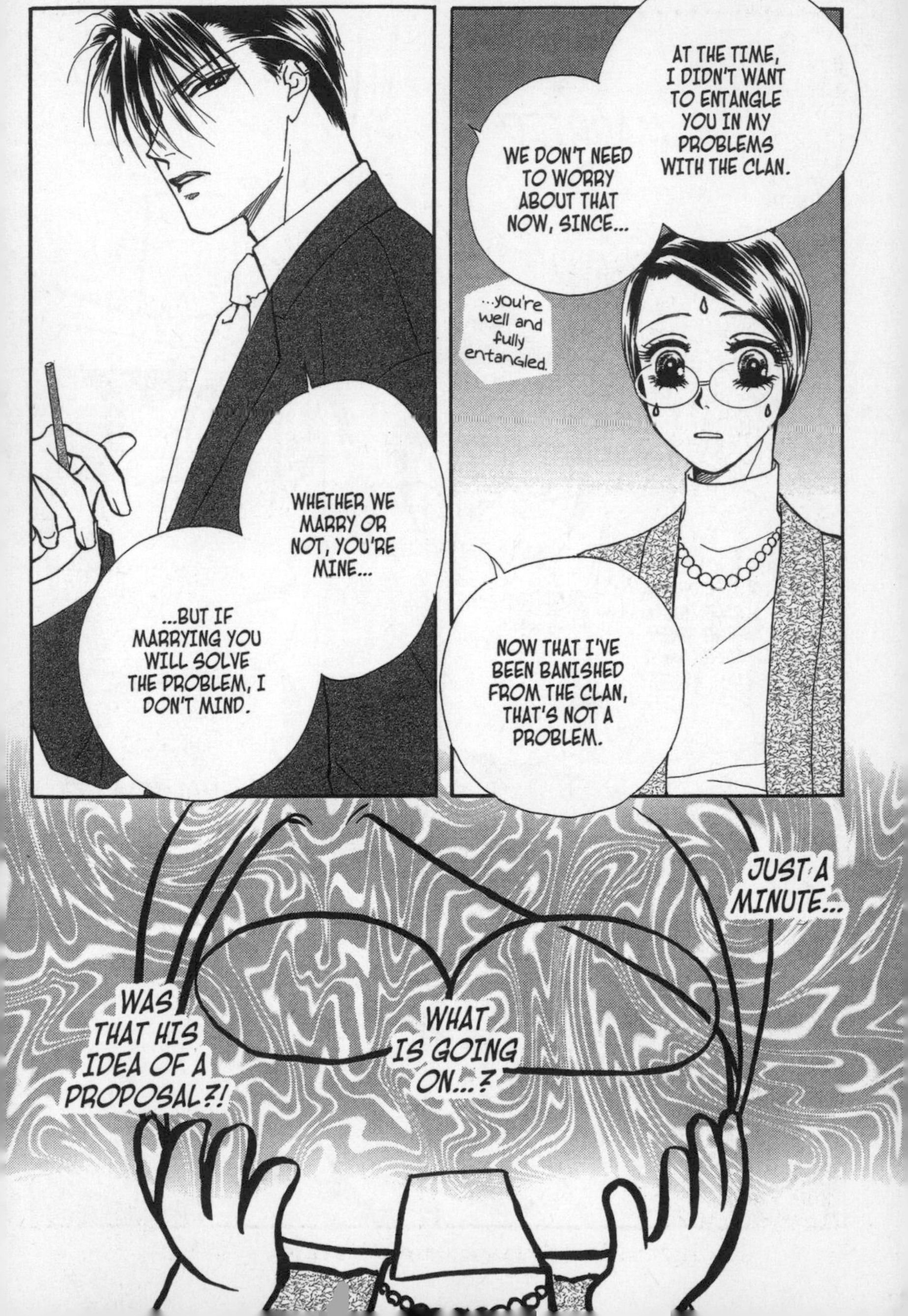
AT THE TIME, I DIDN'T WANT TO ENTANGLE YOU IN MY PROBLEMS WITH THE CLAN.
WE DON'T NEED TO WORRY ABOUT THAT NOW, SINCE...
...you're well and fully entangled.
NOW THAT I'VE BEEN BANISHED FROM THE CLAN, THAT'S NOT A PROBLEM.
WHETHER WE MARRY OR NOT, YOU'RE MINE...
...BUT IF MARRYING YOU WILL SOLVE THE PROBLEM, I DON'T MIND.
JUST A MINUTE...
WHAT IS GOING ON...?
WAS THAT HIS IDEA OF A PROPOSAL?!

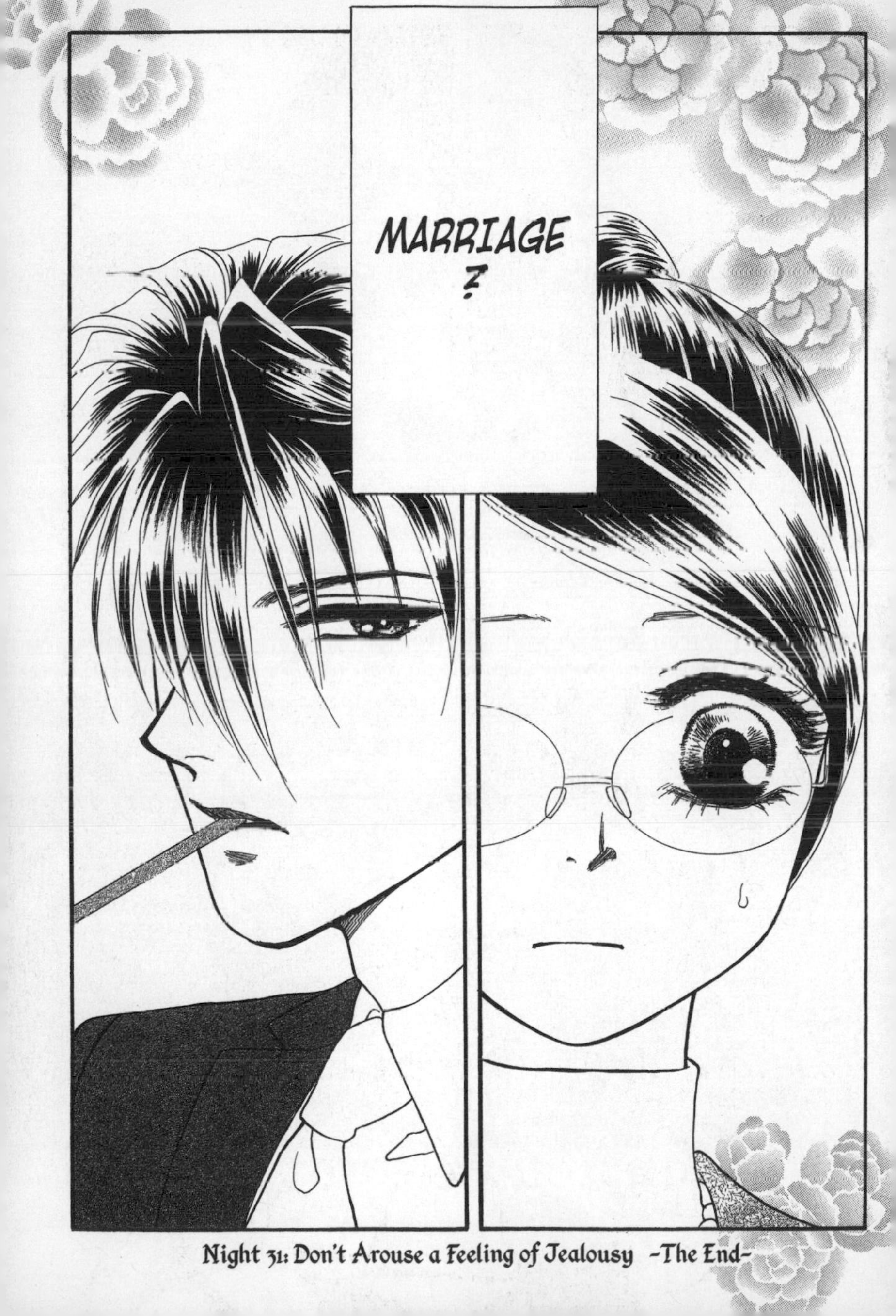
MARRIAGE
?

Night 31: Don't Arouse a Feeling of Jealousy -The End-

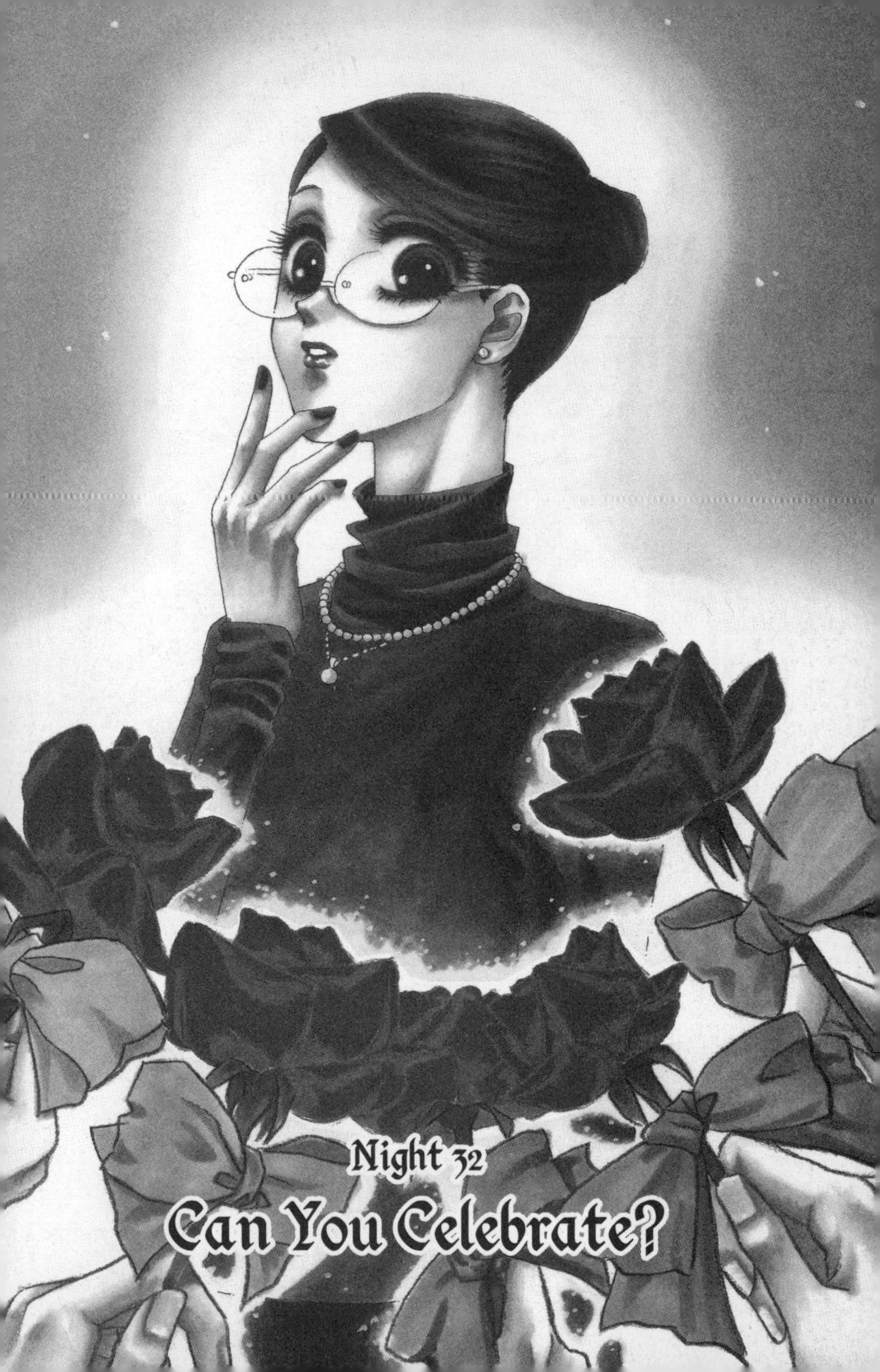
Night 32
Can You Celebrate?

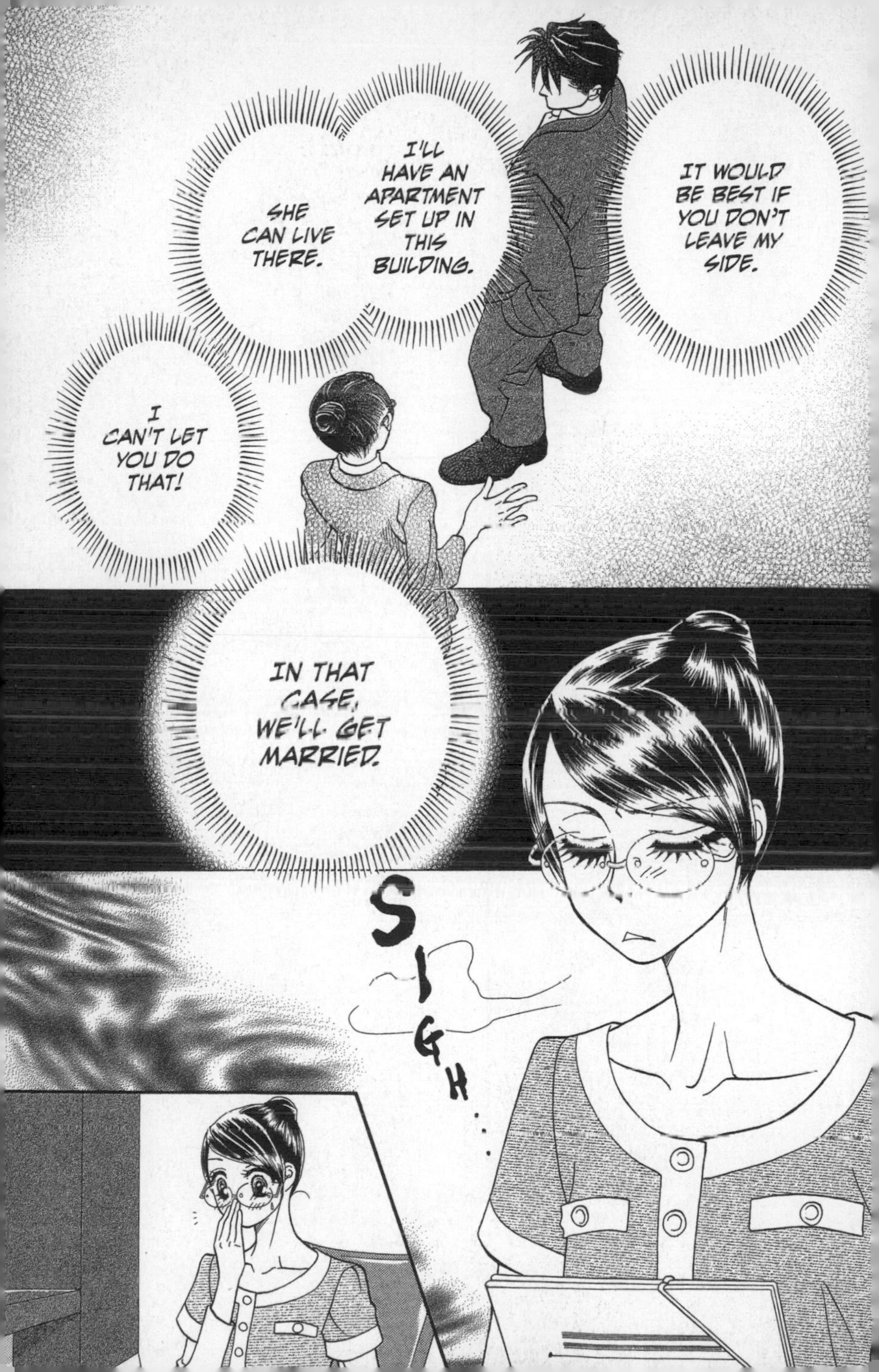
IT WOULD BE BEST IF YOU DON'T LEAVE MY SIDE.
I'LL HAVE AN APARTMENT SET UP IN THIS BUILDING.
SHE CAN LIVE THERE.
I CAN'T LET YOU DO THAT!
IN THAT CASE, WE'LL GET MARRIED.
SIGH...

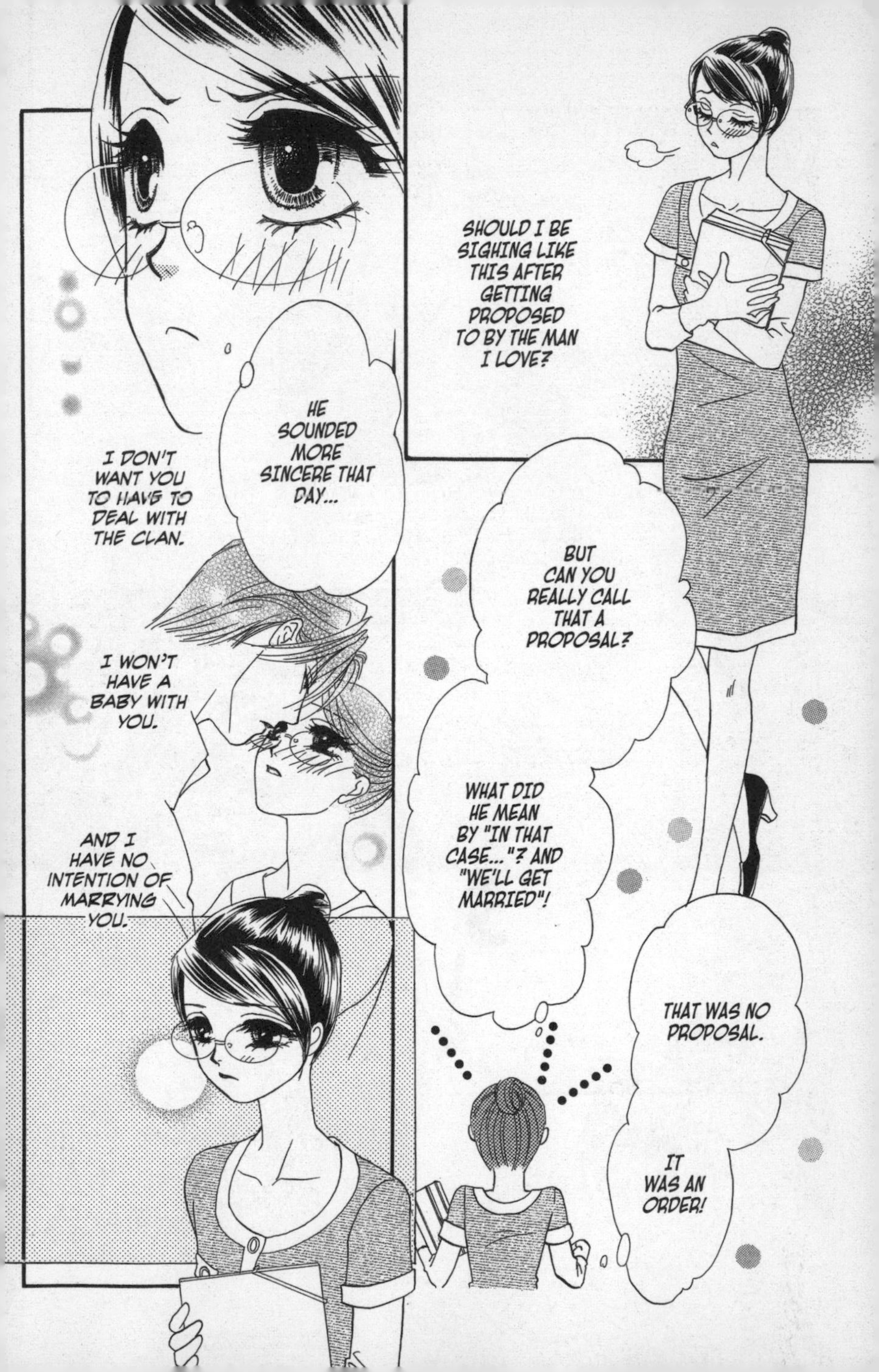
SHOULD I BE SIGHING LIKE THIS AFTER GETTING PROPOSED TO BY THE MAN I LOVE?
HE SOUNDED MORE SINCERE THAT DAY...
I DON'T WANT YOU TO HAVE TO DEAL WITH THE CLAN.
I WON'T HAVE A BABY WITH YOU.
AND I HAVE NO INTENTION OF MARRYING YOU.
BUT CAN YOU REALLY CALL THAT A PROPOSAL?
WHAT DID HE MEAN BY "IN THAT CASE..."? AND "WE'LL GET MARRIED"!
THAT WAS NO PROPOSAL.
IT WAS AN ORDER!

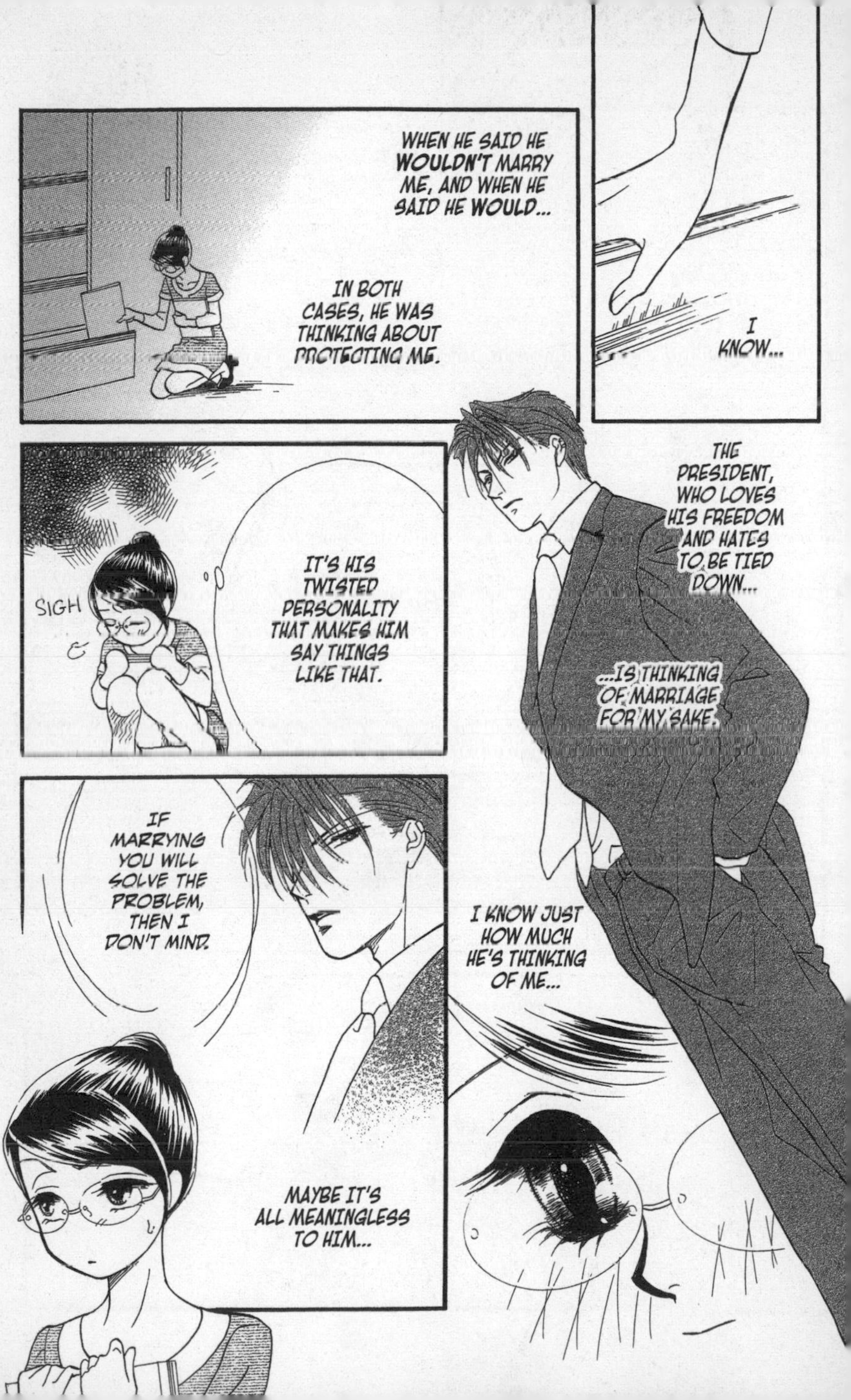
I KNOW...
WHEN HE SAID HE WOULDN'T MARRY ME, AND WHEN HE SAID HE WOULD...
IN BOTH CASES, HE WAS THINKING ABOUT PROTECTING ME.
THE PRESIDENT, WHO LOVES HIS FREEDOM AND HATES TO BE TIED DOWN...
...IS THINKING OF MARRIAGE FOR MY SAKE.
IT'S HIS TWISTED PERSONALITY THAT MAKES HIM SAY THINGS LIKE THAT.
SIGH
IF MARRYING YOU WILL SOLVE THE PROBLEM, THEN I DON'T MIND.
I KNOW JUST HOW MUCH HE'S THINKING OF ME...
MAYBE IT'S ALL MEANINGLESS TO HIM...

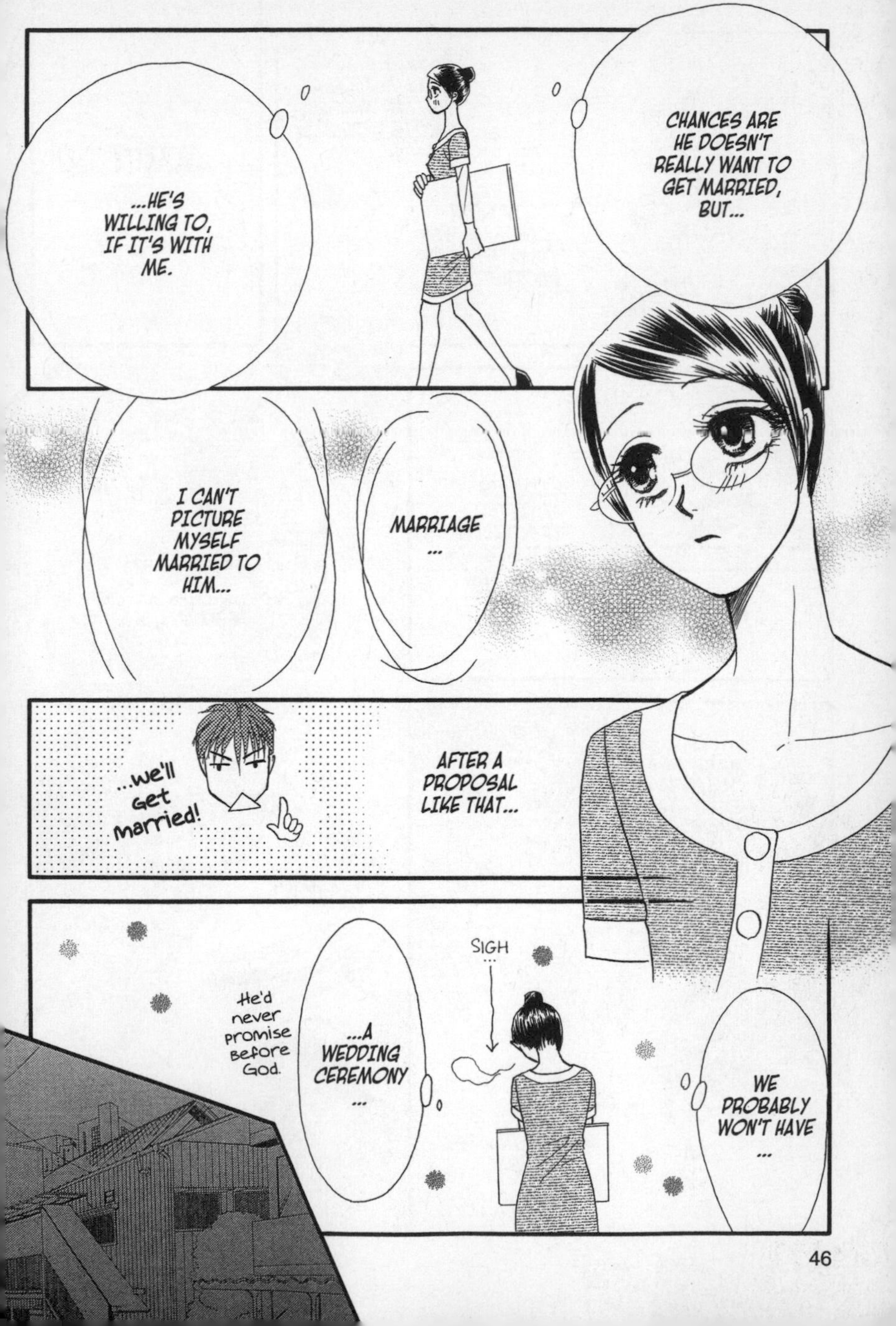
CHANCES ARE HE DOESN'T REALLY WANT TO GET MARRIED, BUT...
...HE'S WILLING TO, IF IT'S WITH ME.
MARRIAGE ...
I CAN'T PICTURE MYSELF MARRIED TO HIM...
AFTER A PROPOSAL LIKE THAT...
...we'll get married!
WE PROBABLY WON'T HAVE ...
SIGH ...
...A WEDDING CEREMONY ...
He'd never promise before God.

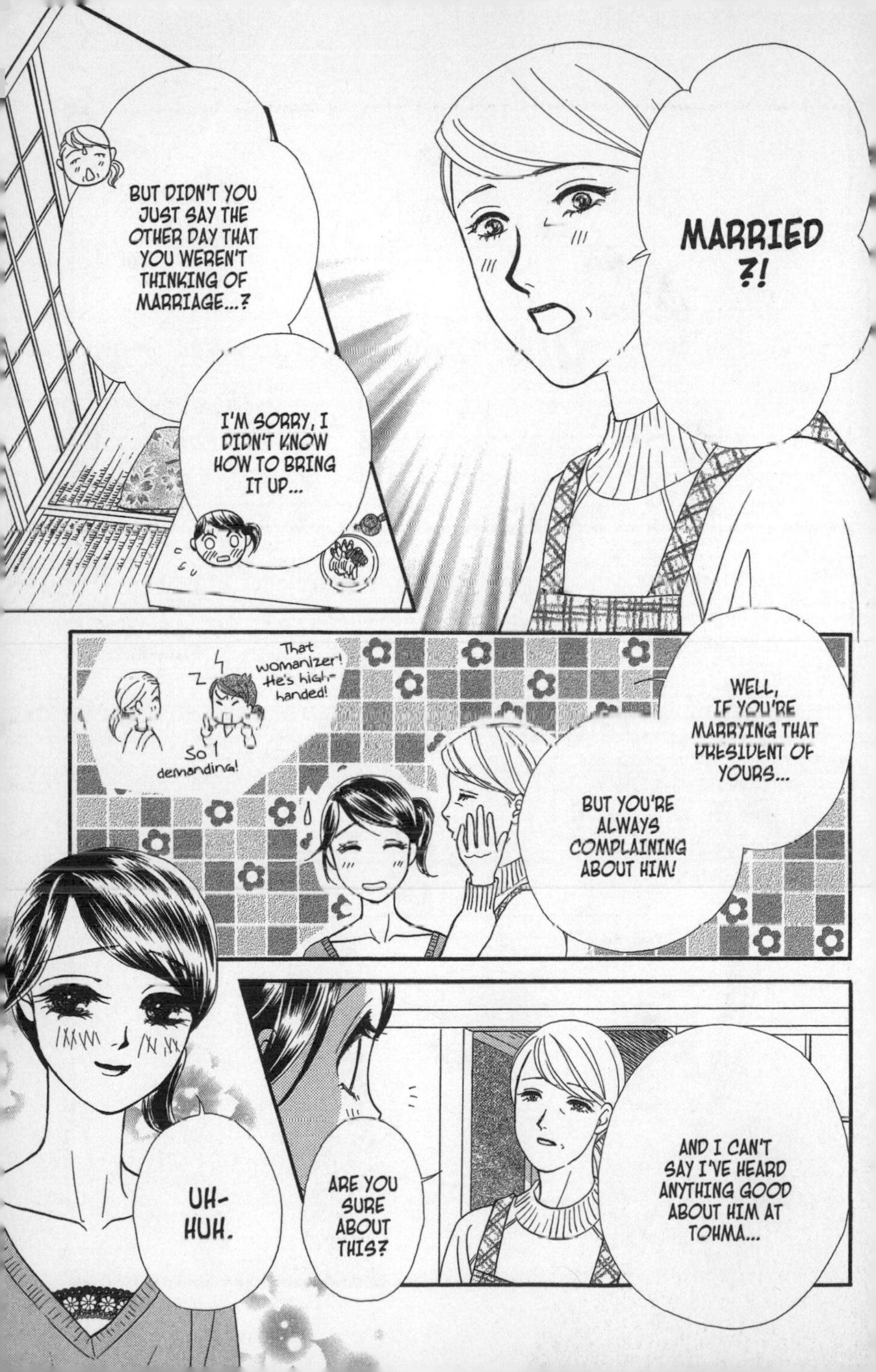
MARRIED ?!
BUT DIDN'T YOU JUST SAY THE OTHER DAY THAT YOU WEREN'T THINKING OF MARRIAGE...?
I'M SORRY, I DIDN'T KNOW HOW TO BRING IT UP...
WELL, IF YOU'RE MARRYING THAT PRESIDENT OF YOURS...
BUT YOU'RE ALWAYS COMPLAINING ABOUT HIM!
That womanizer! He's high-handed!
So demanding!
AND I CAN'T SAY I'VE HEARD ANYTHING GOOD ABOUT HIM AT TOHMA...
ARE YOU SURE ABOUT THIS?
UH-HUH.

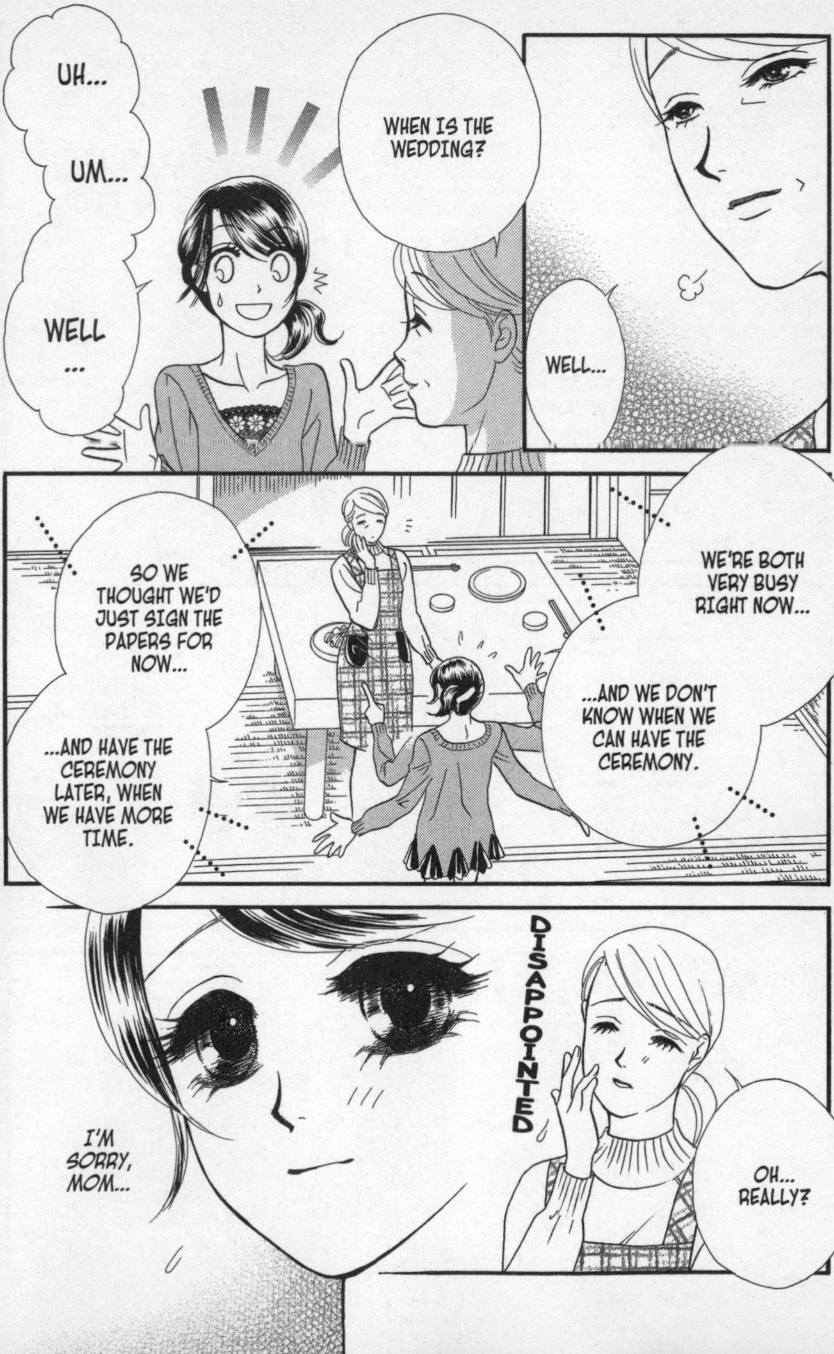
WELL...
WHEN IS THE WEDDING?
UH...
UM...
WELL...
WE'RE BOTH VERY BUSY RIGHT NOW...
...AND WE DON'T KNOW WHEN WE CAN HAVE THE CEREMONY.
SO WE THOUGHT WE'D JUST SIGN THE PAPERS FOR NOW...
...AND HAVE THE CEREMONY LATER, WHEN WE HAVE MORE TIME.
DISAPPOINTED
OH... REALLY?
I'M SORRY, MOM...

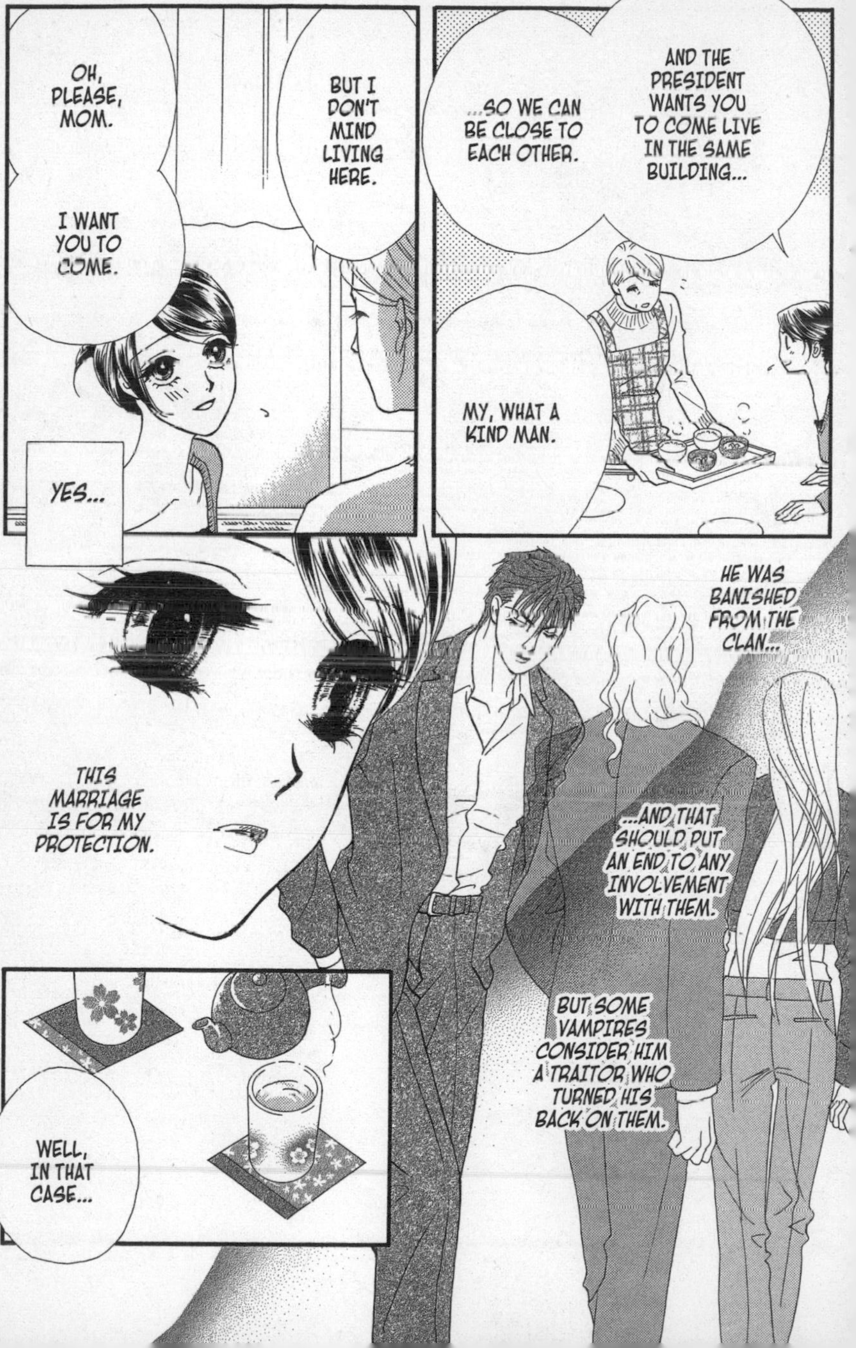
AND THE PRESIDENT WANTS YOU TO COME LIVE IN THE SAME BUILDING...
...SO WE CAN BE CLOSE TO EACH OTHER.
MY, WHAT A KIND MAN.
BUT I DON'T MIND LIVING HERE.
OH, PLEASE, MOM.
I WANT YOU TO COME.
YES...
HE WAS BANISHED FROM THE CLAN...
...AND THAT SHOULD PUT AN END TO ANY INVOLVEMENT WITH THEM.
BUT SOME VAMPIRES CONSIDER HIM A TRAITOR WHO TURNED HIS BACK ON THEM.
THIS MARRIAGE IS FOR MY PROTECTION.
WELL, IN THAT CASE...

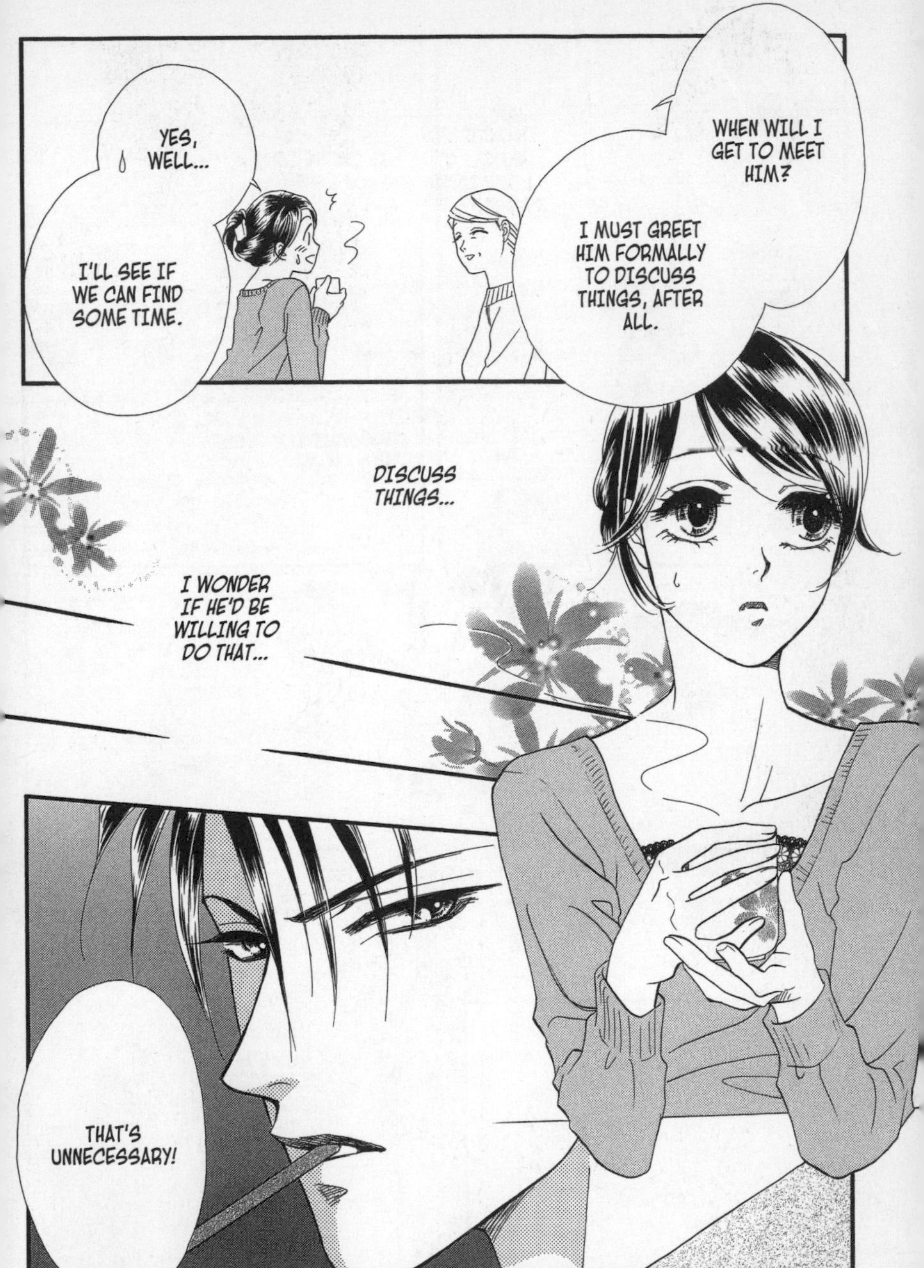
WHEN WILL I GET TO MEET HIM?
I MUST GREET HIM FORMALLY TO DISCUSS THINGS, AFTER ALL.
YES, WELL...
I'LL SEE IF WE CAN FIND SOME TIME.
DISCUSS THINGS...
I WONDER IF HE'D BE WILLING TO DO THAT...
THAT'S UNNECESSARY!

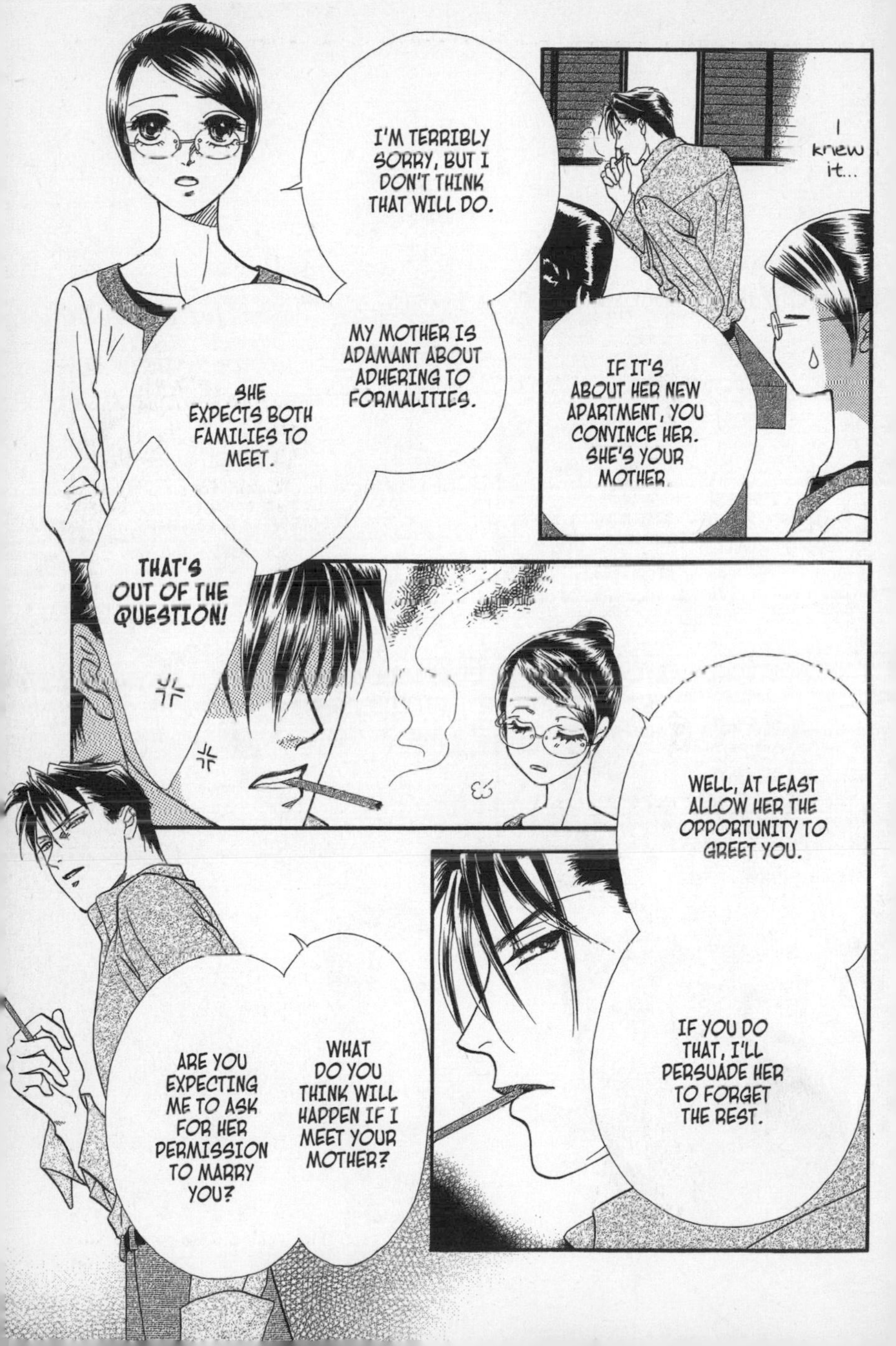
I knew it...
IF IT'S ABOUT HER NEW APARTMENT, YOU CONVINCE HER. SHE'S YOUR MOTHER.
I'M TERRIBLY SORRY, BUT I DON'T THINK THAT WILL DO.
MY MOTHER IS ADAMANT ABOUT ADHERING TO FORMALITIES.
SHE EXPECTS BOTH FAMILIES TO MEET.
THAT'S OUT OF THE QUESTION!
WELL, AT LEAST ALLOW HER THE OPPORTUNITY TO GREET YOU.
IF YOU DO THAT, I'LL PERSUADE HER TO FORGET THE REST.
WHAT DO YOU THINK WILL HAPPEN IF I MEET YOUR MOTHER?
ARE YOU EXPECTING ME TO ASK FOR HER PERMISSION TO MARRY YOU?

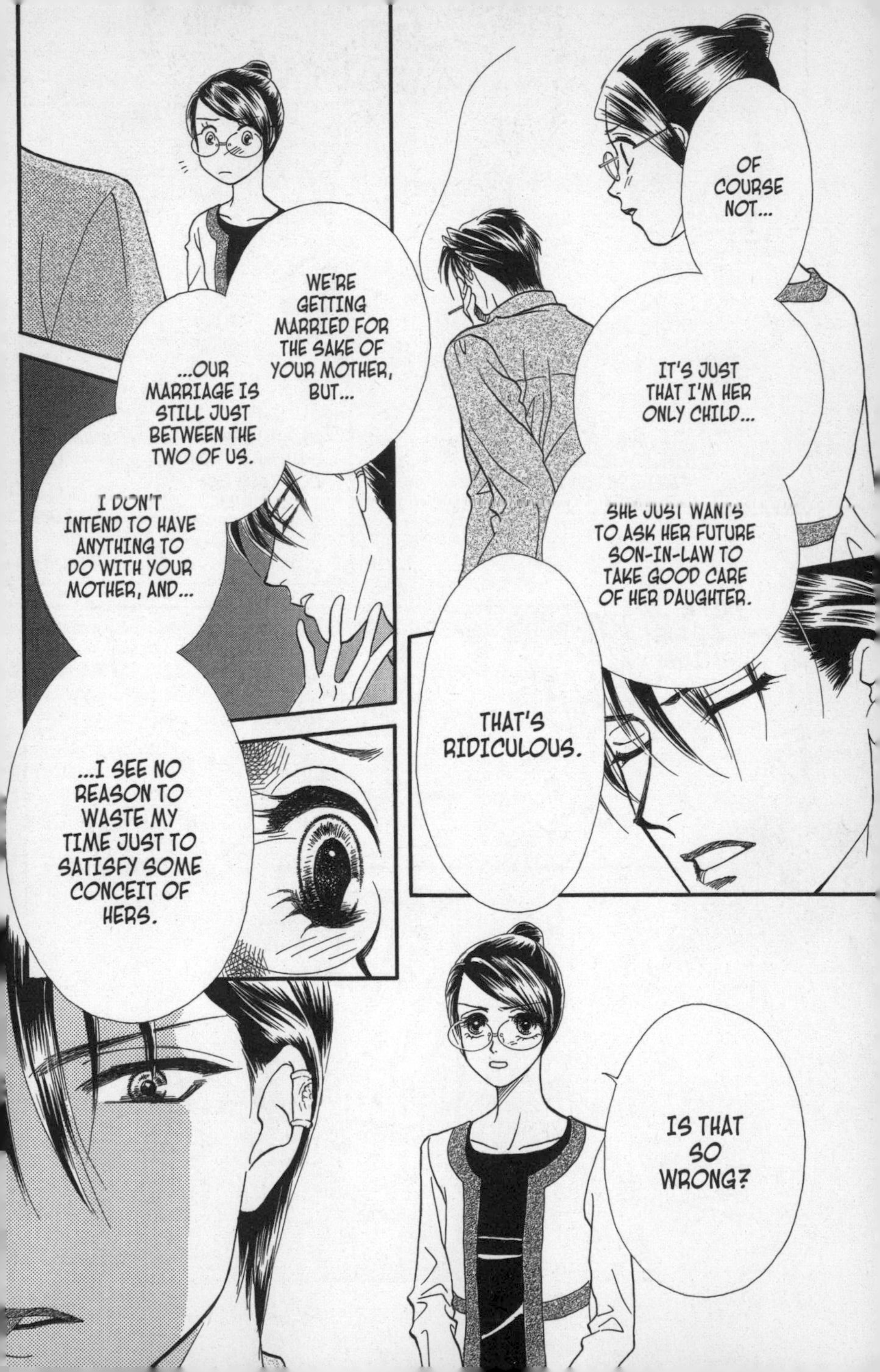
OF COURSE NOT...
IT'S JUST THAT I'M HER ONLY CHILD...
SHE JUST WANTS TO ASK HER FUTURE SON-IN-LAW TO TAKE GOOD CARE OF HER DAUGHTER.
THAT'S RIDICULOUS.
WE'RE GETTING MARRIED FOR THE SAKE OF YOUR MOTHER, BUT...
...OUR MARRIAGE IS STILL JUST BETWEEN THE TWO OF US.
I DON'T INTEND TO HAVE ANYTHING TO DO WITH YOUR MOTHER, AND...
...I SEE NO REASON TO WASTE MY TIME JUST TO SATISFY SOME CONCEIT OF HERS.
IS THAT SO WRONG?

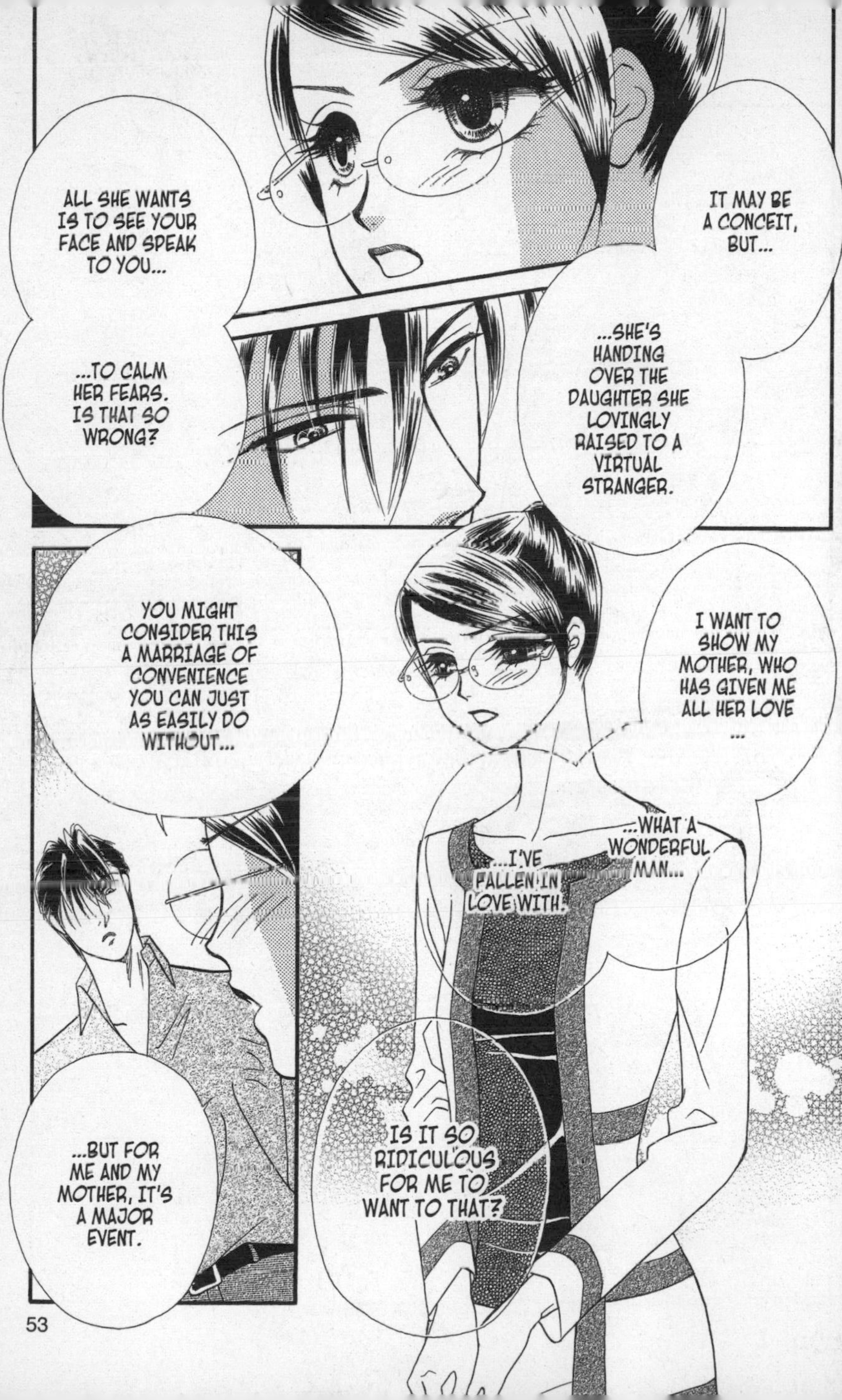
IT MAY BE A CONCEIT, BUT...
...SHE'S HANDING OVER THE DAUGHTER SHE LOVINGLY RAISED TO A VIRTUAL STRANGER.
ALL SHE WANTS IS TO SEE YOUR FACE AND SPEAK TO YOU...
...TO CALM HER FEARS. IS THAT SO WRONG?
I WANT TO SHOW MY MOTHER, WHO HAS GIVEN ME ALL HER LOVE ...
...WHAT A WONDERFUL MAN...
...I'VE FALLEN IN LOVE WITH.
IS IT SO RIDICULOUS FOR ME TO WANT TO THAT?
YOU MIGHT CONSIDER THIS A MARRIAGE OF CONVENIENCE YOU CAN JUST AS EASILY DO WITHOUT...
...BUT FOR ME AND MY MOTHER, IT'S A MAJOR EVENT.

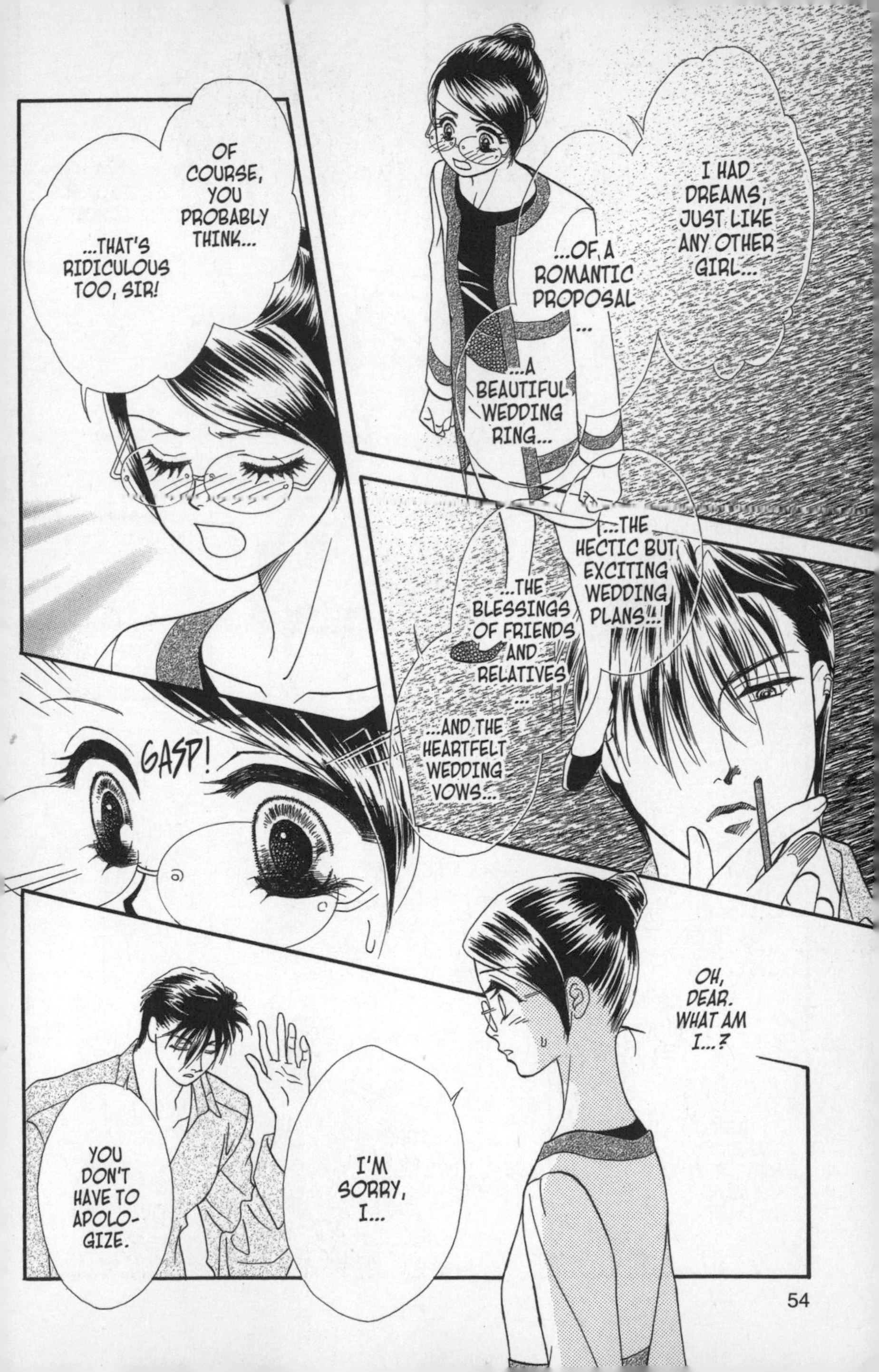
I HAD DREAMS, JUST LIKE ANY OTHER GIRL...
...OF A ROMANTIC PROPOSAL...
...A BEAUTIFUL WEDDING RING...
...THE HECTIC BUT EXCITING WEDDING PLANS...
...THE BLESSINGS OF FRIENDS AND RELATIVES...
...AND THE HEARTFELT WEDDING VOWS...
OF COURSE, YOU PROBABLY THINK...
...THAT'S RIDICULOUS TOO, SIR!
GASP!
OH, DEAR. WHAT AM I...?
I'M SORRY, I...
YOU DON'T HAVE TO APOLO-GIZE.

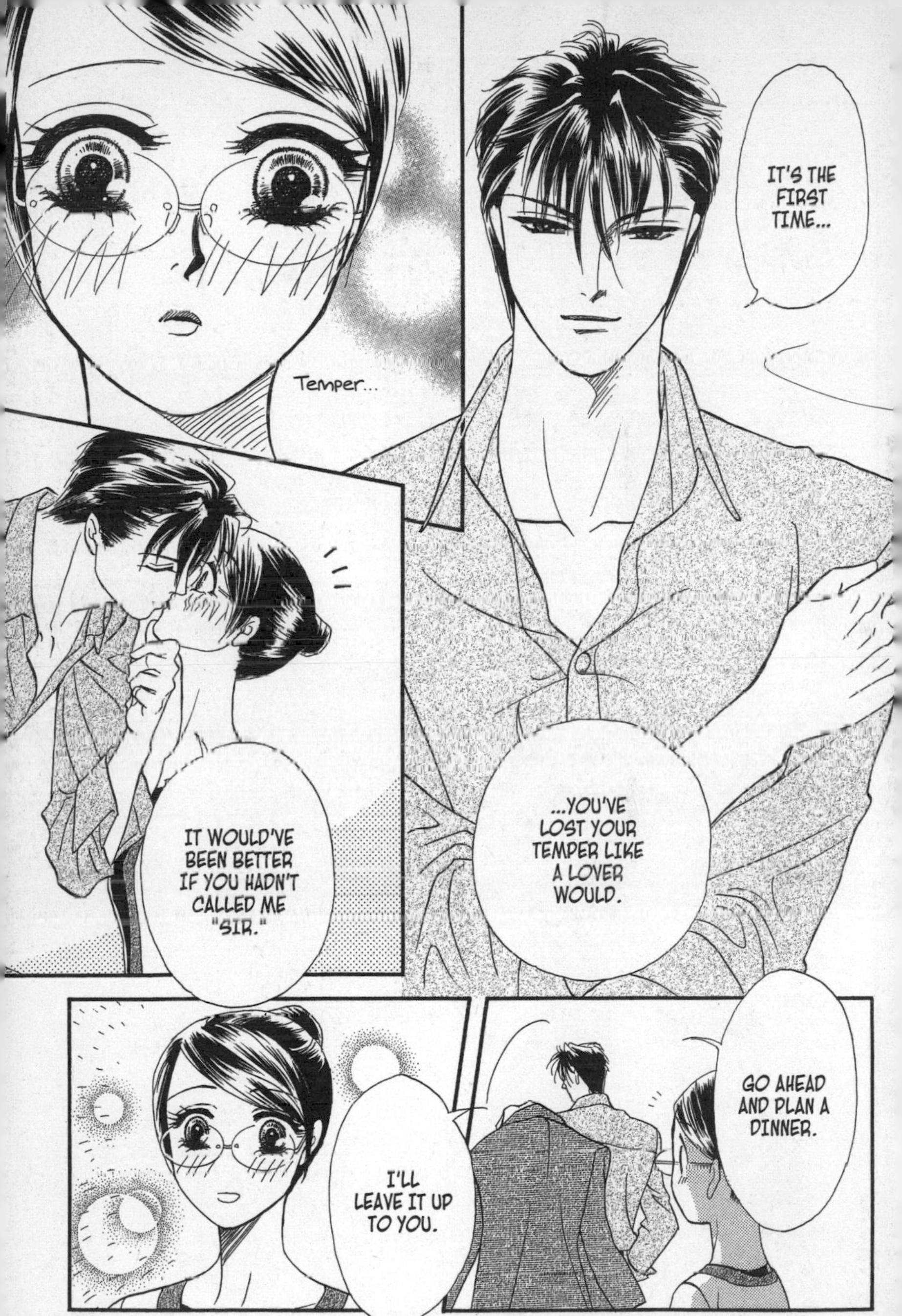
IT'S THE FIRST TIME...
...YOU'VE LOST YOUR TEMPER LIKE A LOVER WOULD.
Temper...
IT WOULD'VE BEEN BETTER IF YOU HADN'T CALLED ME "SIR."
GO AHEAD AND PLAN A DINNER.
I'LL LEAVE IT UP TO YOU.

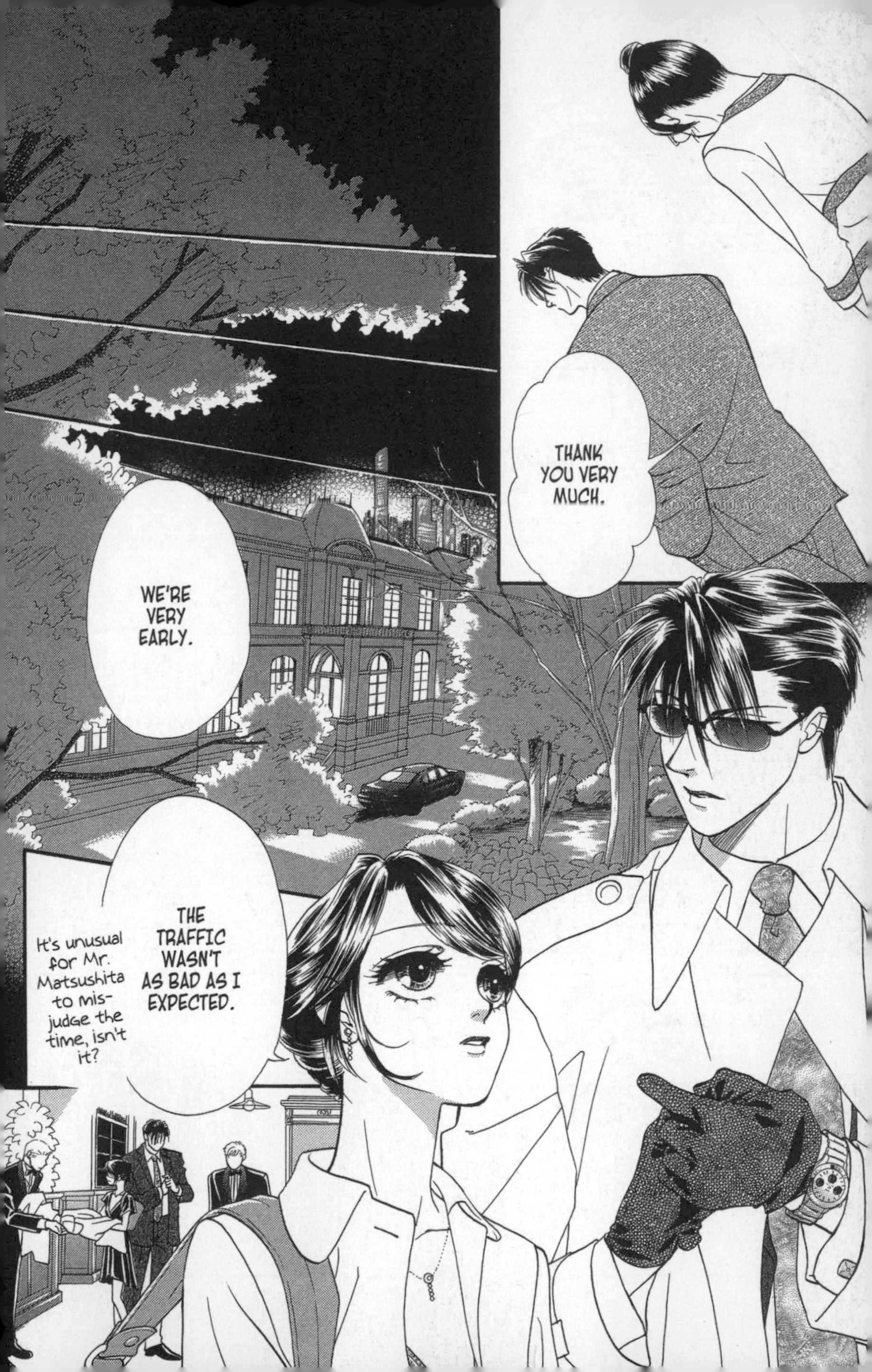
THANK YOU VERY MUCH.
WE'RE VERY EARLY.
THE TRAFFIC WASN'T AS BAD AS I EXPECTED.
It's unusual for Mr. Matsushita to mis-judge the time, isn't it?

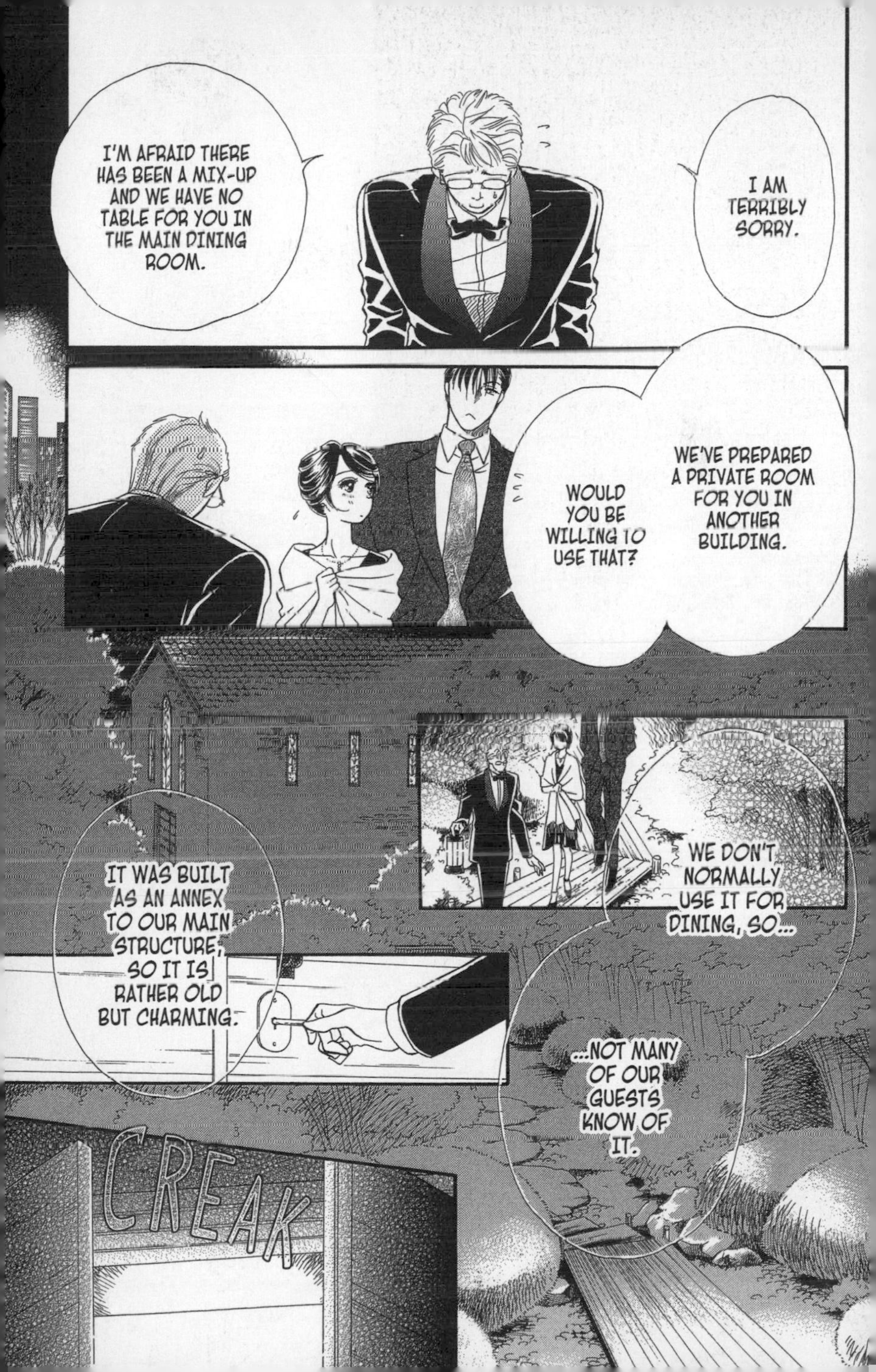
I AM TERRIBLY SORRY.
I'M AFRAID THERE HAS BEEN A MIX-UP AND WE HAVE NO TABLE FOR YOU IN THE MAIN DINING ROOM.
WE'VE PREPARED A PRIVATE ROOM FOR YOU IN ANOTHER BUILDING.
WOULD YOU BE WILLING TO USE THAT?
WE DON'T NORMALLY USE IT FOR DINING, SO...
...NOT MANY OF OUR GUESTS KNOW OF IT.
IT WAS BUILT AS AN ANNEX TO OUR MAIN STRUCTURE, SO IT IS RATHER OLD BUT CHARMING.
CREAK

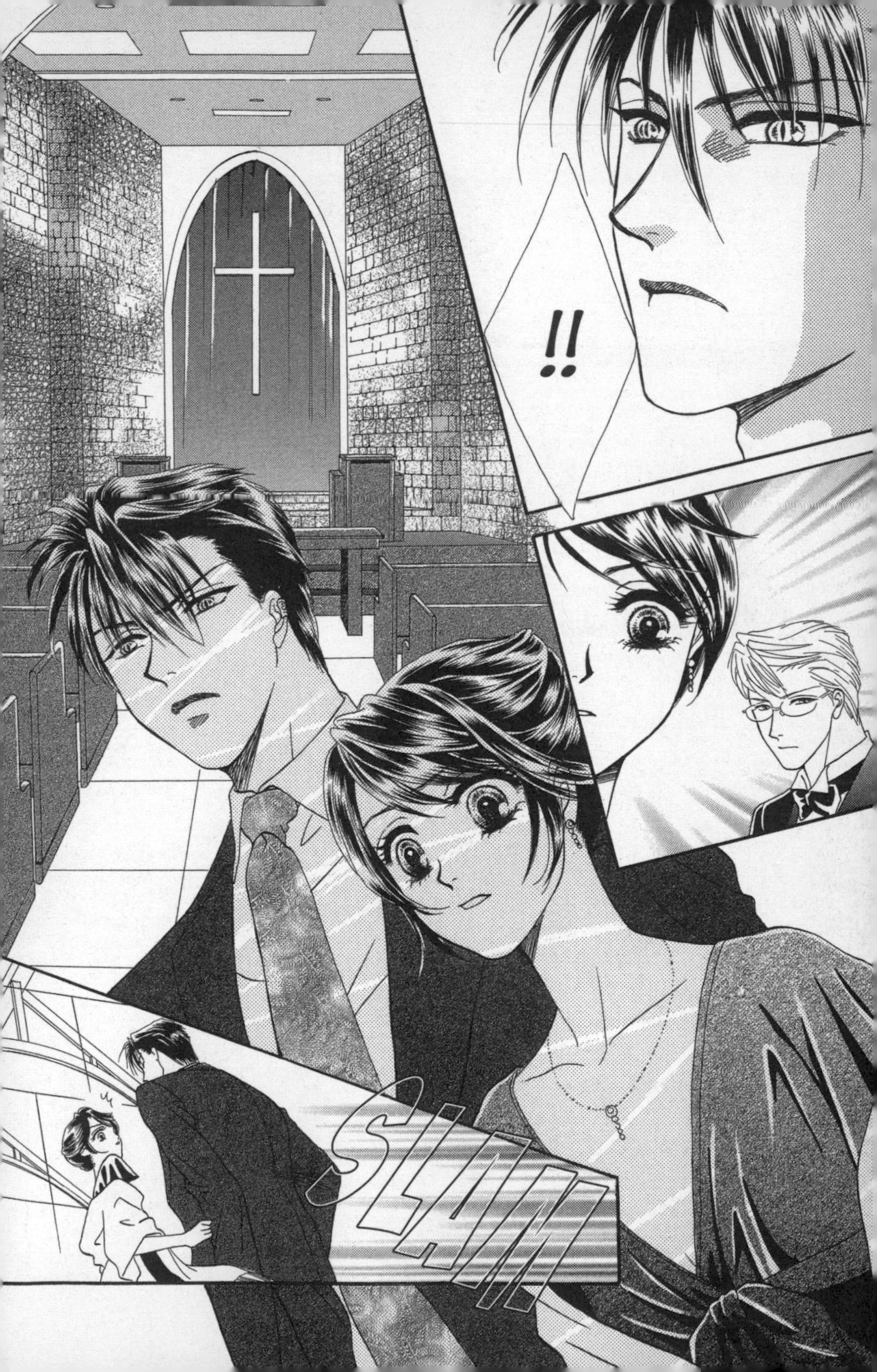
!!
SLAM

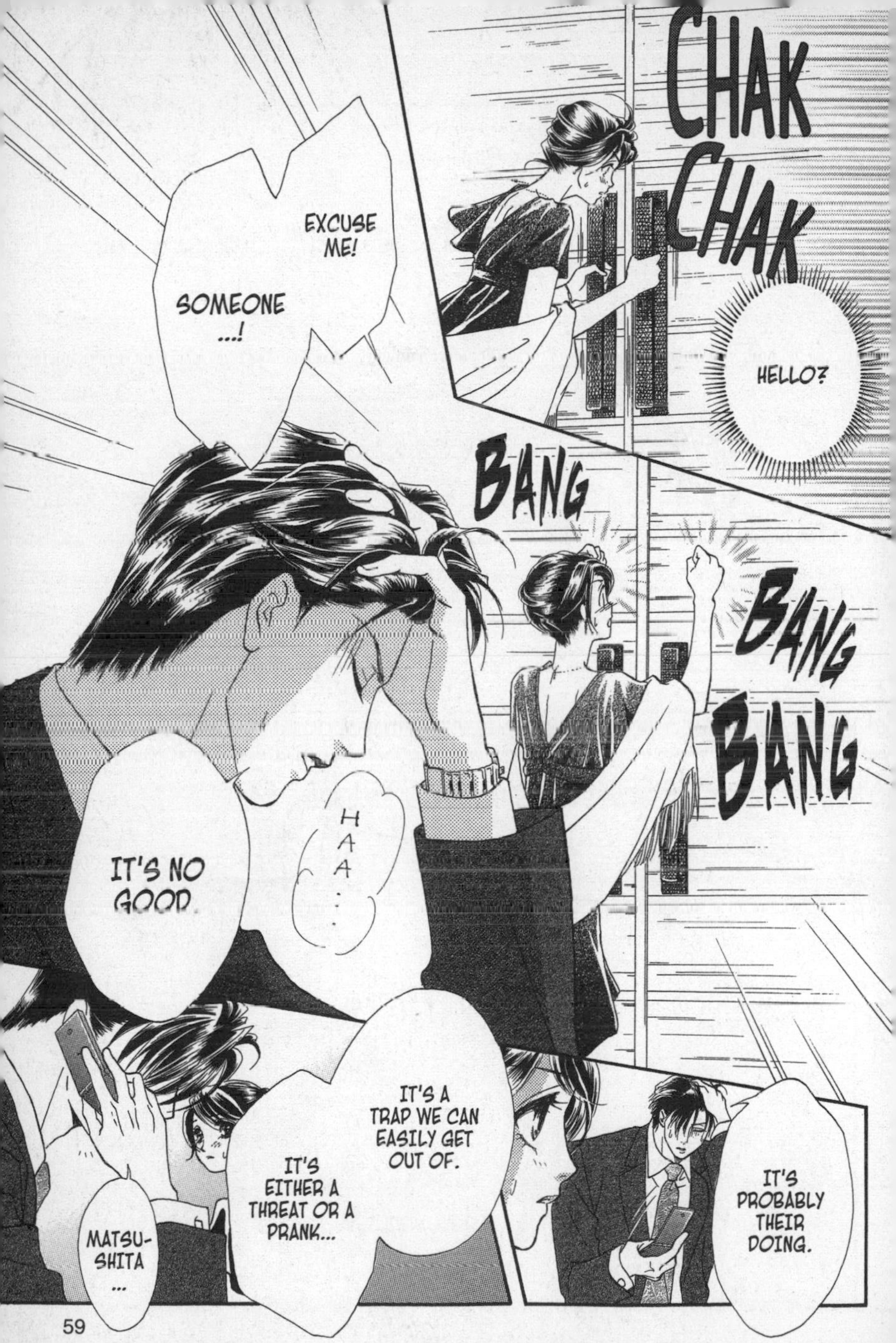
CHAK CHAK
HELLO?
EXCUSE ME!
SOMEONE ...!
BANG
BANG BANG BANG
HAA...
IT'S NO GOOD.
IT'S PROBABLY THEIR DOING.
IT'S A TRAP WE CAN EASILY GET OUT OF.
IT'S EITHER A THREAT OR A PRANK...
MATSU-SHITA ...

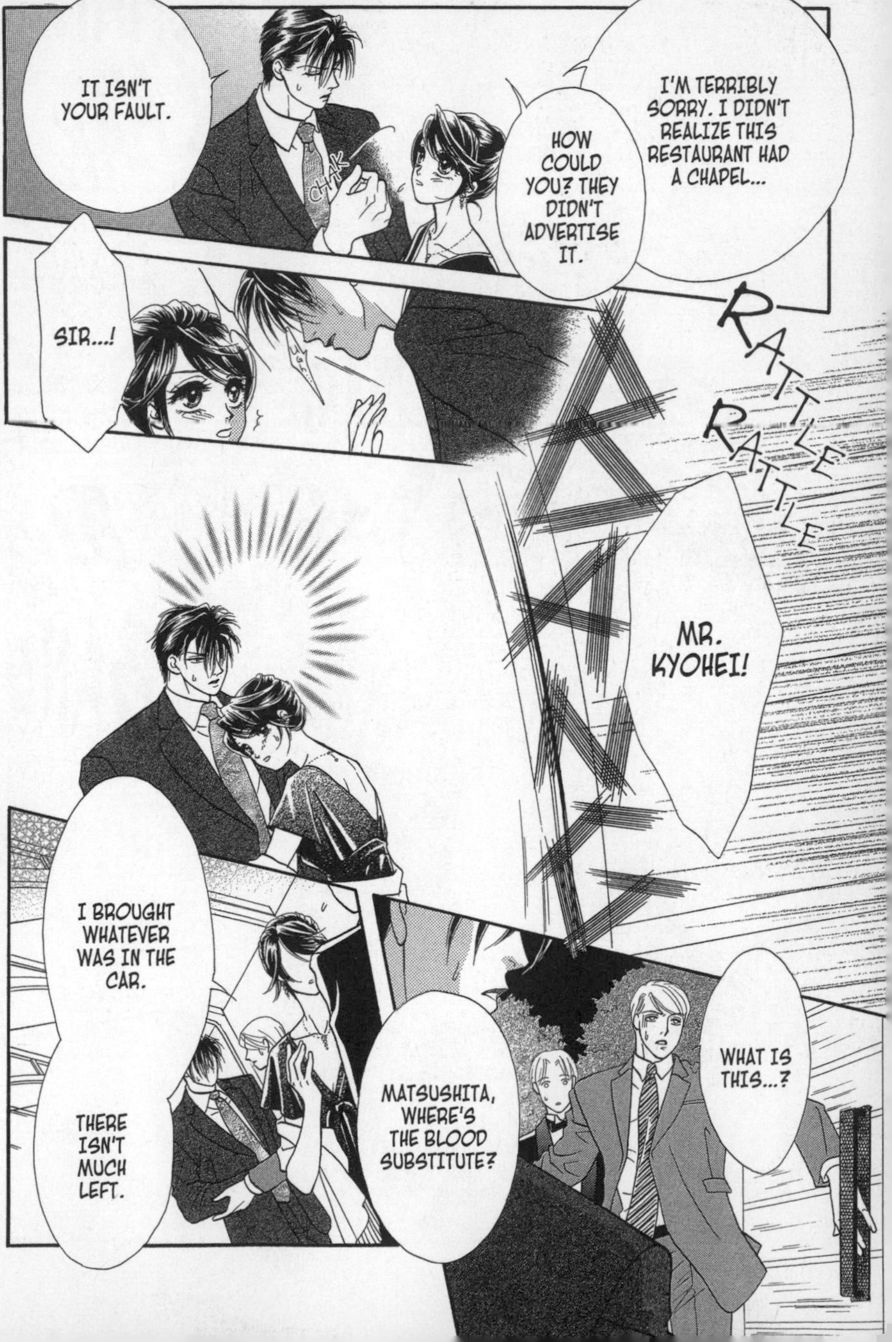
I'M TERRIBLY SORRY. I DIDN'T REALIZE THIS RESTAURANT HAD A CHAPEL...
HOW COULD YOU? THEY DIDN'T ADVERTISE IT.
CHAK
IT ISN'T YOUR FAULT.
SIR...!
RATTLE RATTLE
MR. KYOHEI!
WHAT IS THIS...?
MATSUSHITA, WHERE'S THE BLOOD SUBSTITUTE?
I BROUGHT WHATEVER WAS IN THE CAR.
THERE ISN'T MUCH LEFT.

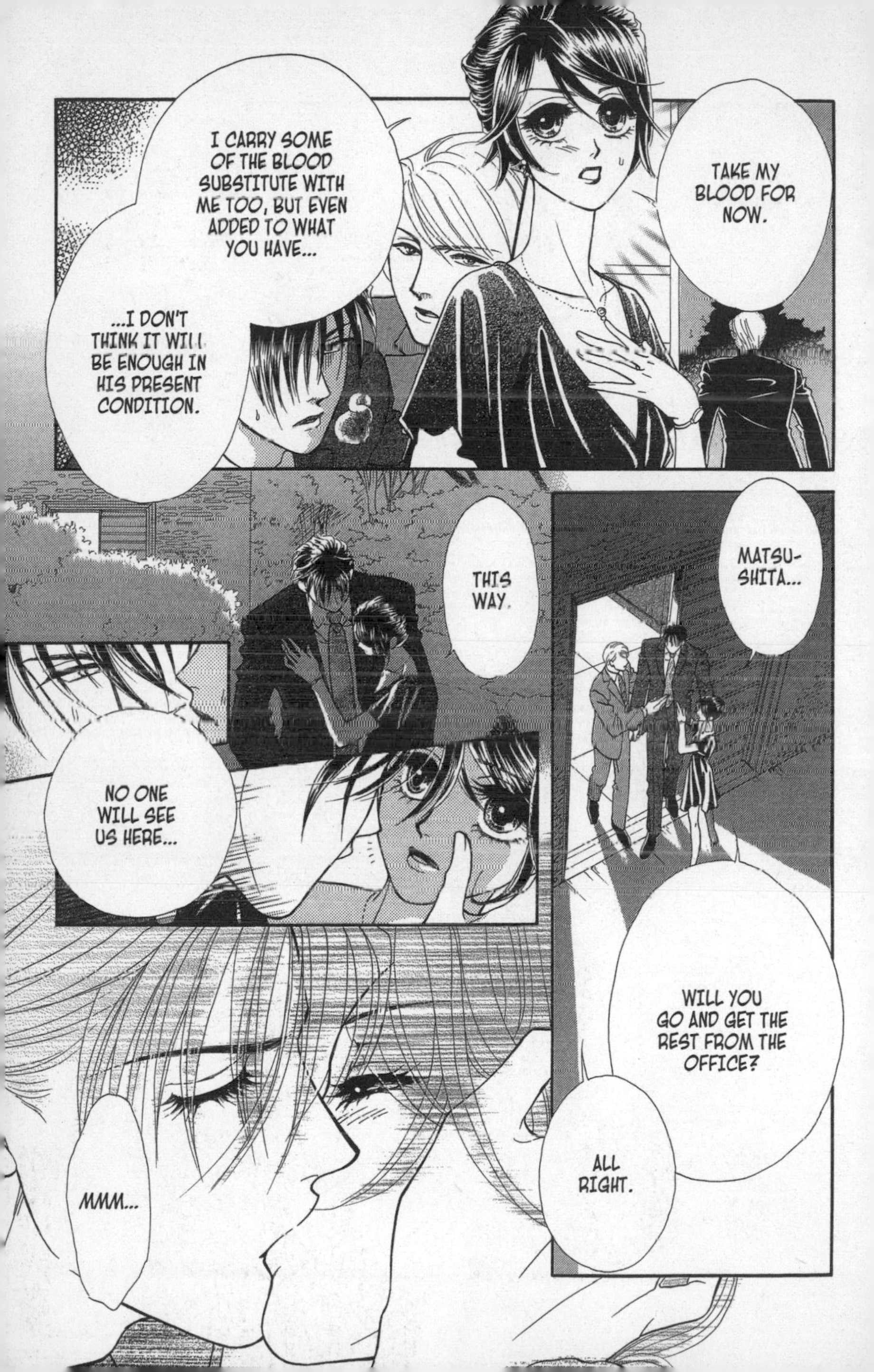
TAKE MY BLOOD FOR NOW.
I CARRY SOME OF THE BLOOD SUBSTITUTE WITH ME TOO, BUT EVEN ADDED TO WHAT YOU HAVE...
...I DON'T THINK IT WILL BE ENOUGH IN HIS PRESENT CONDITION.
MATSU-SHITA...
WILL YOU GO AND GET THE REST FROM THE OFFICE?
ALL RIGHT.
THIS WAY.
NO ONE WILL SEE US HERE...
MMM...

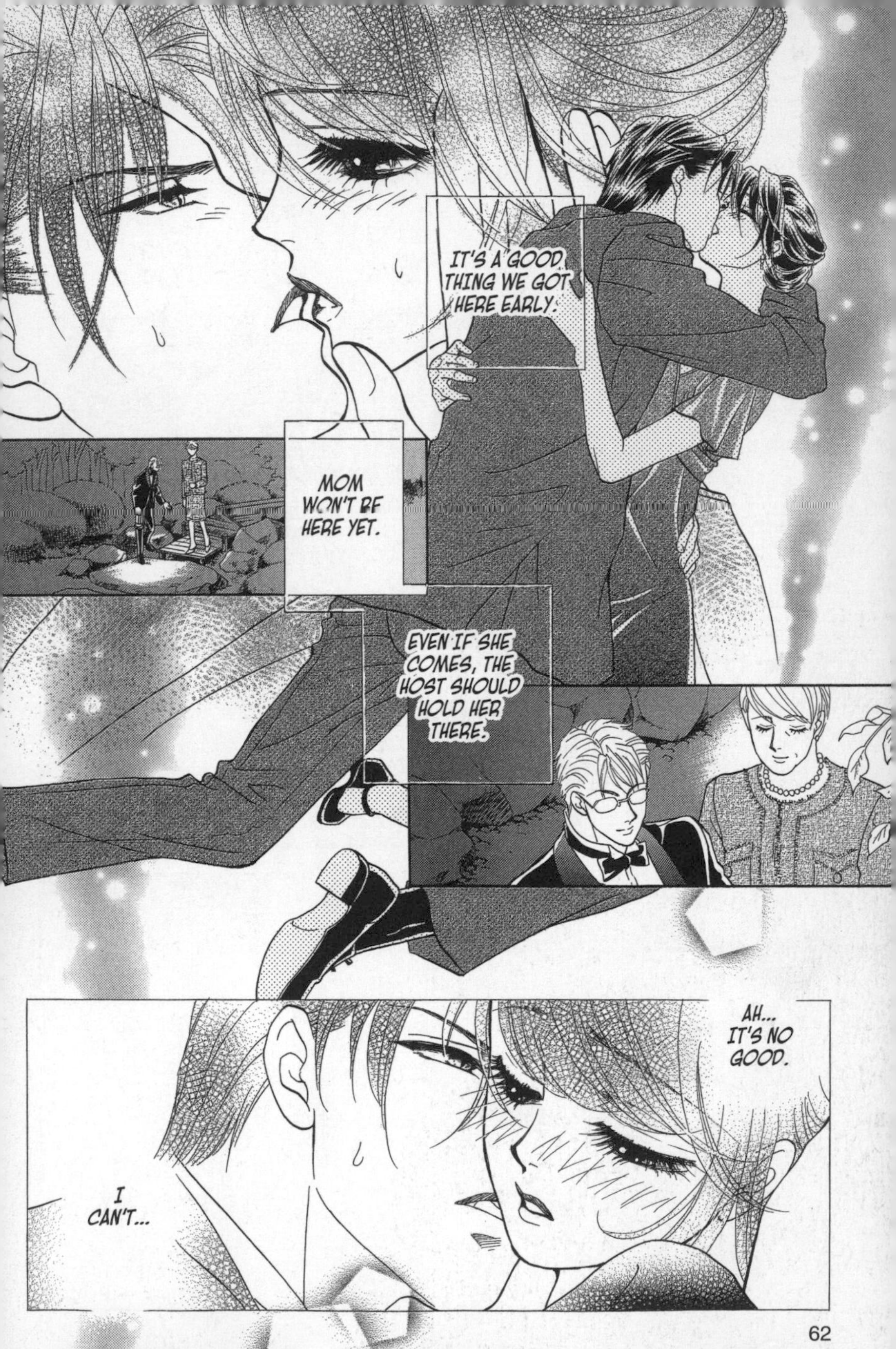
IT'S A GOOD THING WE GOT HERE EARLY.
MOM WON'T BE HERE YET.
EVEN IF SHE COMES, THE HOST SHOULD HOLD HER THERE.
AH... IT'S NO GOOD.
I CAN'T...

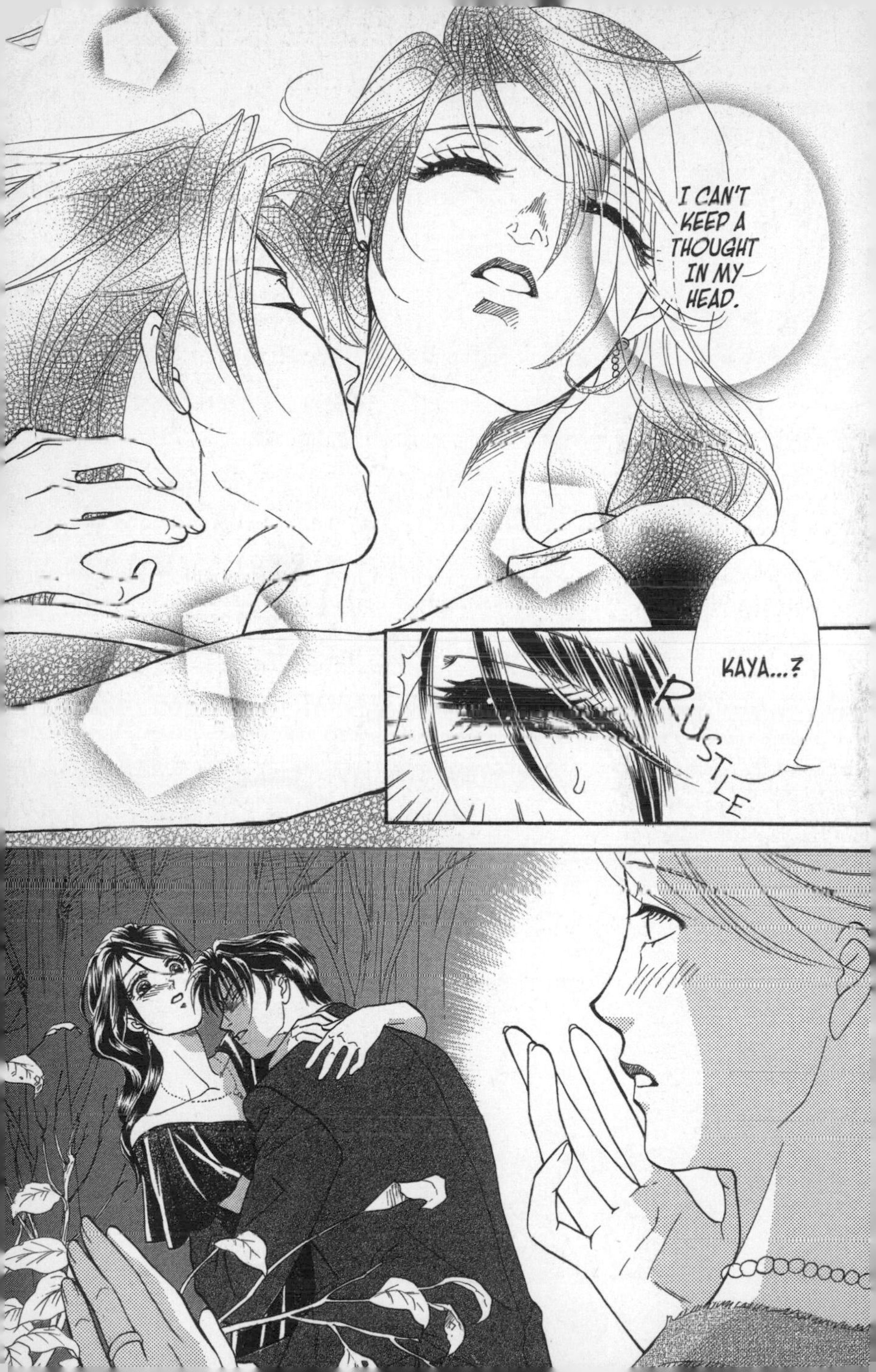
I CAN'T KEEP A THOUGHT IN MY HEAD.
KAYA...?
RUSTLE

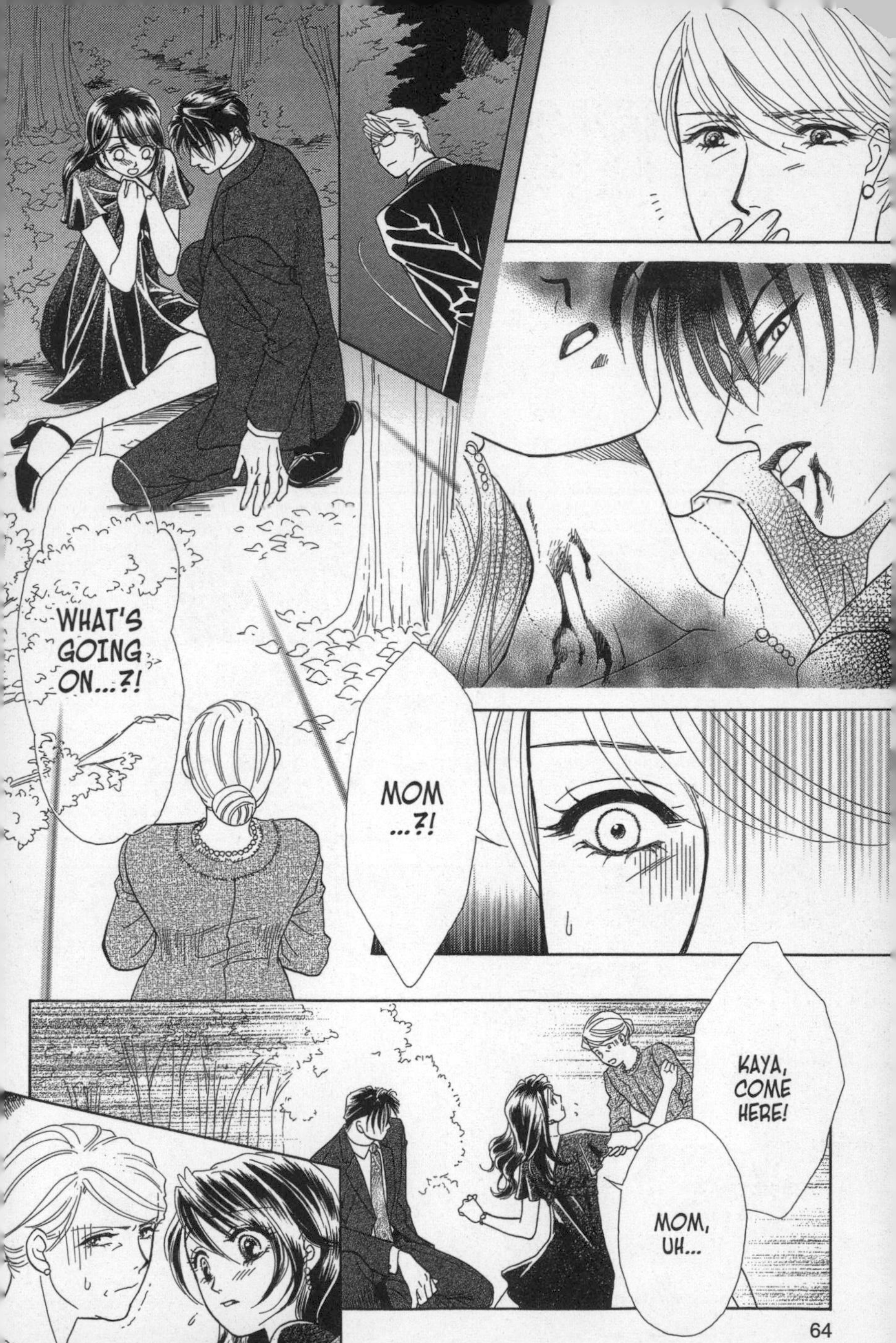
MOM ...?!
WHAT'S GOING ON...?!
KAYA, COME HERE!
MOM, UH...

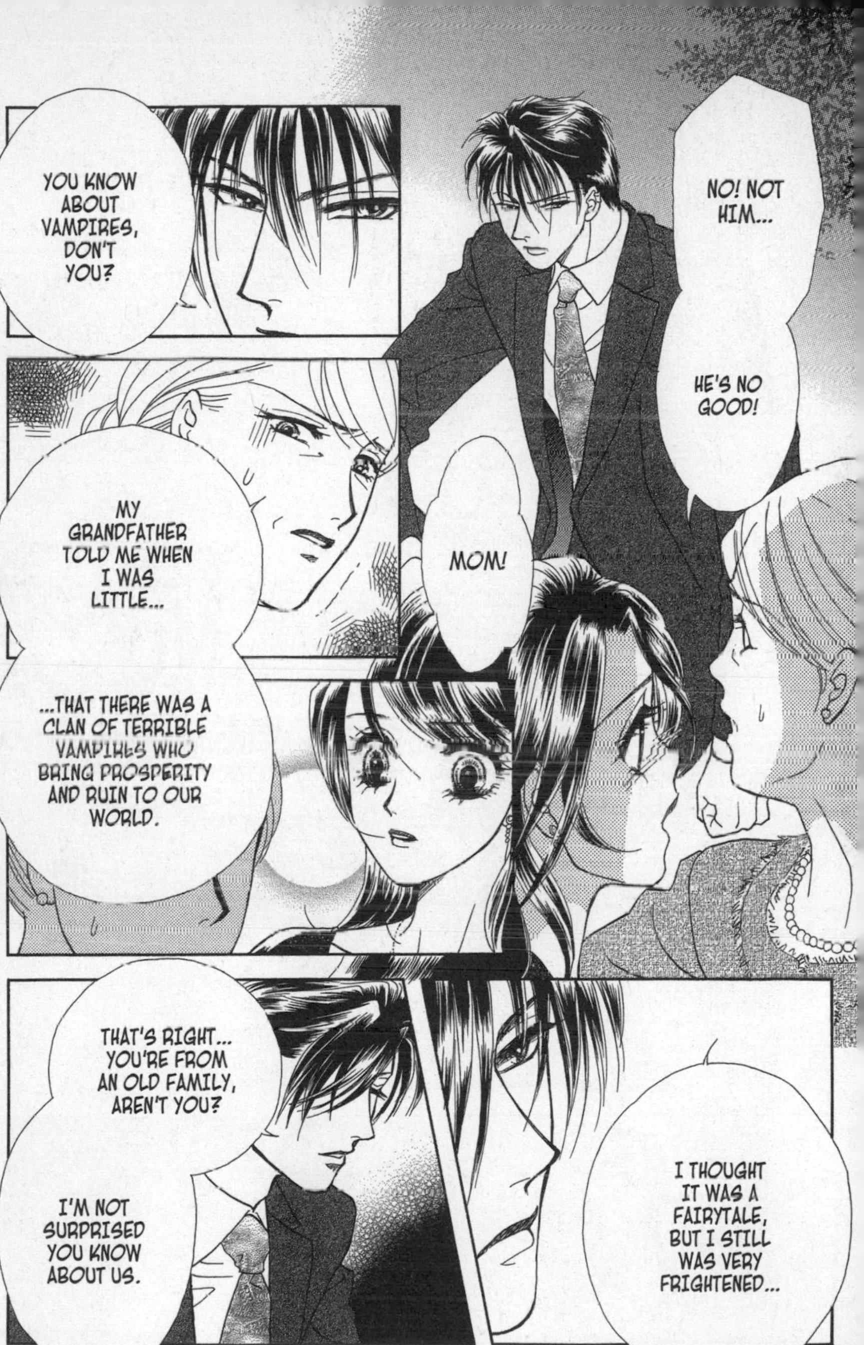
NO! NOT HIM...
HE'S NO GOOD!
MOM!
YOU KNOW ABOUT VAMPIRES, DON'T YOU?
MY GRANDFATHER TOLD ME WHEN I WAS LITTLE...
...THAT THERE WAS A CLAN OF TERRIBLE VAMPIRES WHO BRING PROSPERITY AND RUIN TO OUR WORLD.
I THOUGHT IT WAS A FAIRYTALE, BUT I STILL WAS VERY FRIGHTENED...
THAT'S RIGHT... YOU'RE FROM AN OLD FAMILY, AREN'T YOU?
I'M NOT SURPRISED YOU KNOW ABOUT US.

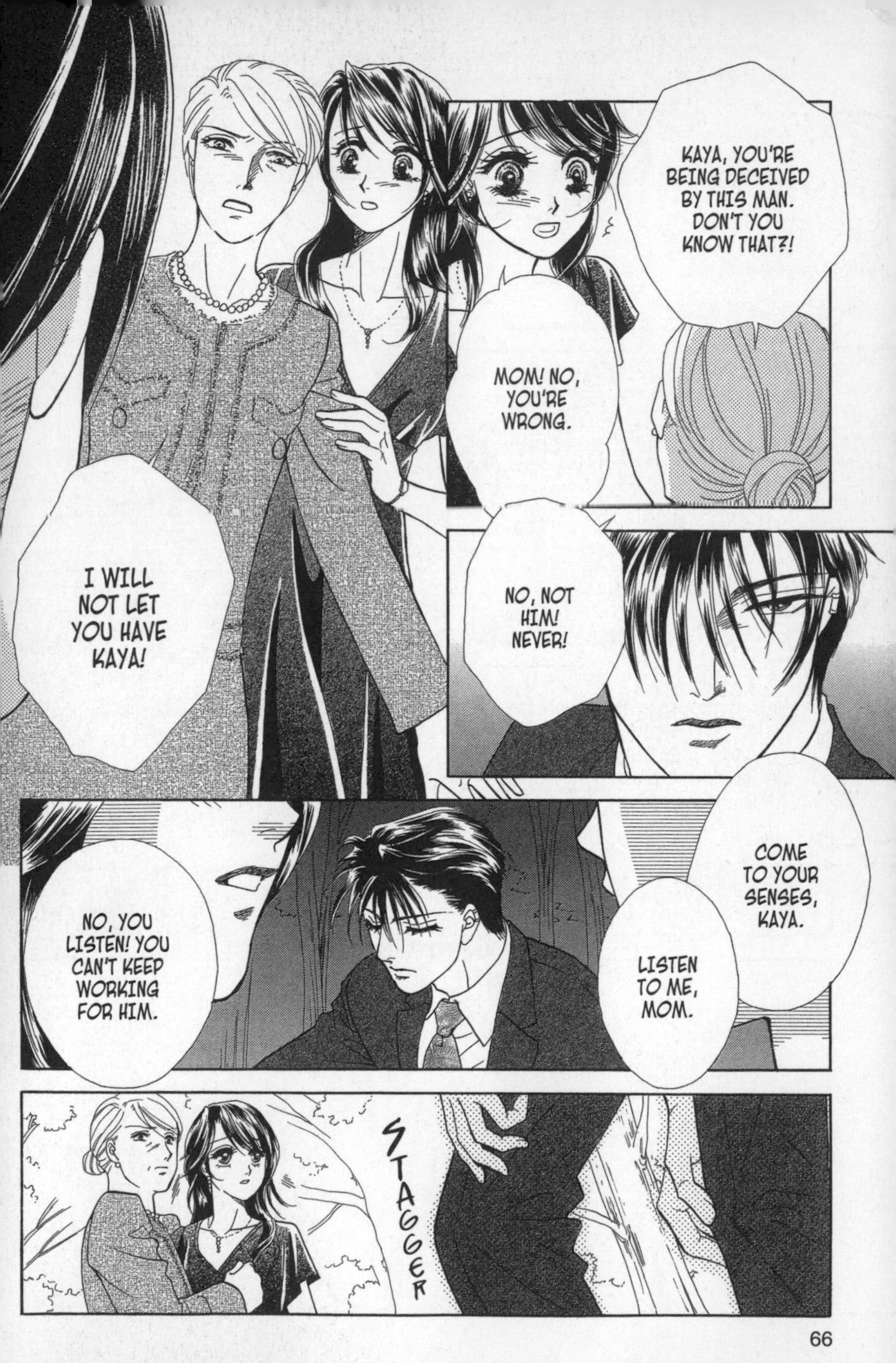
KAYA, YOU'RE BEING DECEIVED BY THIS MAN. DON'T YOU KNOW THAT?!
MOM! NO, YOU'RE WRONG.
NO, NOT HIM! NEVER!
I WILL NOT LET YOU HAVE KAYA!
COME TO YOUR SENSES, KAYA.
LISTEN TO ME, MOM.
NO, YOU LISTEN! YOU CAN'T KEEP WORKING FOR HIM.
STAGGER

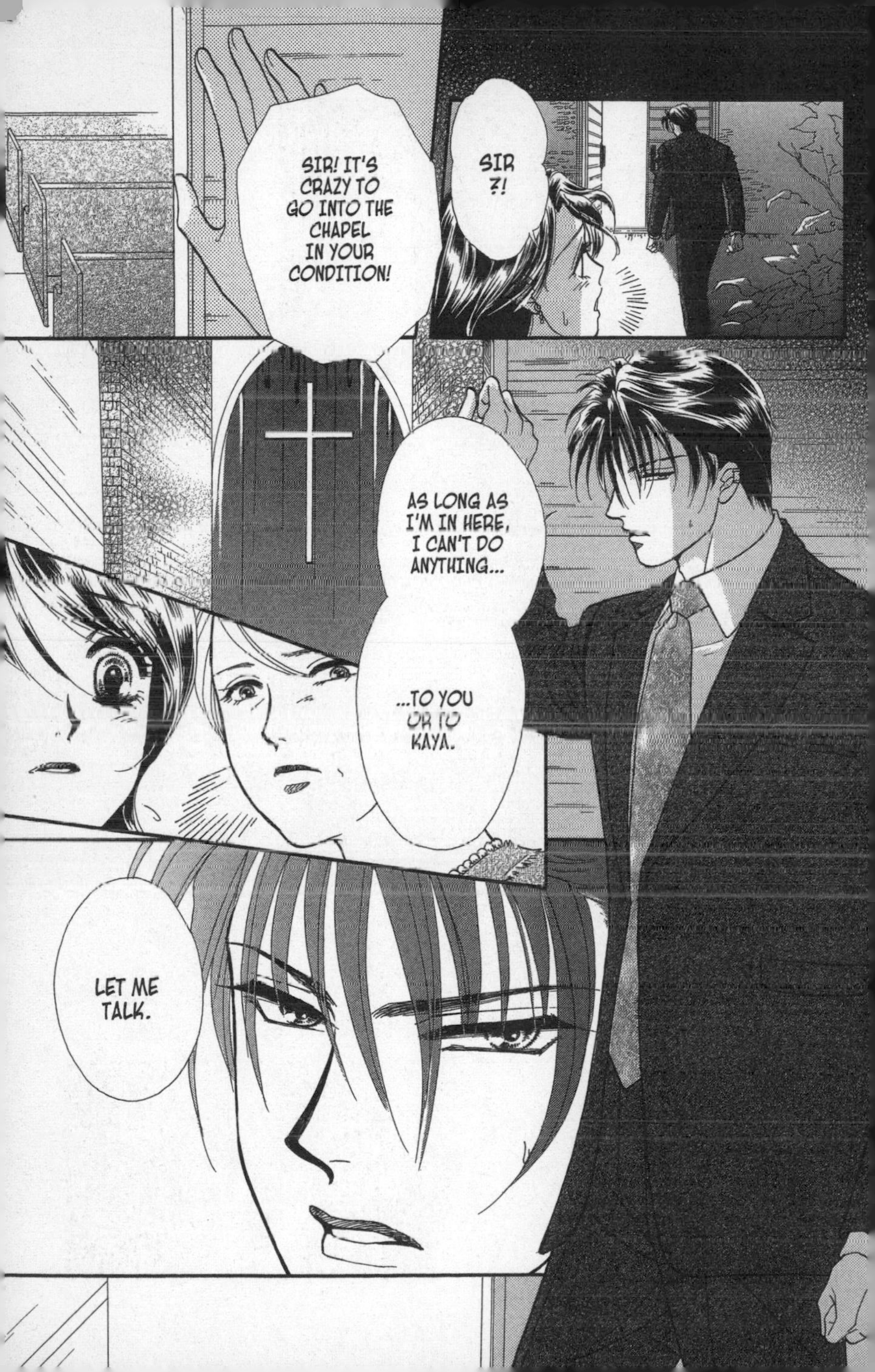
SIR ?!
SIR! IT'S CRAZY TO GO INTO THE CHAPEL IN YOUR CONDITION!
AS LONG AS I'M IN HERE, I CAN'T DO ANYTHING...
...TO YOU OR TO KAYA.
LET ME TALK.

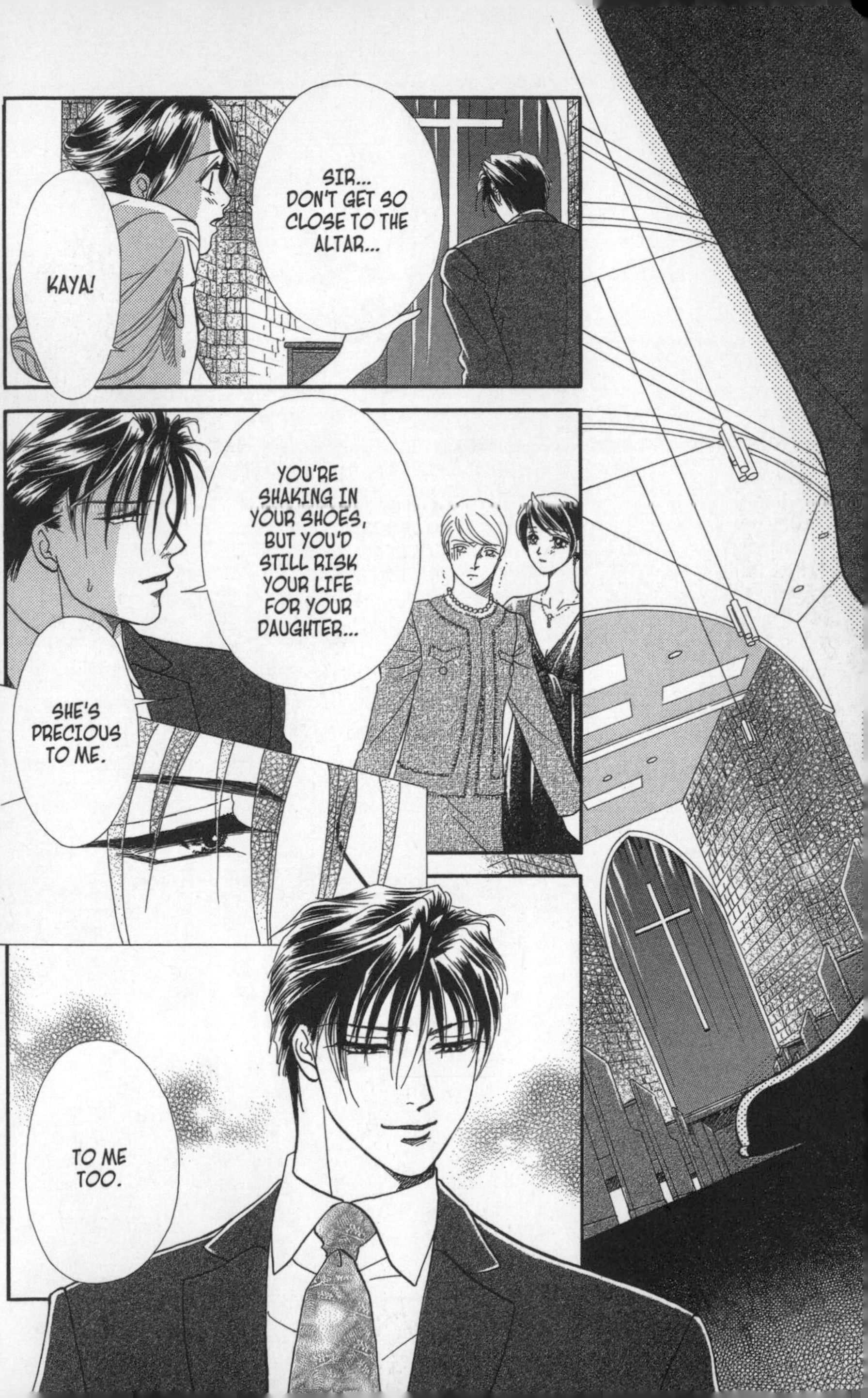
SIR... DON'T GET SO CLOSE TO THE ALTAR...
KAYA!
YOU'RE SHAKING IN YOUR SHOES, BUT YOU'D STILL RISK YOUR LIFE FOR YOUR DAUGHTER...
SHE'S PRECIOUS TO ME.
TO ME TOO.

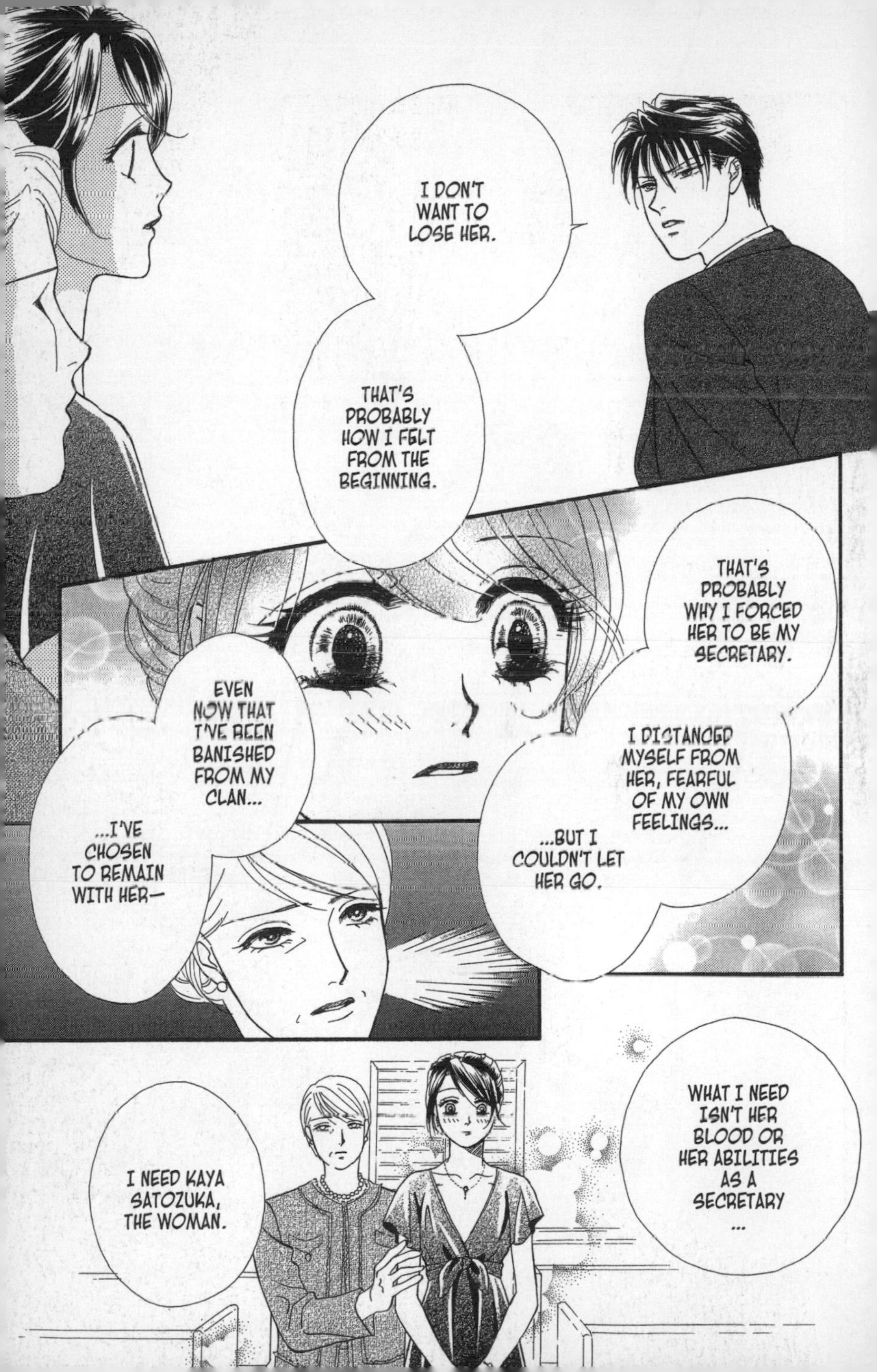
I DON'T WANT TO LOSE HER.
THAT'S PROBABLY HOW I FELT FROM THE BEGINNING.
THAT'S PROBABLY WHY I FORCED HER TO BE MY SECRETARY.
I DISTANCED MYSELF FROM HER, FEARFUL OF MY OWN FEELINGS...
...BUT I COULDN'T LET HER GO.
EVEN NOW THAT I'VE BEEN BANISHED FROM MY CLAN...
...I'VE CHOSEN TO REMAIN WITH HER—
WHAT I NEED ISN'T HER BLOOD OR HER ABILITIES AS A SECRETARY ...
I NEED KAYA SATOZUKA, THE WOMAN.

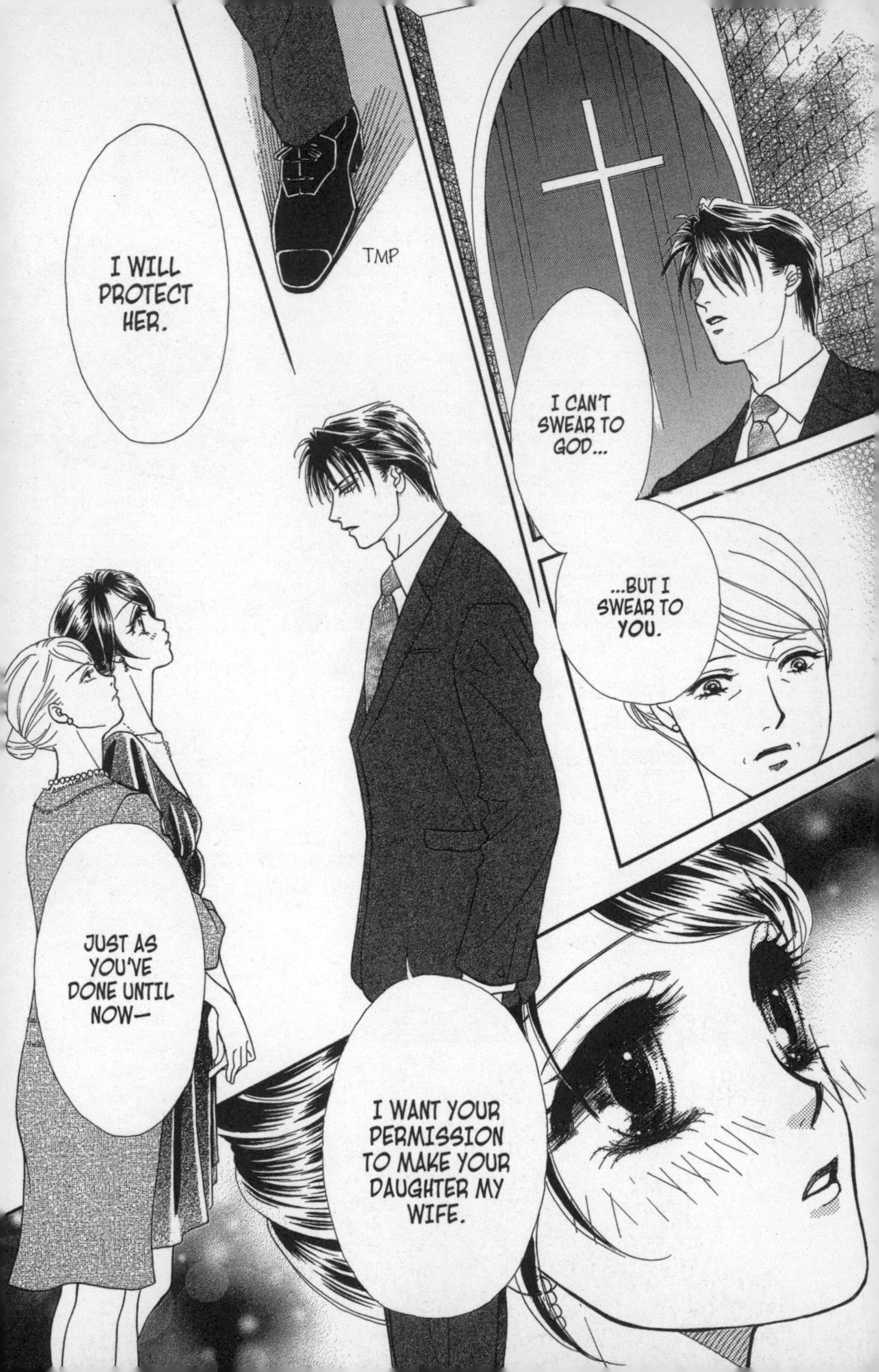
I CAN'T SWEAR TO GOD...
TMP
...BUT I SWEAR TO YOU.
I WILL PROTECT HER.
JUST AS YOU'VE DONE UNTIL NOW—
I WANT YOUR PERMISSION TO MAKE YOUR DAUGHTER MY WIFE.

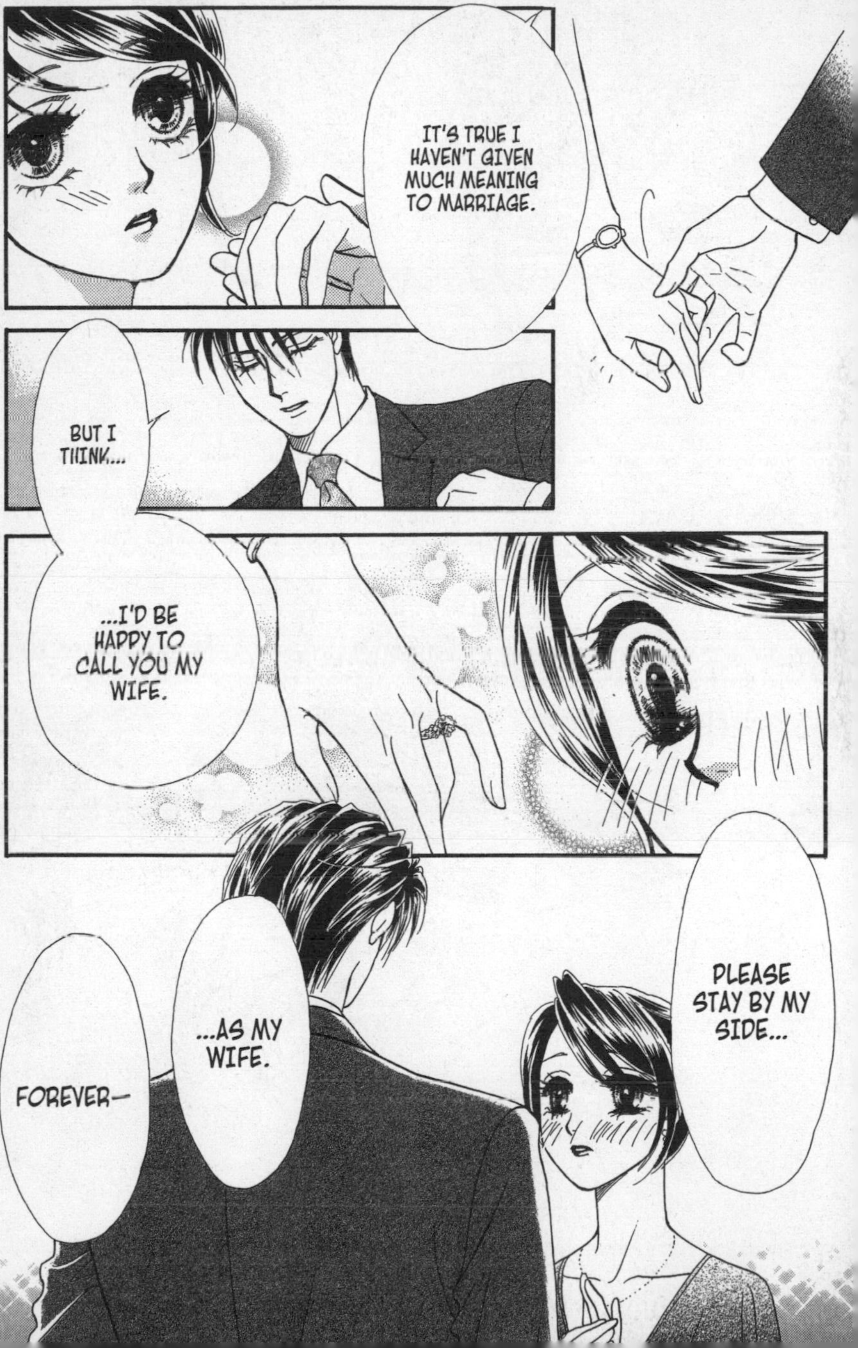
IT'S TRUE I HAVEN'T GIVEN MUCH MEANING TO MARRIAGE.
BUT I THINK...
...I'D BE HAPPY TO CALL YOU MY WIFE.
PLEASE STAY BY MY SIDE...
...AS MY WIFE.
FOREVER—

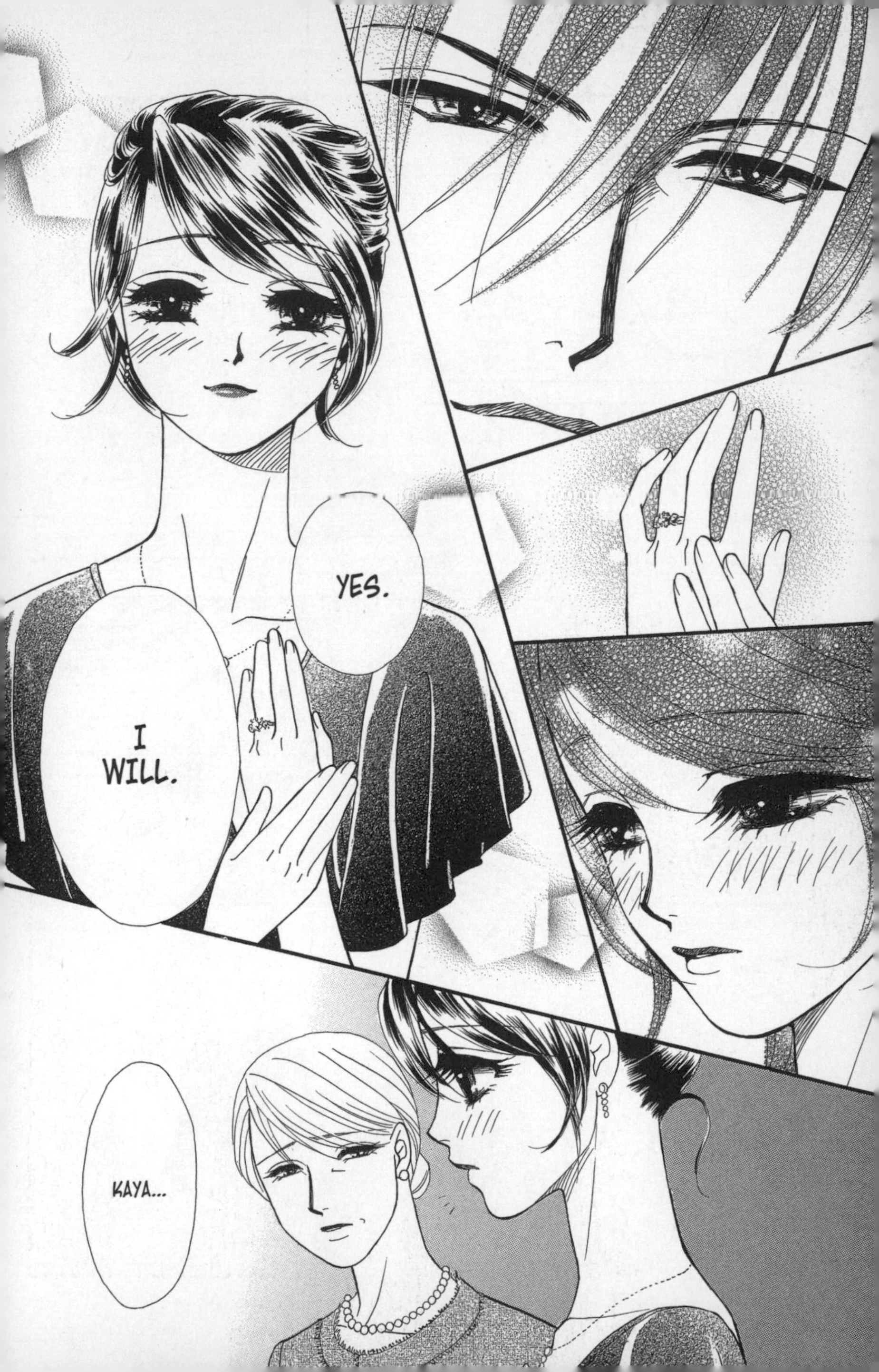
YES.
I WILL.
KAYA...

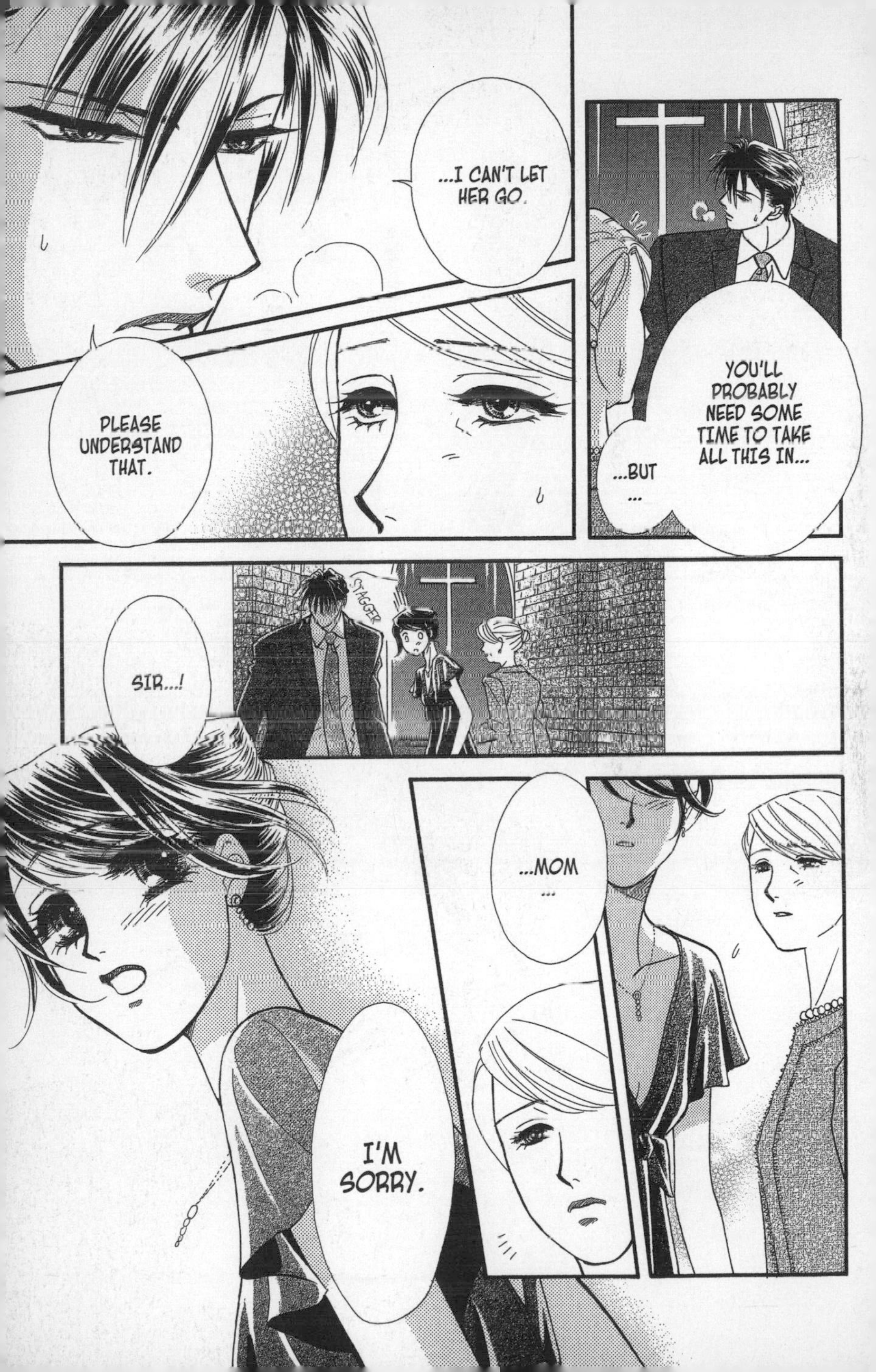
YOU'LL PROBABLY NEED SOME TIME TO TAKE ALL THIS IN...
...BUT ...
...I CAN'T LET HER GO.
PLEASE UNDERSTAND THAT.
STAGGER
SIR...!
...MOM ...
I'M SORRY.

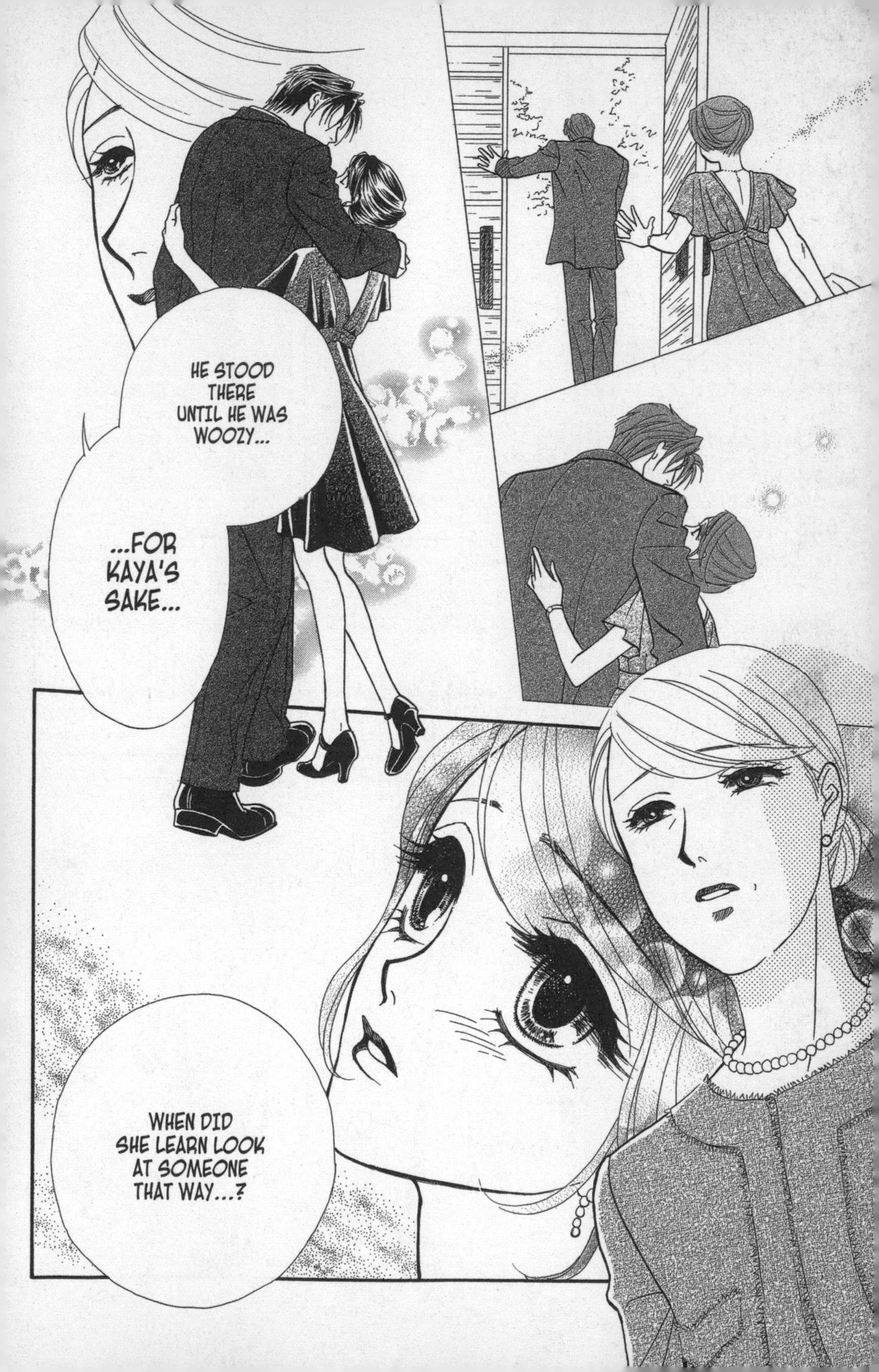
HE STOOD THERE UNTIL HE WAS WOOZY...
...FOR KAYA'S SAKE...
WHEN DID SHE LEARN LOOK AT SOMEONE THAT WAY...?

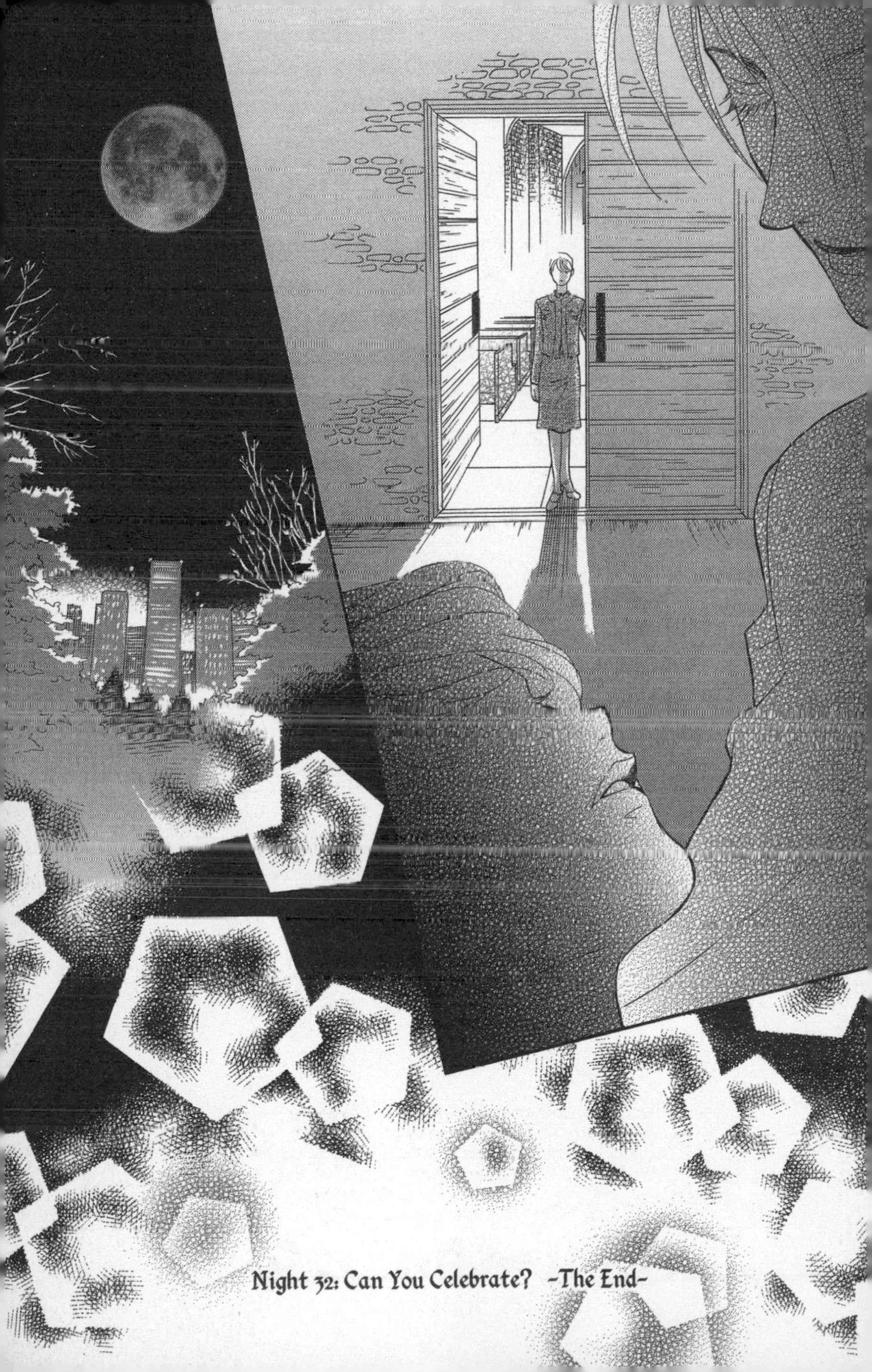

Night 32: Can You Celebrate? -The End-

— Can You Celebrate? —

The engagement ring Kyohei gave her.
It's rather simple. Kyohei is accustomed to
giving women jewelry, but I wonder what look
he wore on his face when he chose this ring.

# Night 33
# Please Don't Hold Me

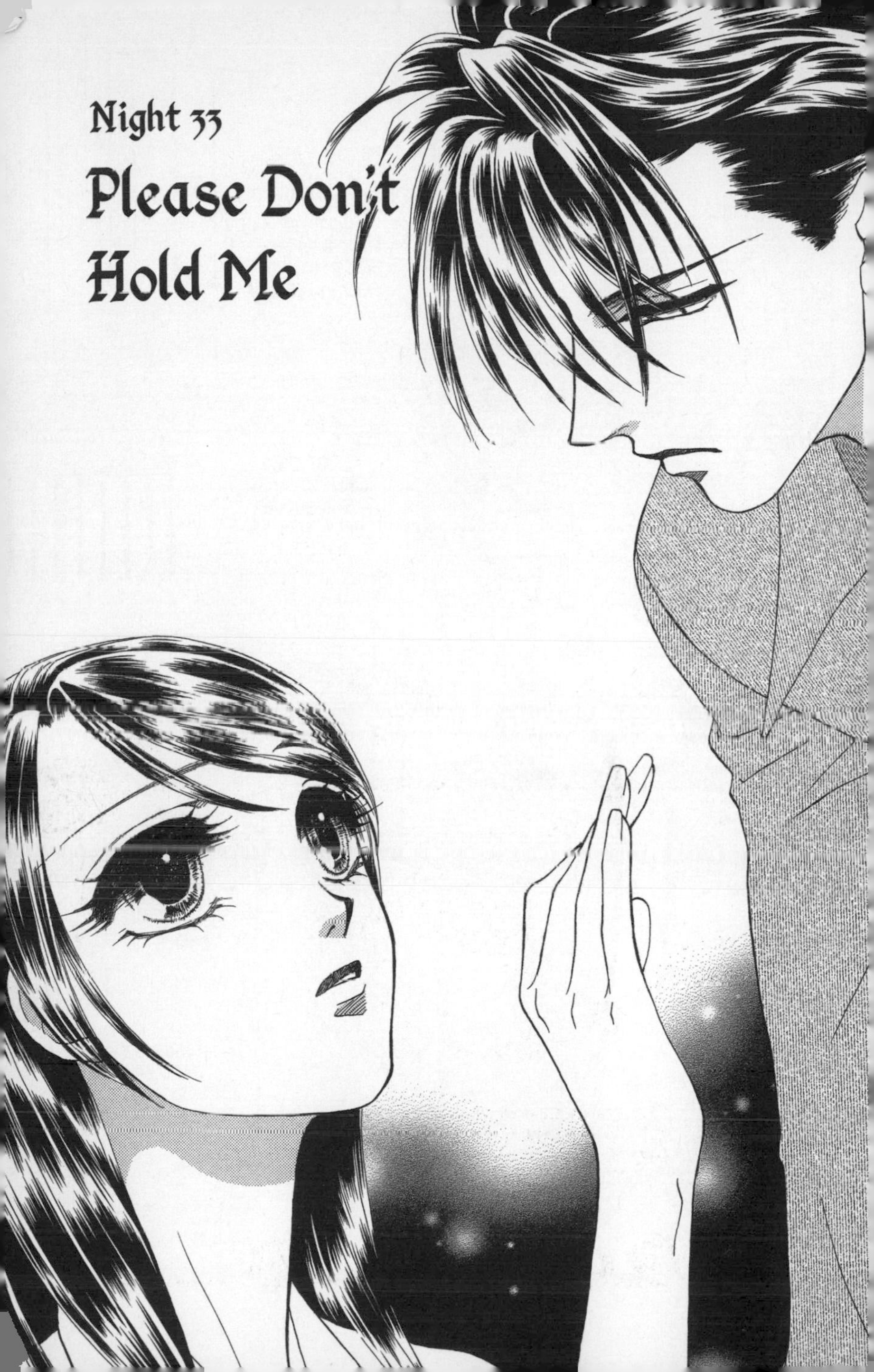

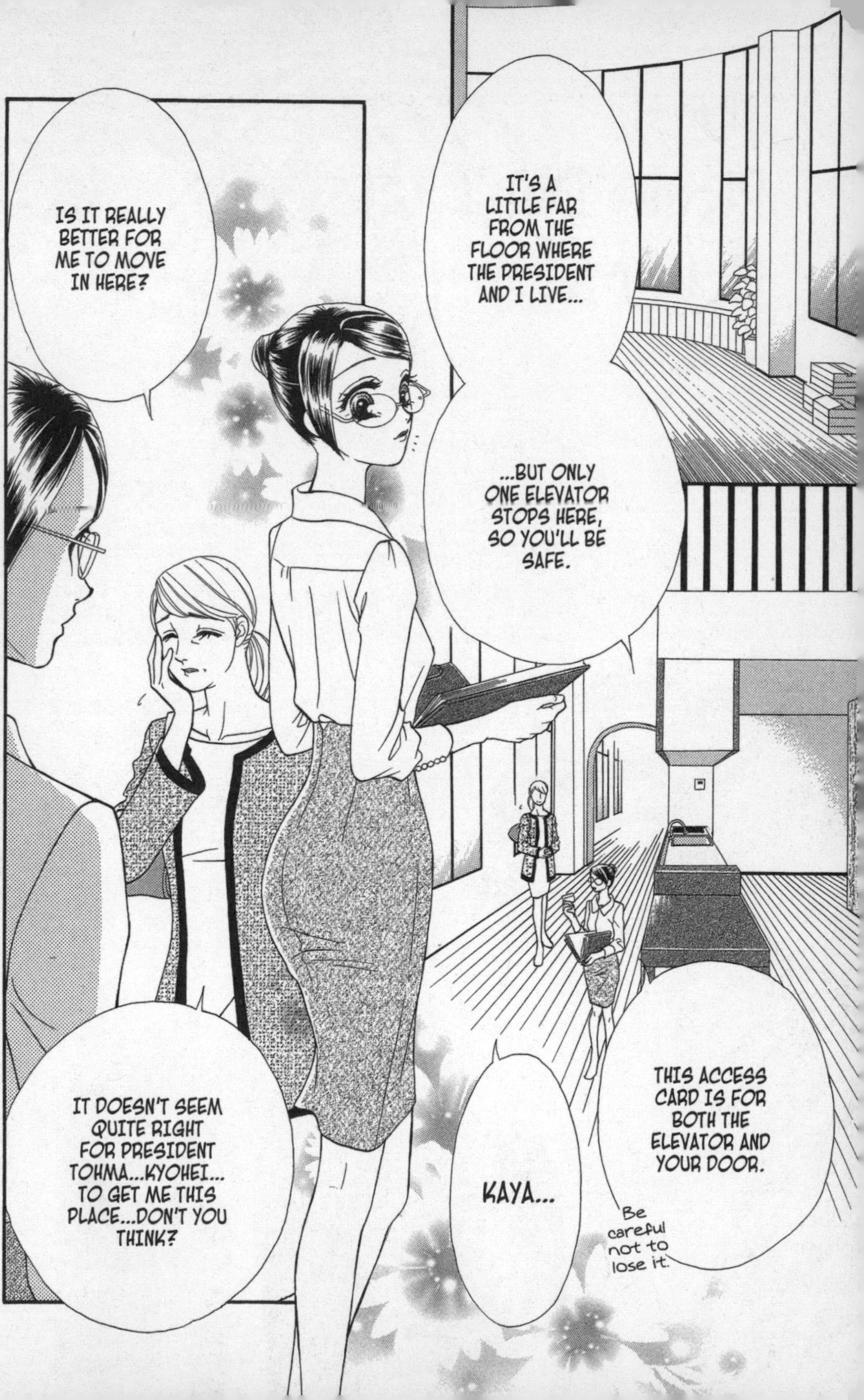
IT'S A LITTLE FAR FROM THE FLOOR WHERE THE PRESIDENT AND I LIVE...
...BUT ONLY ONE ELEVATOR STOPS HERE, SO YOU'LL BE SAFE.
THIS ACCESS CARD IS FOR BOTH THE ELEVATOR AND YOUR DOOR.
Be careful not to lose it.
KAYA...
IS IT REALLY BETTER FOR ME TO MOVE IN HERE?
IT DOESN'T SEEM QUITE RIGHT FOR PRESIDENT TOHMA...KYOHEI... TO GET ME THIS PLACE...DON'T YOU THINK?

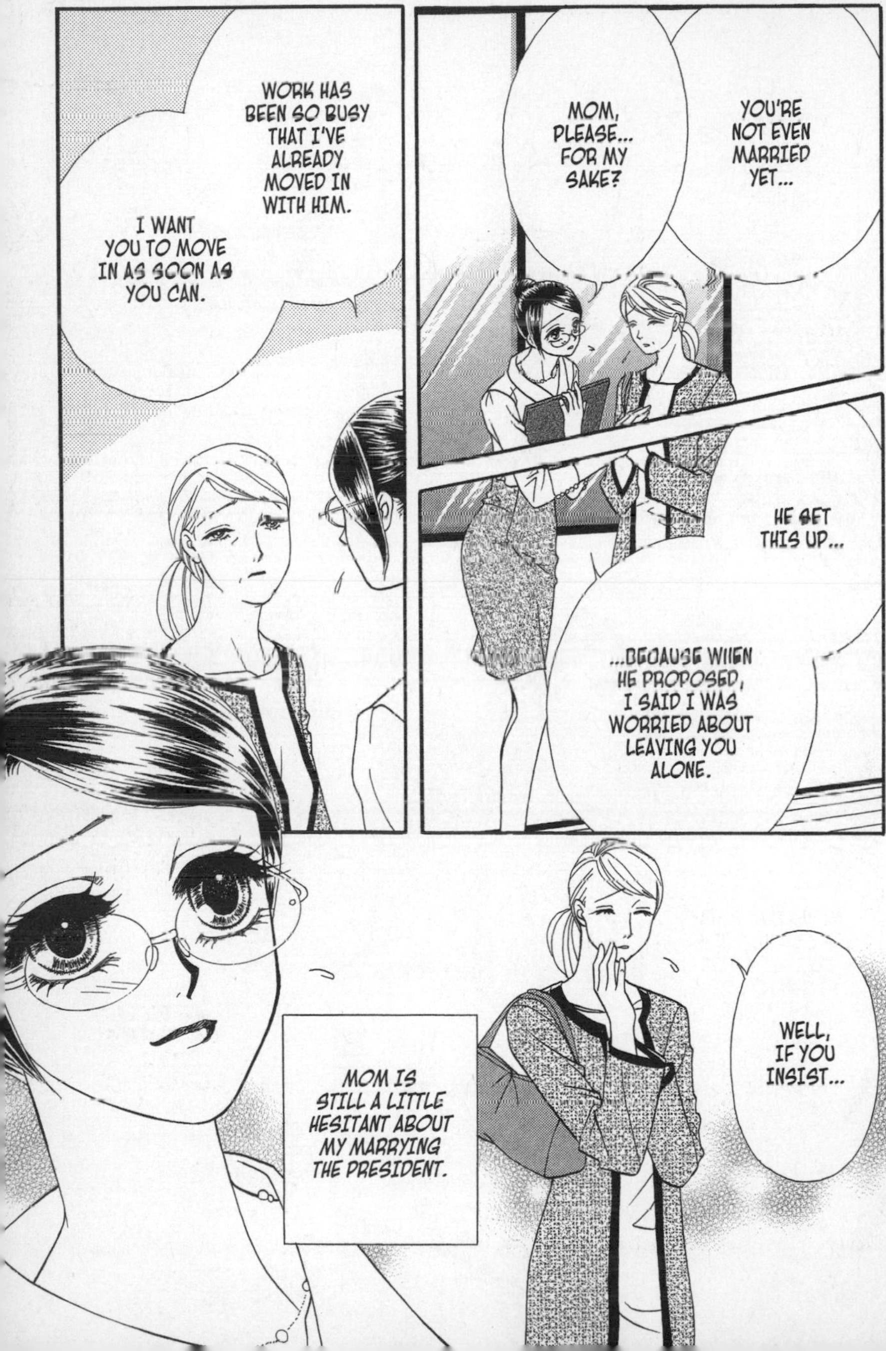
YOU'RE NOT EVEN MARRIED YET...
MOM, PLEASE... FOR MY SAKE?
HE SET THIS UP...
...BECAUSE WHEN HE PROPOSED, I SAID I WAS WORRIED ABOUT LEAVING YOU ALONE.
WORK HAS BEEN SO BUSY THAT I'VE ALREADY MOVED IN WITH HIM.
I WANT YOU TO MOVE IN AS SOON AS YOU CAN.
WELL, IF YOU INSIST...
MOM IS STILL A LITTLE HESITANT ABOUT MY MARRYING THE PRESIDENT.

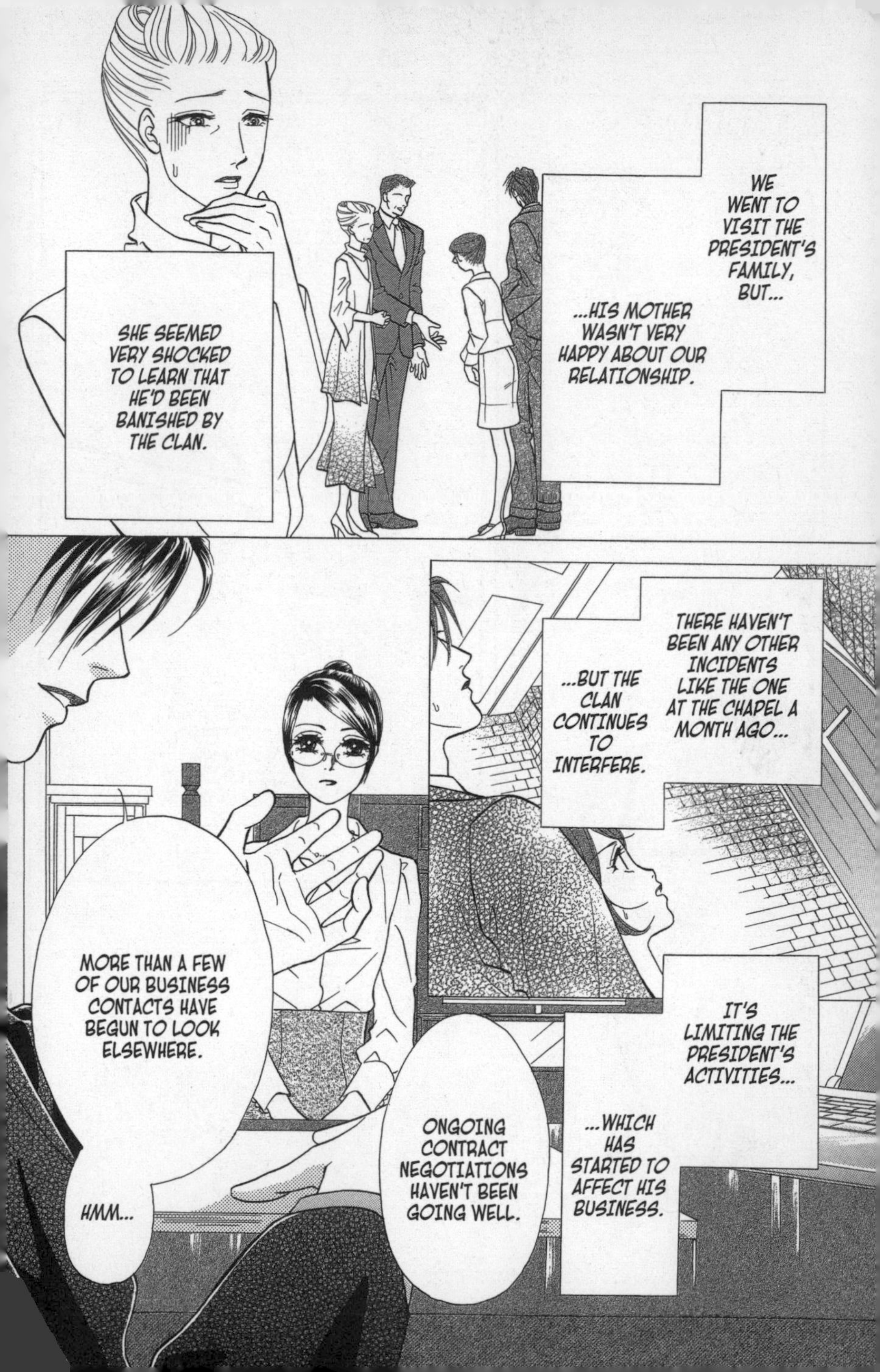
WE WENT TO VISIT THE PRESIDENT'S FAMILY, BUT...
...HIS MOTHER WASN'T VERY HAPPY ABOUT OUR RELATIONSHIP.
SHE SEEMED VERY SHOCKED TO LEARN THAT HE'D BEEN BANISHED BY THE CLAN.
THERE HAVEN'T BEEN ANY OTHER INCIDENTS LIKE THE ONE AT THE CHAPEL A MONTH AGO...
...BUT THE CLAN CONTINUES TO INTERFERE.
IT'S LIMITING THE PRESIDENT'S ACTIVITIES...
...WHICH HAS STARTED TO AFFECT HIS BUSINESS.
ONGOING CONTRACT NEGOTIATIONS HAVEN'T BEEN GOING WELL.
MORE THAN A FEW OF OUR BUSINESS CONTACTS HAVE BEGUN TO LOOK ELSEWHERE.
HMM...

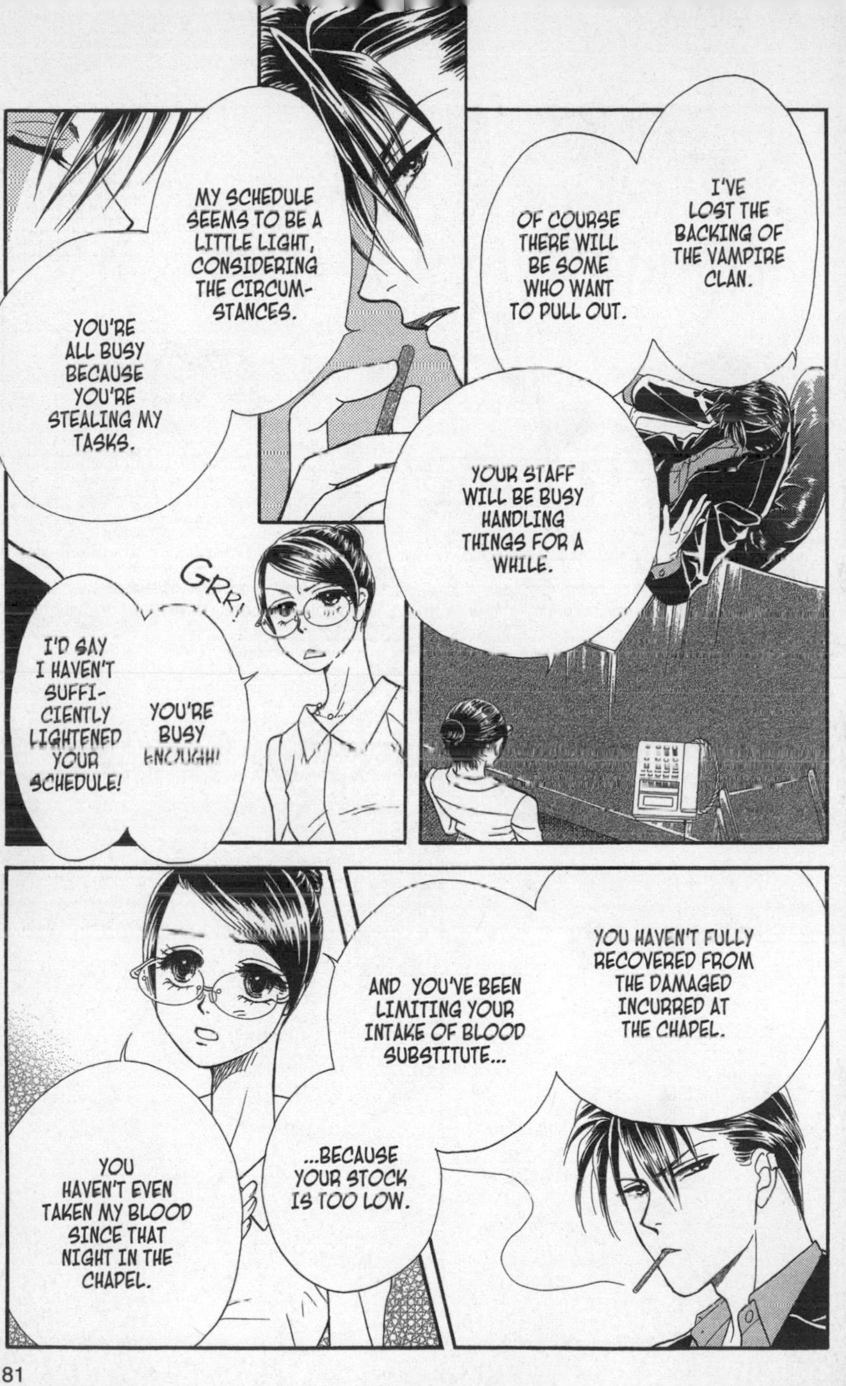
I'VE LOST THE BACKING OF THE VAMPIRE CLAN.
OF COURSE THERE WILL BE SOME WHO WANT TO PULL OUT.
YOUR STAFF WILL BE BUSY HANDLING THINGS FOR A WHILE.
MY SCHEDULE SEEMS TO BE A LITTLE LIGHT, CONSIDERING THE CIRCUM-STANCES.
YOU'RE ALL BUSY BECAUSE YOU'RE STEALING MY TASKS.
GRR!
YOU'RE BUSY ENOUGH!
I'D SAY I HAVEN'T SUFFI-CIENTLY LIGHTENED YOUR SCHEDULE!
YOU HAVEN'T FULLY RECOVERED FROM THE DAMAGED INCURRED AT THE CHAPEL.
AND YOU'VE BEEN LIMITING YOUR INTAKE OF BLOOD SUBSTITUTE...
...BECAUSE YOUR STOCK IS TOO LOW.
YOU HAVEN'T EVEN TAKEN MY BLOOD SINCE THAT NIGHT IN THE CHAPEL.

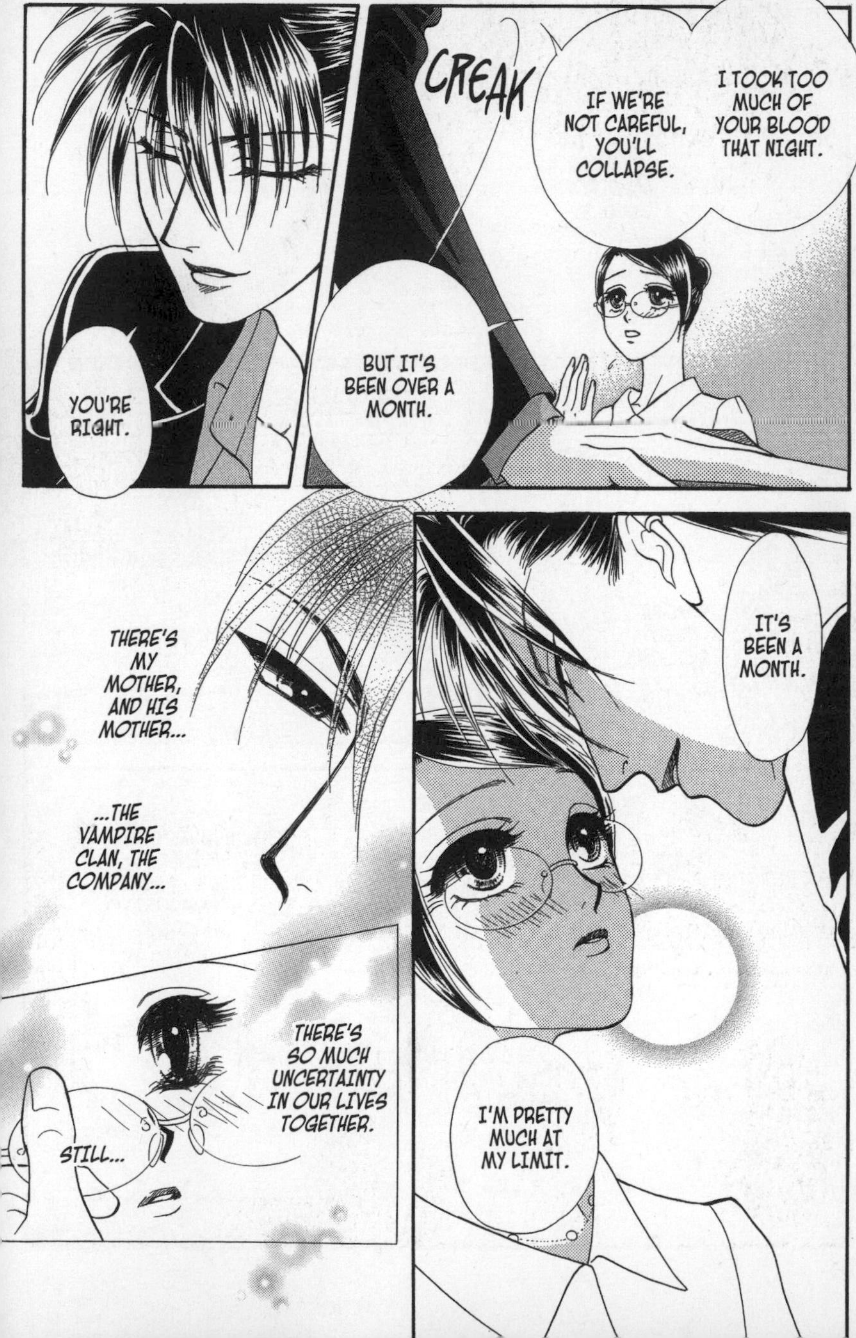
CREAK
I TOOK TOO MUCH OF YOUR BLOOD THAT NIGHT.
IF WE'RE NOT CAREFUL, YOU'LL COLLAPSE.
BUT IT'S BEEN OVER A MONTH.
YOU'RE RIGHT.
IT'S BEEN A MONTH.
I'M PRETTY MUCH AT MY LIMIT.
THERE'S MY MOTHER, AND HIS MOTHER...
...THE VAMPIRE CLAN, THE COMPANY...
THERE'S SO MUCH UNCERTAINTY IN OUR LIVES TOGETHER.
STILL...

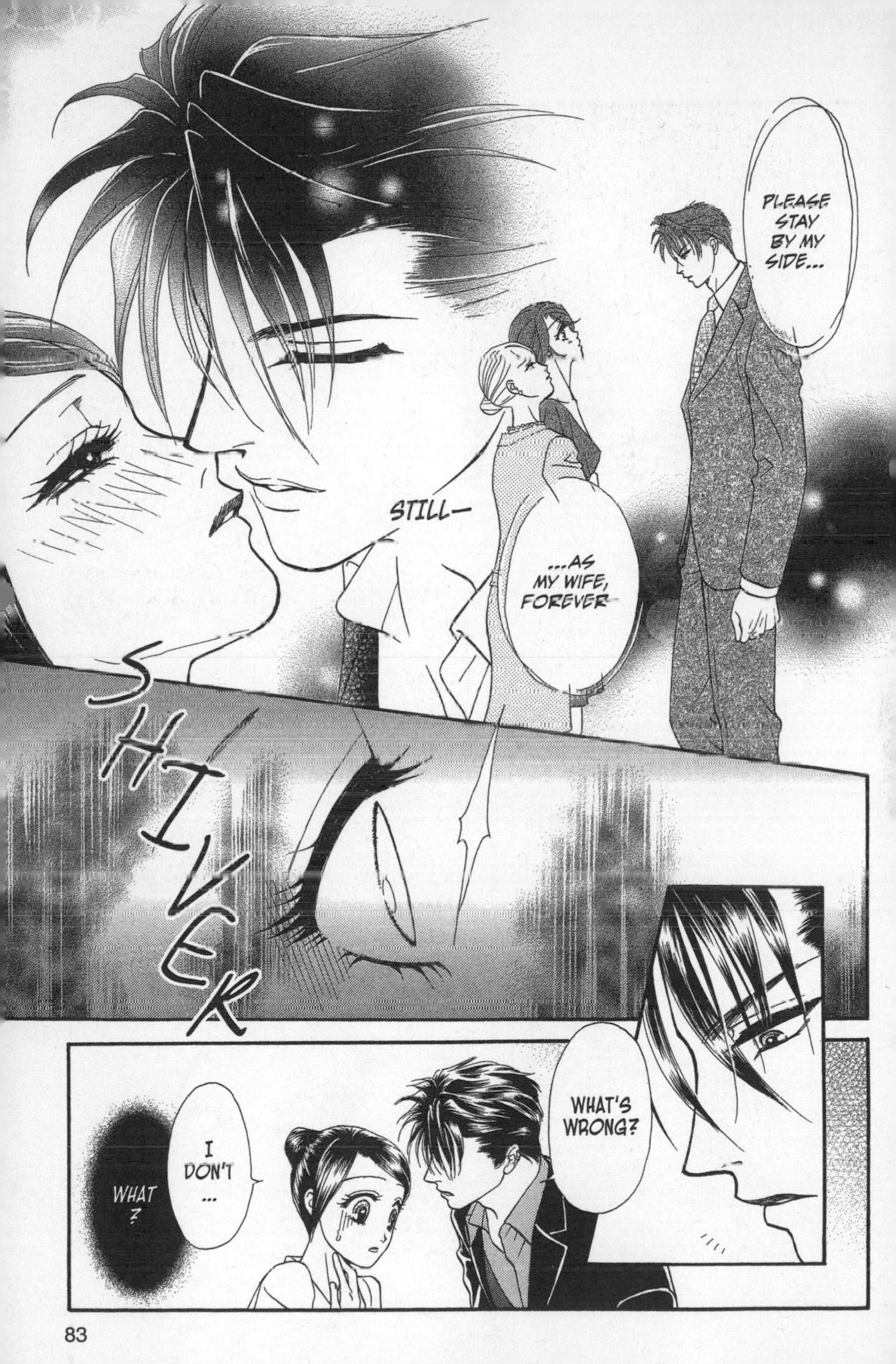
PLEASE STAY BY MY SIDE...
...AS MY WIFE, FOREVER
STILL—
SHIVER
WHAT'S WRONG?
I DON'T ...
WHAT ?

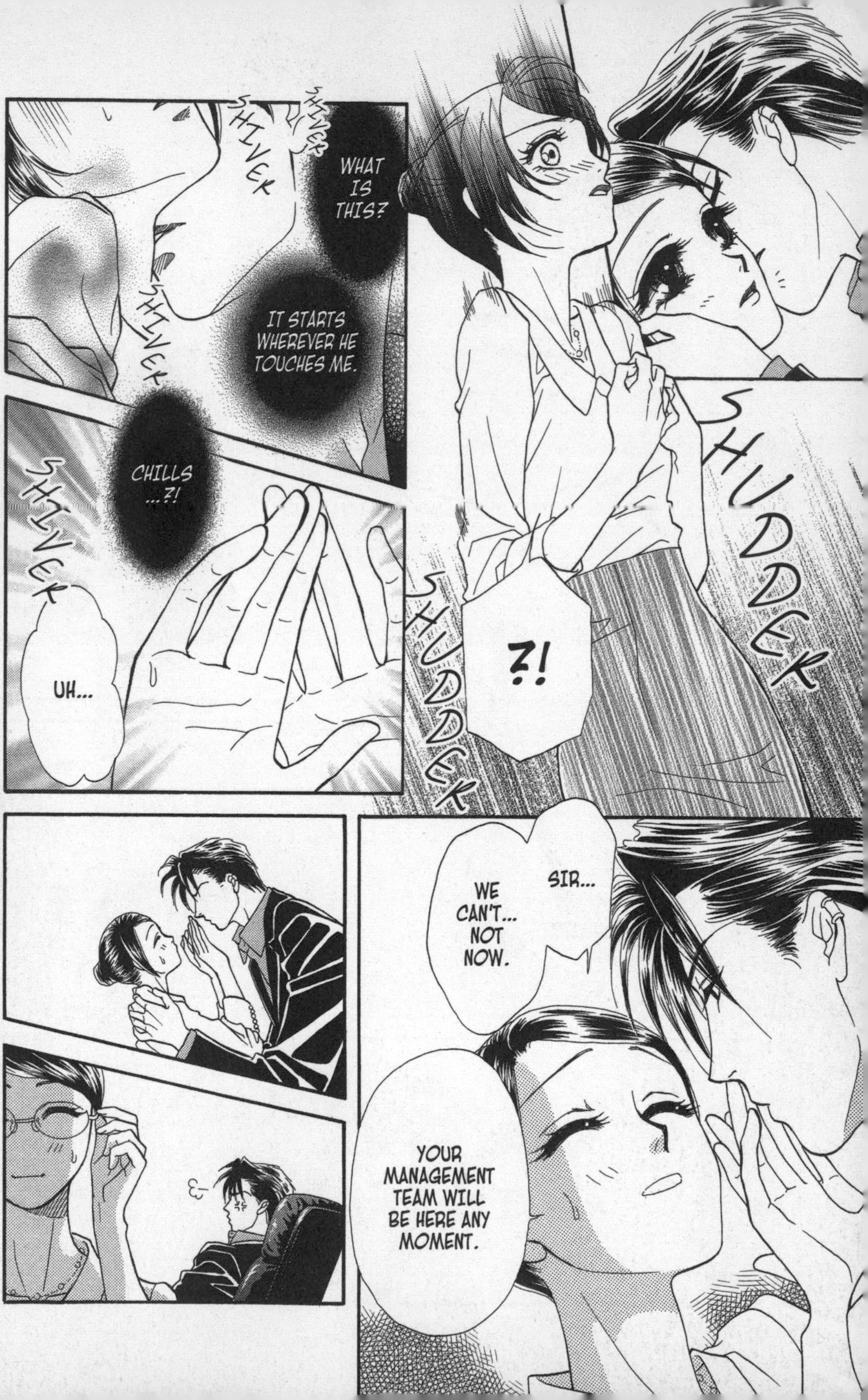
SHUDDER
SHUDDER
?!
SHIVER
SHIVER
WHAT IS THIS?
IT STARTS WHEREVER HE TOUCHES ME.
SHIVER
CHILLS ...?!
SHIVER
UH...
SIR...
WE CAN'T... NOT NOW.
YOUR MANAGEMENT TEAM WILL BE HERE ANY MOMENT.

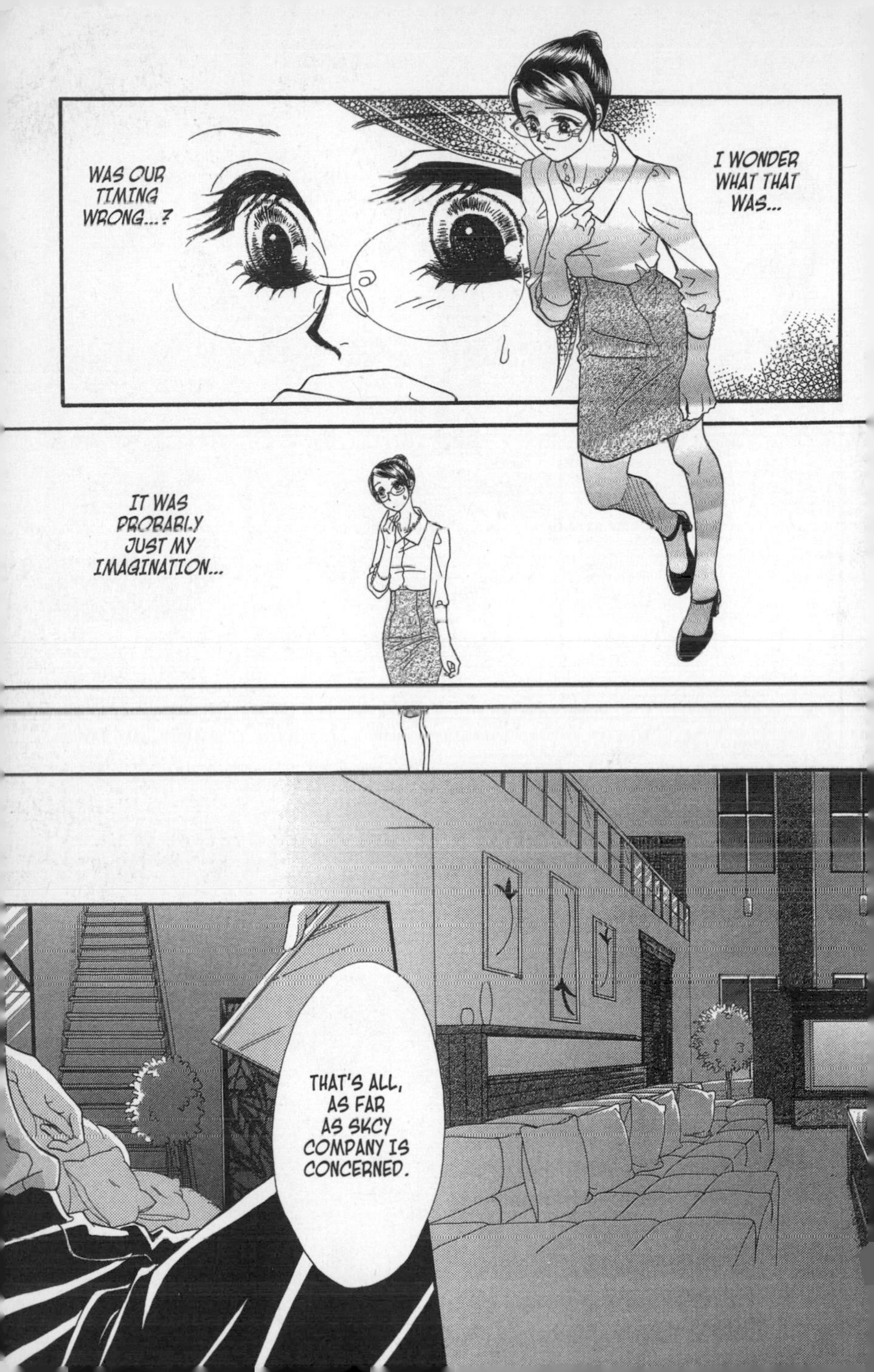
I WONDER WHAT THAT WAS...
WAS OUR TIMING WRONG...?
IT WAS PROBABLY JUST MY IMAGINATION...
THAT'S ALL, AS FAR AS SKCY COMPANY IS CONCERNED.

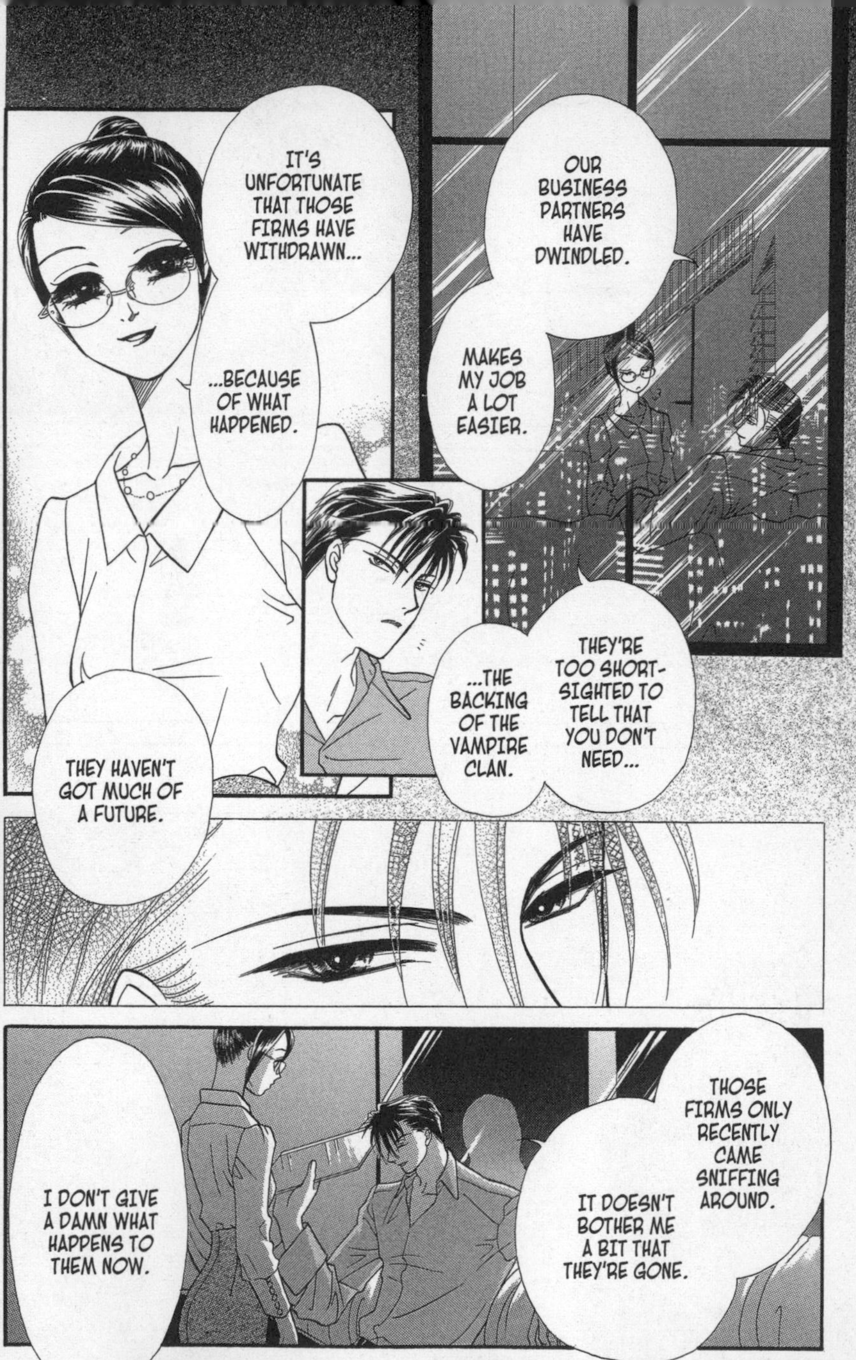
OUR BUSINESS PARTNERS HAVE DWINDLED.
MAKES MY JOB A LOT EASIER.
IT'S UNFORTUNATE THAT THOSE FIRMS HAVE WITHDRAWN...
...BECAUSE OF WHAT HAPPENED.
THEY'RE TOO SHORT-SIGHTED TO TELL THAT YOU DON'T NEED...
...THE BACKING OF THE VAMPIRE CLAN.
THEY HAVEN'T GOT MUCH OF A FUTURE.
THOSE FIRMS ONLY RECENTLY CAME SNIFFING AROUND.
IT DOESN'T BOTHER ME A BIT THAT THEY'RE GONE.
I DON'T GIVE A DAMN WHAT HAPPENS TO THEM NOW.

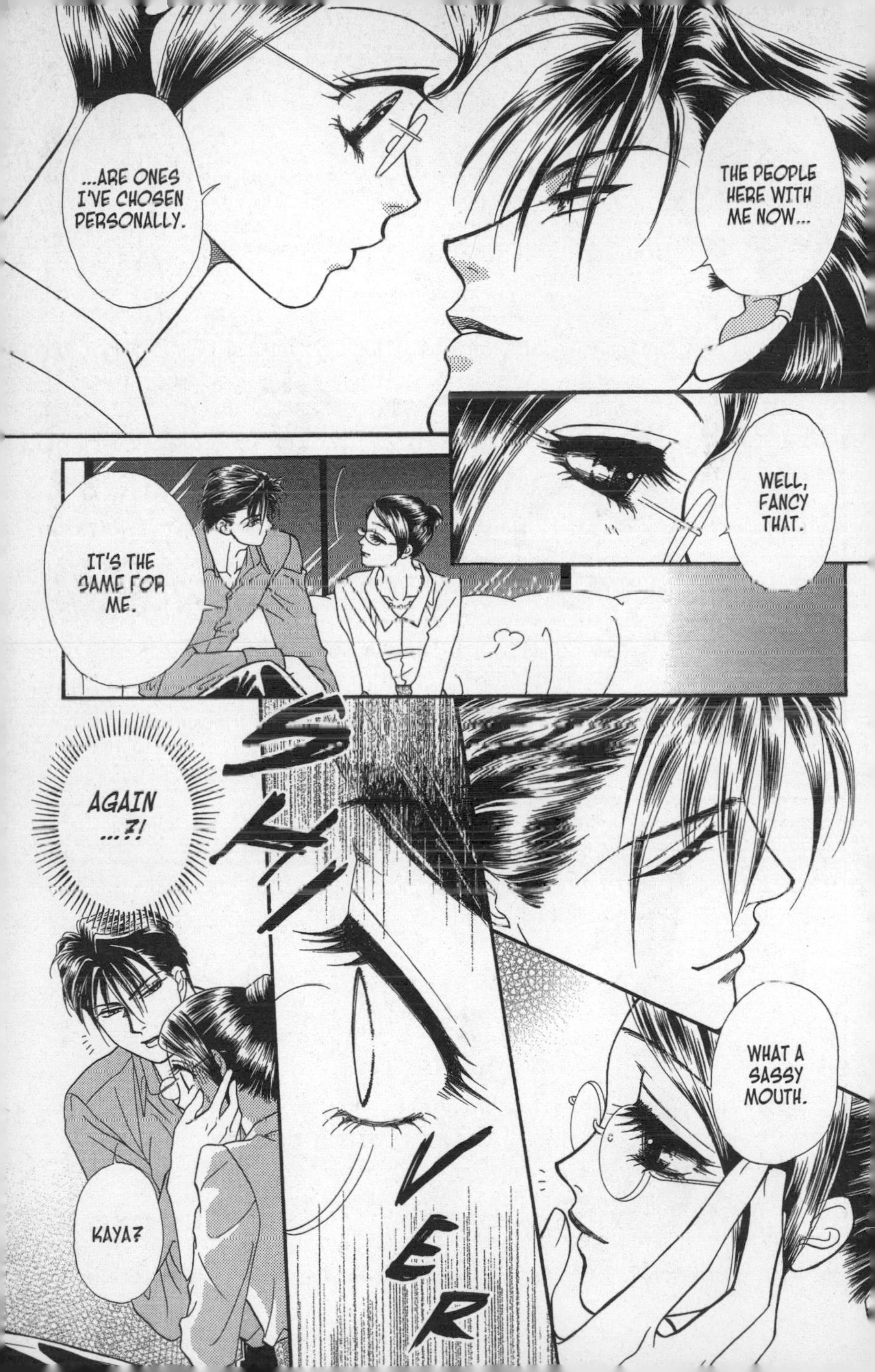
THE PEOPLE HERE WITH ME NOW...
...ARE ONES I'VE CHOSEN PERSONALLY.
WELL, FANCY THAT.
IT'S THE SAME FOR ME.
WHAT A SASSY MOUTH.
SHIVER
AGAIN ...?!
KAYA?

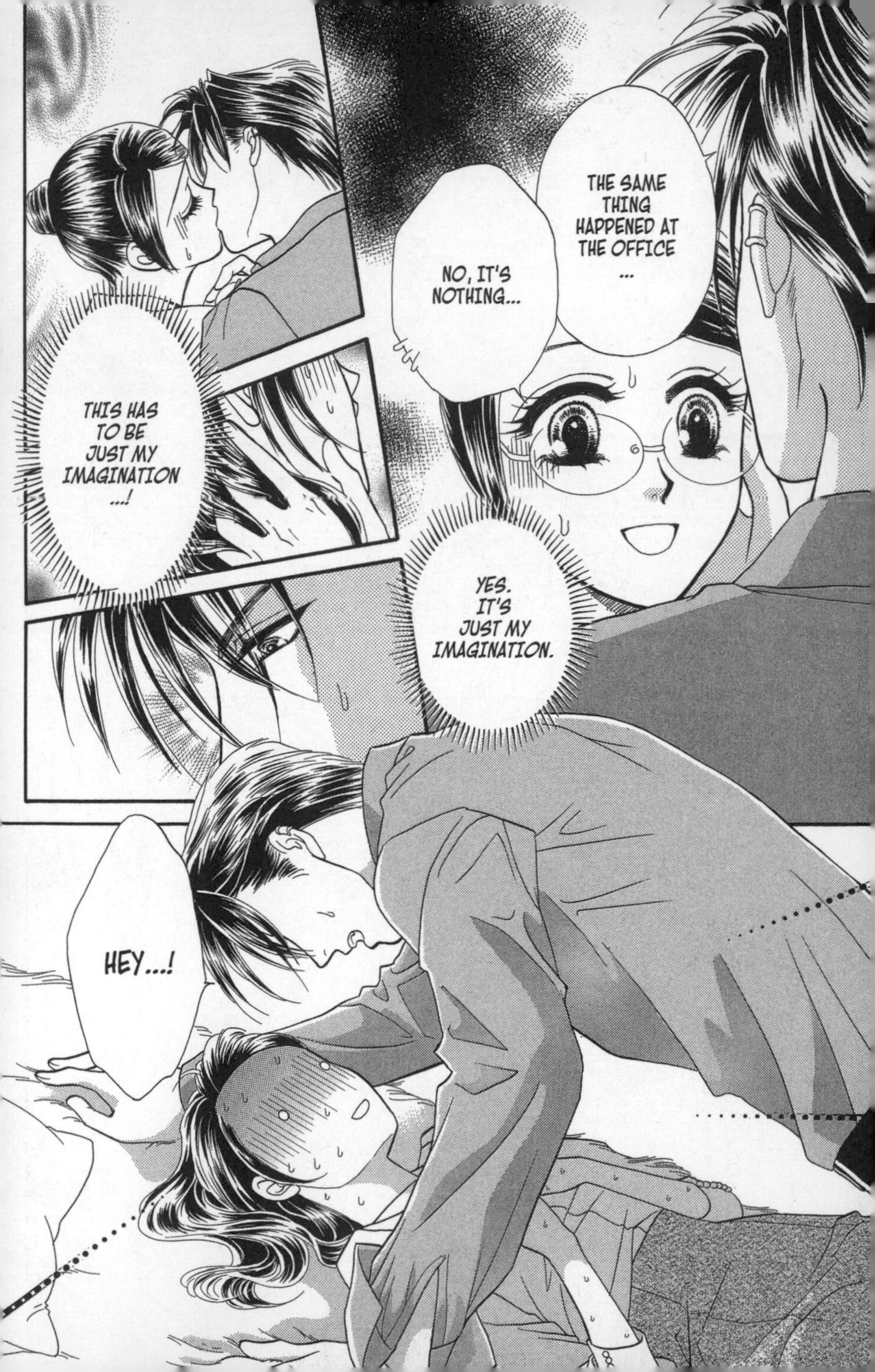
THE SAME THING HAPPENED AT THE OFFICE ...
NO, IT'S NOTHING...
YES. IT'S JUST MY IMAGINATION.
THIS HAS TO BE JUST MY IMAGINATION ...!
HEY...!

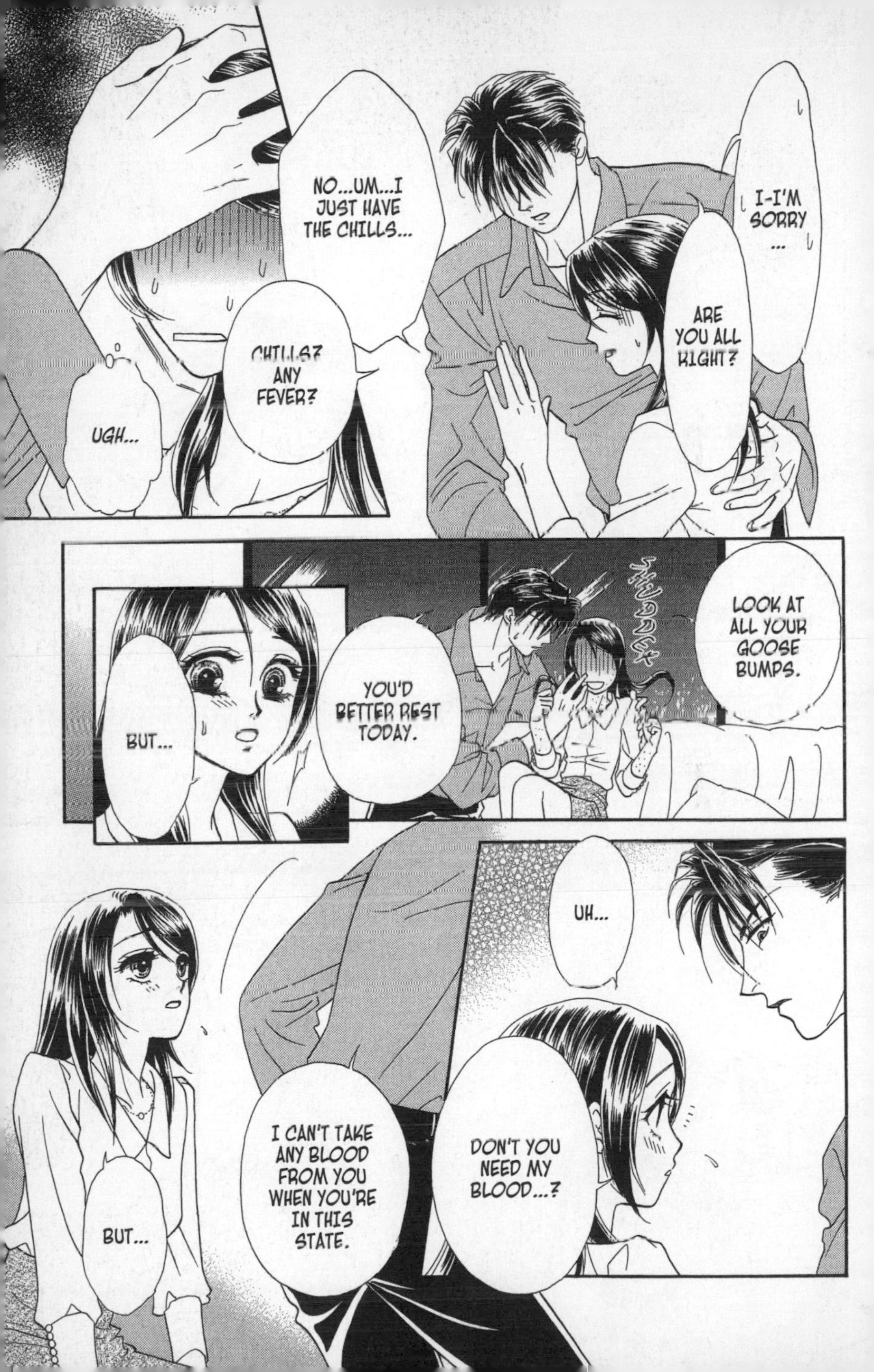
I-I'M SORRY ...
ARE YOU ALL RIGHT?
NO...UM...I JUST HAVE THE CHILLS...
CHILLS? ANY FEVER?
UGH...
LOOK AT ALL YOUR GOOSE BUMPS.
SHUDDER
YOU'D BETTER REST TODAY.
BUT...
UH...
DON'T YOU NEED MY BLOOD...?
I CAN'T TAKE ANY BLOOD FROM YOU WHEN YOU'RE IN THIS STATE.
BUT...

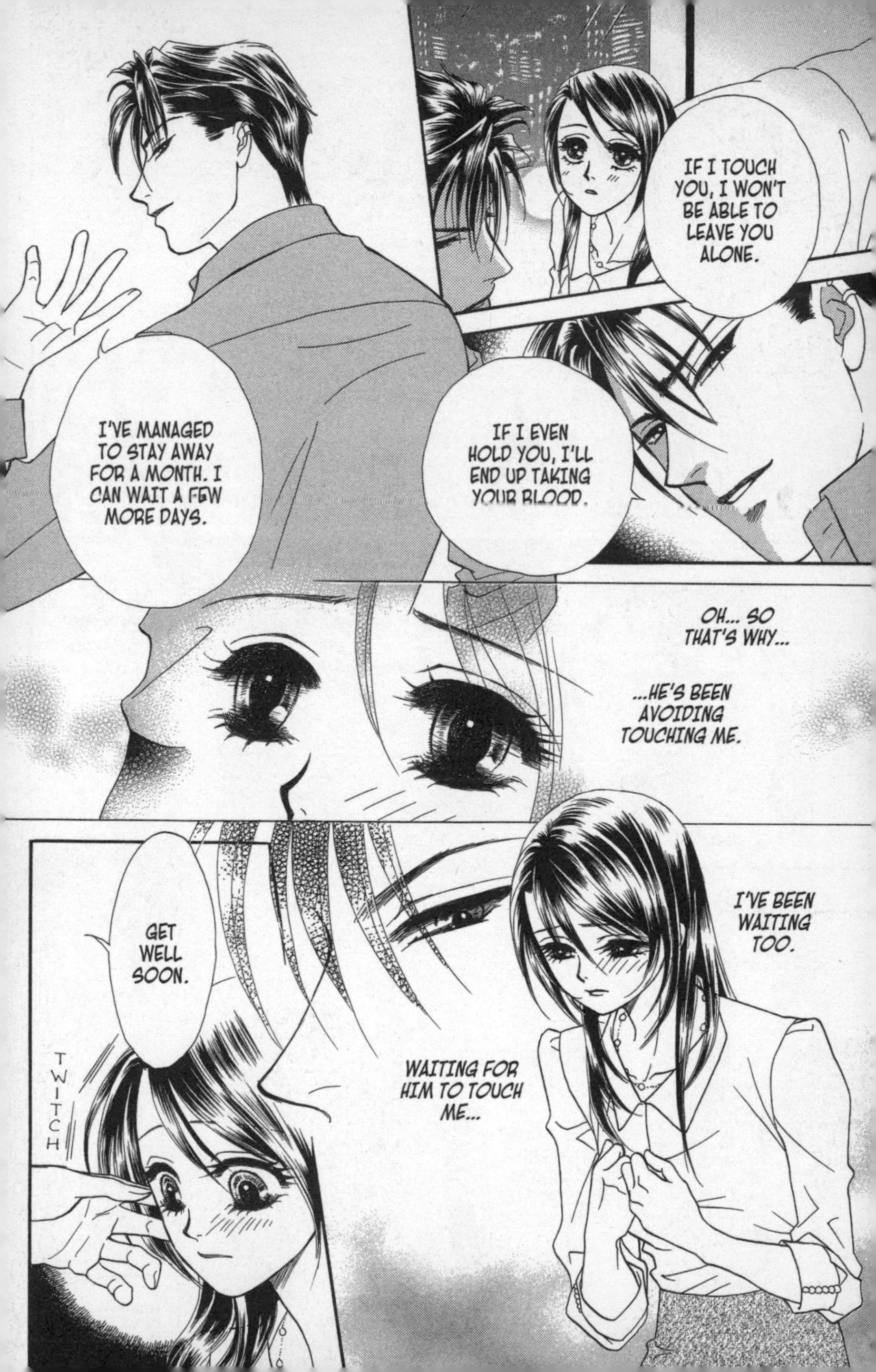
IF I TOUCH YOU, I WON'T BE ABLE TO LEAVE YOU ALONE.
IF I EVEN HOLD YOU, I'LL END UP TAKING YOUR BLOOD.
I'VE MANAGED TO STAY AWAY FOR A MONTH. I CAN WAIT A FEW MORE DAYS.
OH... SO THAT'S WHY...
...HE'S BEEN AVOIDING TOUCHING ME.
I'VE BEEN WAITING TOO.
WAITING FOR HIM TO TOUCH ME...
GET WELL SOON.
TWITCH

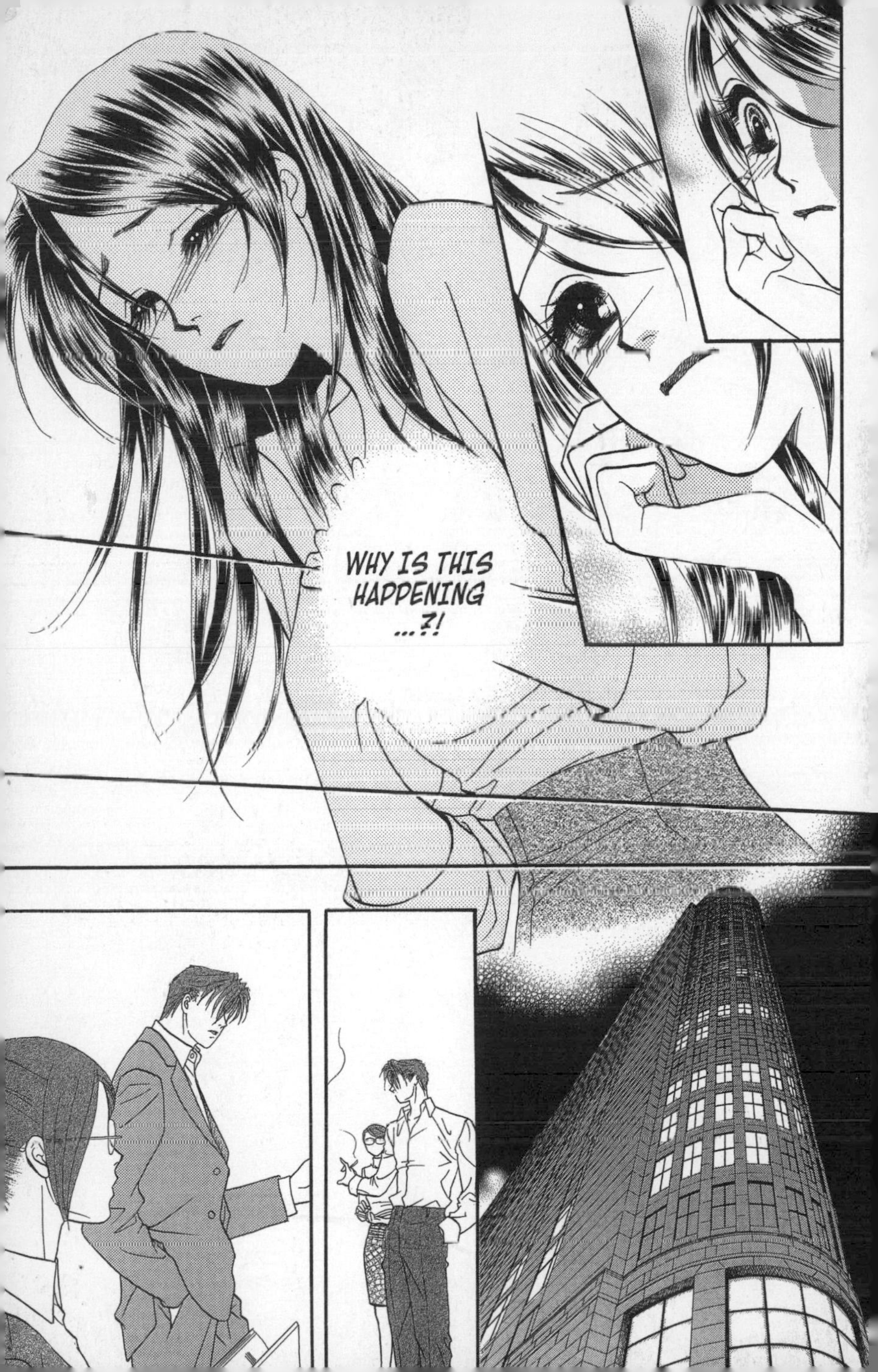
WHY IS THIS HAPPENING ...?!

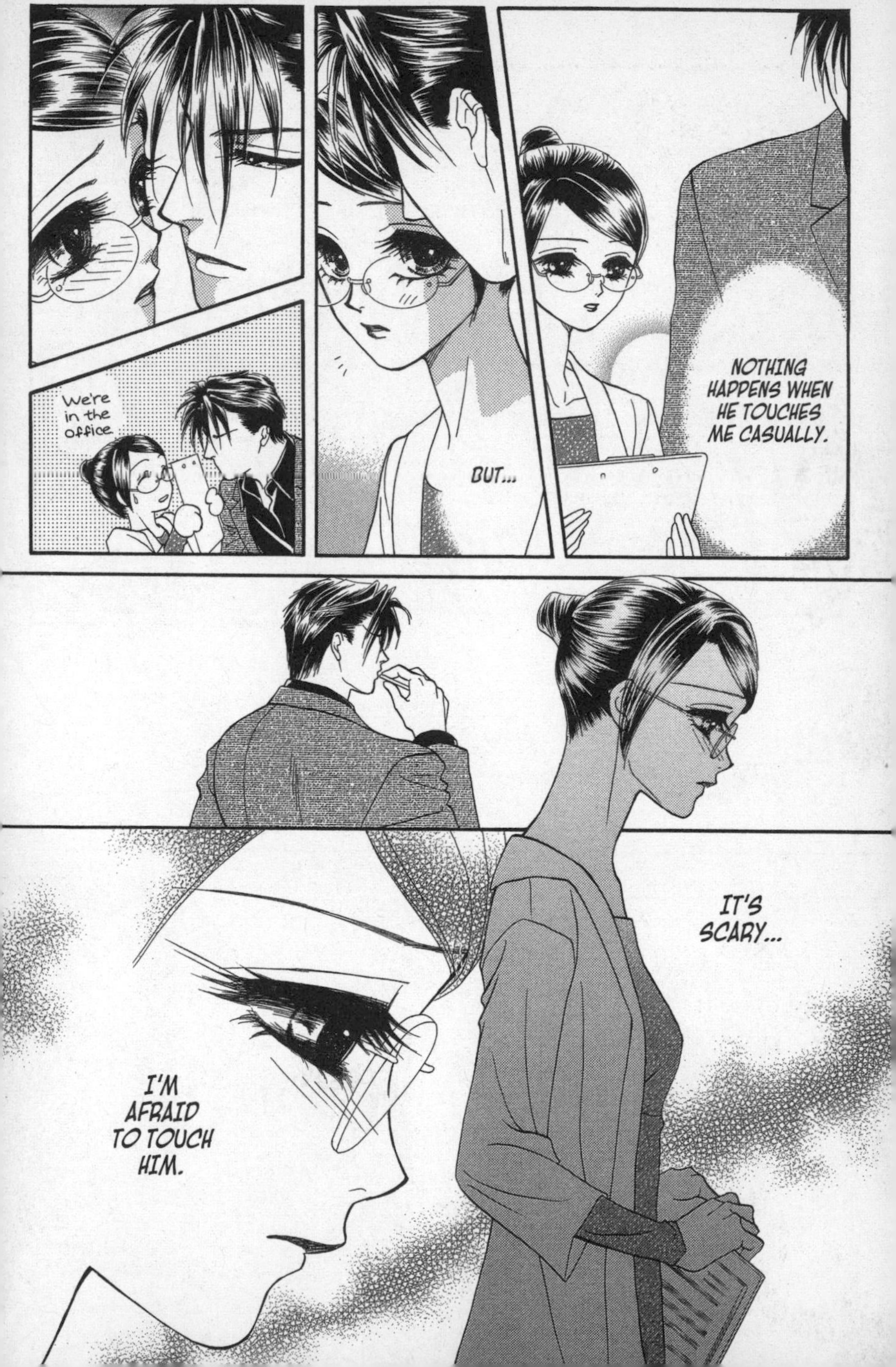
NOTHING HAPPENS WHEN HE TOUCHES ME CASUALLY.
BUT...
We're in the office.
IT'S SCARY...
I'M AFRAID TO TOUCH HIM.

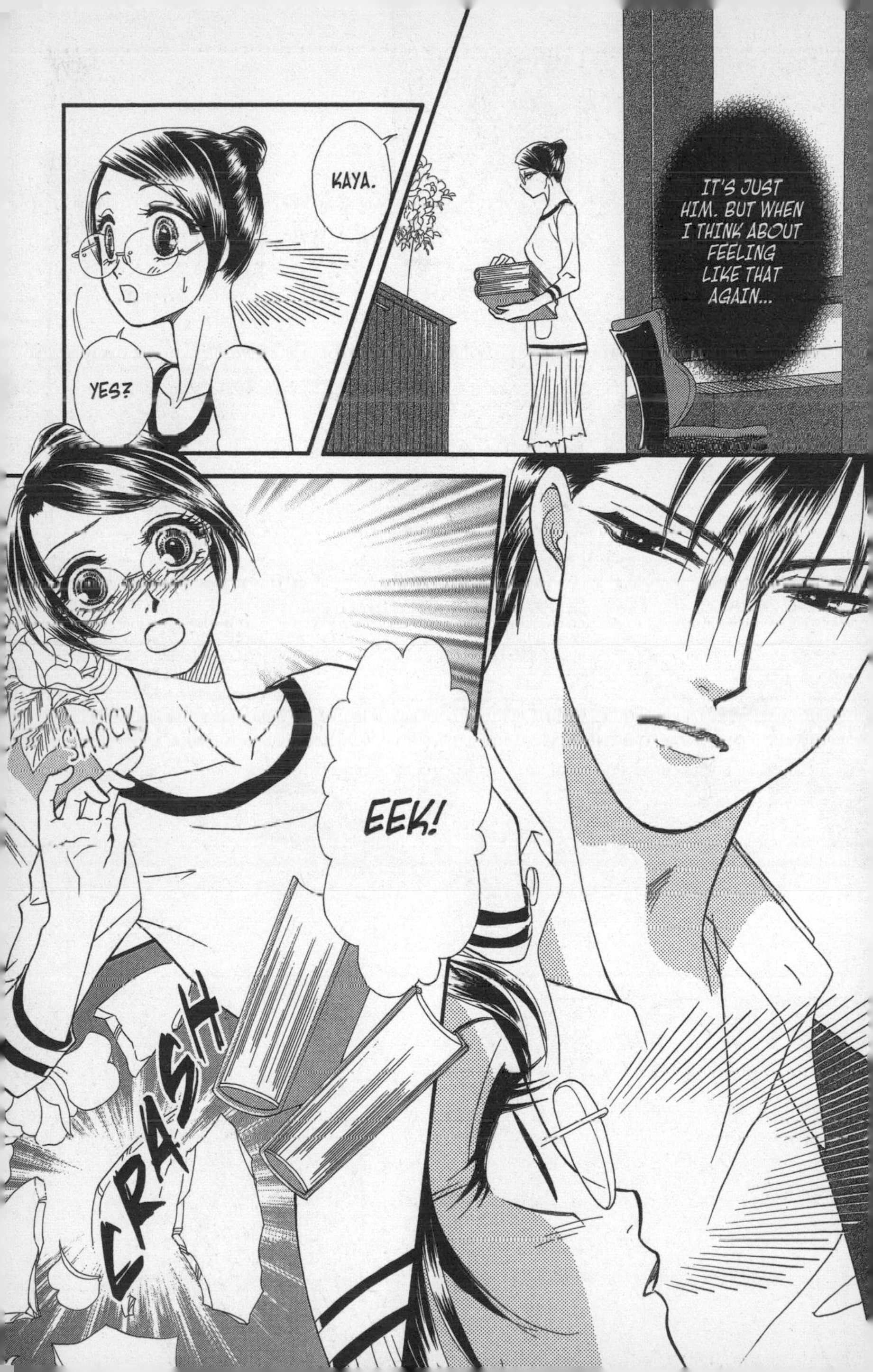
IT'S JUST HIM. BUT WHEN I THINK ABOUT FEELING LIKE THAT AGAIN...
KAYA.
YES?
SHOCK
EEK!
CRASH

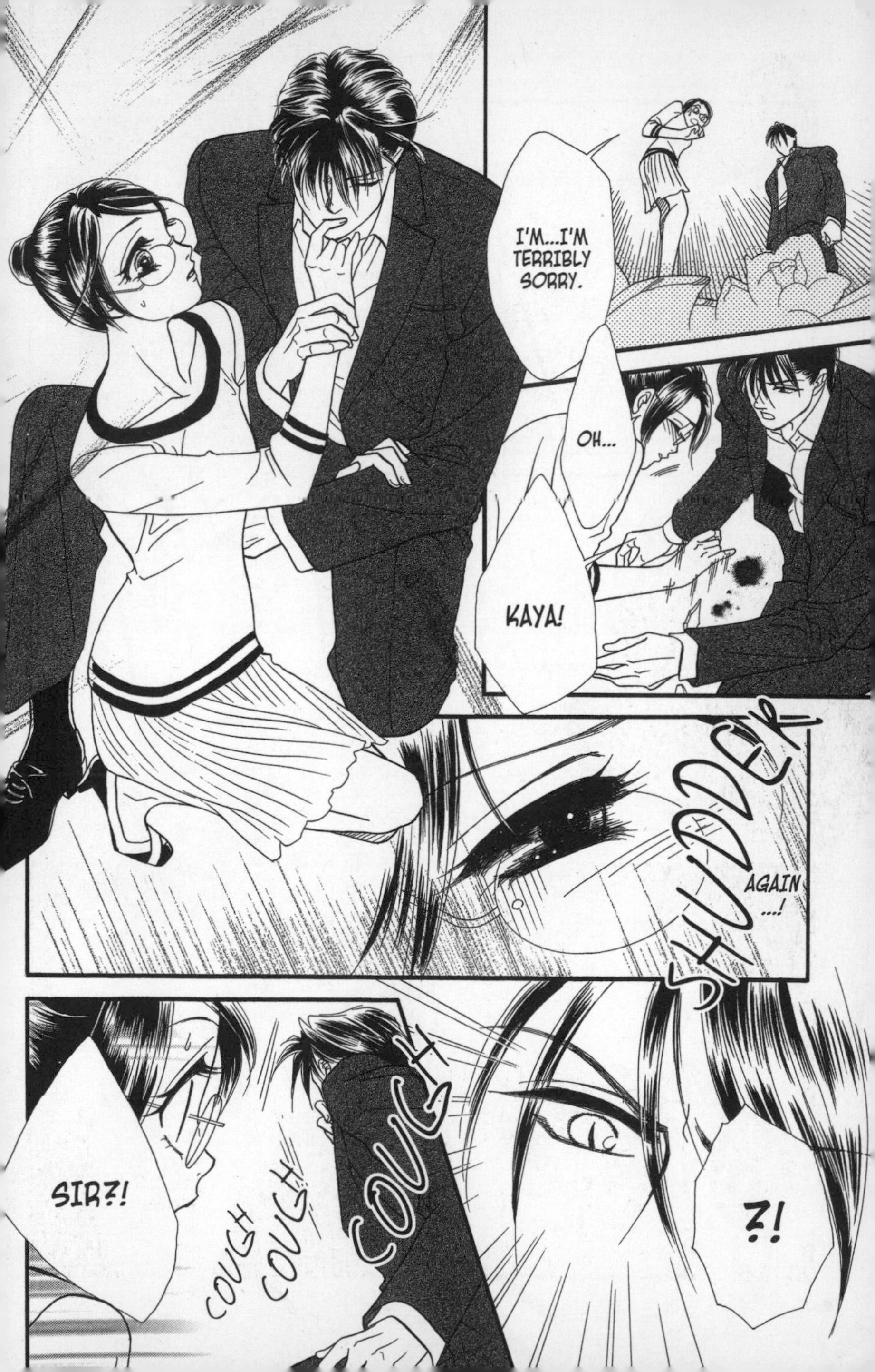
I'M...I'M TERRIBLY SORRY.
OH...
KAYA!
SHUDDER
AGAIN...!
?!
COUGH
COUGH
COUGH
SIR?!

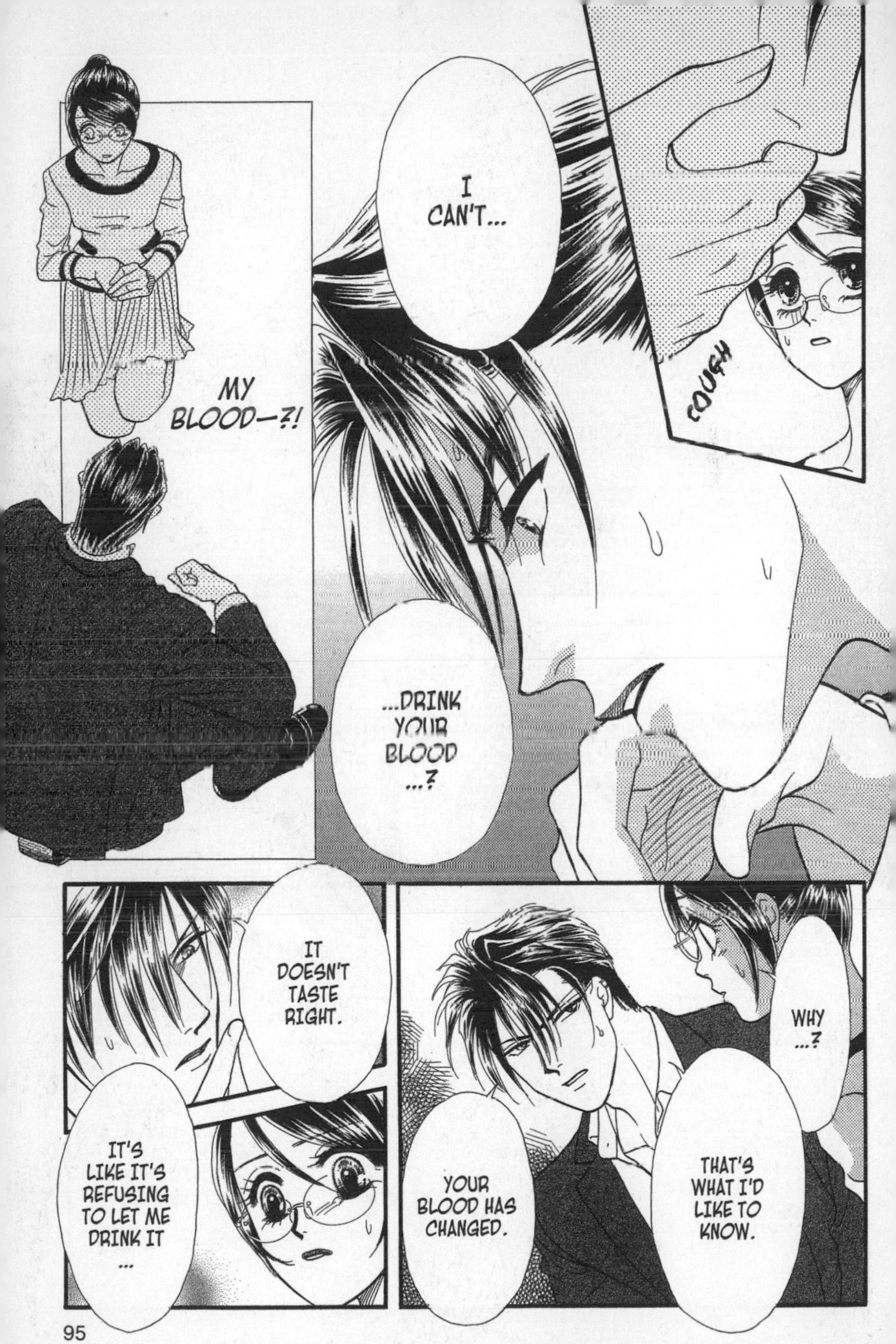
COUGH
I CAN'T...
...DRINK YOUR BLOOD ...?
MY BLOOD—?!
WHY ...?
THAT'S WHAT I'D LIKE TO KNOW.
YOUR BLOOD HAS CHANGED.
IT DOESN'T TASTE RIGHT.
IT'S LIKE IT'S REFUSING TO LET ME DRINK IT ...

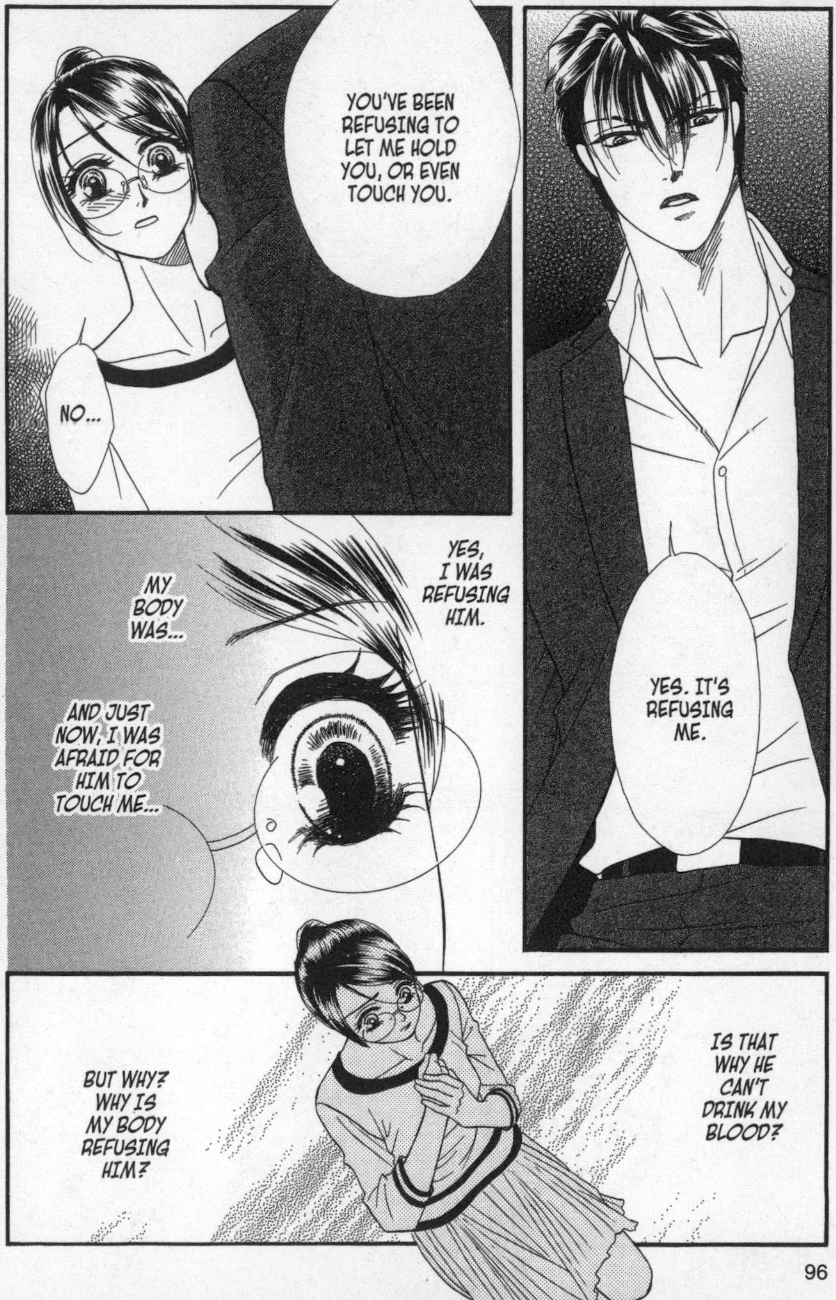
YES. IT'S REFUSING ME.
YOU'VE BEEN REFUSING TO LET ME HOLD YOU, OR EVEN TOUCH YOU.
NO...
YES, I WAS REFUSING HIM.
MY BODY WAS...
AND JUST NOW, I WAS AFRAID FOR HIM TO TOUCH ME...
IS THAT WHY HE CAN'T DRINK MY BLOOD?
BUT WHY? WHY IS MY BODY REFUSING HIM?

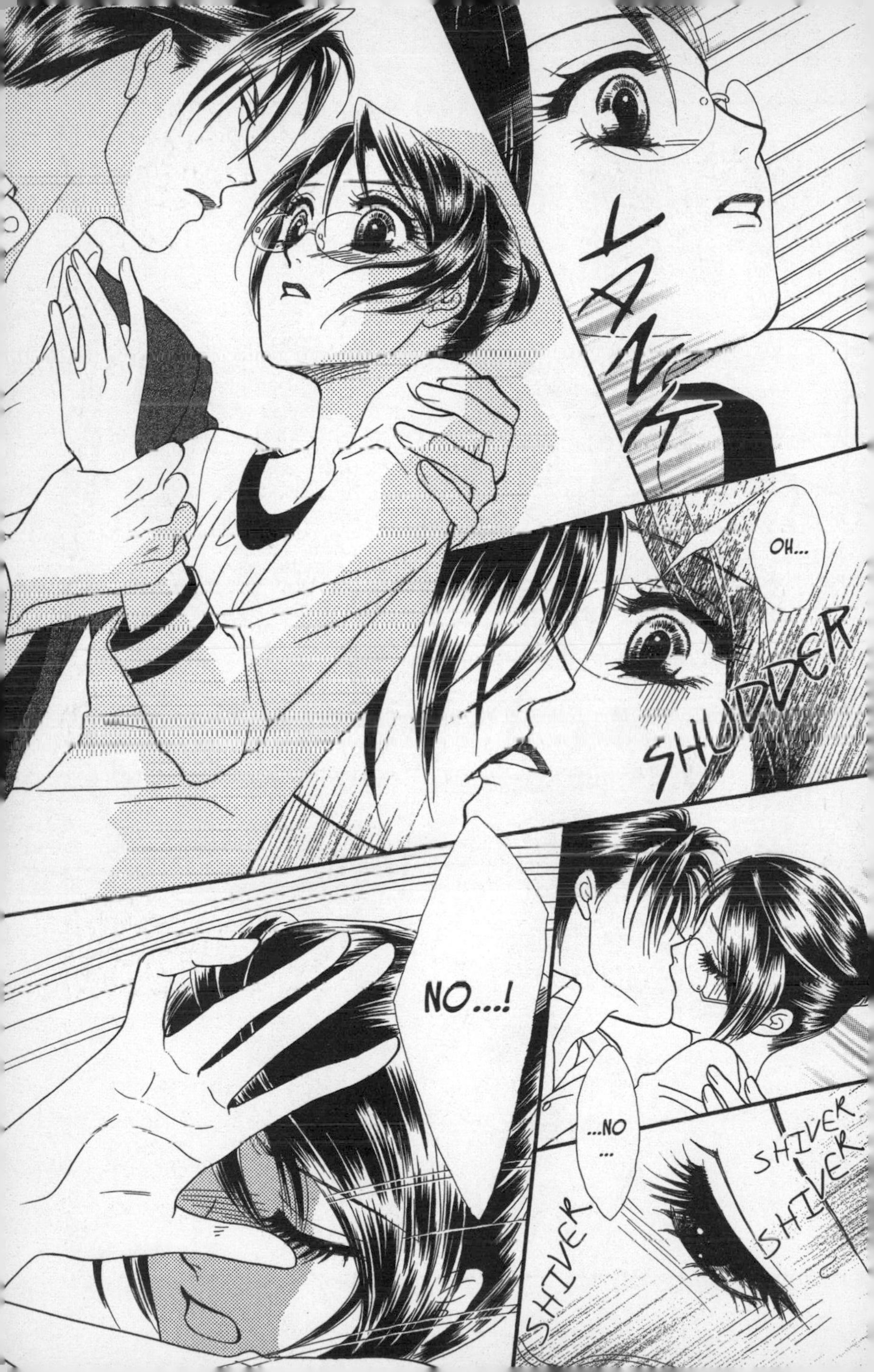
YANK
OH...
SHUDDER
...NO ...
SHIVER
SHIVER
SHIVER
NO...!

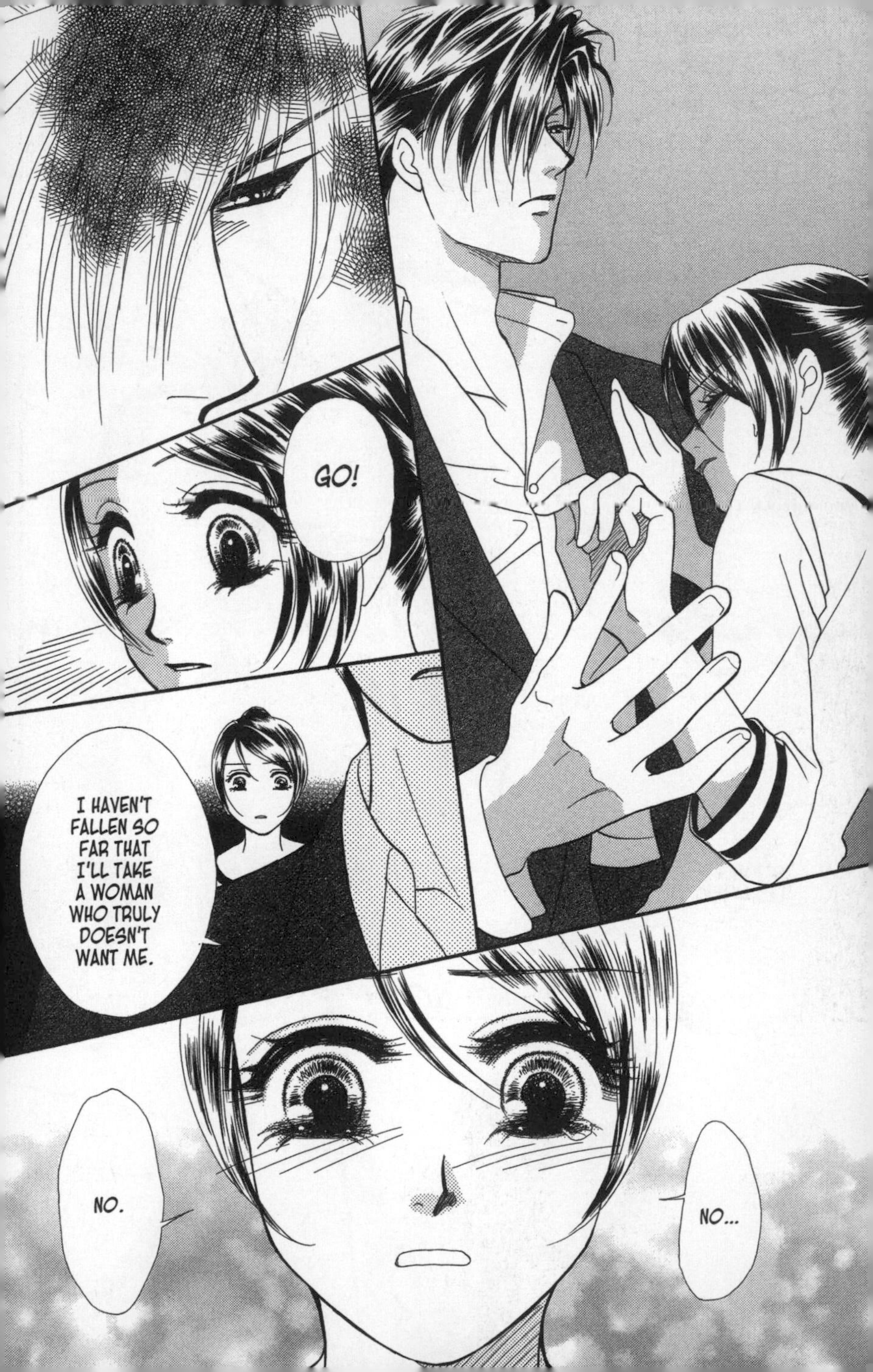
GO!
I HAVEN'T FALLEN SO FAR THAT I'LL TAKE A WOMAN WHO TRULY DOESN'T WANT ME.
NO...
NO.

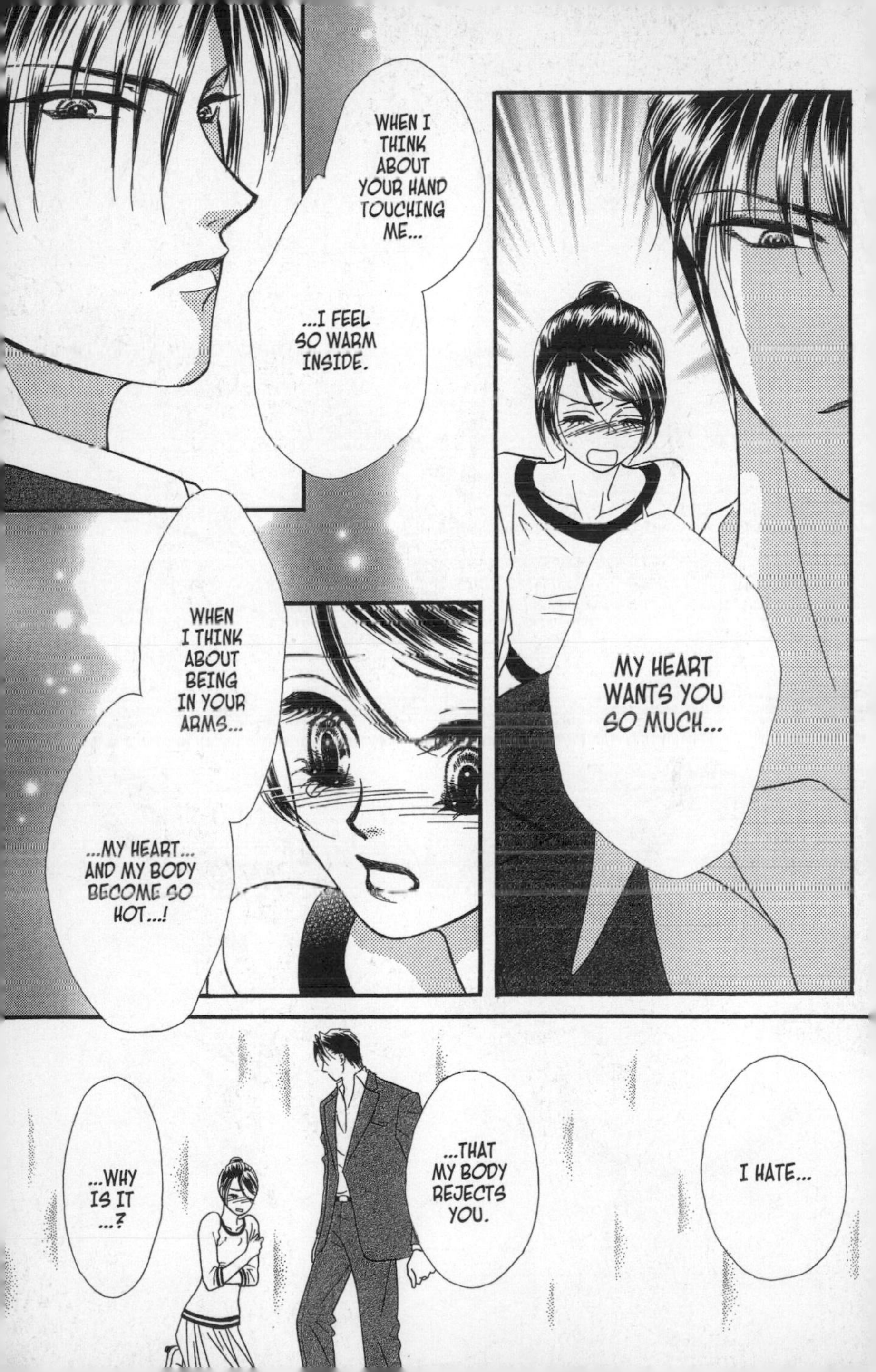
MY HEART WANTS YOU SO MUCH...
WHEN I THINK ABOUT YOUR HAND TOUCHING ME...
...I FEEL SO WARM INSIDE.
WHEN I THINK ABOUT BEING IN YOUR ARMS...
...MY HEART... AND MY BODY BECOME SO HOT...!
I HATE...
...THAT MY BODY REJECTS YOU.
...WHY IS IT ...?

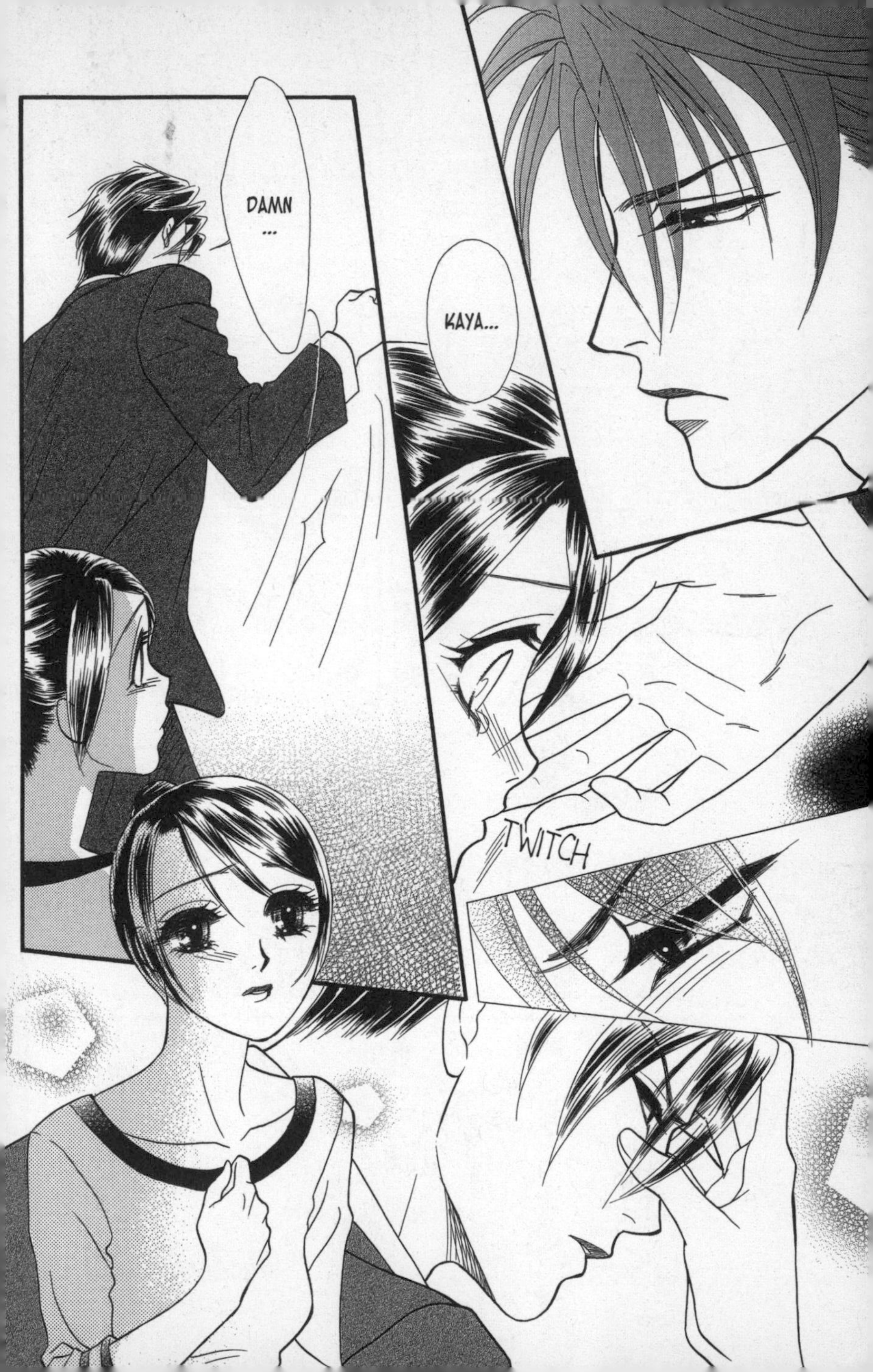
KAYA...
TWITCH
DAMN ...

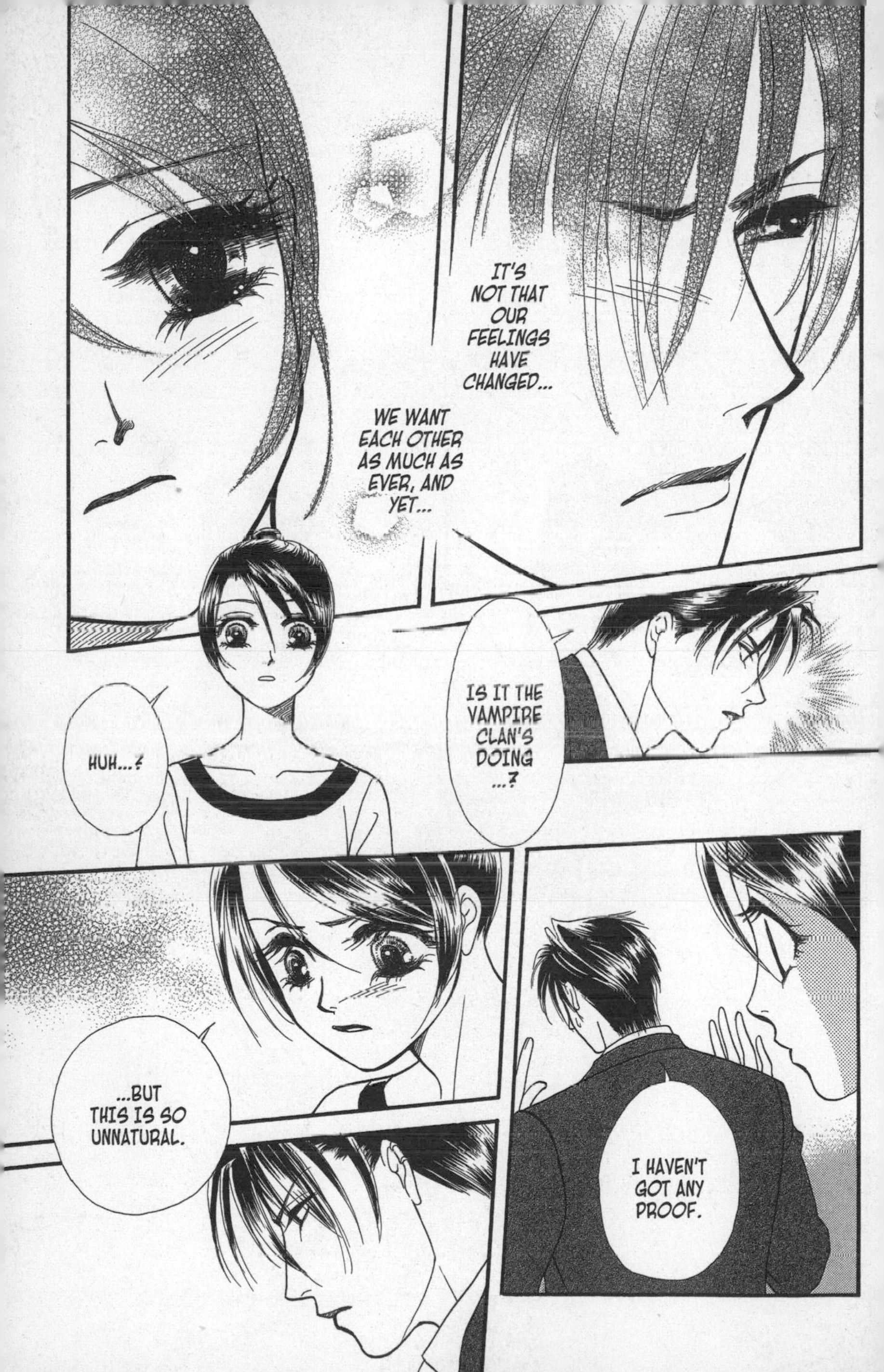
IT'S NOT THAT OUR FEELINGS HAVE CHANGED...
WE WANT EACH OTHER AS MUCH AS EVER, AND YET...
IS IT THE VAMPIRE CLAN'S DOING ...?
HUH...?
I HAVEN'T GOT ANY PROOF.
...BUT THIS IS SO UNNATURAL.

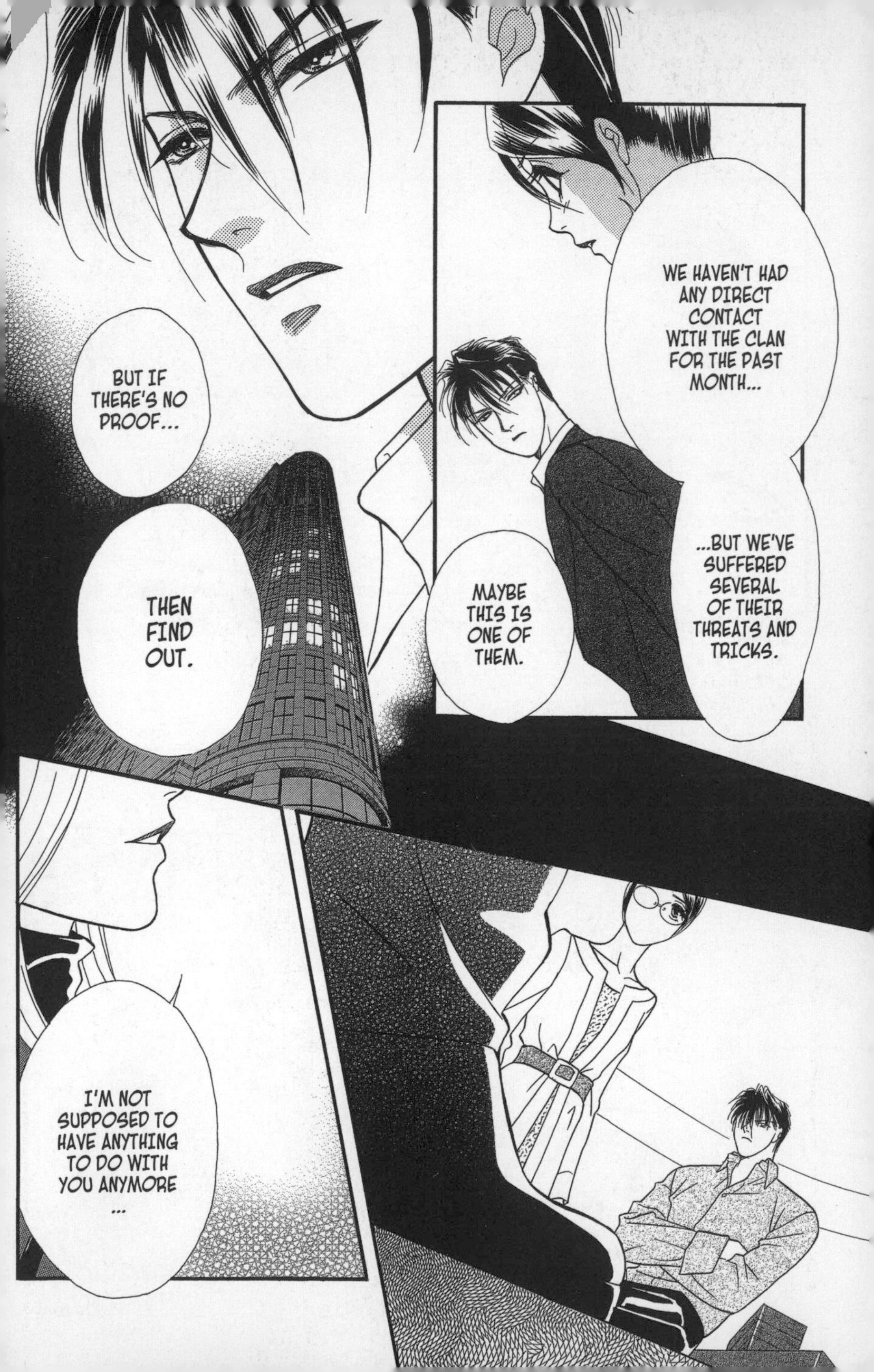
WE HAVEN'T HAD ANY DIRECT CONTACT WITH THE CLAN FOR THE PAST MONTH...
...BUT WE'VE SUFFERED SEVERAL OF THEIR THREATS AND TRICKS.
MAYBE THIS IS ONE OF THEM.
BUT IF THERE'S NO PROOF...
THEN FIND OUT.
I'M NOT SUPPOSED TO HAVE ANYTHING TO DO WITH YOU ANYMORE
...

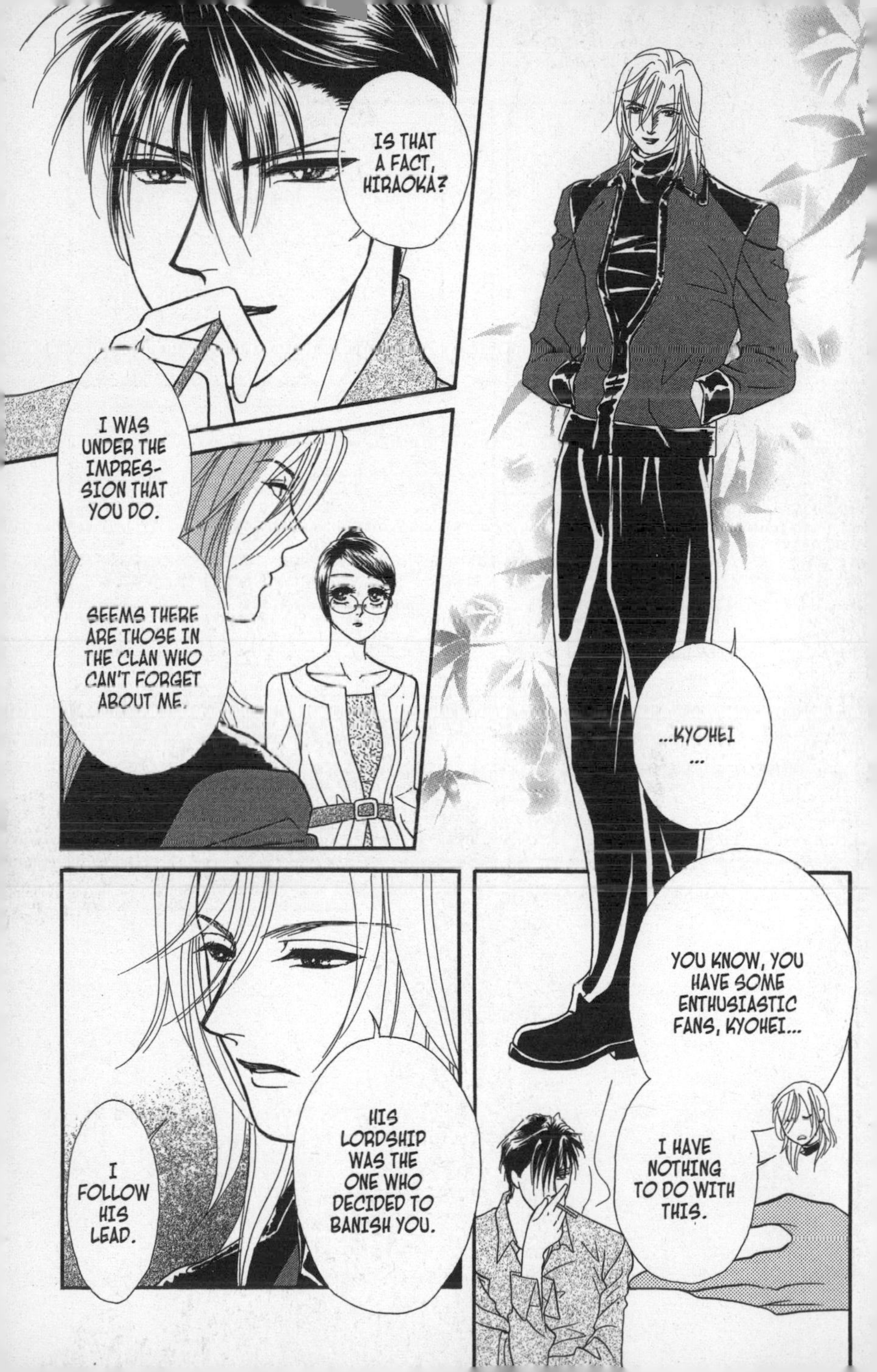
...KYOHEI ...
IS THAT A FACT, HIRAOKA?
I WAS UNDER THE IMPRESSION THAT YOU DO.
SEEMS THERE ARE THOSE IN THE CLAN WHO CAN'T FORGET ABOUT ME.
YOU KNOW, YOU HAVE SOME ENTHUSIASTIC FANS, KYOHEI...
I HAVE NOTHING TO DO WITH THIS.
HIS LORDSHIP WAS THE ONE WHO DECIDED TO BANISH YOU.
I FOLLOW HIS LEAD.

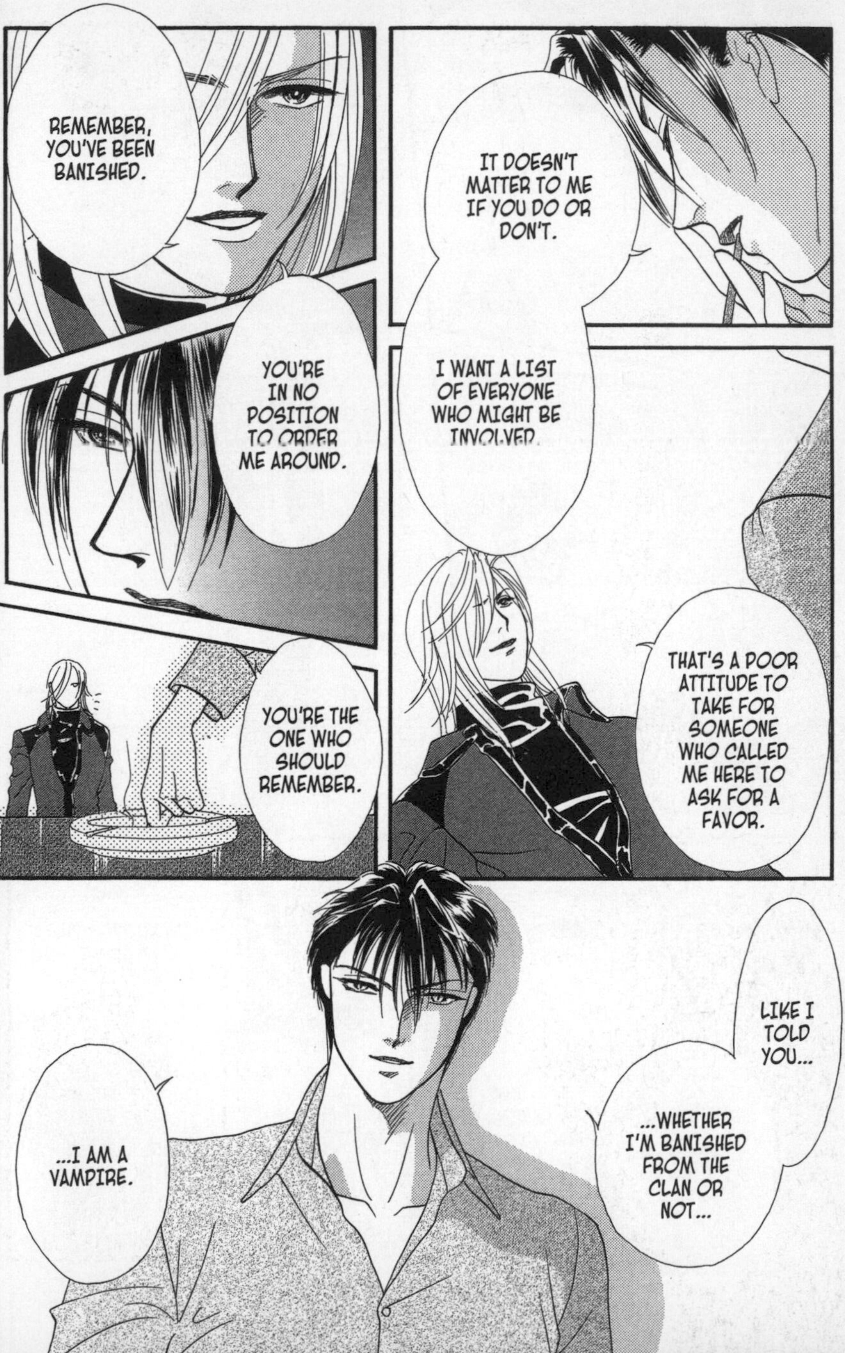
IT DOESN'T MATTER TO ME IF YOU DO OR DON'T.
I WANT A LIST OF EVERYONE WHO MIGHT BE INVOLVED.
THAT'S A POOR ATTITUDE TO TAKE FOR SOMEONE WHO CALLED ME HERE TO ASK FOR A FAVOR.
REMEMBER, YOU'VE BEEN BANISHED.
YOU'RE IN NO POSITION TO ORDER ME AROUND.
YOU'RE THE ONE WHO SHOULD REMEMBER.
LIKE I TOLD YOU...
...WHETHER I'M BANISHED FROM THE CLAN OR NOT...
...I AM A VAMPIRE.

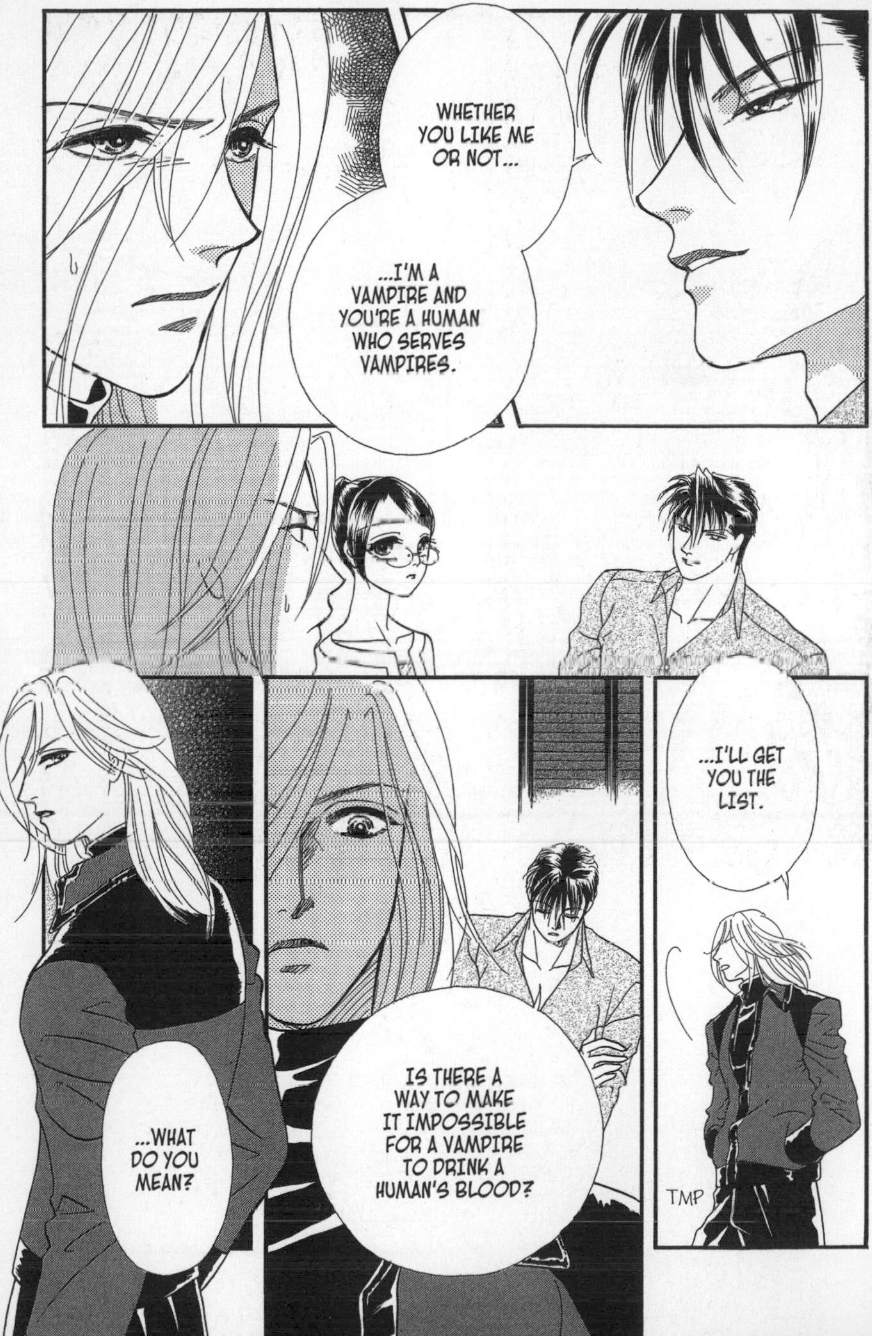
WHETHER YOU LIKE ME OR NOT...
...I'M A VAMPIRE AND YOU'RE A HUMAN WHO SERVES VAMPIRES.
...I'LL GET YOU THE LIST.
TMP
IS THERE A WAY TO MAKE IT IMPOSSIBLE FOR A VAMPIRE TO DRINK A HUMAN'S BLOOD?
...WHAT DO YOU MEAN?

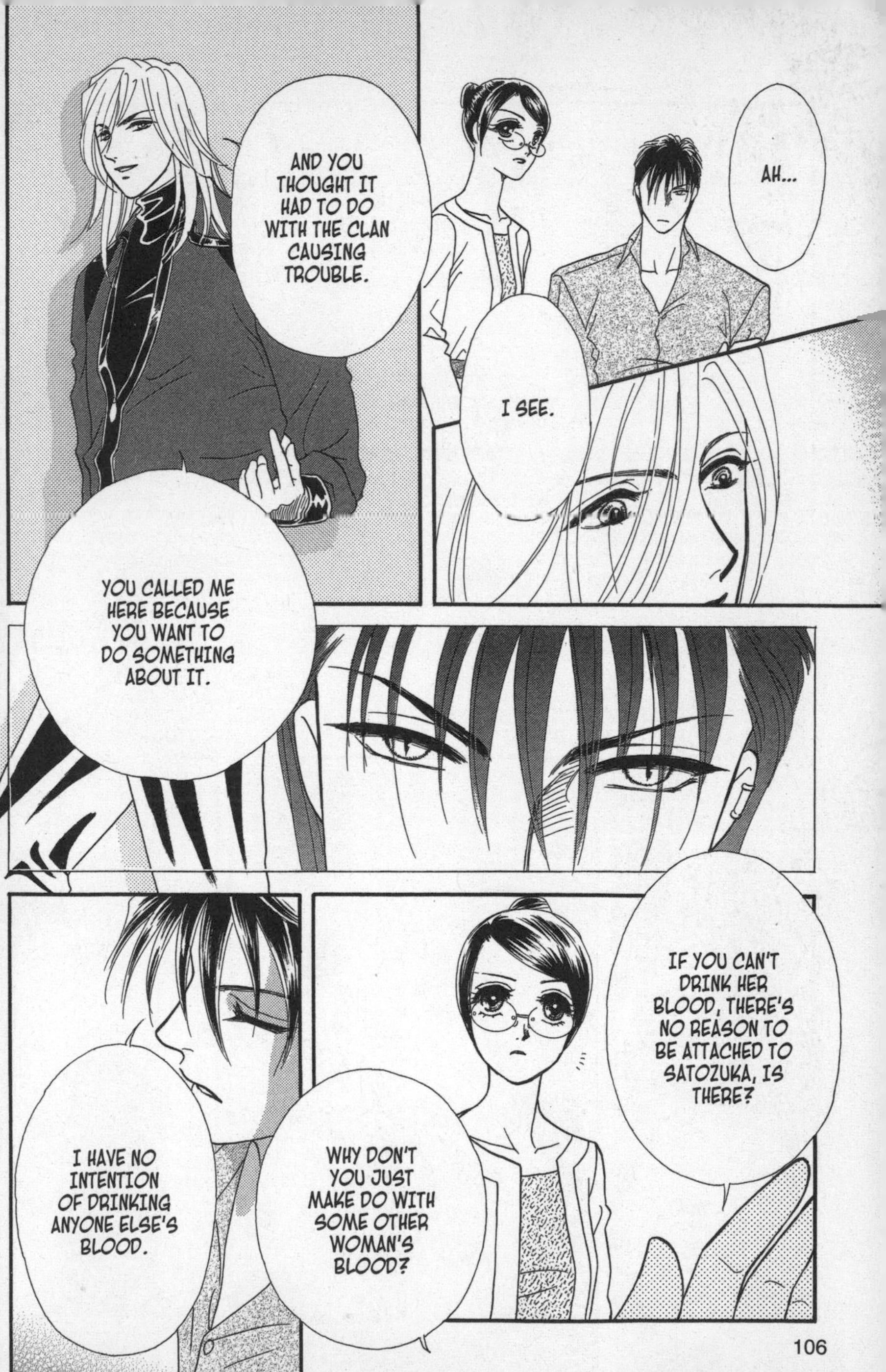
AH...
I SEE.
AND YOU THOUGHT IT HAD TO DO WITH THE CLAN CAUSING TROUBLE.
YOU CALLED ME HERE BECAUSE YOU WANT TO DO SOMETHING ABOUT IT.
IF YOU CAN'T DRINK HER BLOOD, THERE'S NO REASON TO BE ATTACHED TO SATOZUKA, IS THERE?
WHY DON'T YOU JUST MAKE DO WITH SOME OTHER WOMAN'S BLOOD?
I HAVE NO INTENTION OF DRINKING ANYONE ELSE'S BLOOD.

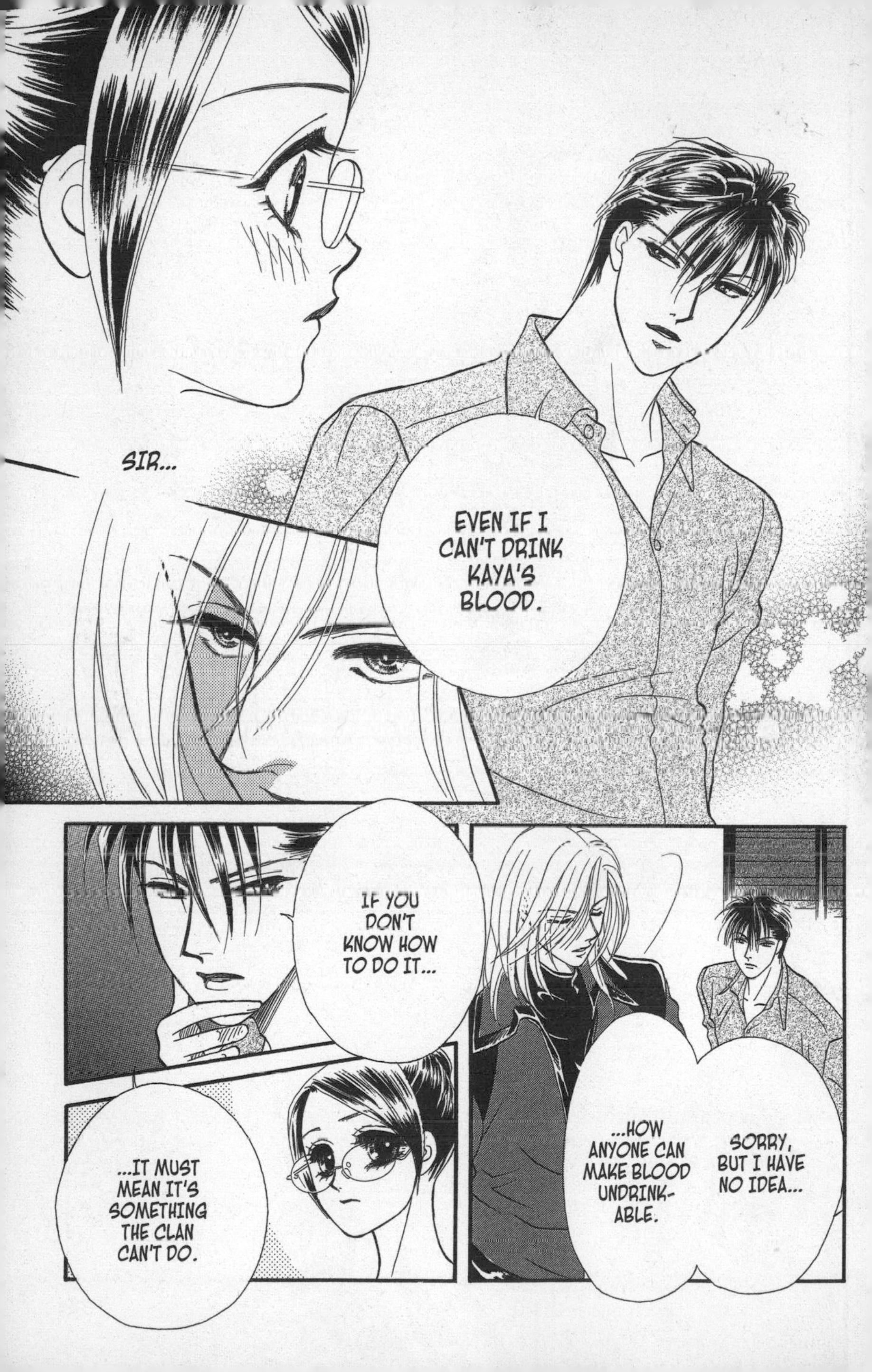
EVEN IF I CAN'T DRINK KAYA'S BLOOD.
SIR...
SORRY, BUT I HAVE NO IDEA...
...HOW ANYONE CAN MAKE BLOOD UNDRINK-ABLE.
IF YOU DON'T KNOW HOW TO DO IT...
...IT MUST MEAN IT'S SOMETHING THE CLAN CAN'T DO.

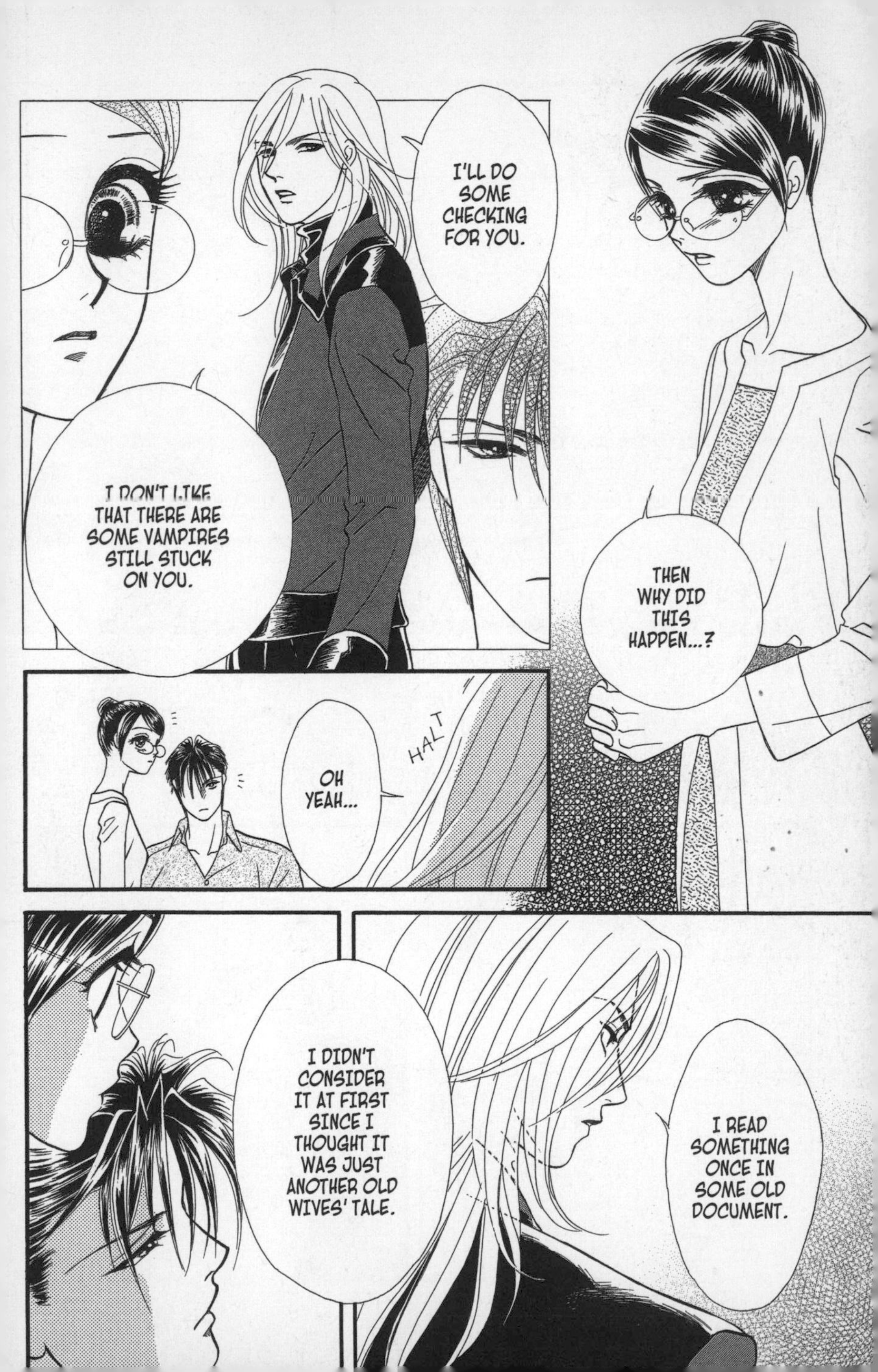
THEN WHY DID THIS HAPPEN...?
I'LL DO SOME CHECKING FOR YOU.
I DON'T LIKE THAT THERE ARE SOME VAMPIRES STILL STUCK ON YOU.
HALT
OH YEAH...
I READ SOMETHING ONCE IN SOME OLD DOCUMENT.
I DIDN'T CONSIDER IT AT FIRST SINCE I THOUGHT IT WAS JUST ANOTHER OLD WIVES' TALE.

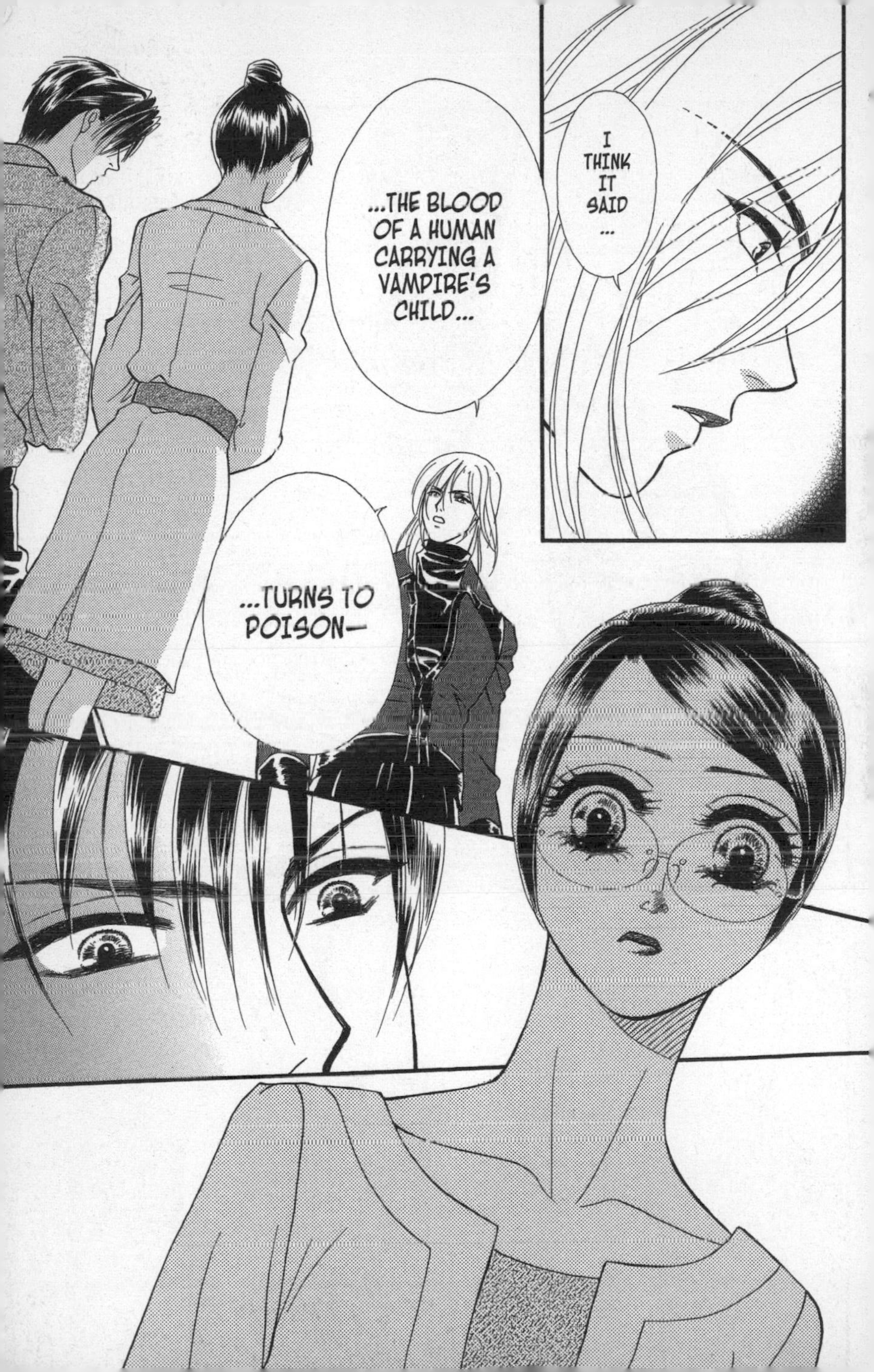
I THINK IT SAID ...
...THE BLOOD OF A HUMAN CARRYING A VAMPIRE'S CHILD...
...TURNS TO POISON—

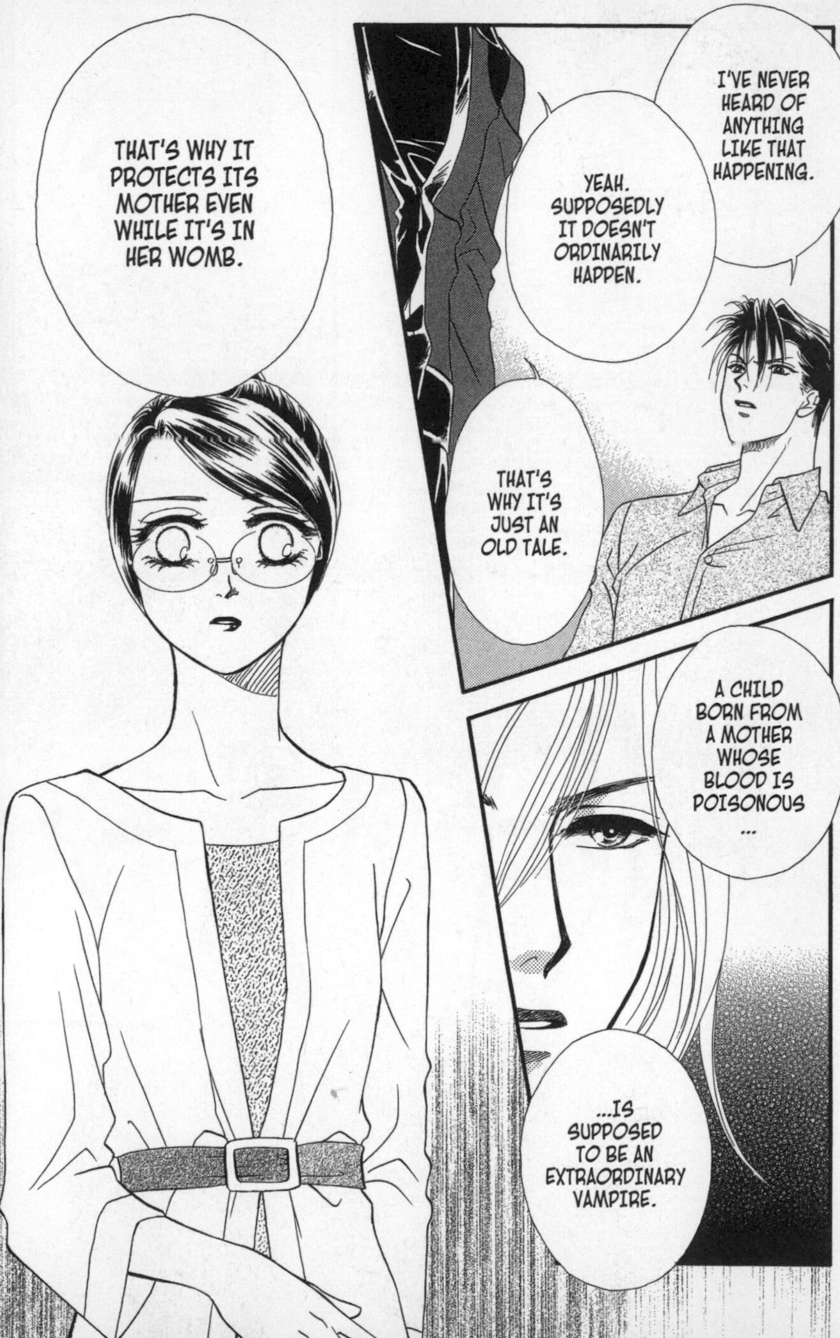
I'VE NEVER HEARD OF ANYTHING LIKE THAT HAPPENING.
YEAH. SUPPOSEDLY IT DOESN'T ORDINARILY HAPPEN.
THAT'S WHY IT'S JUST AN OLD TALE.
A CHILD BORN FROM A MOTHER WHOSE BLOOD IS POISONOUS ...
...IS SUPPOSED TO BE AN EXTRAORDINARY VAMPIRE.
THAT'S WHY IT PROTECTS ITS MOTHER EVEN WHILE IT'S IN HER WOMB.

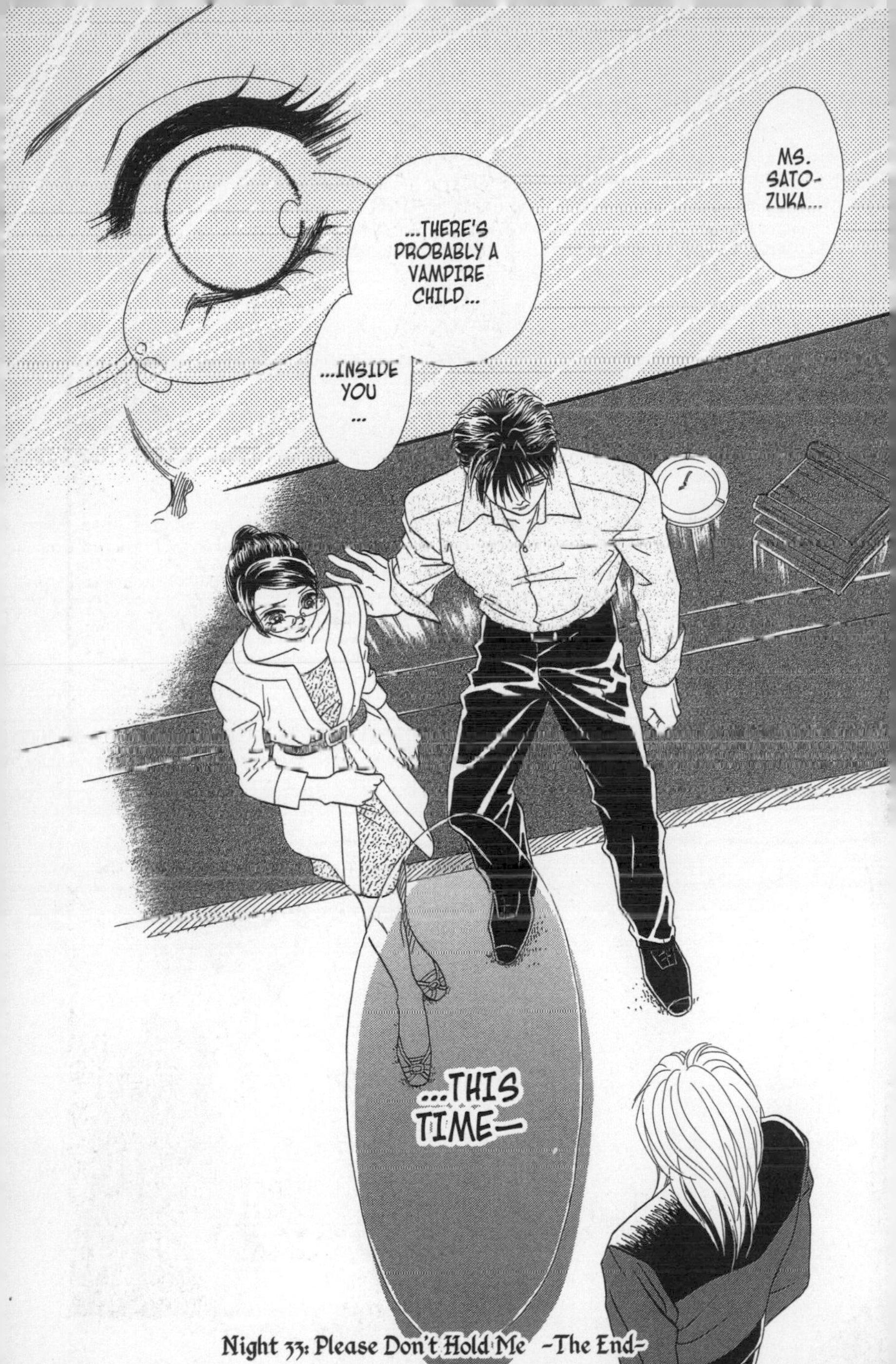
MS. SATO-ZUKA...
...THERE'S PROBABLY A VAMPIRE CHILD...
...INSIDE YOU ...
...THIS TIME—

Night 33: Please Don't Hold Me -The End-

## – Please Don't Hold Me –

Kyohei licks Kaya's Blood and spits it out. How rude! Those around me didn't like that scene. (smile) I think if it actually happened to someone, it would be quite a shock.

## – I am Your Secretary Forever –

Is Kaya really pregnant this time?! This is the final chapter. Vampires have trouble Bearing children, But sometimes if the couple gets along well, they may end up with two children like Kyohei's parents. Kyohei and Kaya may have gotten pregnant By chance, But whether they will have many children or not, only God knows. However it turns out, I'm sure Kyohei will do his Best...whether they are fruitful or not. (smile)

Night 31: Don't Arouse a Feeling of Jealousy preview ▲

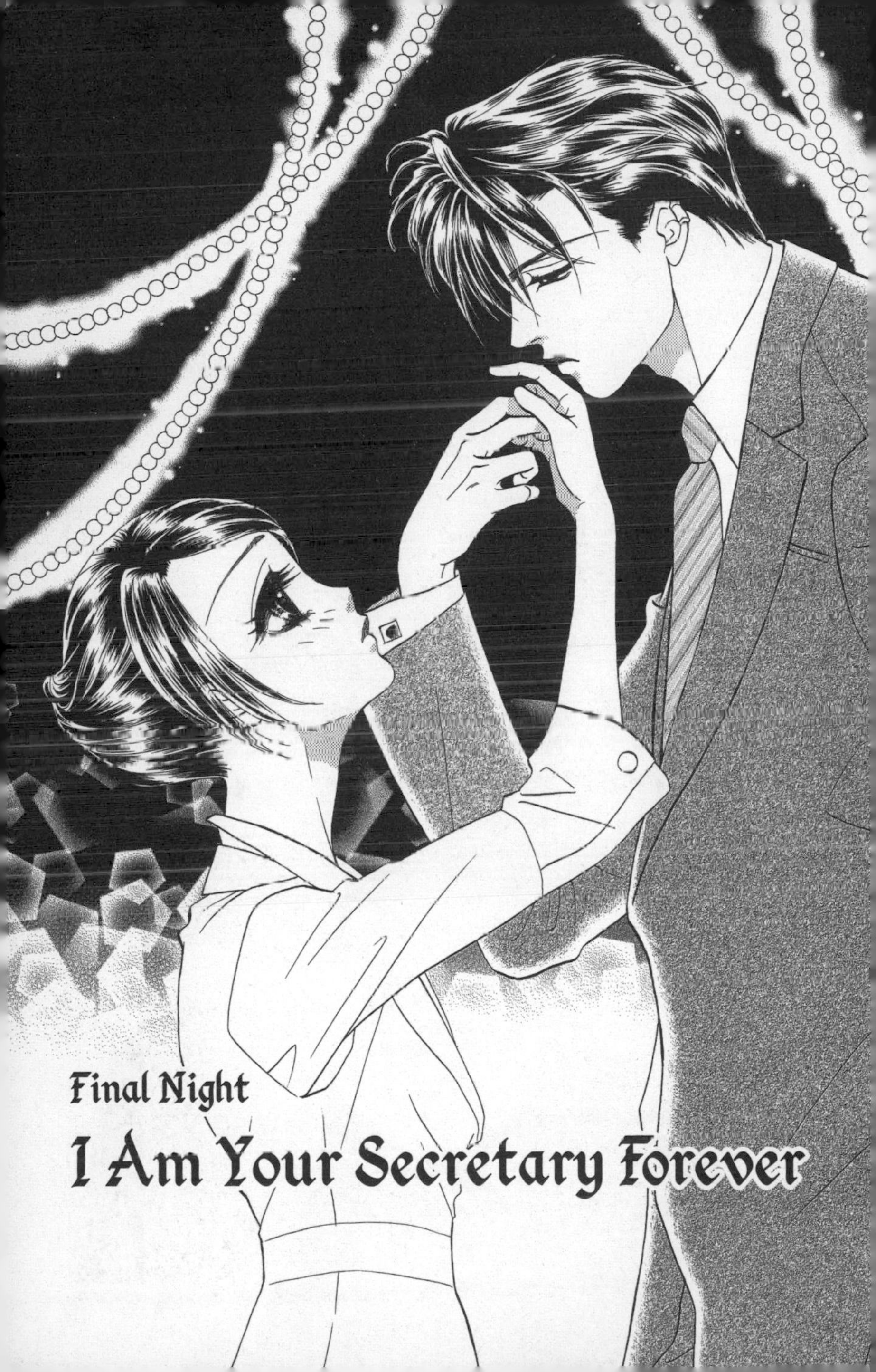

## Final Night

# I Am Your Secretary Forever

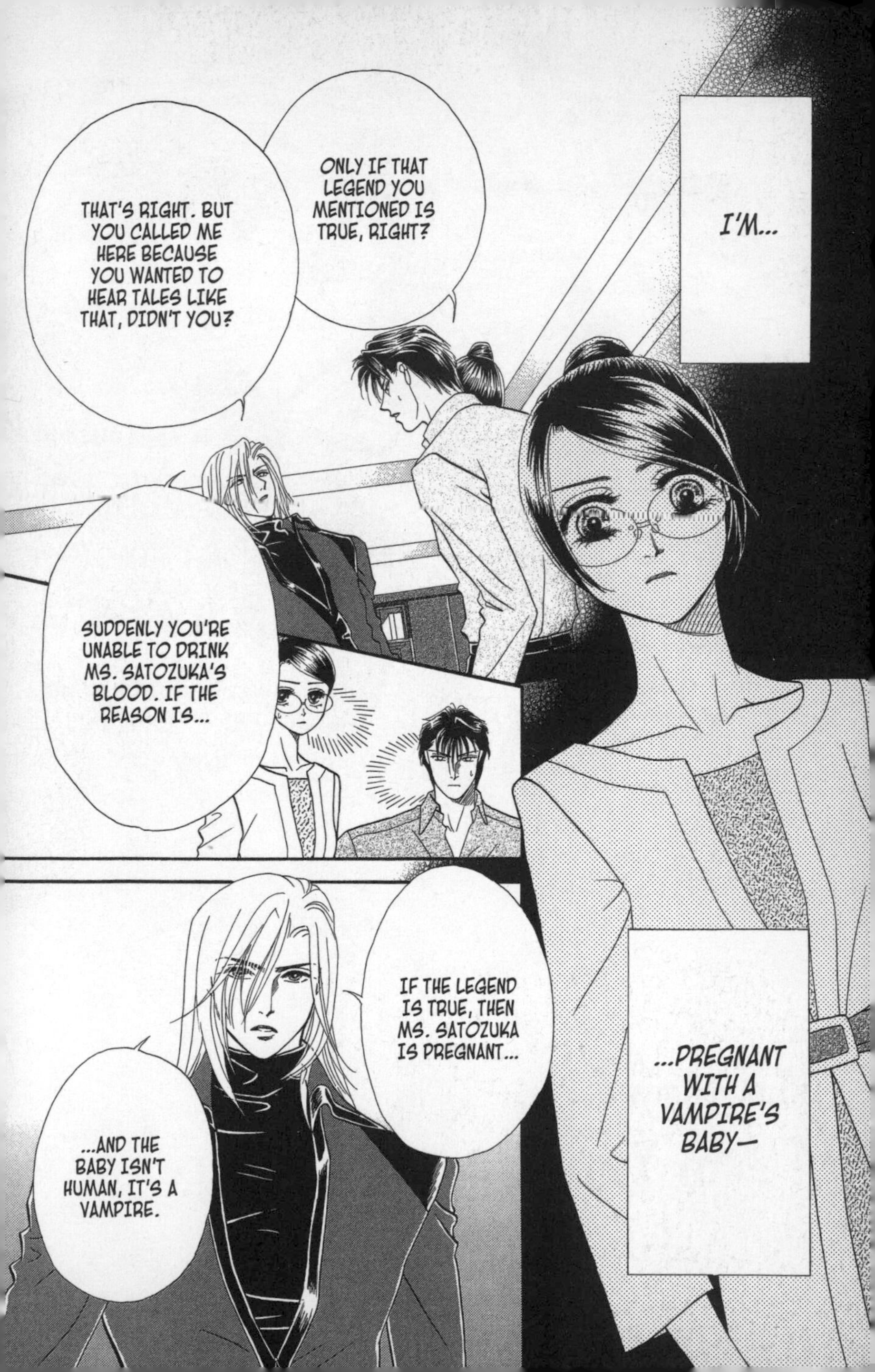
I'M...
...PREGNANT WITH A VAMPIRE'S BABY—
ONLY IF THAT LEGEND YOU MENTIONED IS TRUE, RIGHT?
THAT'S RIGHT. BUT YOU CALLED ME HERE BECAUSE YOU WANTED TO HEAR TALES LIKE THAT, DIDN'T YOU?
SUDDENLY YOU'RE UNABLE TO DRINK MS. SATOZUKA'S BLOOD. IF THE REASON IS...
IF THE LEGEND IS TRUE, THEN MS. SATOZUKA IS PREGNANT...
...AND THE BABY ISN'T HUMAN, IT'S A VAMPIRE.

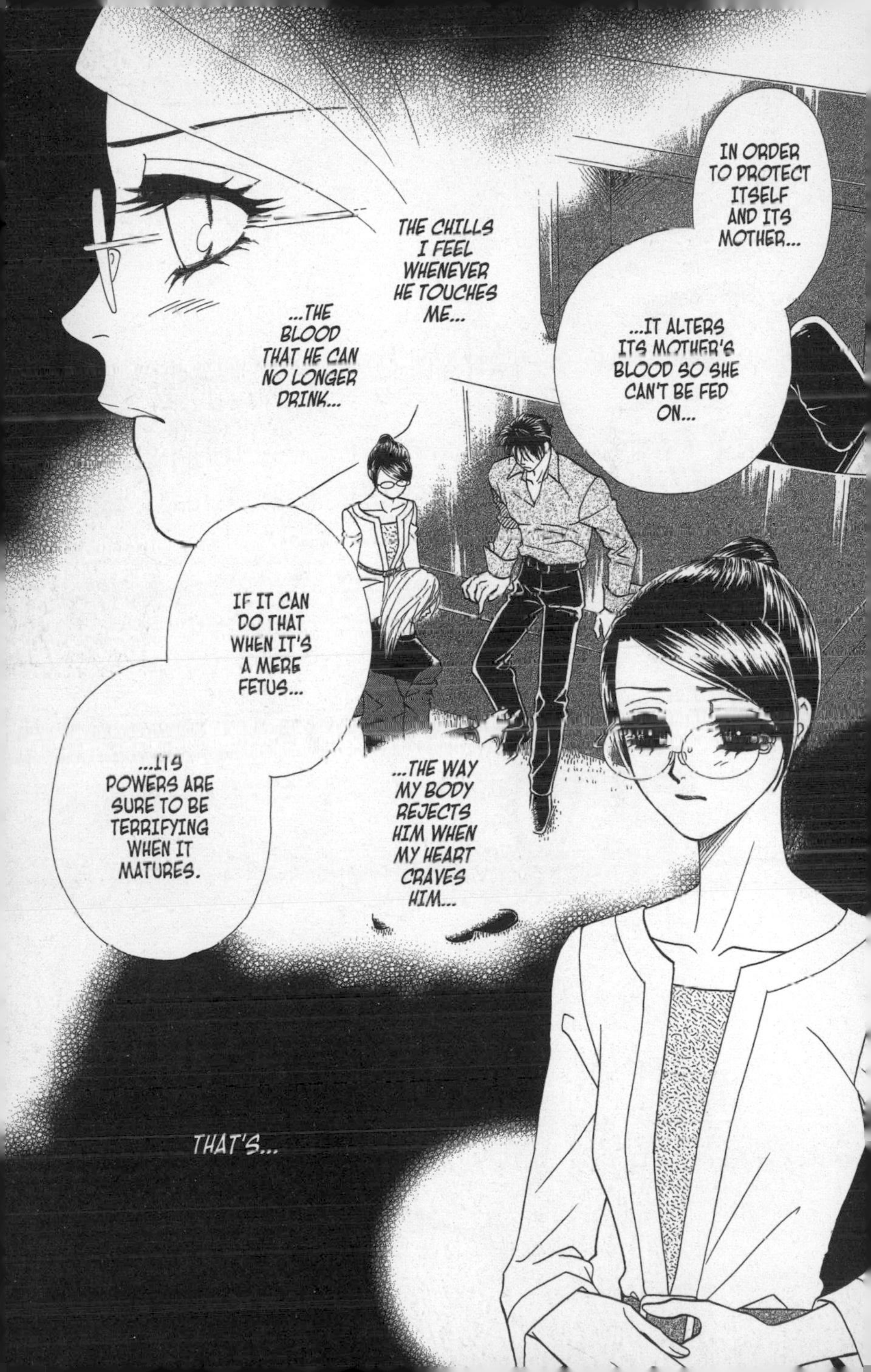
IN ORDER TO PROTECT ITSELF AND ITS MOTHER...
...IT ALTERS ITS MOTHER'S BLOOD SO SHE CAN'T BE FED ON...
THE CHILLS I FEEL WHENEVER HE TOUCHES ME...
...THE BLOOD THAT HE CAN NO LONGER DRINK...
IF IT CAN DO THAT WHEN IT'S A MERE FETUS...
...ITS POWERS ARE SURE TO BE TERRIFYING WHEN IT MATURES.
...THE WAY MY BODY REJECTS HIM WHEN MY HEART CRAVES HIM...
THAT'S...

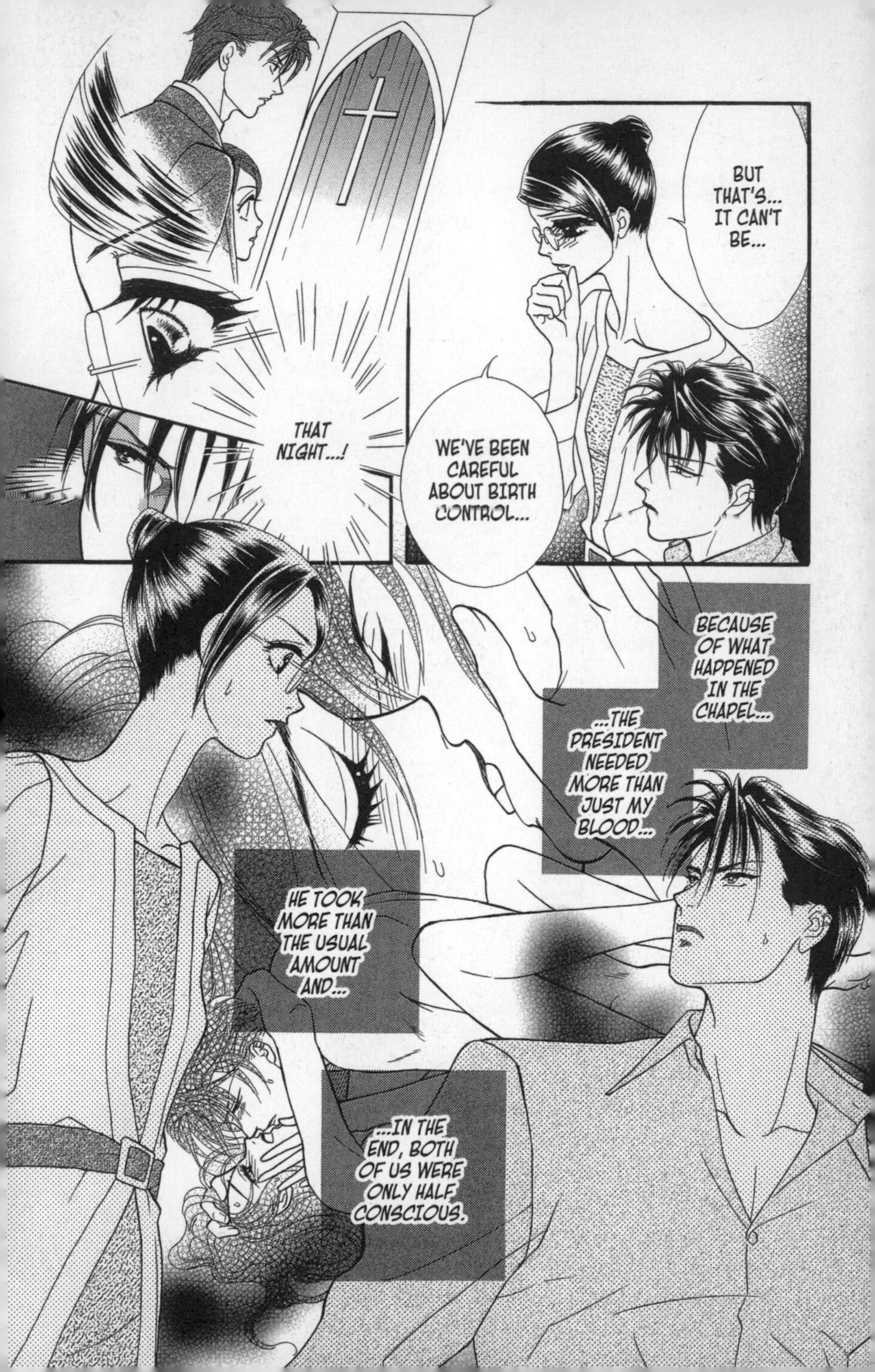
BUT THAT'S... IT CAN'T BE...
WE'VE BEEN CAREFUL ABOUT BIRTH CONTROL...
THAT NIGHT...!
BECAUSE OF WHAT HAPPENED IN THE CHAPEL...
...THE PRESIDENT NEEDED MORE THAN JUST MY BLOOD...
HE TOOK MORE THAN THE USUAL AMOUNT AND...
...IN THE END, BOTH OF US WERE ONLY HALF CONSCIOUS.

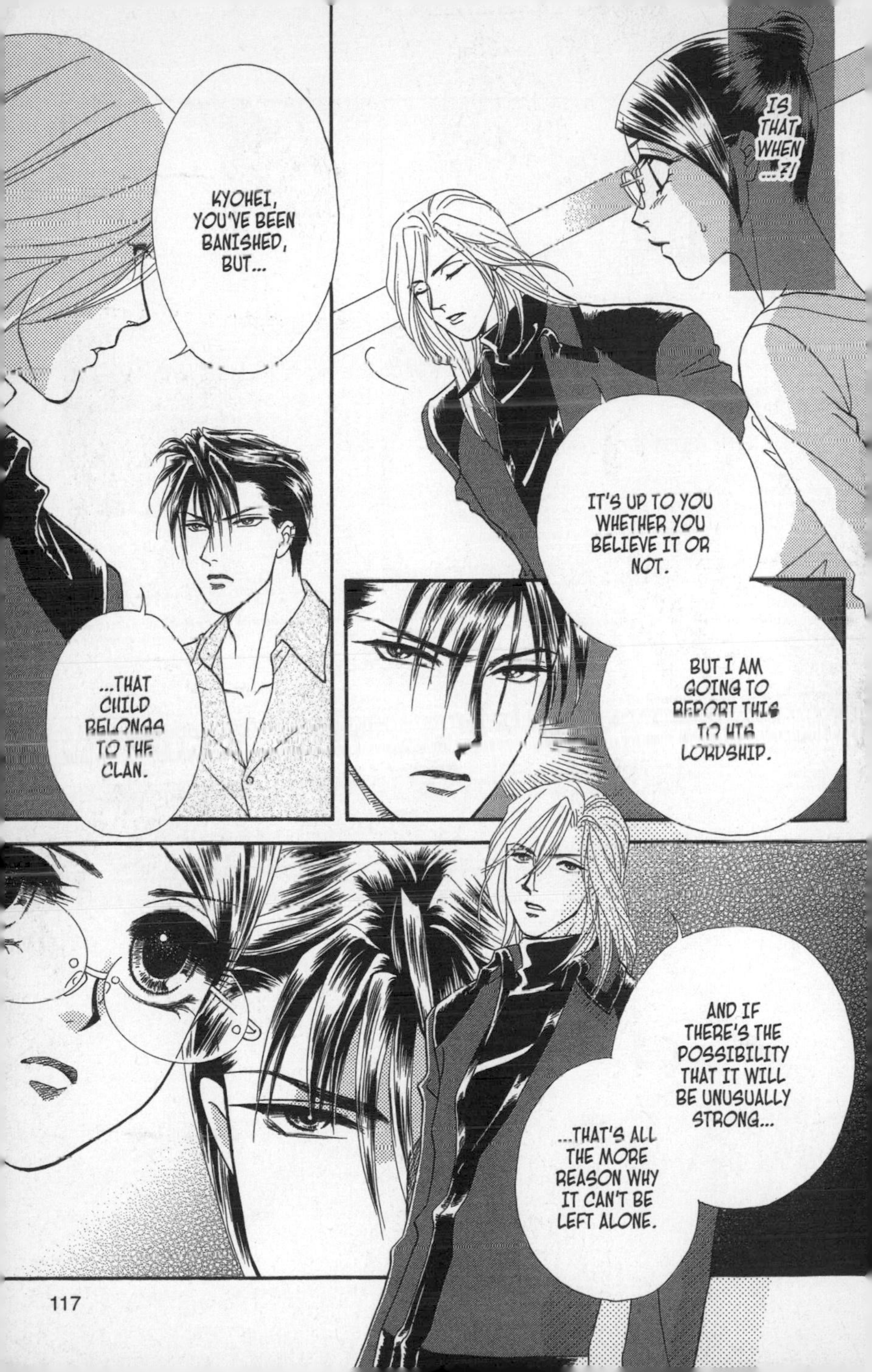
IS THAT WHEN ...?!
KYOHEI, YOU'VE BEEN BANISHED, BUT...
...THAT CHILD BELONGS TO THE CLAN.
IT'S UP TO YOU WHETHER YOU BELIEVE IT OR NOT.
BUT I AM GOING TO REPORT THIS TO HIS LORDSHIP.
AND IF THERE'S THE POSSIBILITY THAT IT WILL BE UNUSUALLY STRONG...
...THAT'S ALL THE MORE REASON WHY IT CAN'T BE LEFT ALONE.

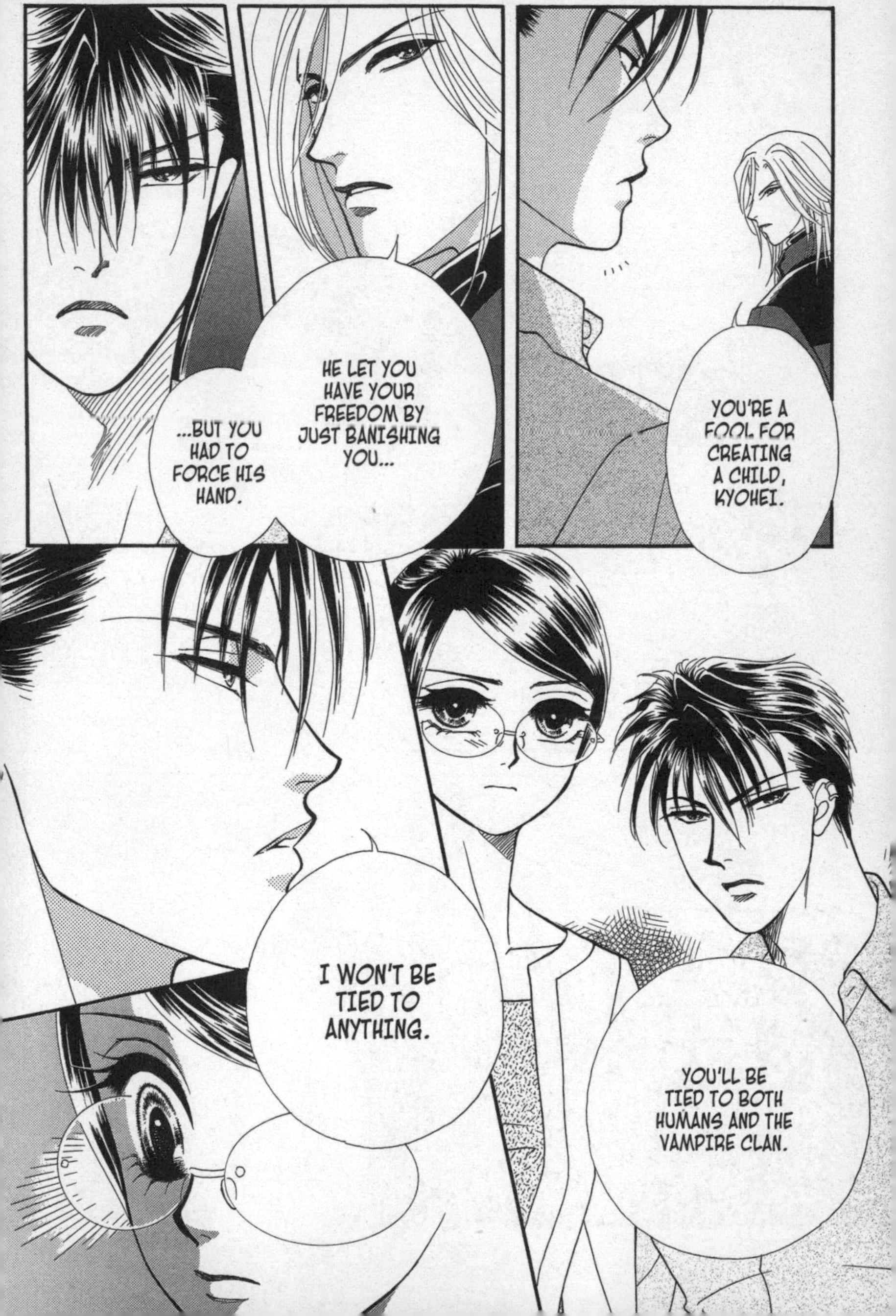
YOU'RE A FOOL FOR CREATING A CHILD, KYOHEI.
HE LET YOU HAVE YOUR FREEDOM BY JUST BANISHING YOU...
...BUT YOU HAD TO FORCE HIS HAND.
YOU'LL BE TIED TO BOTH HUMANS AND THE VAMPIRE CLAN.
I WON'T BE TIED TO ANYTHING.

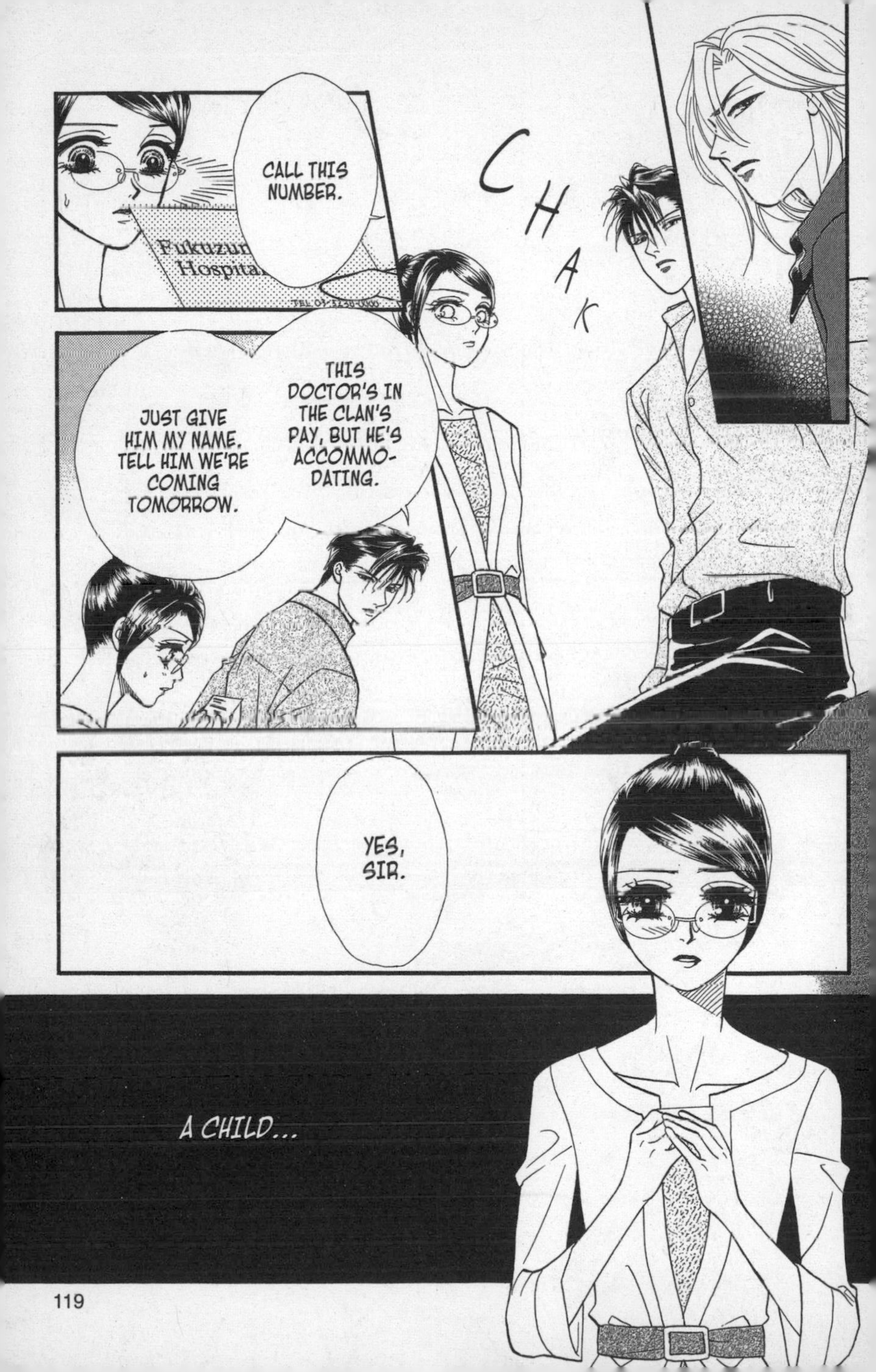
CHAK
CALL THIS NUMBER.
THIS DOCTOR'S IN THE CLAN'S PAY, BUT HE'S ACCOMMO-DATING.
JUST GIVE HIM MY NAME. TELL HIM WE'RE COMING TOMORROW.
YES, SIR.
A CHILD...

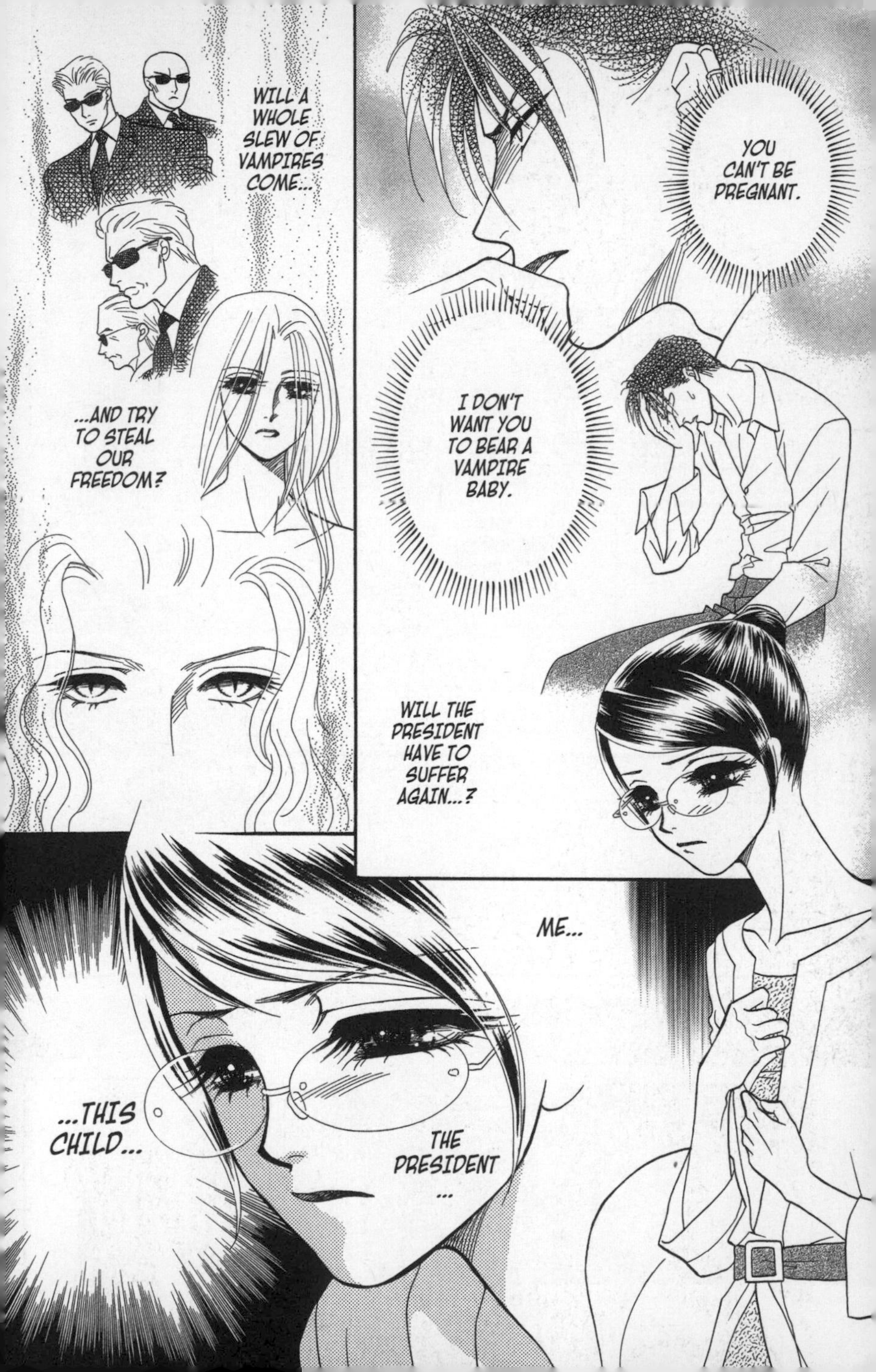
YOU CAN'T BE PREGNANT.
I DON'T WANT YOU TO BEAR A VAMPIRE BABY.
WILL THE PRESIDENT HAVE TO SUFFER AGAIN...?
WILL A WHOLE SLEW OF VAMPIRES COME...
...AND TRY TO STEAL OUR FREEDOM?
ME...
THE PRESIDENT ...
...THIS CHILD...

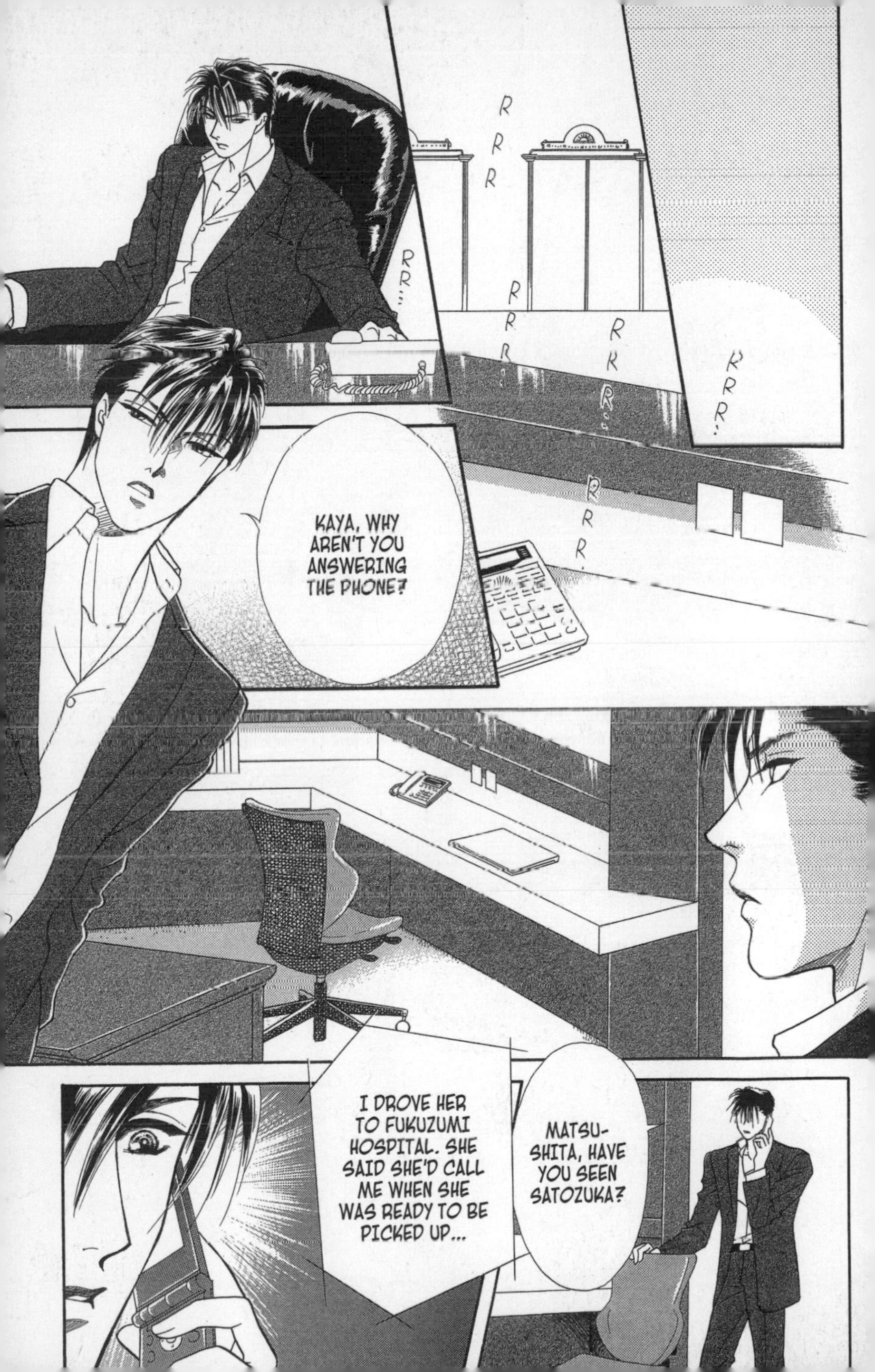
RRR..
RRR..
RRR.
RRR..
RRR
RR..
KAYA, WHY AREN'T YOU ANSWERING THE PHONE?
MATSU-SHITA, HAVE YOU SEEN SATOZUKA?
I DROVE HER TO FUKUZUMI HOSPITAL. SHE SAID SHE'D CALL ME WHEN SHE WAS READY TO BE PICKED UP...

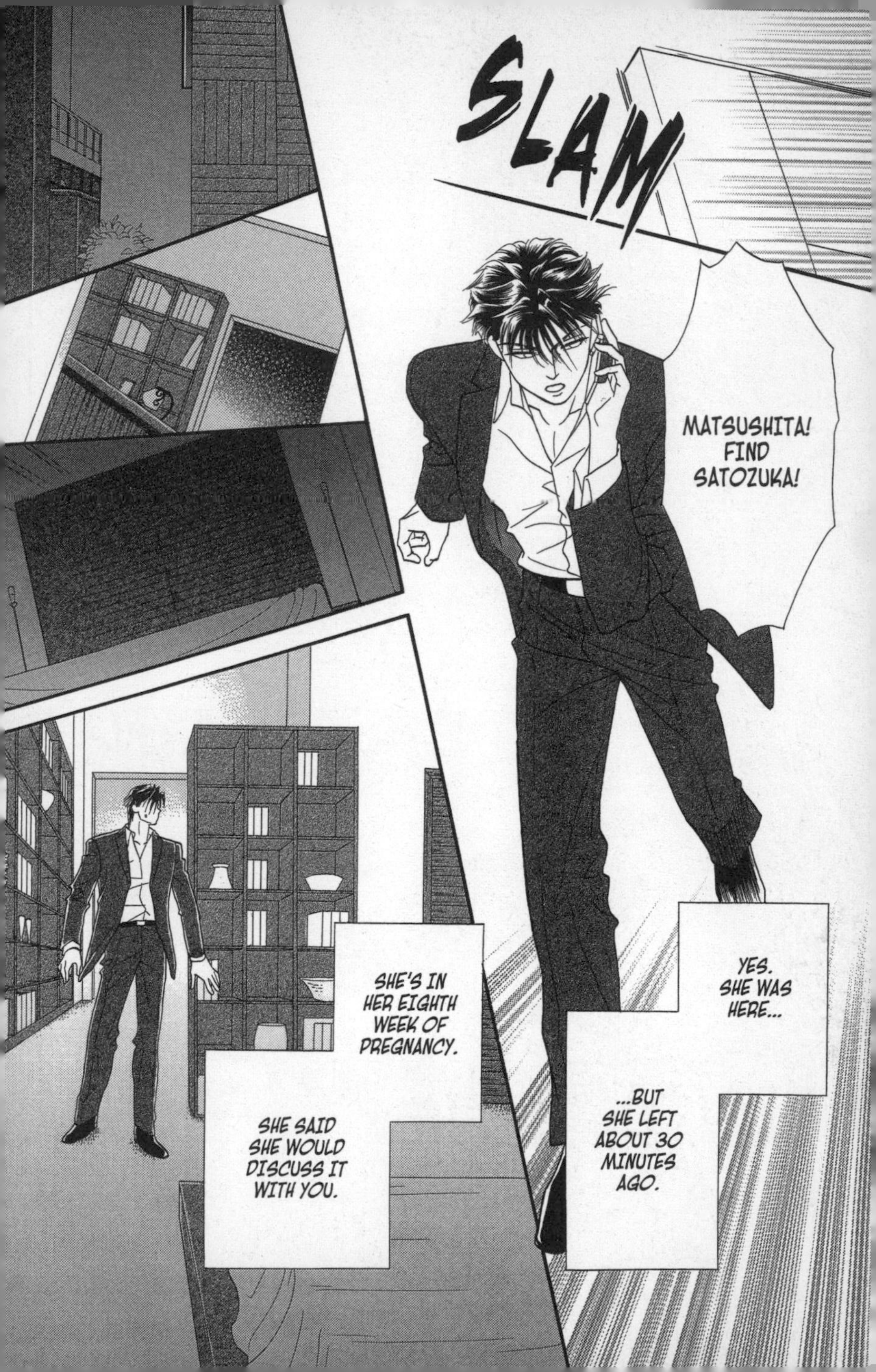
SLAM
MATSUSHITA! FIND SATOZUKA!
YES. SHE WAS HERE...
...BUT SHE LEFT ABOUT 30 MINUTES AGO.
SHE'S IN HER EIGHTH WEEK OF PREGNANCY.
SHE SAID SHE WOULD DISCUSS IT WITH YOU.

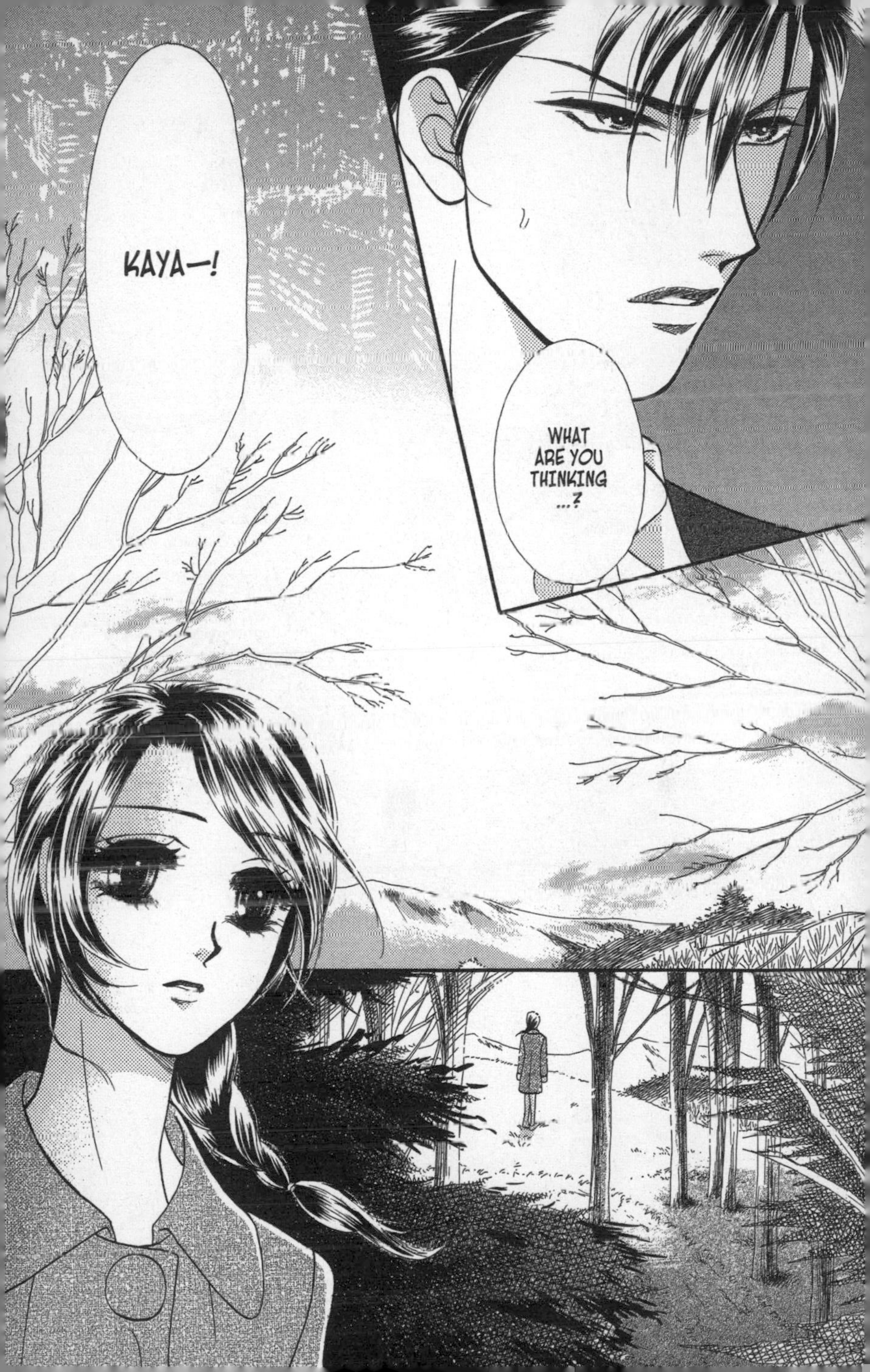
WHAT ARE YOU THINKING ...?
KAYA—!

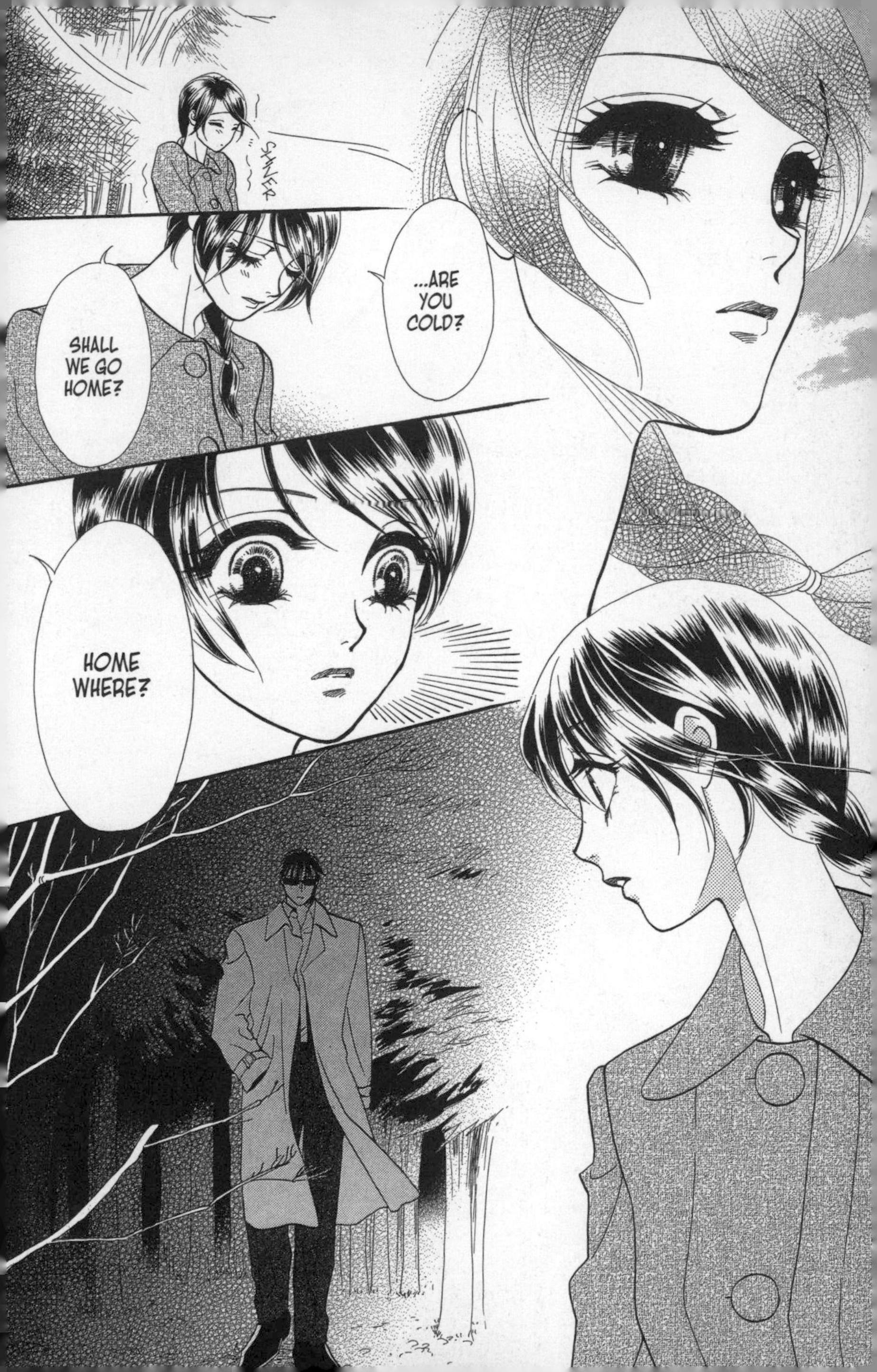
SHIVER
...ARE YOU COLD?
SHALL WE GO HOME?
HOME WHERE?

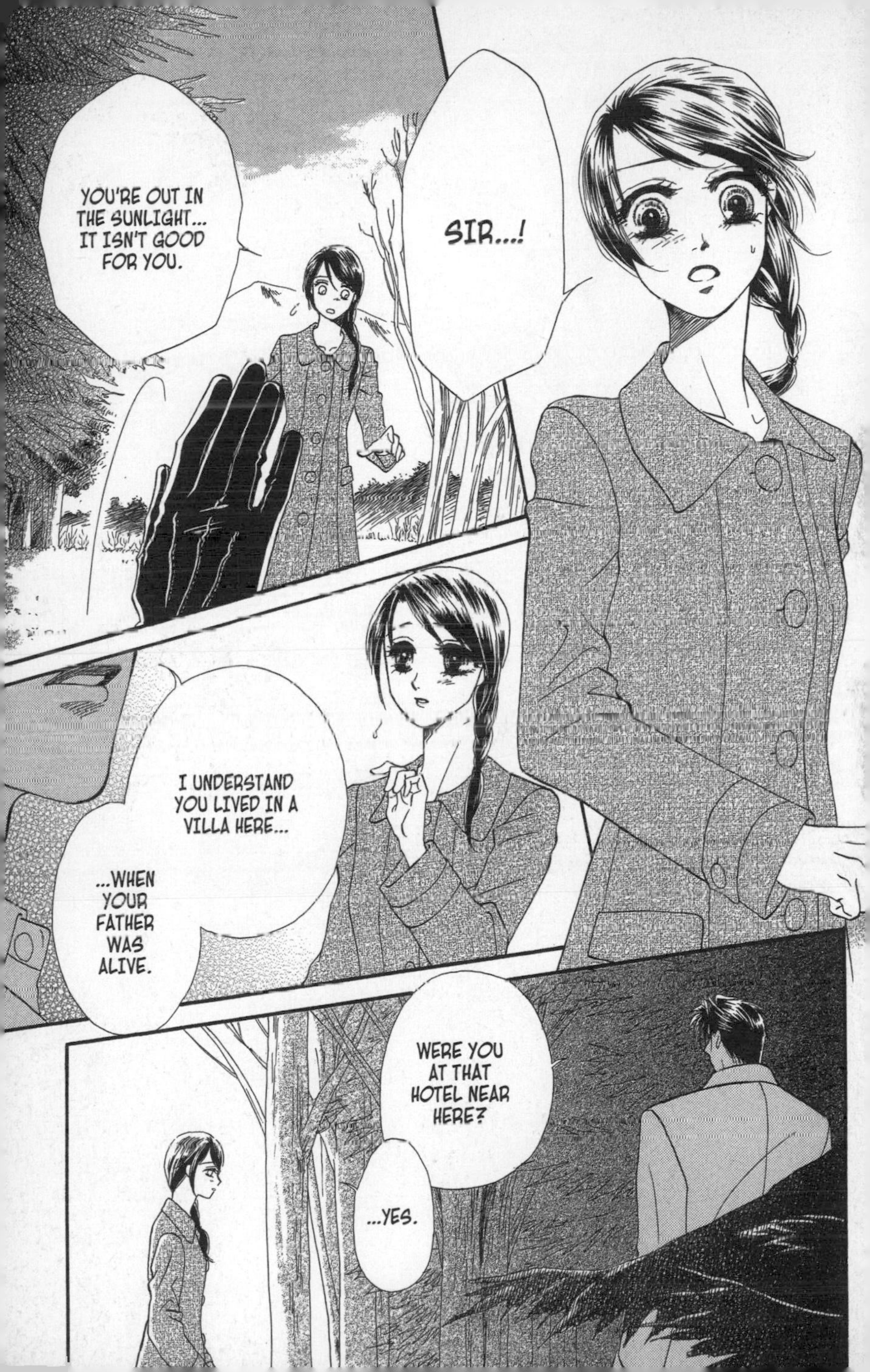
SIR...!
YOU'RE OUT IN THE SUNLIGHT... IT ISN'T GOOD FOR YOU.
I UNDERSTAND YOU LIVED IN A VILLA HERE...
...WHEN YOUR FATHER WAS ALIVE.
WERE YOU AT THAT HOTEL NEAR HERE?
...YES.

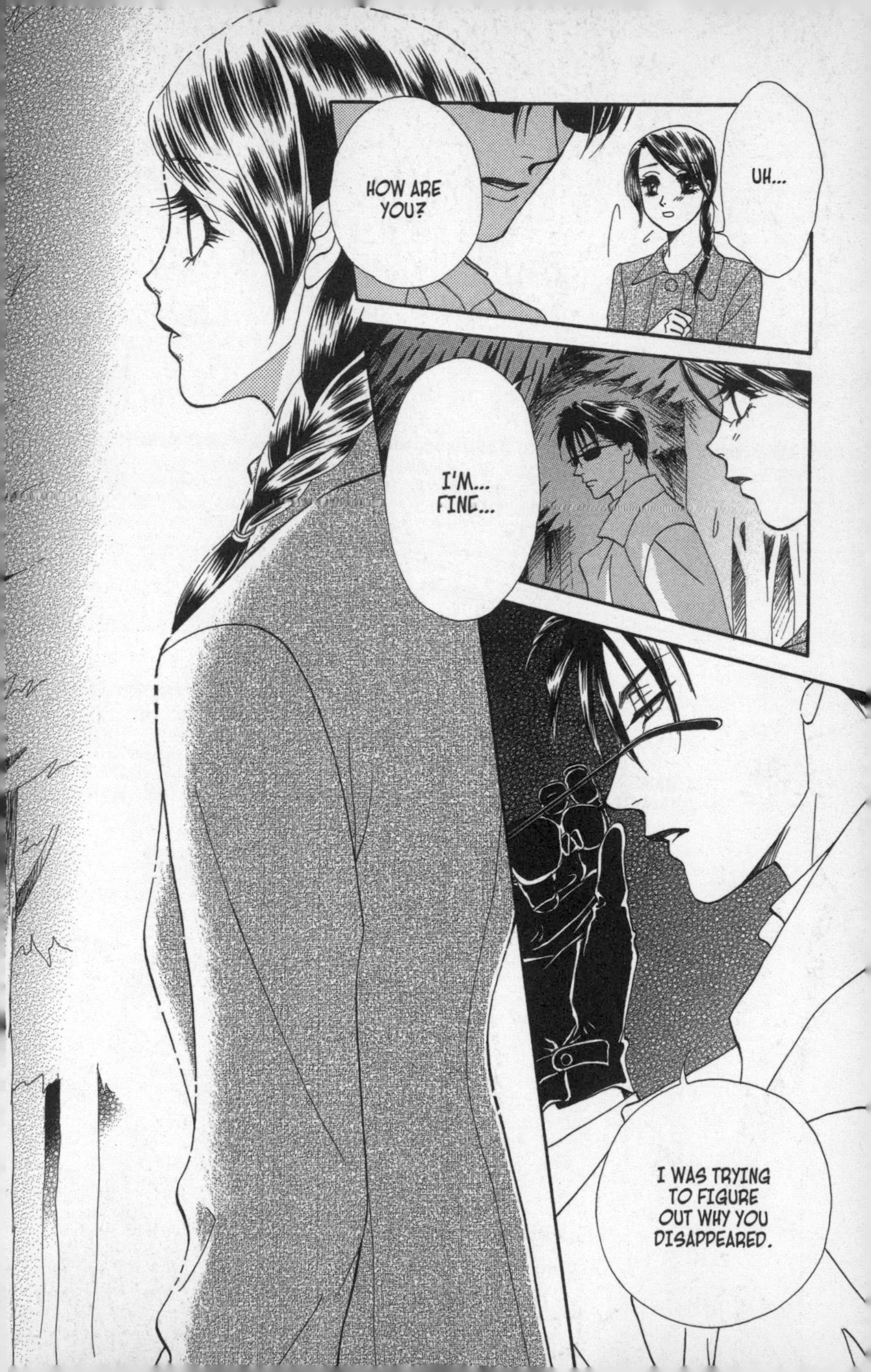
UH...
HOW ARE YOU?
I'M... FINE...
I WAS TRYING TO FIGURE OUT WHY YOU DISAPPEARED.

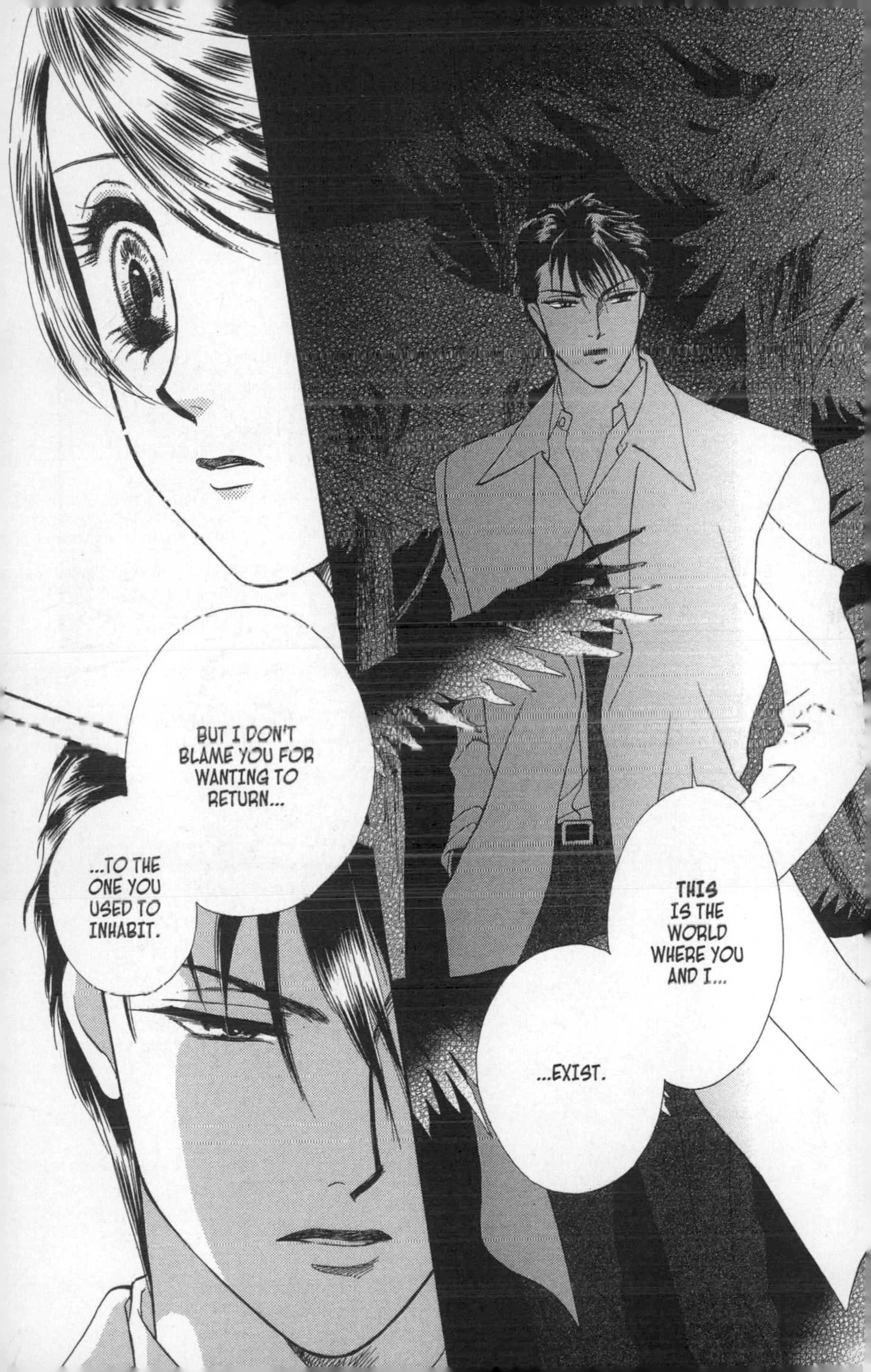
THIS IS THE WORLD WHERE YOU AND I...
...EXIST.
BUT I DON'T BLAME YOU FOR WANTING TO RETURN...
...TO THE ONE YOU USED TO INHABIT.

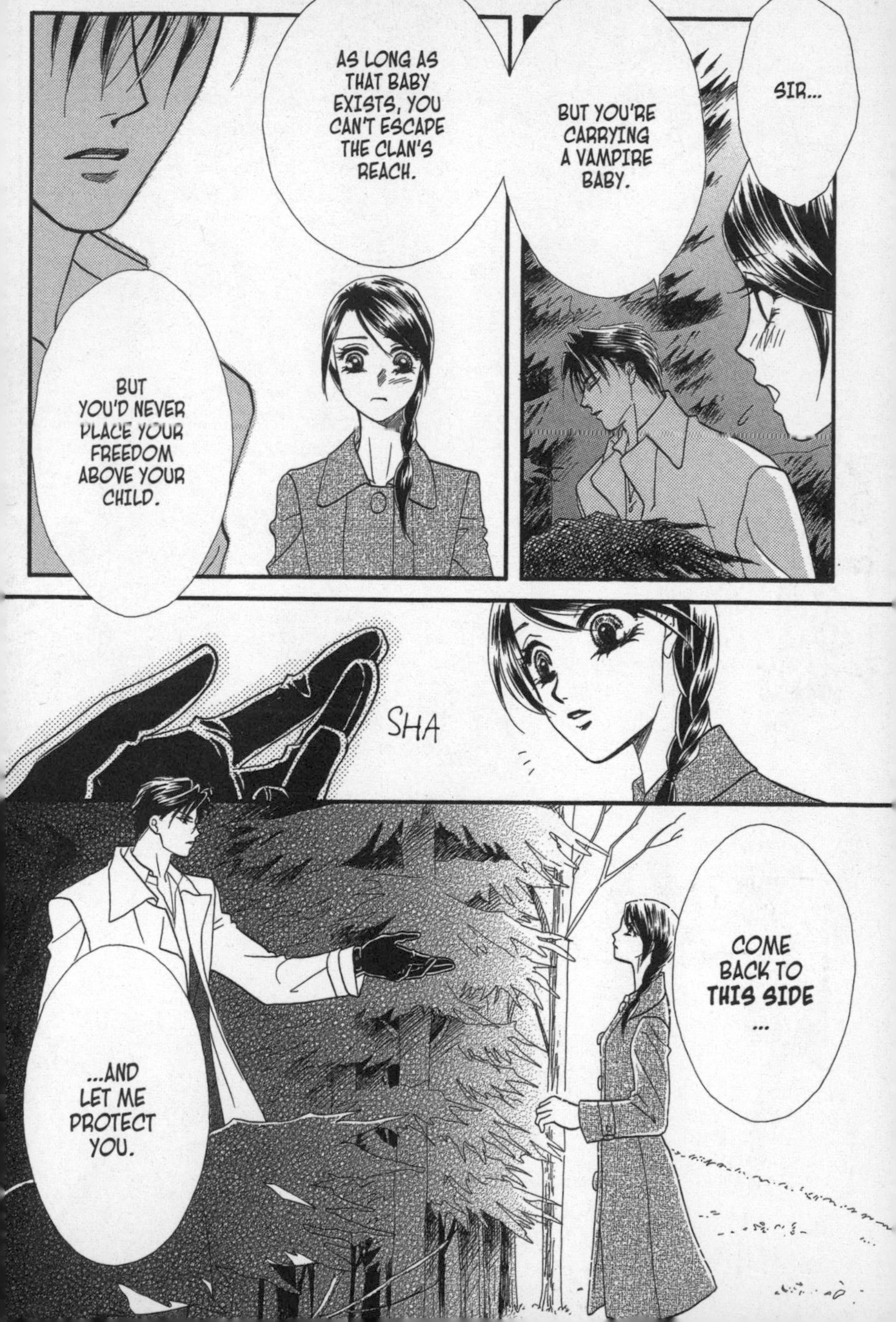
SIR...
BUT YOU'RE CARRYING A VAMPIRE BABY.
AS LONG AS THAT BABY EXISTS, YOU CAN'T ESCAPE THE CLAN'S REACH.
BUT YOU'D NEVER PLACE YOUR FREEDOM ABOVE YOUR CHILD.
SHA
COME BACK TO THIS SIDE...
...AND LET ME PROTECT YOU.

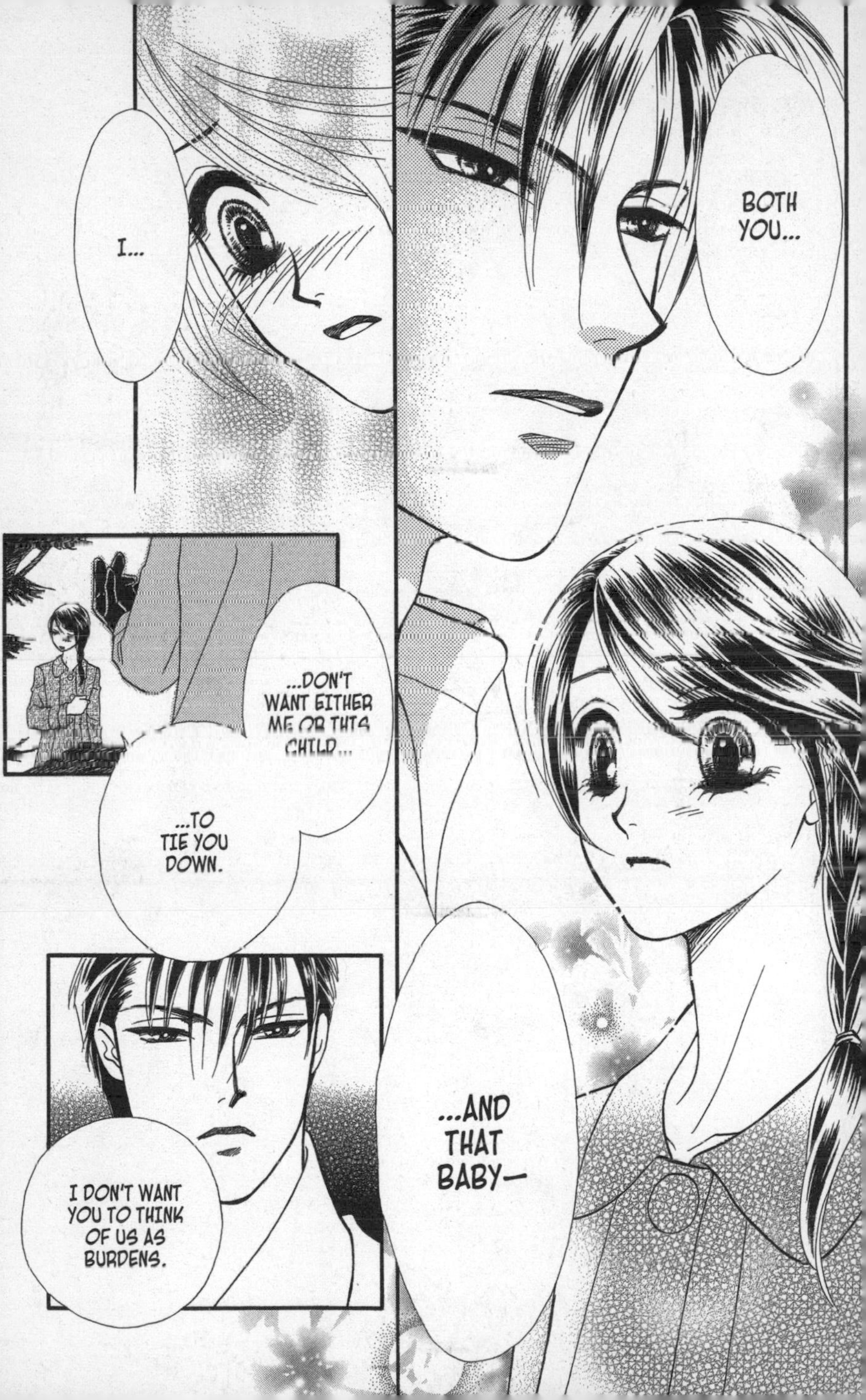
BOTH YOU...
...AND THAT BABY—
I...
...DON'T WANT EITHER ME OR THIS CHILD...
...TO TIE YOU DOWN.
I DON'T WANT YOU TO THINK OF US AS BURDENS.

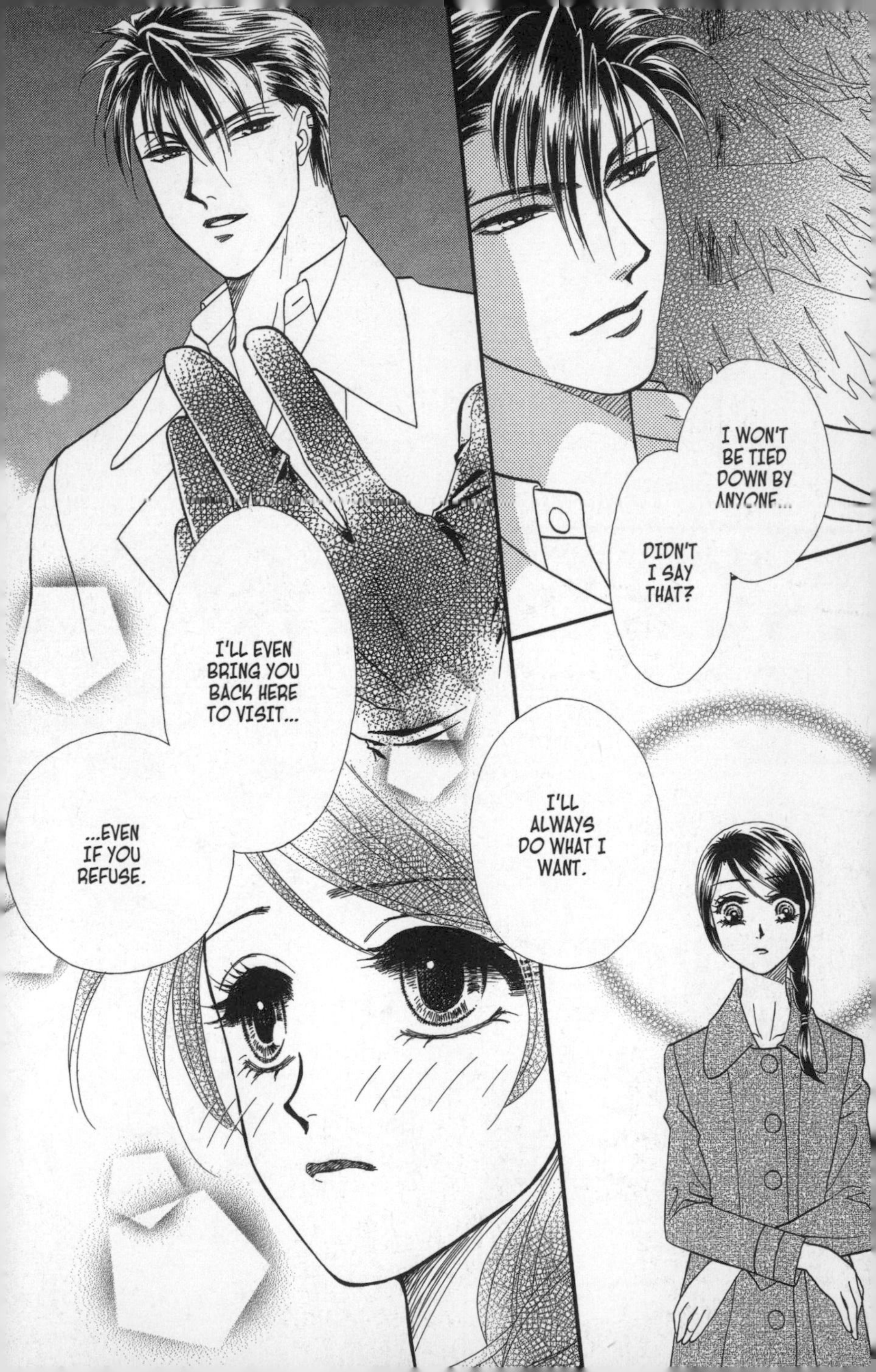
I WON'T BE TIED DOWN BY ANYONE...
DIDN'T I SAY THAT?
I'LL ALWAYS DO WHAT I WANT.
I'LL EVEN BRING YOU BACK HERE TO VISIT...
...EVEN IF YOU REFUSE.

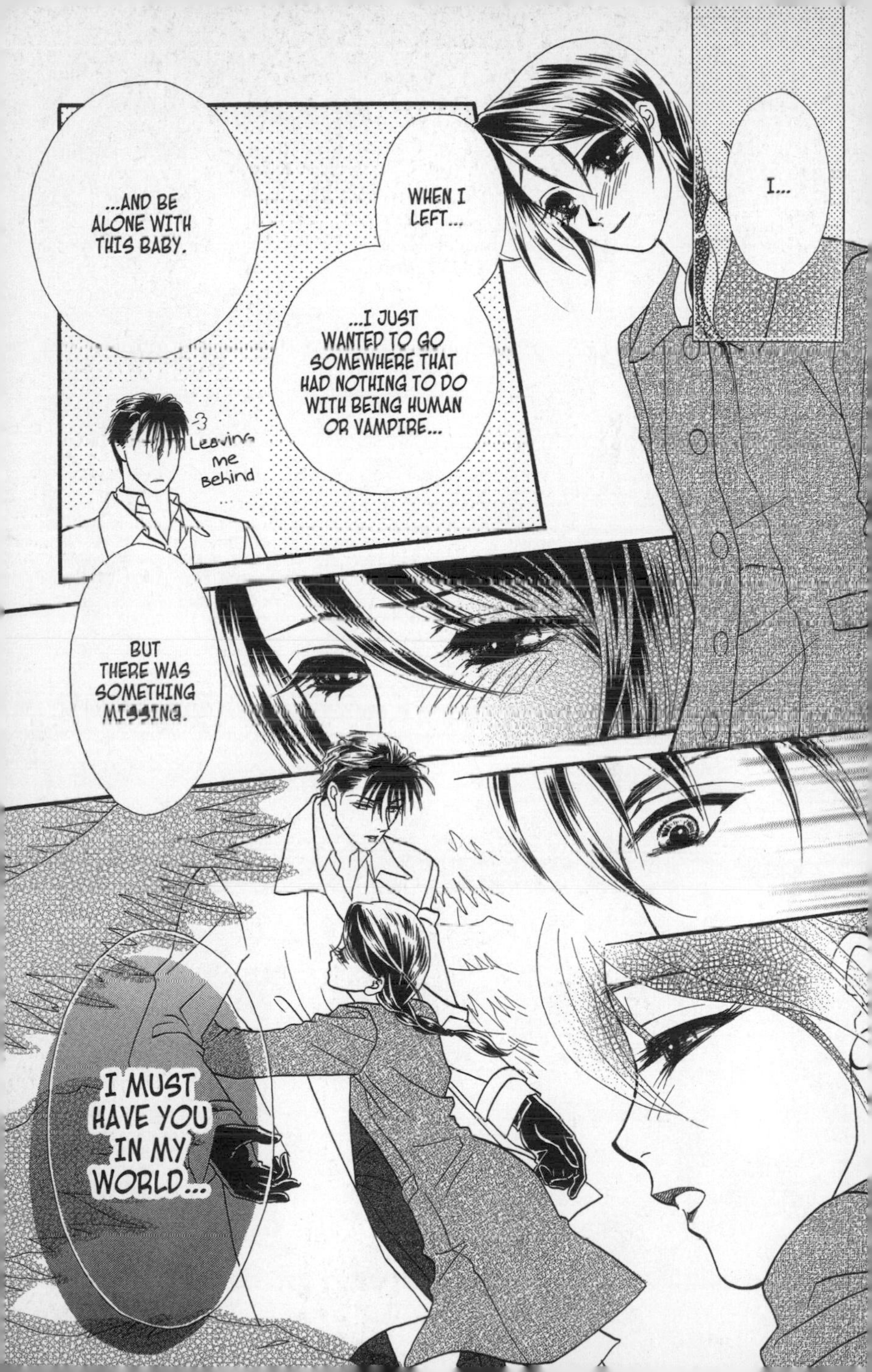
I...
WHEN I LEFT...
...I JUST WANTED TO GO SOMEWHERE THAT HAD NOTHING TO DO WITH BEING HUMAN OR VAMPIRE...
...AND BE ALONE WITH THIS BABY.
Leaving me behind ...
BUT THERE WAS SOMETHING MISSING.
I MUST HAVE YOU IN MY WORLD...

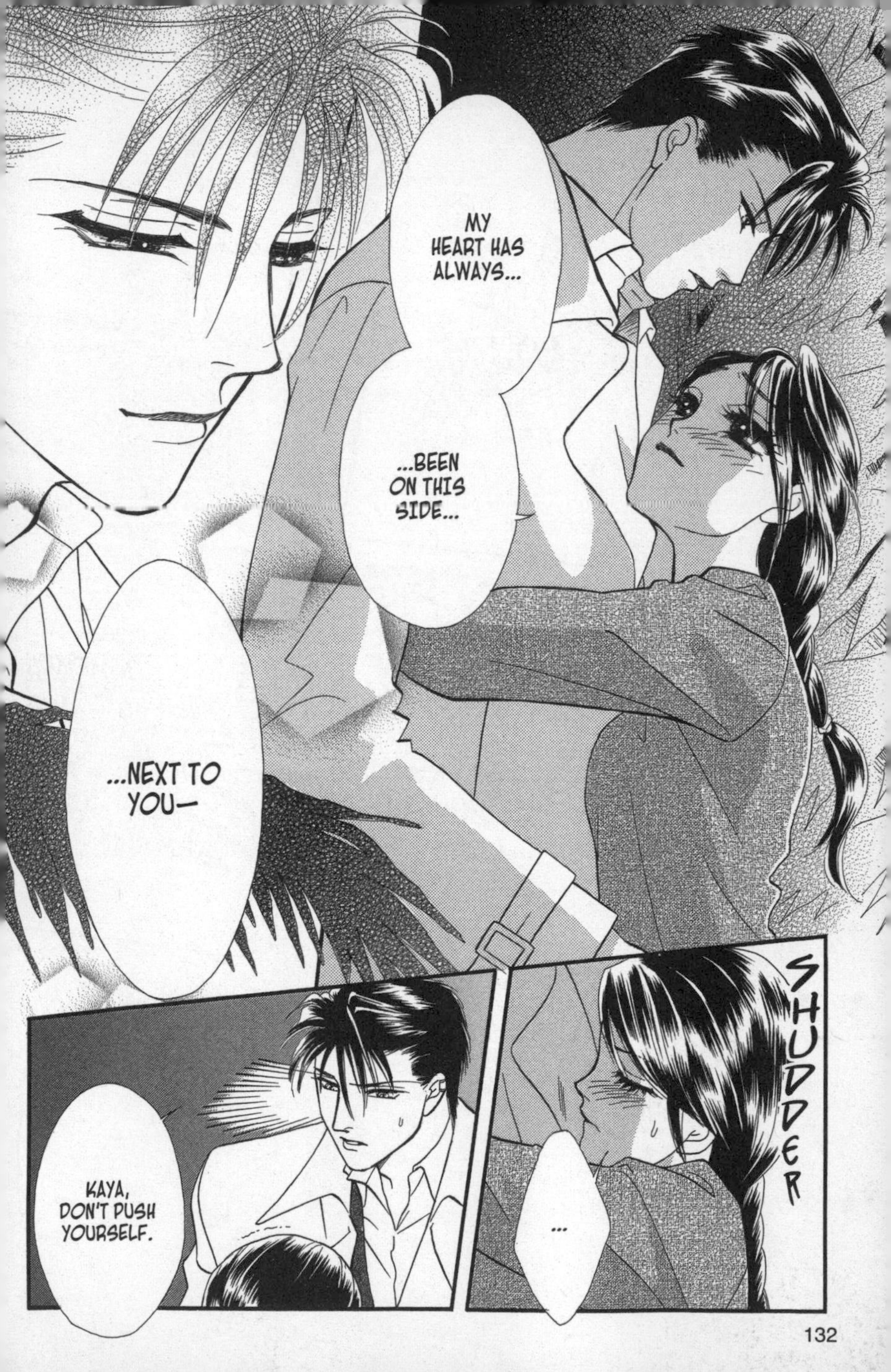
MY HEART HAS ALWAYS...
...BEEN ON THIS SIDE...
...NEXT TO YOU—
SHUDDER
...
KAYA, DON'T PUSH YOURSELF.

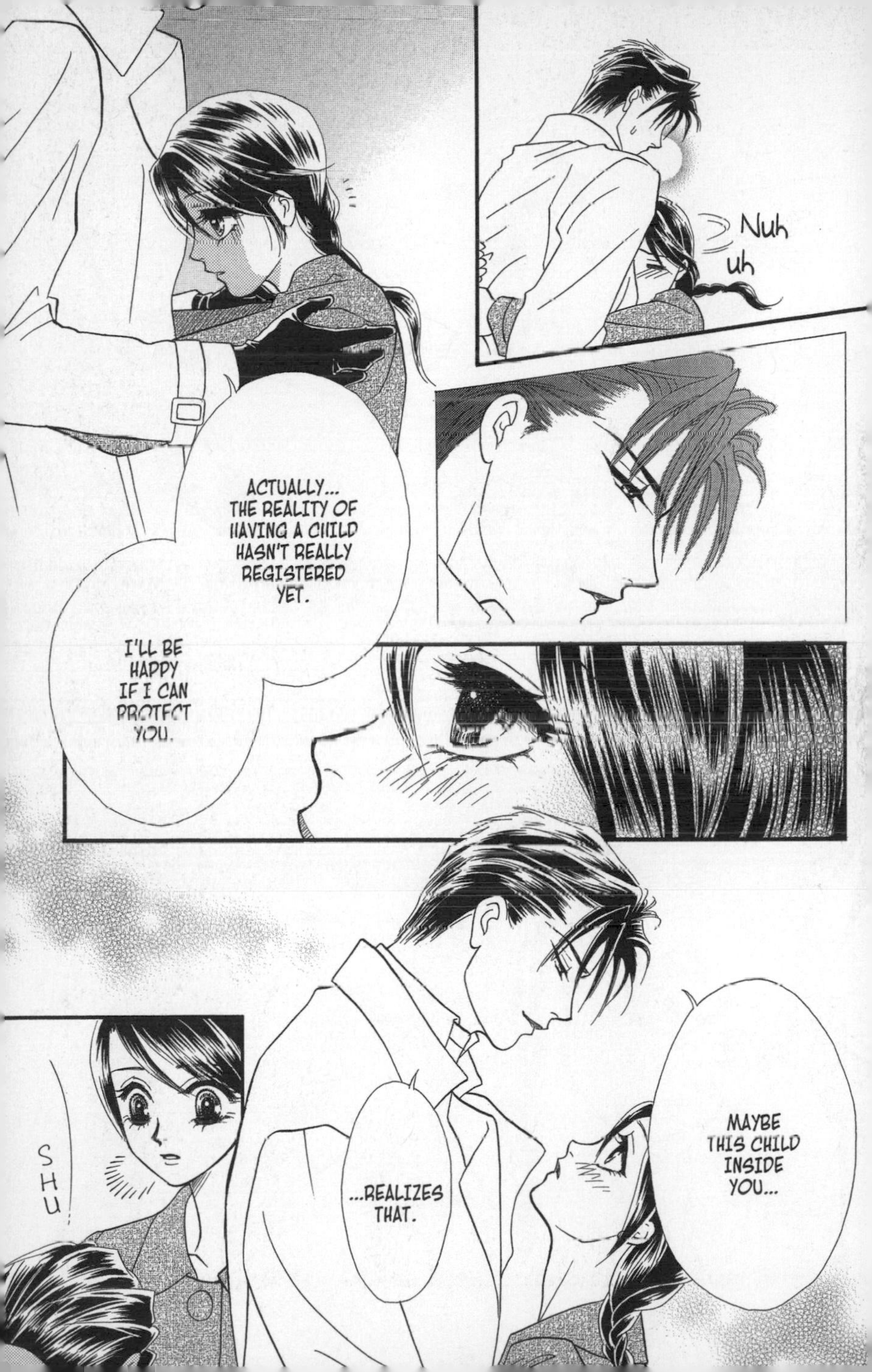
Nuh uh
ACTUALLY... THE REALITY OF HAVING A CHILD HASN'T REALLY REGISTERED YET.
I'LL BE HAPPY IF I CAN PROTECT YOU.
MAYBE THIS CHILD INSIDE YOU...
...REALIZES THAT.
SHU

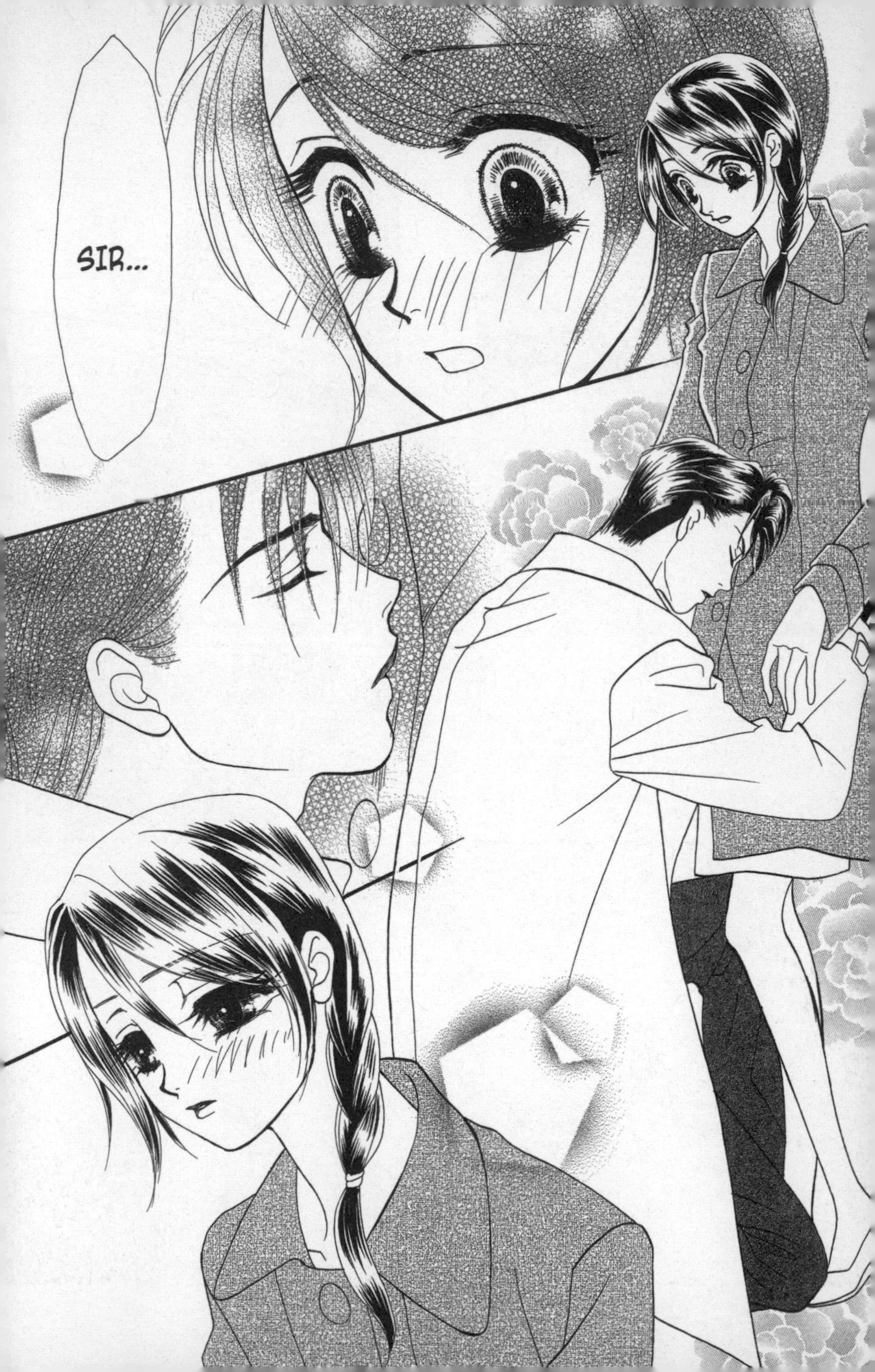
SIR...

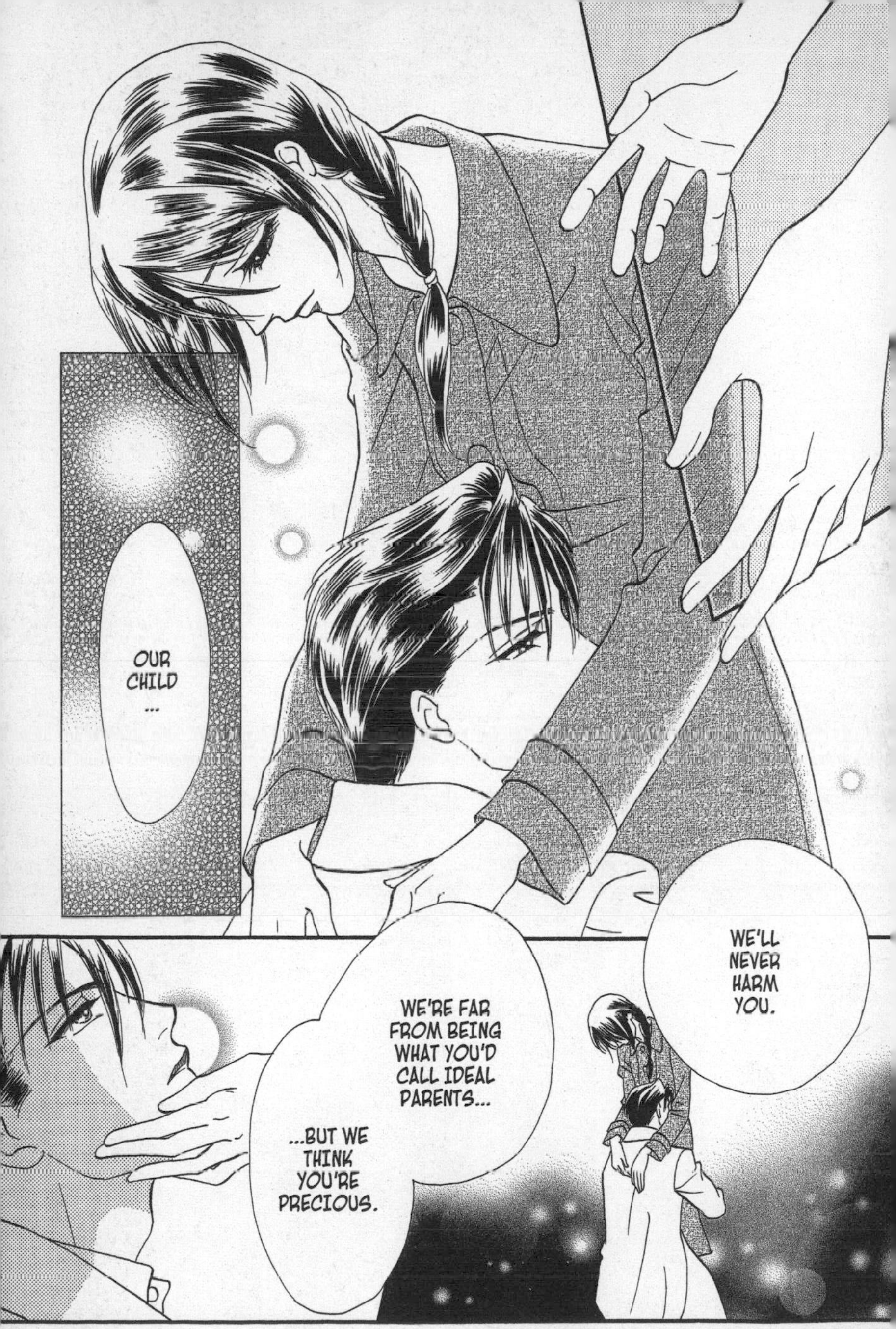
OUR CHILD ...
WE'LL NEVER HARM YOU.
WE'RE FAR FROM BEING WHAT YOU'D CALL IDEAL PARENTS...
...BUT WE THINK YOU'RE PRECIOUS.

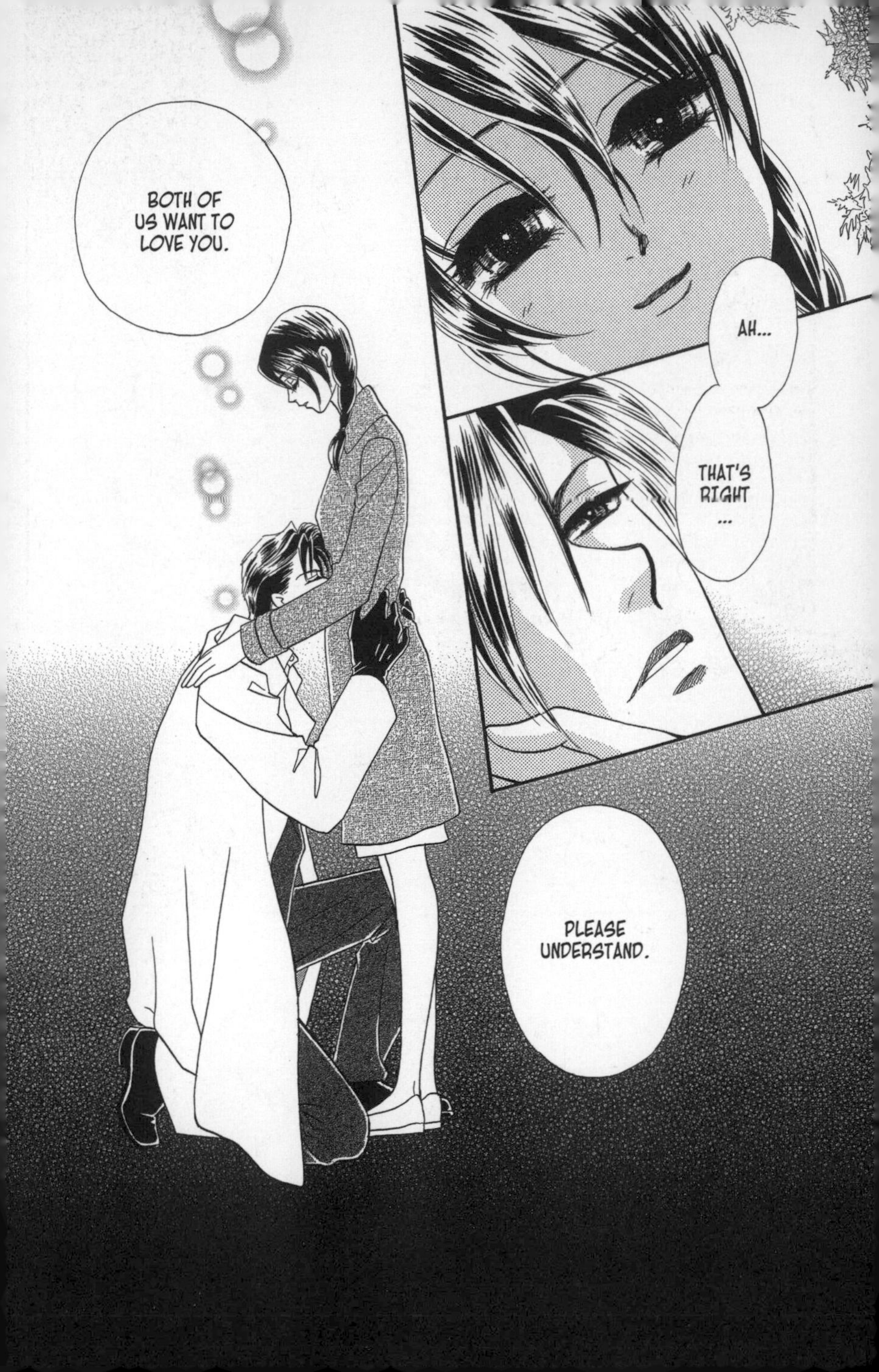
AH...
THAT'S RIGHT ...
BOTH OF US WANT TO LOVE YOU.
PLEASE UNDERSTAND.

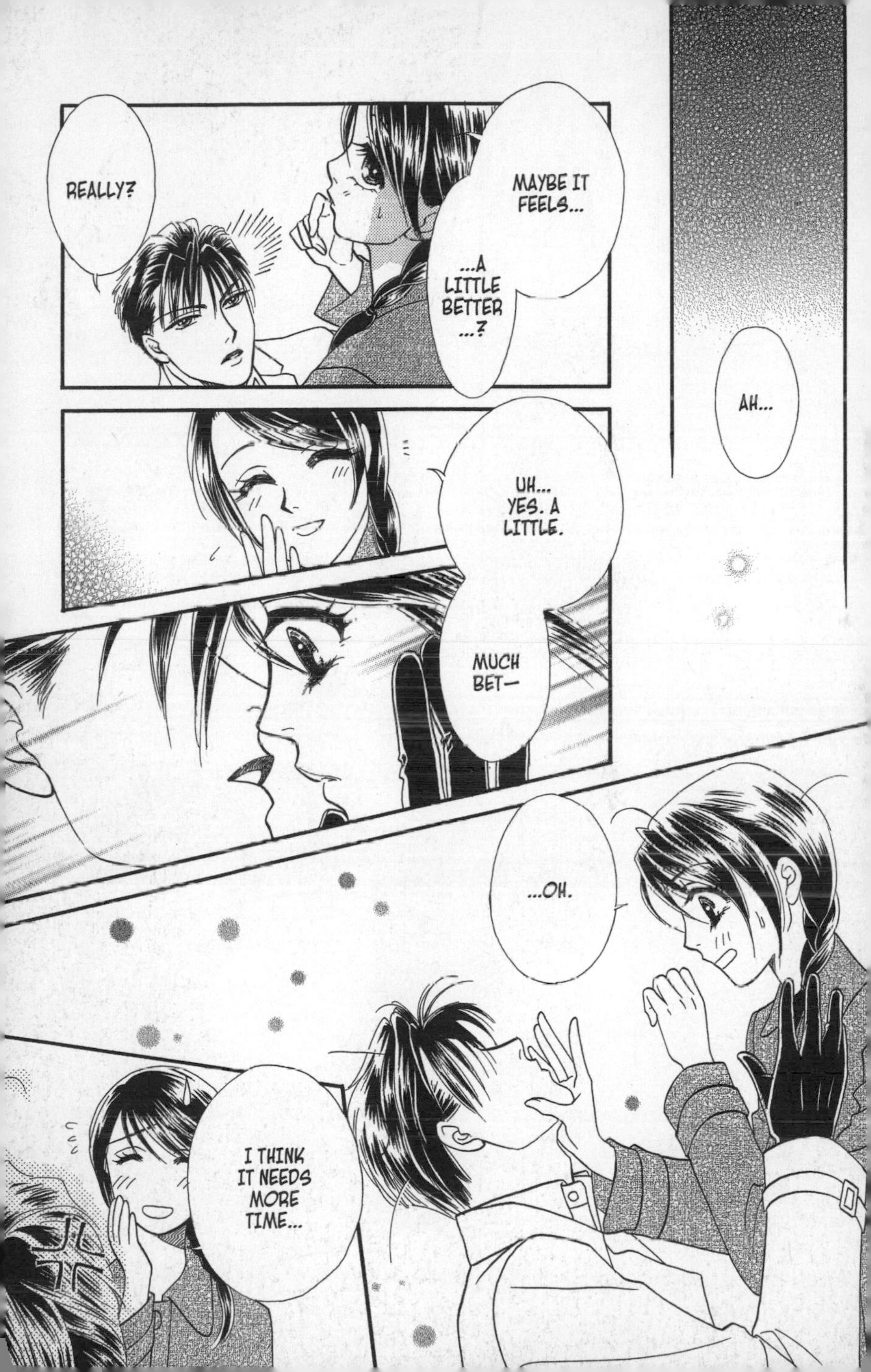
AH...
MAYBE IT FEELS...
...A LITTLE BETTER ...?
REALLY?
UH... YES. A LITTLE.
MUCH BET—
...OH.
I THINK IT NEEDS MORE TIME...

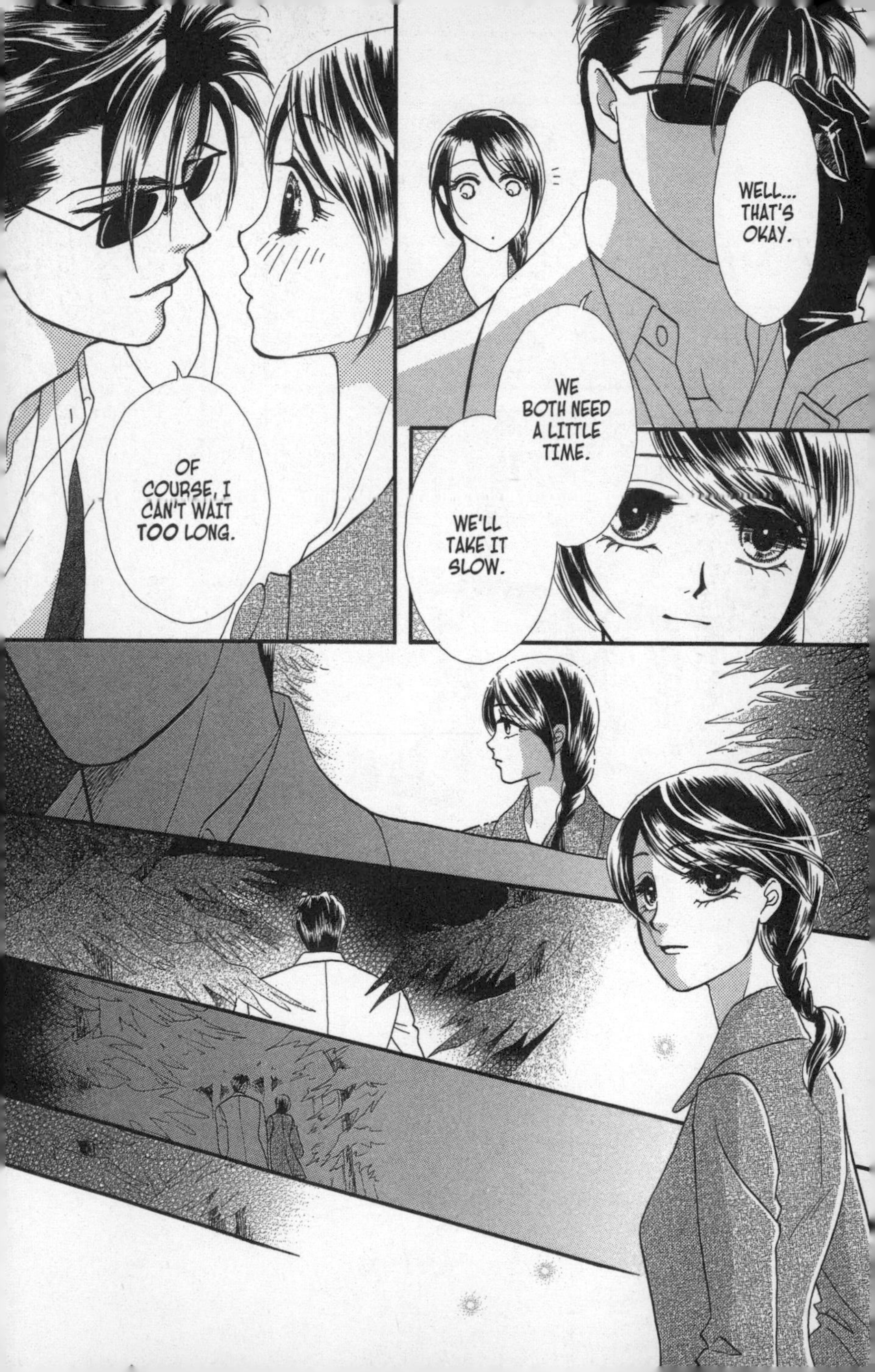
WELL... THAT'S OKAY.
WE BOTH NEED A LITTLE TIME.
WE'LL TAKE IT SLOW.
OF COURSE, I CAN'T WAIT TOO LONG.

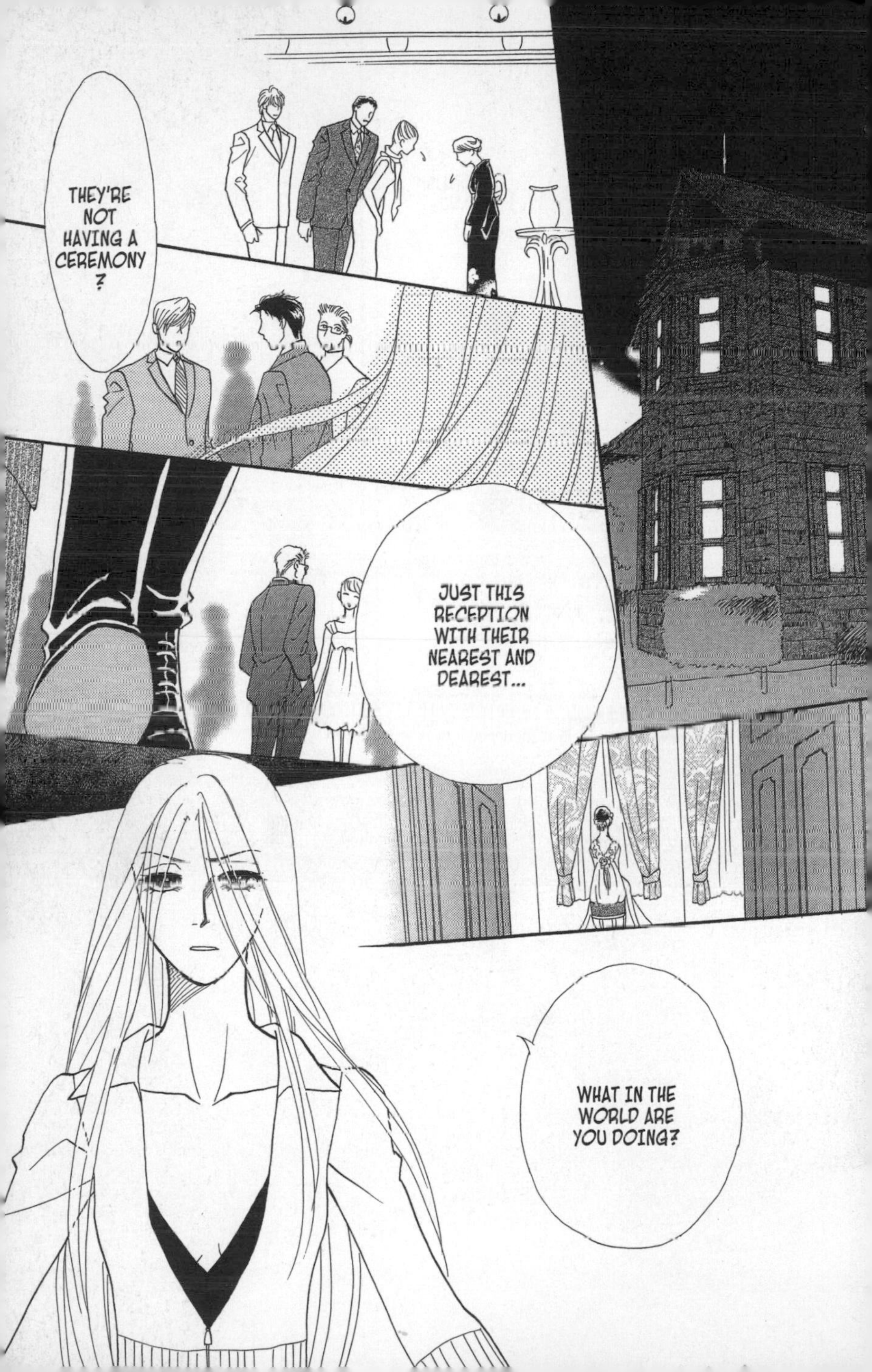
THEY'RE NOT HAVING A CEREMONY?
JUST THIS RECEPTION WITH THEIR NEAREST AND DEAREST...
WHAT IN THE WORLD ARE YOU DOING?

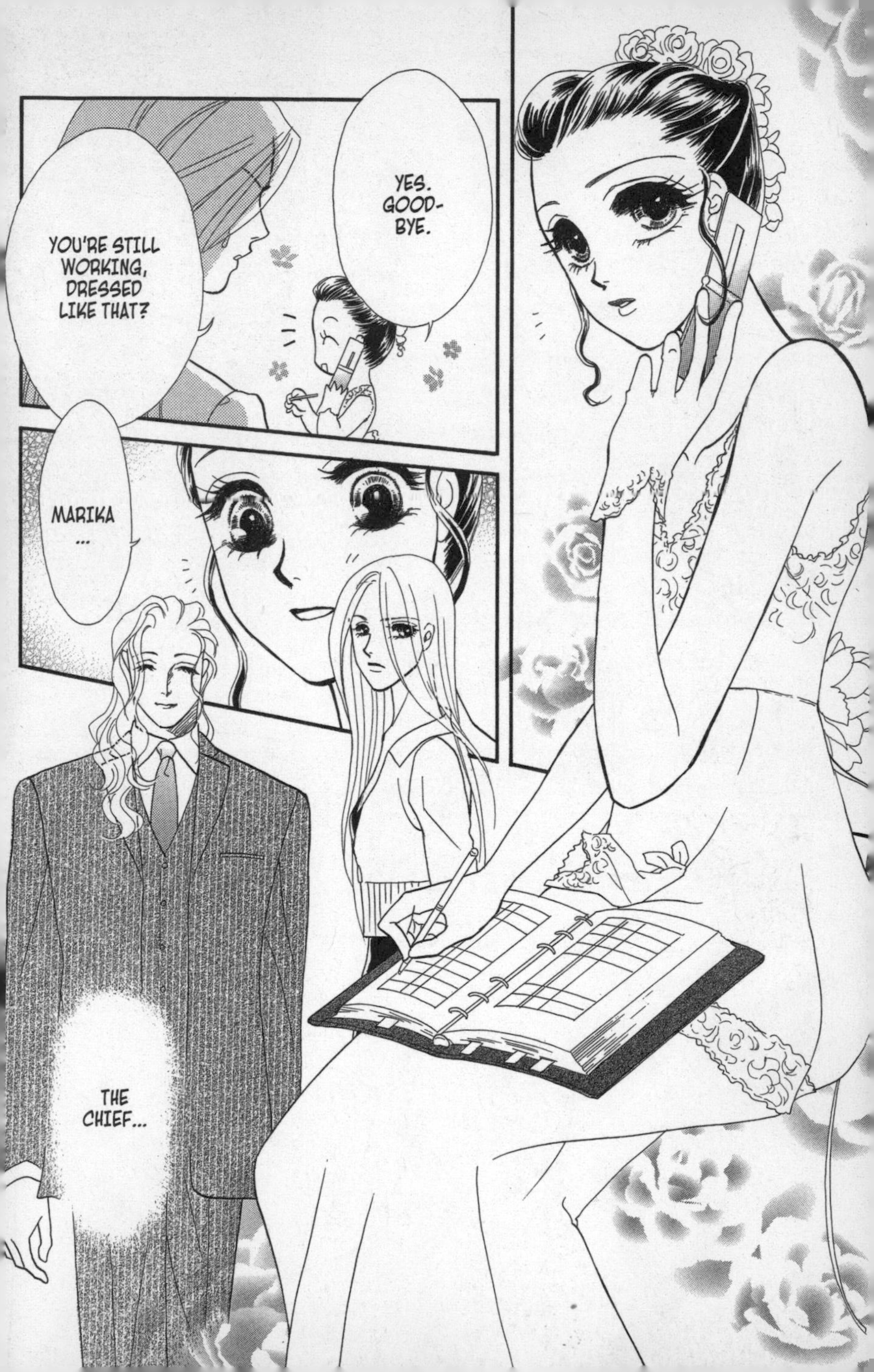
YES. GOOD-BYE.
YOU'RE STILL WORKING, DRESSED LIKE THAT?
MARIKA ...
THE CHIEF...

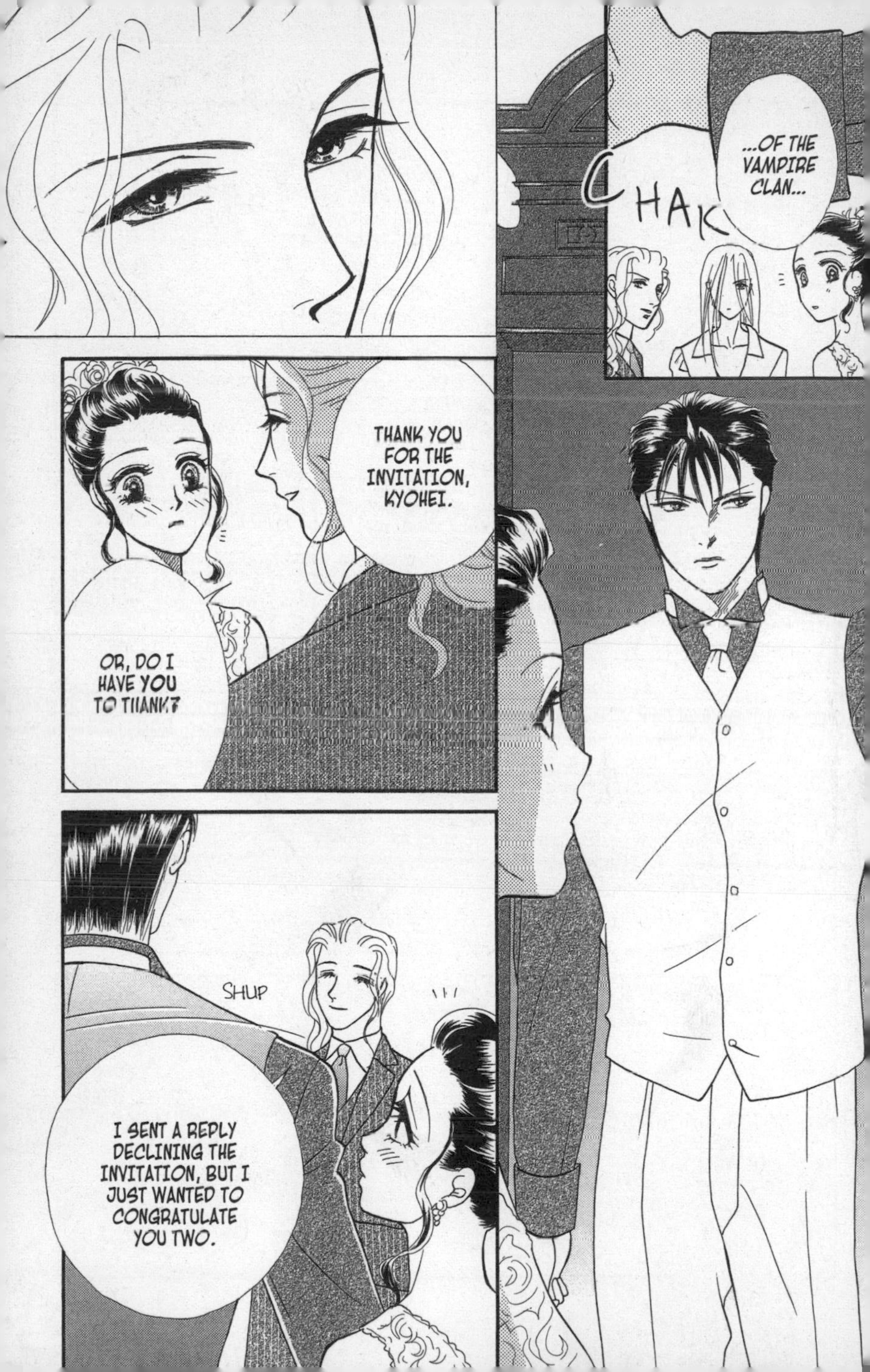
...OF THE VAMPIRE CLAN...
CHAK
THANK YOU FOR THE INVITATION, KYOHEI.
OR, DO I HAVE YOU TO THANK?
SHUP
I SENT A REPLY DECLINING THE INVITATION, BUT I JUST WANTED TO CONGRATULATE YOU TWO.

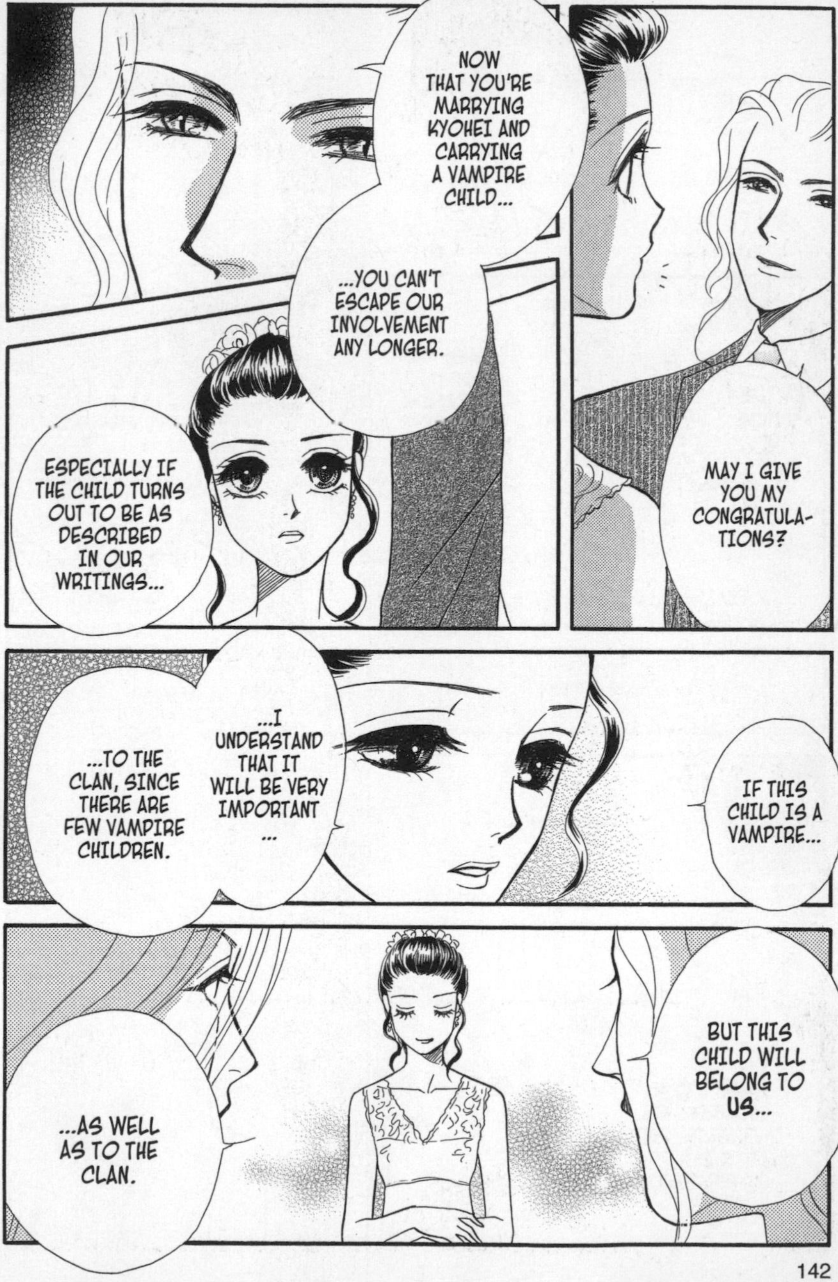
MAY I GIVE YOU MY CONGRATULATIONS?
NOW THAT YOU'RE MARRYING KYOHEI AND CARRYING A VAMPIRE CHILD...
...YOU CAN'T ESCAPE OUR INVOLVEMENT ANY LONGER.
ESPECIALLY IF THE CHILD TURNS OUT TO BE AS DESCRIBED IN OUR WRITINGS...
IF THIS CHILD IS A VAMPIRE...
...I UNDERSTAND THAT IT WILL BE VERY IMPORTANT ...
...TO THE CLAN, SINCE THERE ARE FEW VAMPIRE CHILDREN.
BUT THIS CHILD WILL BELONG TO US...
...AS WELL AS TO THE CLAN.

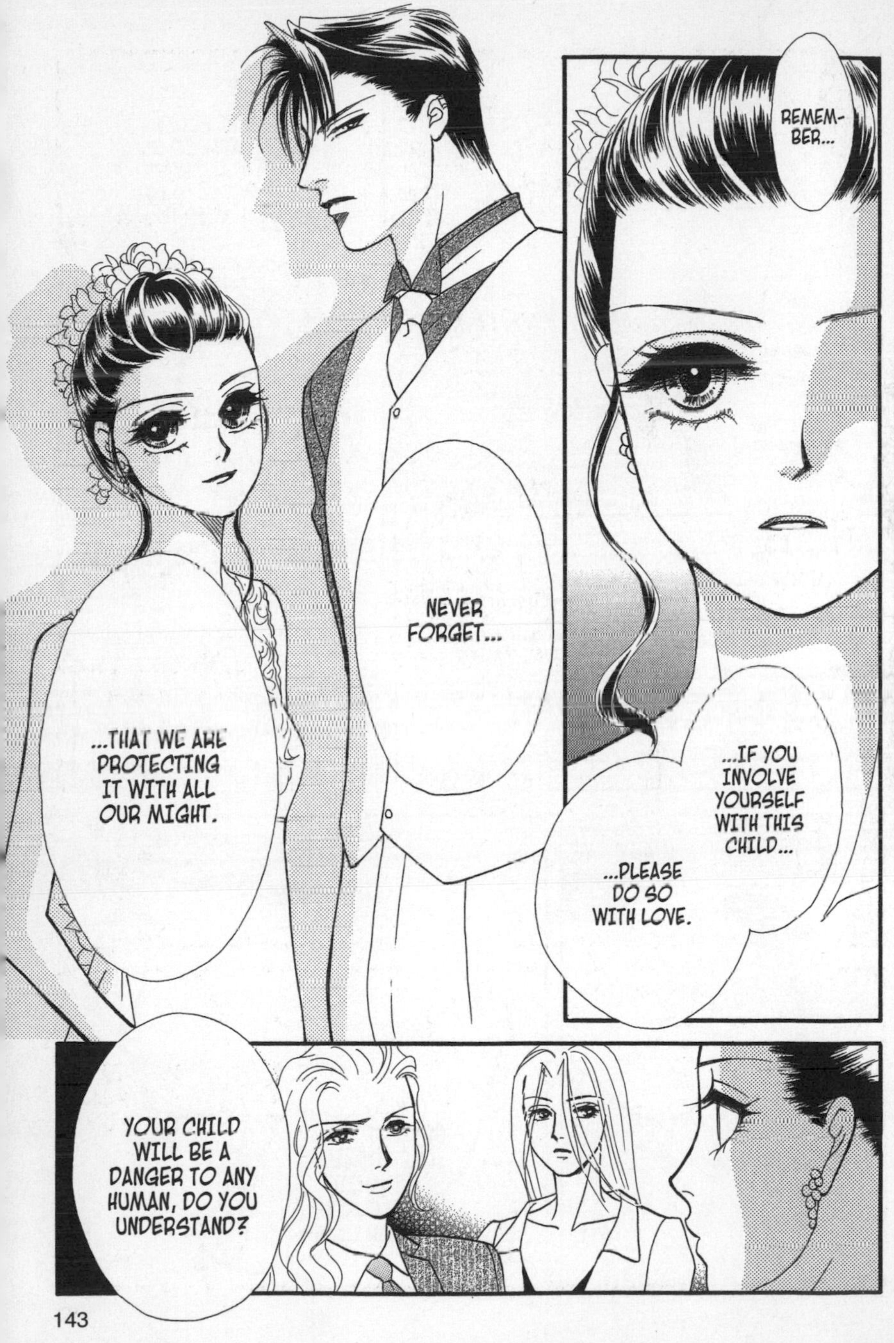
REMEMBER...
...IF YOU INVOLVE YOURSELF WITH THIS CHILD...
...PLEASE DO SO WITH LOVE.
NEVER FORGET...
...THAT WE ARE PROTECTING IT WITH ALL OUR MIGHT.
YOUR CHILD WILL BE A DANGER TO ANY HUMAN, DO YOU UNDERSTAND?

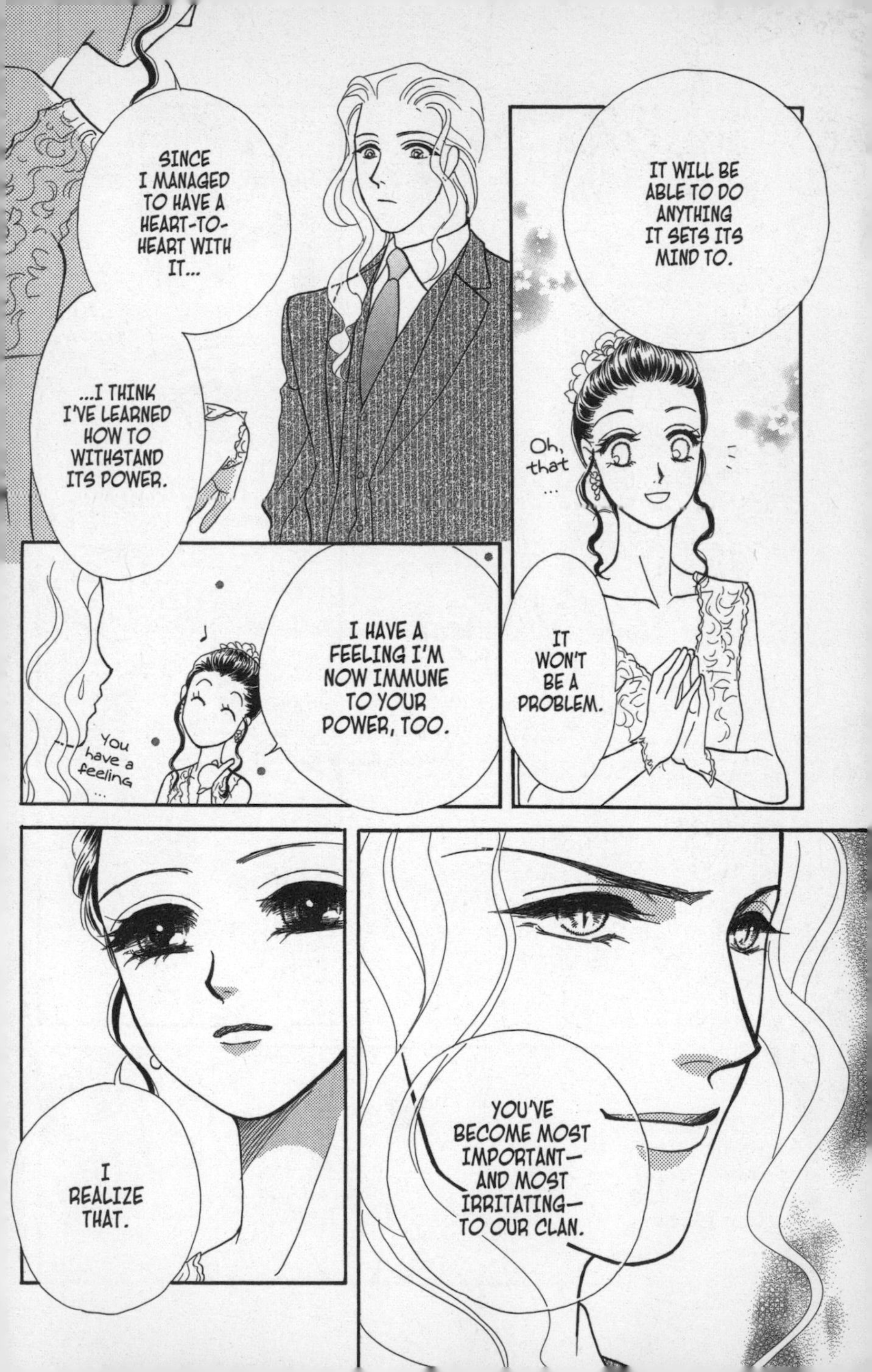
SINCE I MANAGED TO HAVE A HEART-TO-HEART WITH IT...
...I THINK I'VE LEARNED HOW TO WITHSTAND ITS POWER.
IT WILL BE ABLE TO DO ANYTHING IT SETS ITS MIND TO.
Oh, that...
IT WON'T BE A PROBLEM.
I HAVE A FEELING I'M NOW IMMUNE TO YOUR POWER, TOO.
You have a feeling...
YOU'VE BECOME MOST IMPORTANT—AND MOST IRRITATING—TO OUR CLAN.
I REALIZE THAT.

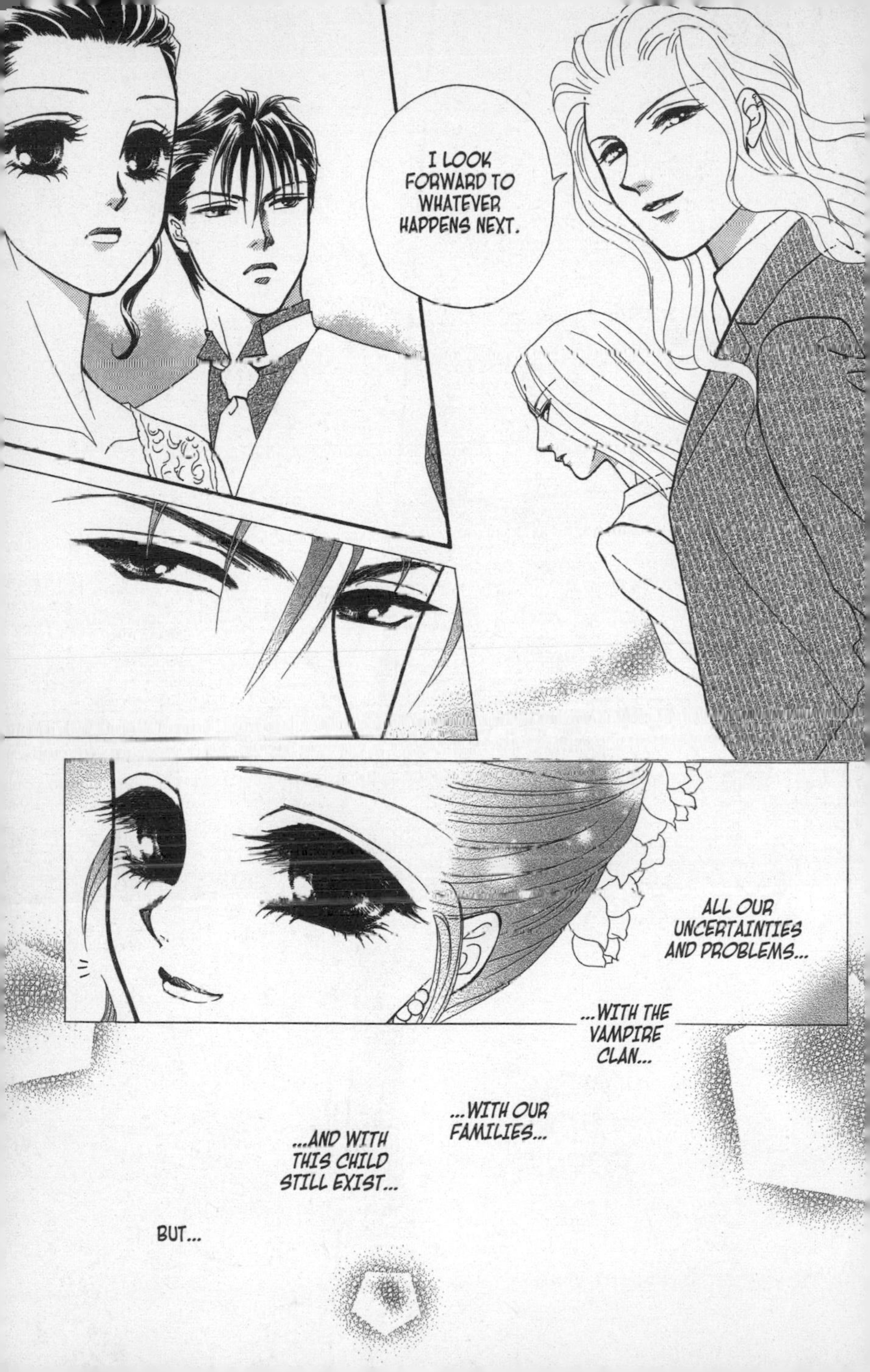
I LOOK FORWARD TO WHATEVER HAPPENS NEXT.
ALL OUR UNCERTAINTIES AND PROBLEMS...
...WITH THE VAMPIRE CLAN...
...WITH OUR FAMILIES...
...AND WITH THIS CHILD STILL EXIST...
BUT...

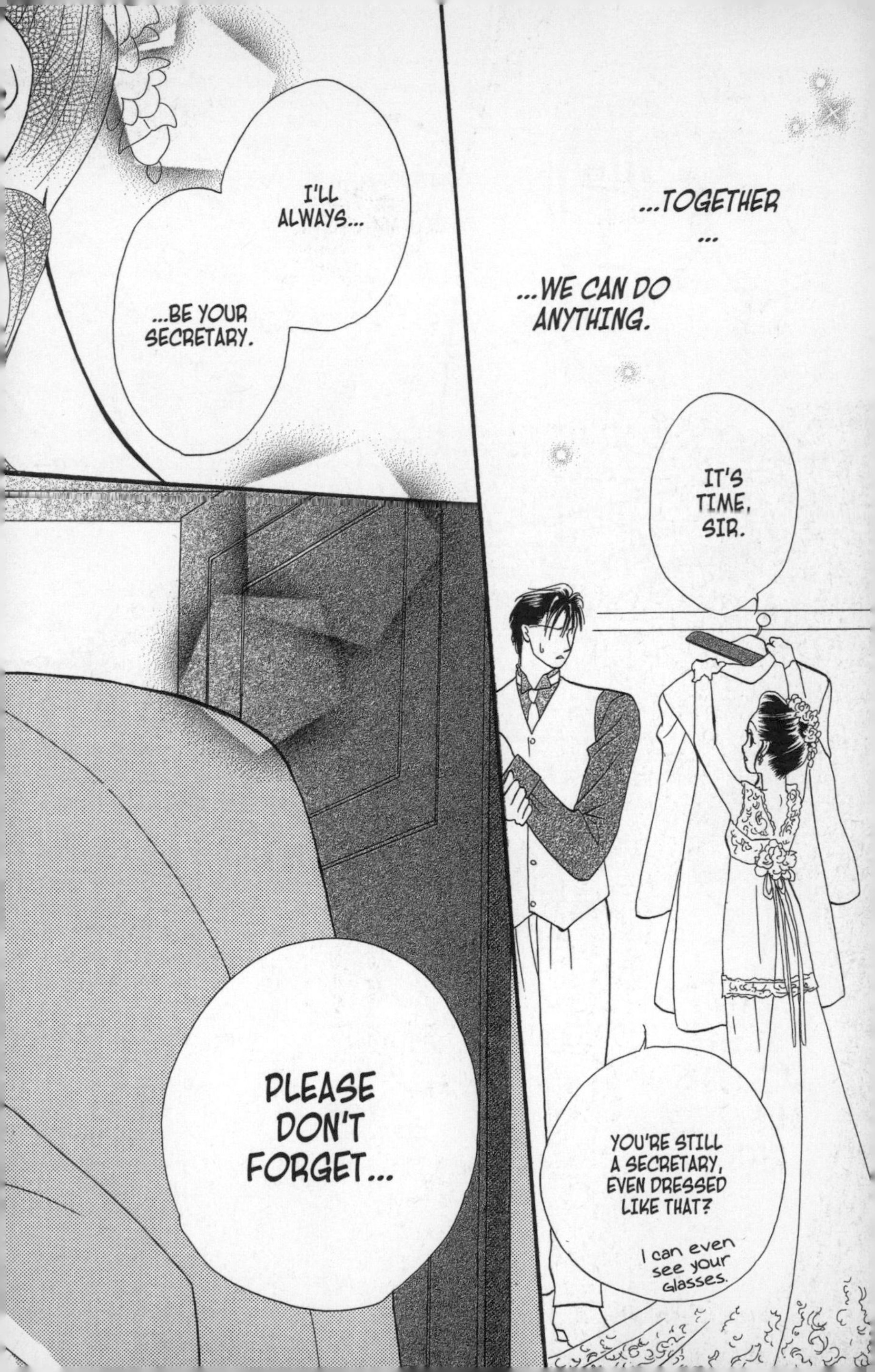
...TOGETHER
...
...WE CAN DO ANYTHING.
IT'S TIME, SIR.
YOU'RE STILL A SECRETARY, EVEN DRESSED LIKE THAT?
I can even see your glasses.
I'LL ALWAYS...
...BE YOUR SECRETARY.
PLEASE DON'T FORGET...

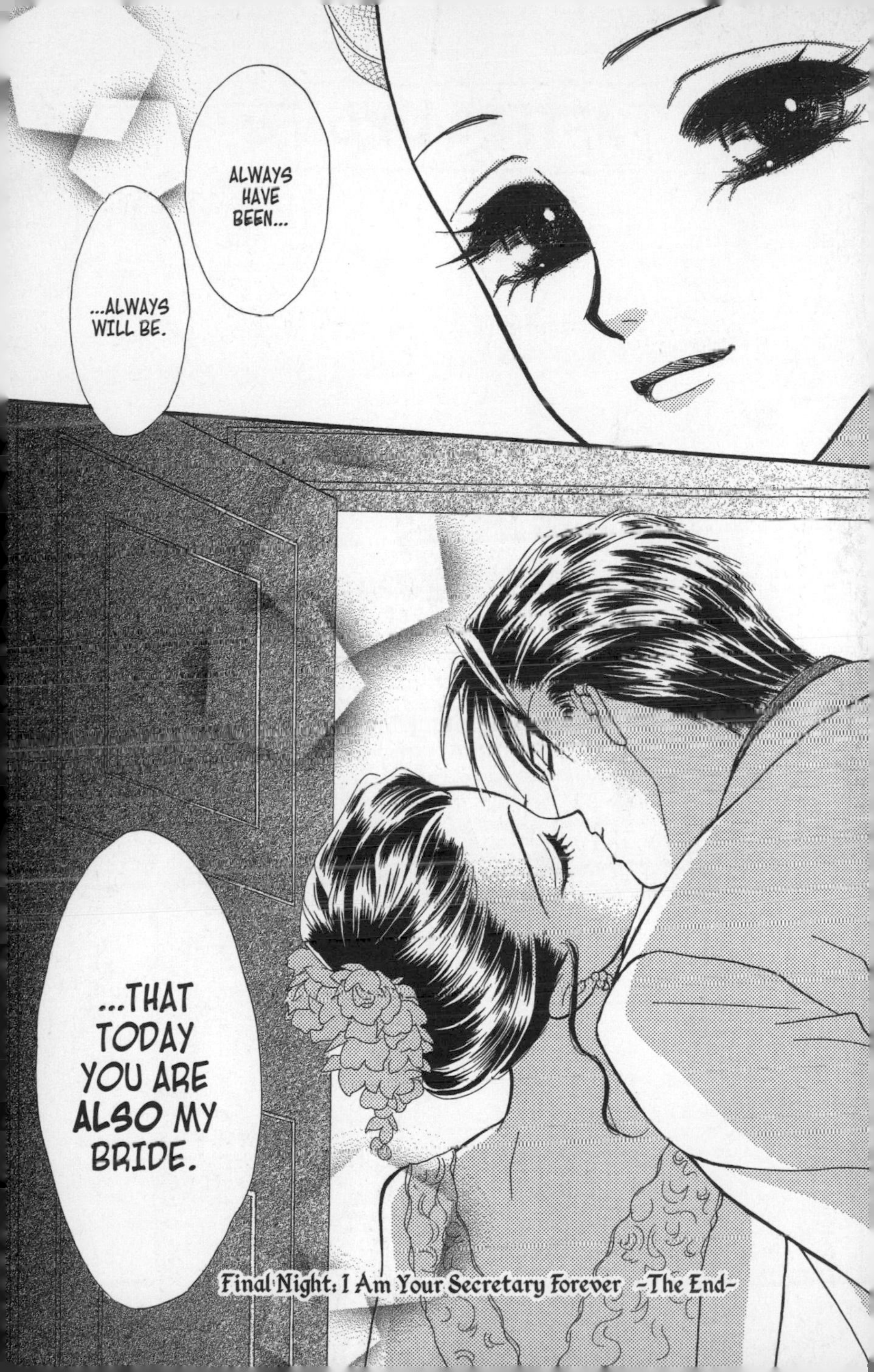
ALWAYS HAVE BEEN...
...ALWAYS WILL BE.
...THAT TODAY YOU ARE ALSO MY BRIDE.
Final Night: I Am Your Secretary Forever -The End-

# AFTERWORD

Hello! This is Tomu Ohmi!

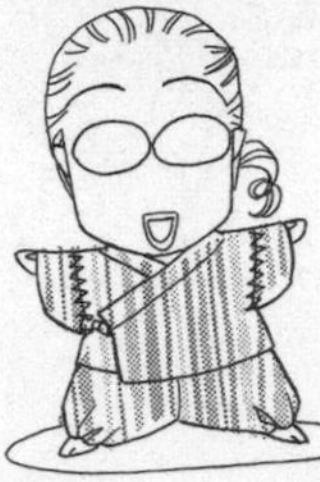

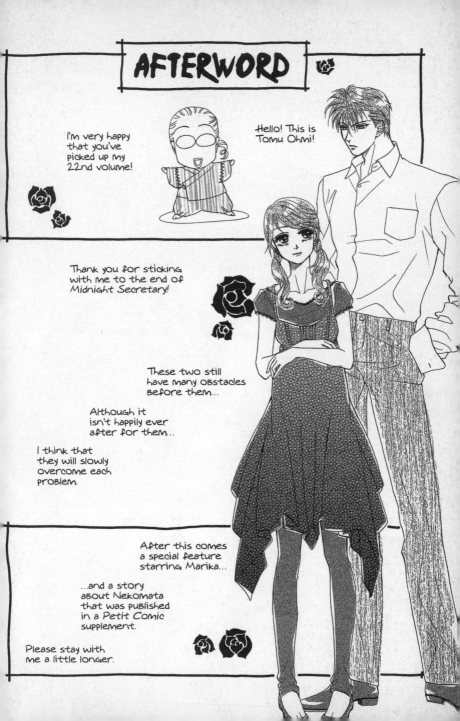

I'm very happy that you've picked up my 22nd volume!

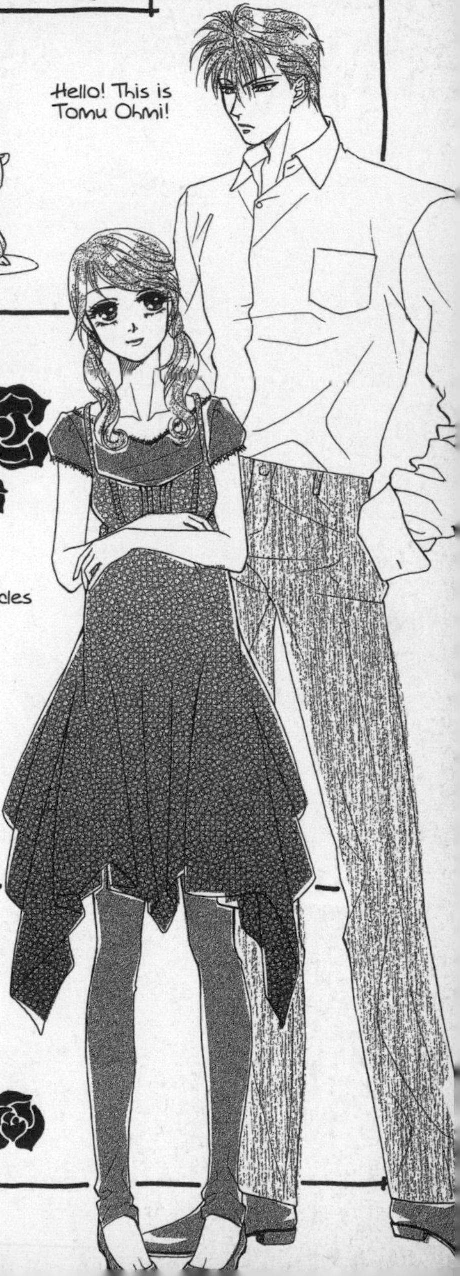

Thank you for sticking with me to the end of Midnight Secretary!

These two still have many obstacles before them...

Although it isn't happily ever after for them...

I think that they will slowly overcome each problem.

After this comes a special feature starring Marika...

...and a story about Nekomata that was published in a *Petit Comic* supplement.

Please stay with me a little longer.

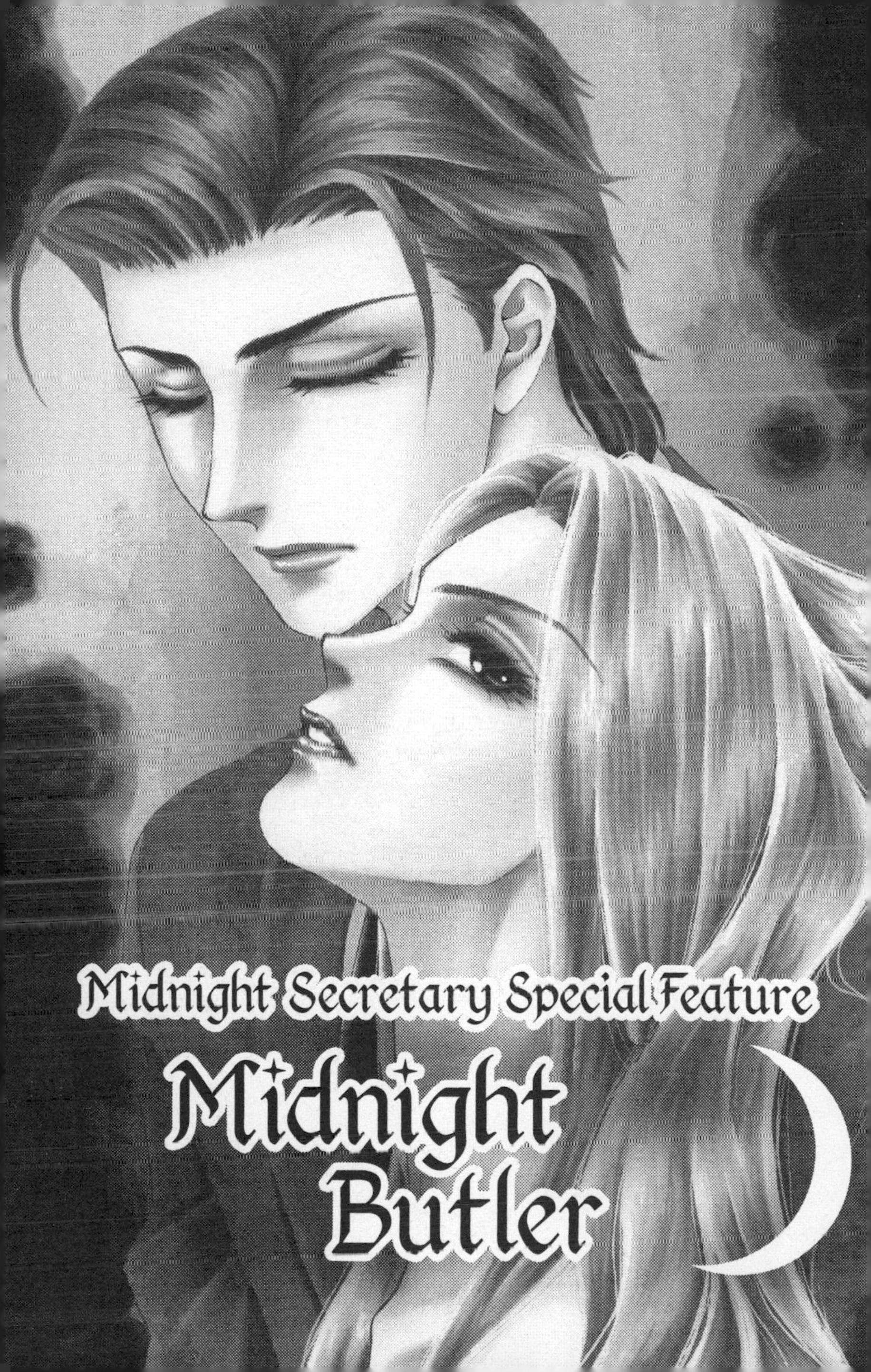
Midnight Secretary Special Feature
Midnight Butler

I hope to see you all in another
*Petit Comic* magazine...

My thanks to everyone who
helped me with this manga, and
to all the readers.

I may not be able to answer
right away, but if possible, please
let me know your thoughts.

Tomu Ohmi
c/o Shojo Beat
Published by VIZ Media, LLC
P.O. Box 77010
San Francisco, CA 94107

You can also email your thoughts
to *Petit Comics* HP address. I
shouldn't say this is in lieu of a
reply, but I'd like to send you a
New Year's greeting card, so
please include your address.

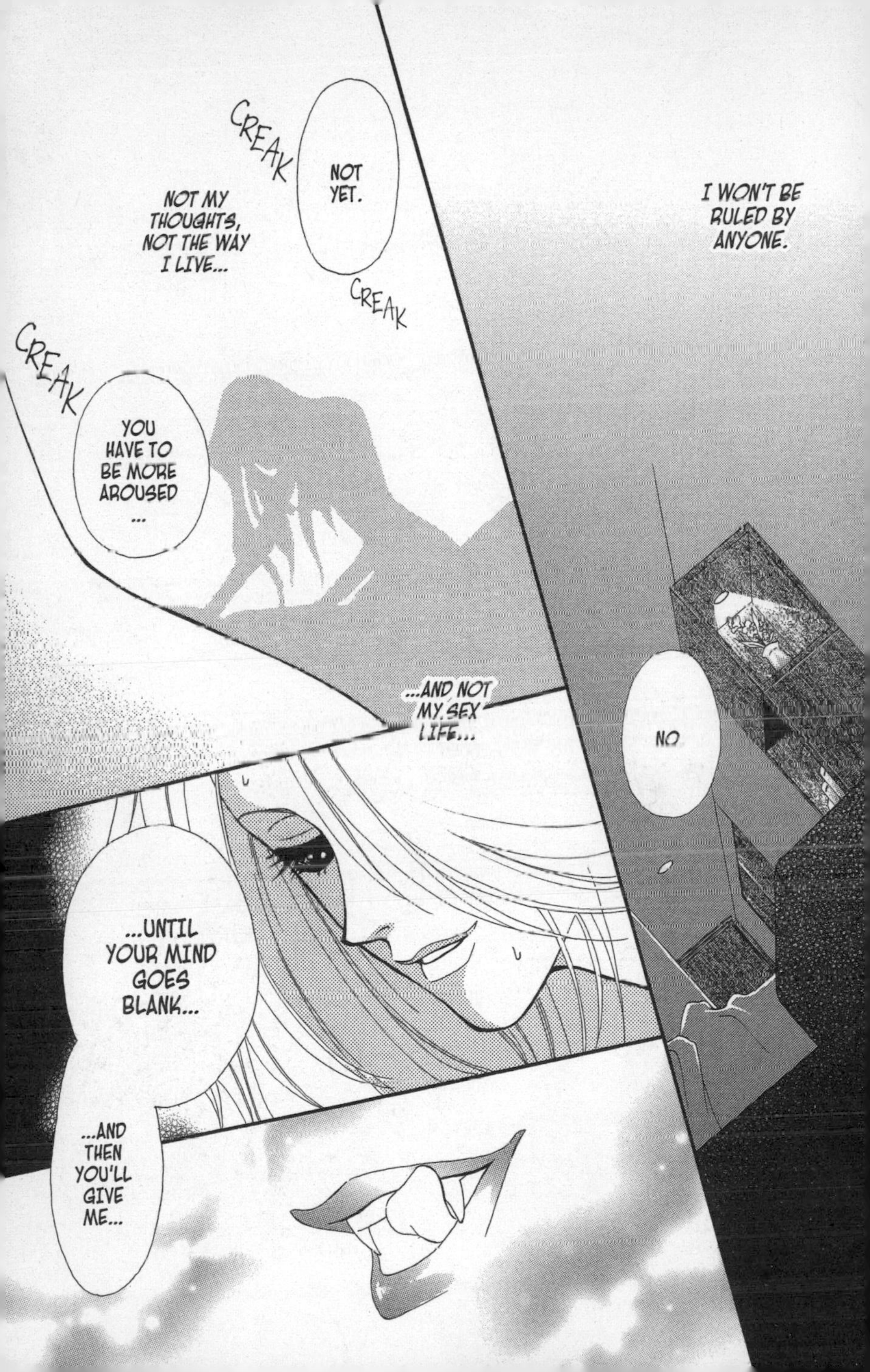
I WON'T BE RULED BY ANYONE.
NO.
CREAK
NOT YET.
NOT MY THOUGHTS, NOT THE WAY I LIVE...
CREAK
CREAK
YOU HAVE TO BE MORE AROUSED ...
...AND NOT MY SEX LIFE...
...UNTIL YOUR MIND GOES BLANK...
...AND THEN YOU'LL GIVE ME...

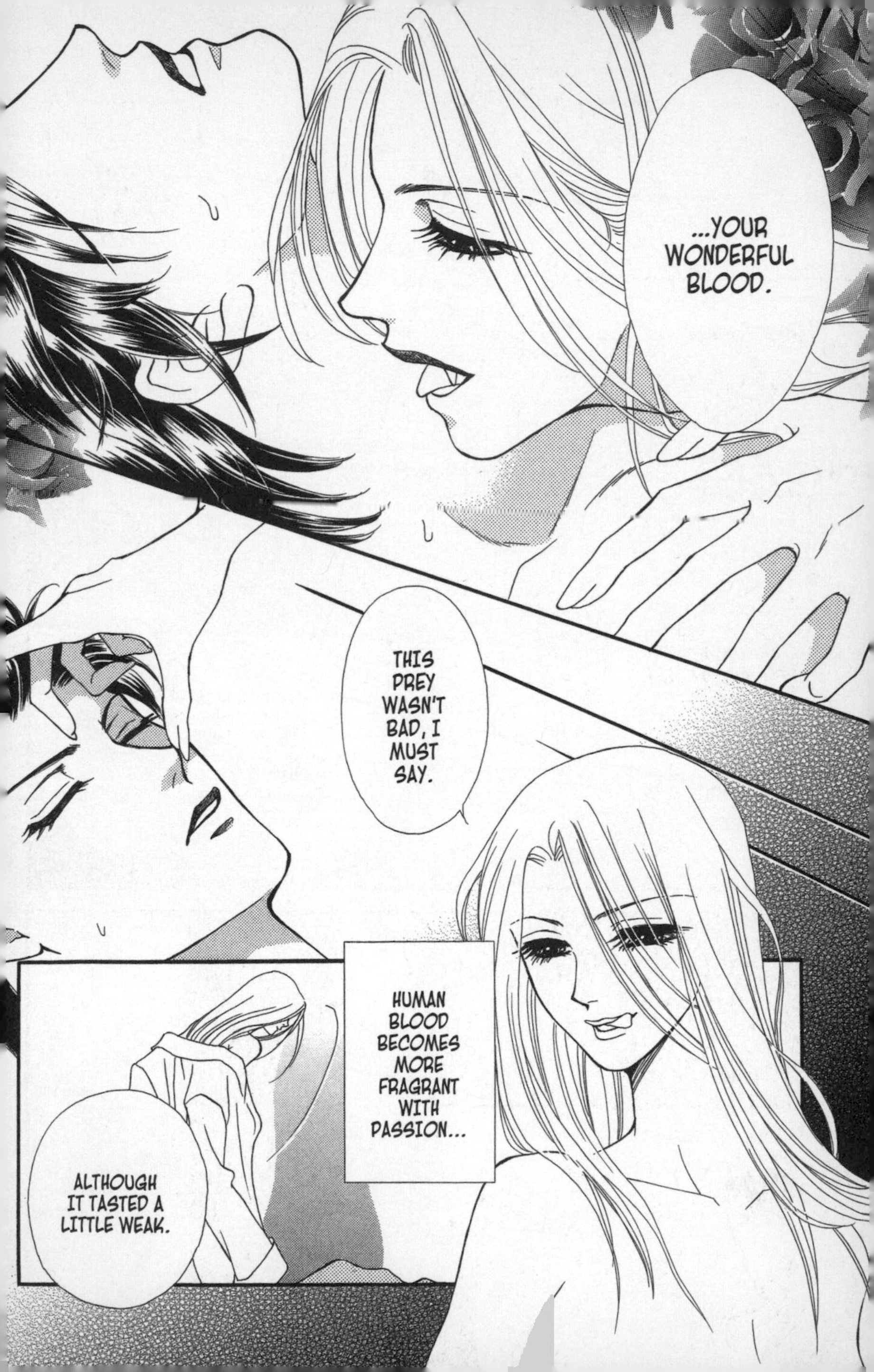
...YOUR WONDERFUL BLOOD.
THIS PREY WASN'T BAD, I MUST SAY.
HUMAN BLOOD BECOMES MORE FRAGRANT WITH PASSION...
ALTHOUGH IT TASTED A LITTLE WEAK.

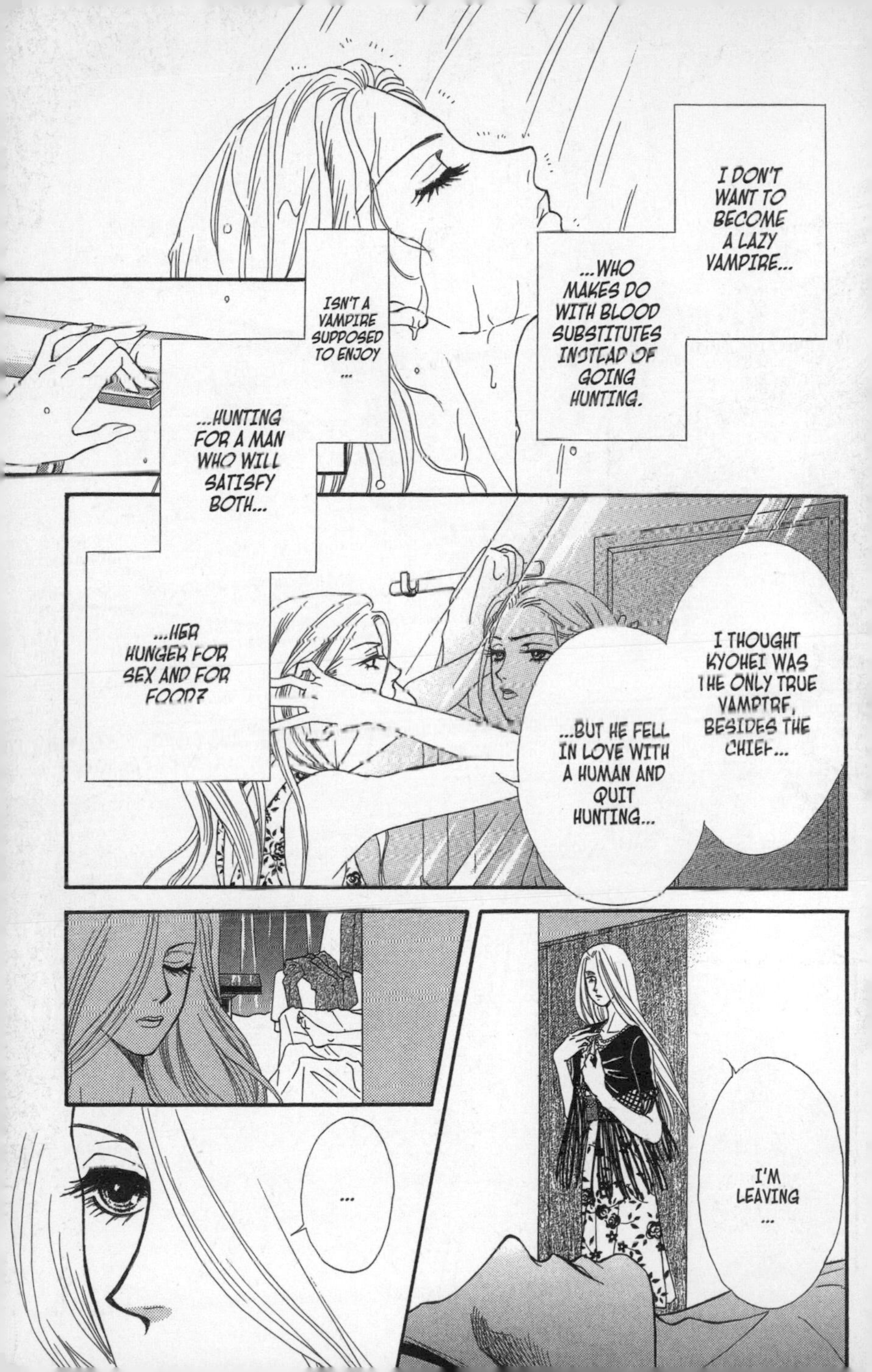
I DON'T WANT TO BECOME A LAZY VAMPIRE...
...WHO MAKES DO WITH BLOOD SUBSTITUTES INSTEAD OF GOING HUNTING.
ISN'T A VAMPIRE SUPPOSED TO ENJOY ...
...HUNTING FOR A MAN WHO WILL SATISFY BOTH...
...HER HUNGER FOR SEX AND FOR FOOD?
I THOUGHT KYOHEI WAS THE ONLY TRUE VAMPIRE, BESIDES THE CHIEF...
...BUT HE FELL IN LOVE WITH A HUMAN AND QUIT HUNTING...
I'M LEAVING ...
...

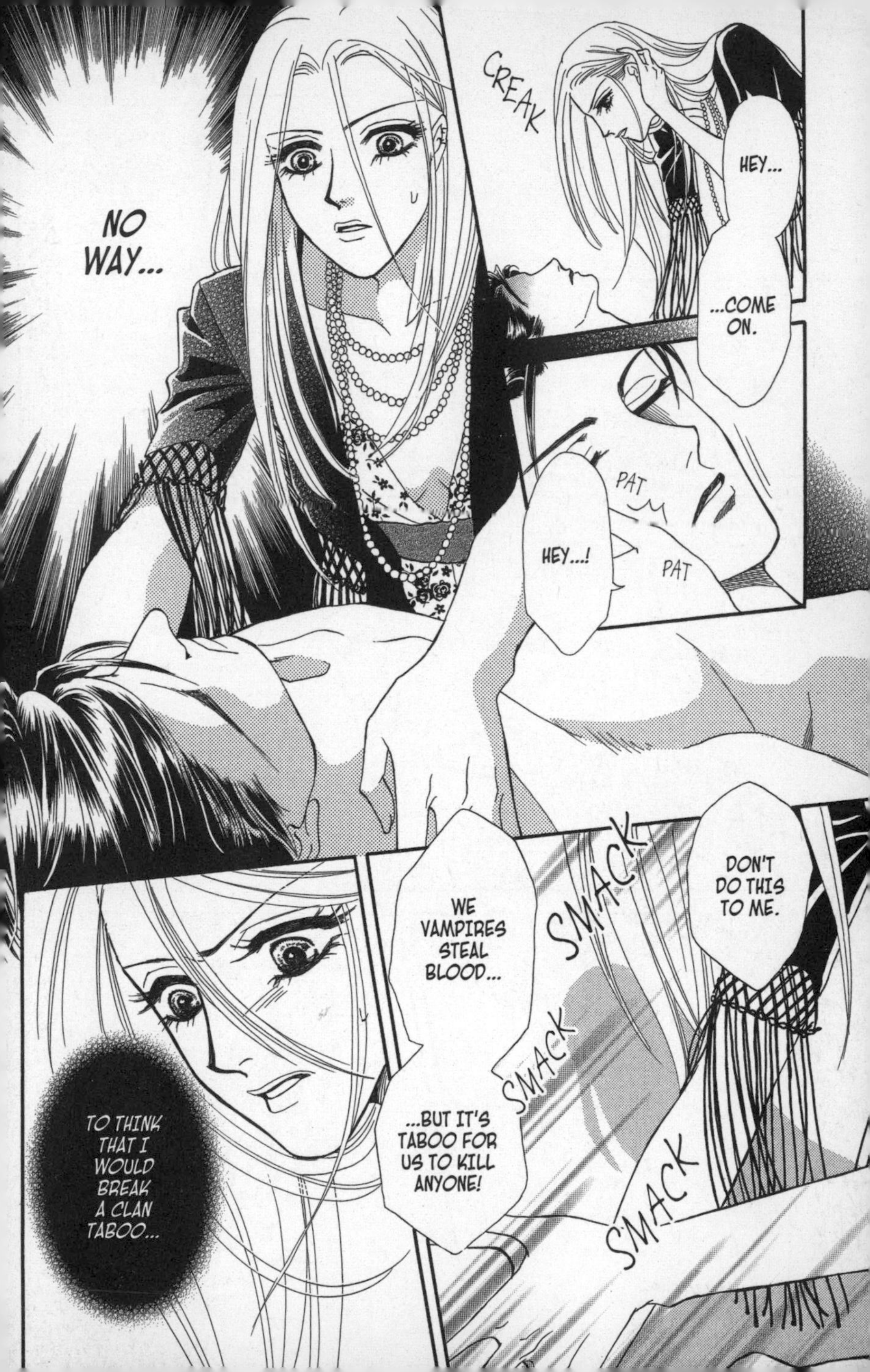
CREAK
HEY...
...COME ON.
PAT
PAT
HEY...!
NO WAY...
SMACK
SMACK
SMACK
SMACK
DON'T DO THIS TO ME.
WE VAMPIRES STEAL BLOOD...
...BUT IT'S TABOO FOR US TO KILL ANYONE!
TO THINK THAT I WOULD BREAK A CLAN TABOO...

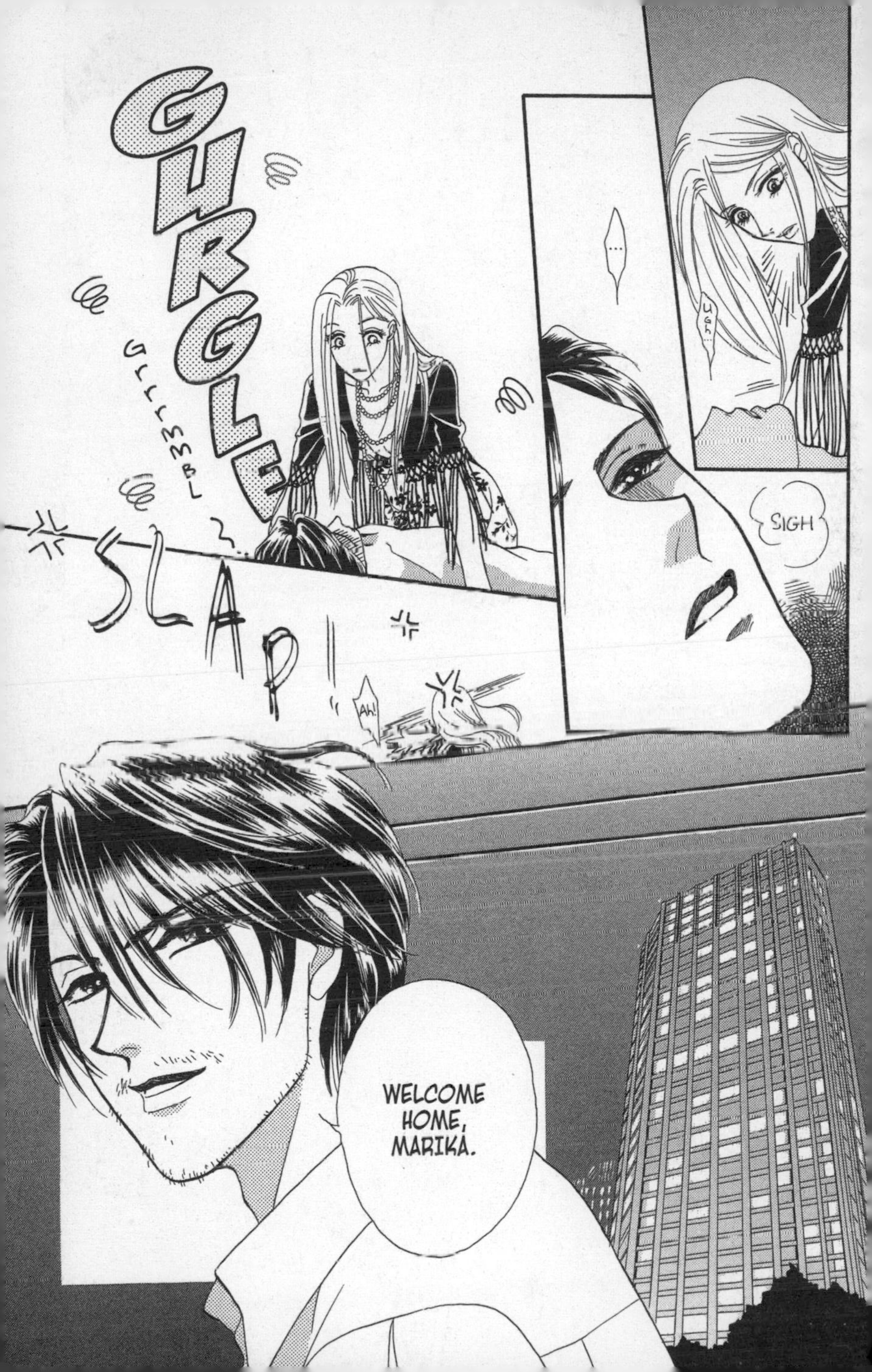
...
Ugh...
SIGH
GURGLE
Grrrrmbl
SLAP!!
Ah!
WELCOME HOME, MARIKA.

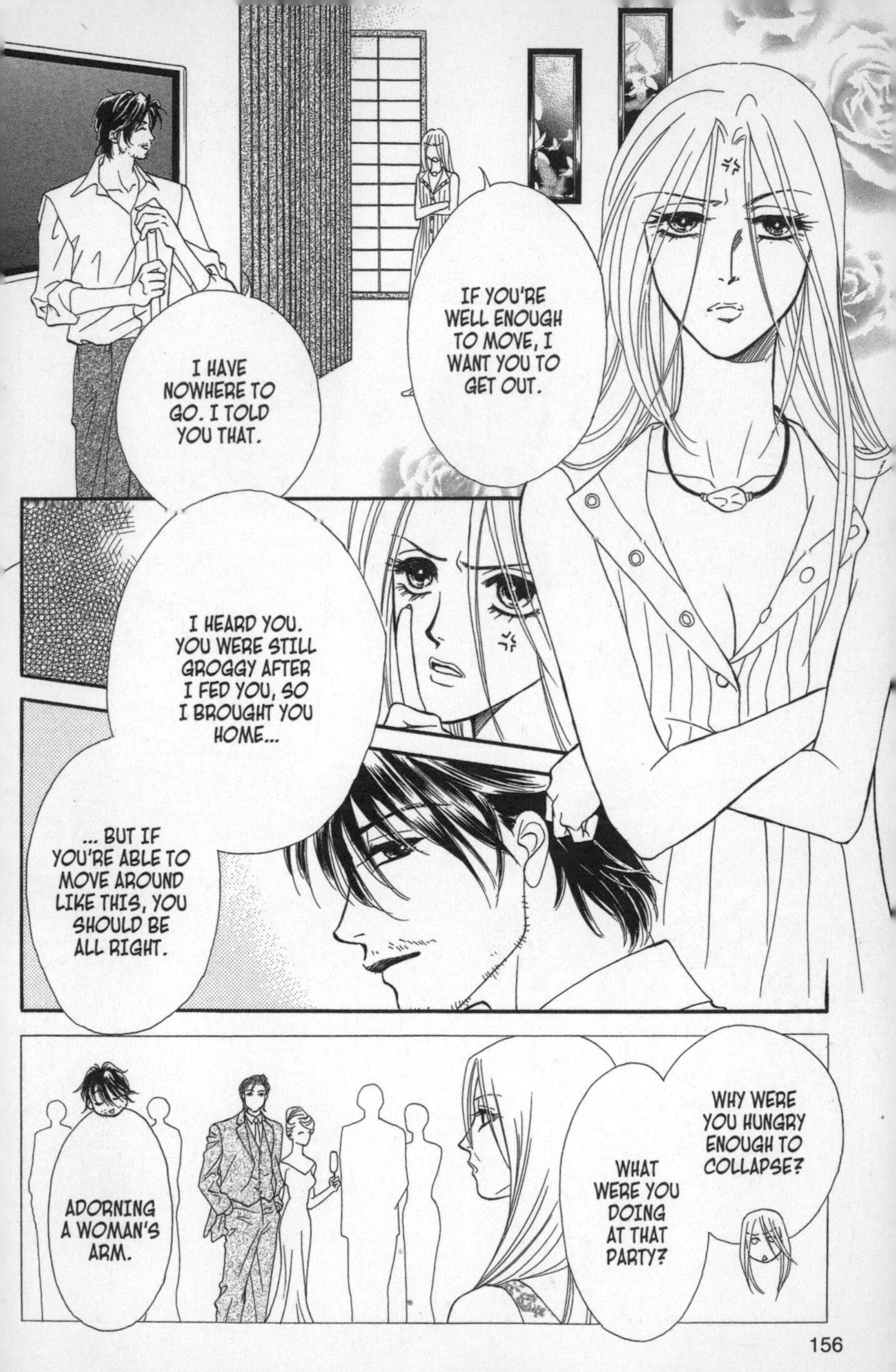
IF YOU'RE WELL ENOUGH TO MOVE, I WANT YOU TO GET OUT.
I HAVE NOWHERE TO GO. I TOLD YOU THAT.
I HEARD YOU. YOU WERE STILL GROGGY AFTER I FED YOU, SO I BROUGHT YOU HOME...
... BUT IF YOU'RE ABLE TO MOVE AROUND LIKE THIS, YOU SHOULD BE ALL RIGHT.
WHY WERE YOU HUNGRY ENOUGH TO COLLAPSE?
WHAT WERE YOU DOING AT THAT PARTY?
ADORNING A WOMAN'S ARM.

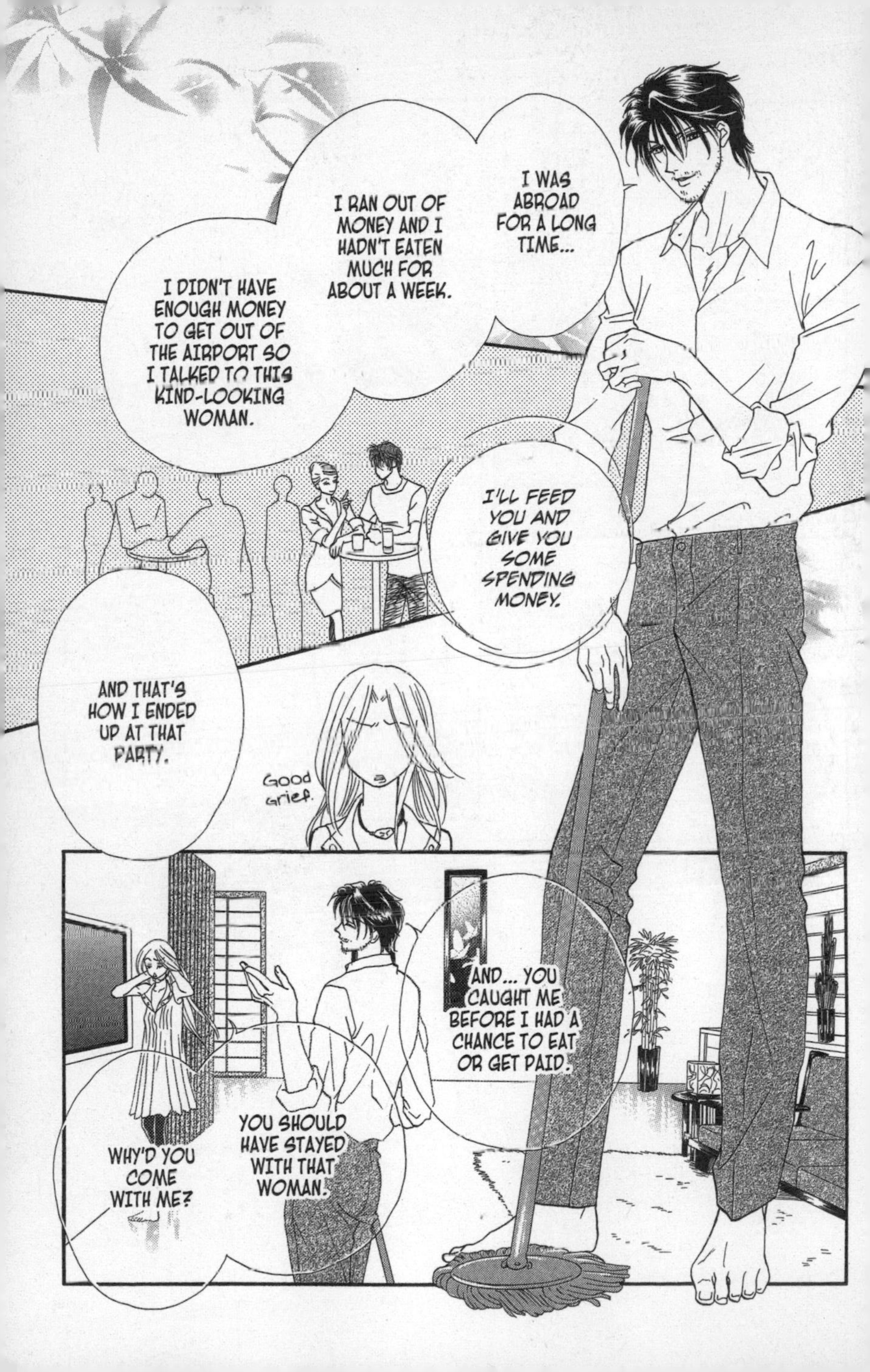
I WAS ABROAD FOR A LONG TIME...
I RAN OUT OF MONEY AND I HADN'T EATEN MUCH FOR ABOUT A WEEK.
I DIDN'T HAVE ENOUGH MONEY TO GET OUT OF THE AIRPORT SO I TALKED TO THIS KIND-LOOKING WOMAN.
I'LL FEED YOU AND GIVE YOU SOME SPENDING MONEY.
AND THAT'S HOW I ENDED UP AT THAT PARTY.
Good grief.
AND... YOU CAUGHT ME BEFORE I HAD A CHANCE TO EAT OR GET PAID.
YOU SHOULD HAVE STAYED WITH THAT WOMAN.
WHY'D YOU COME WITH ME?

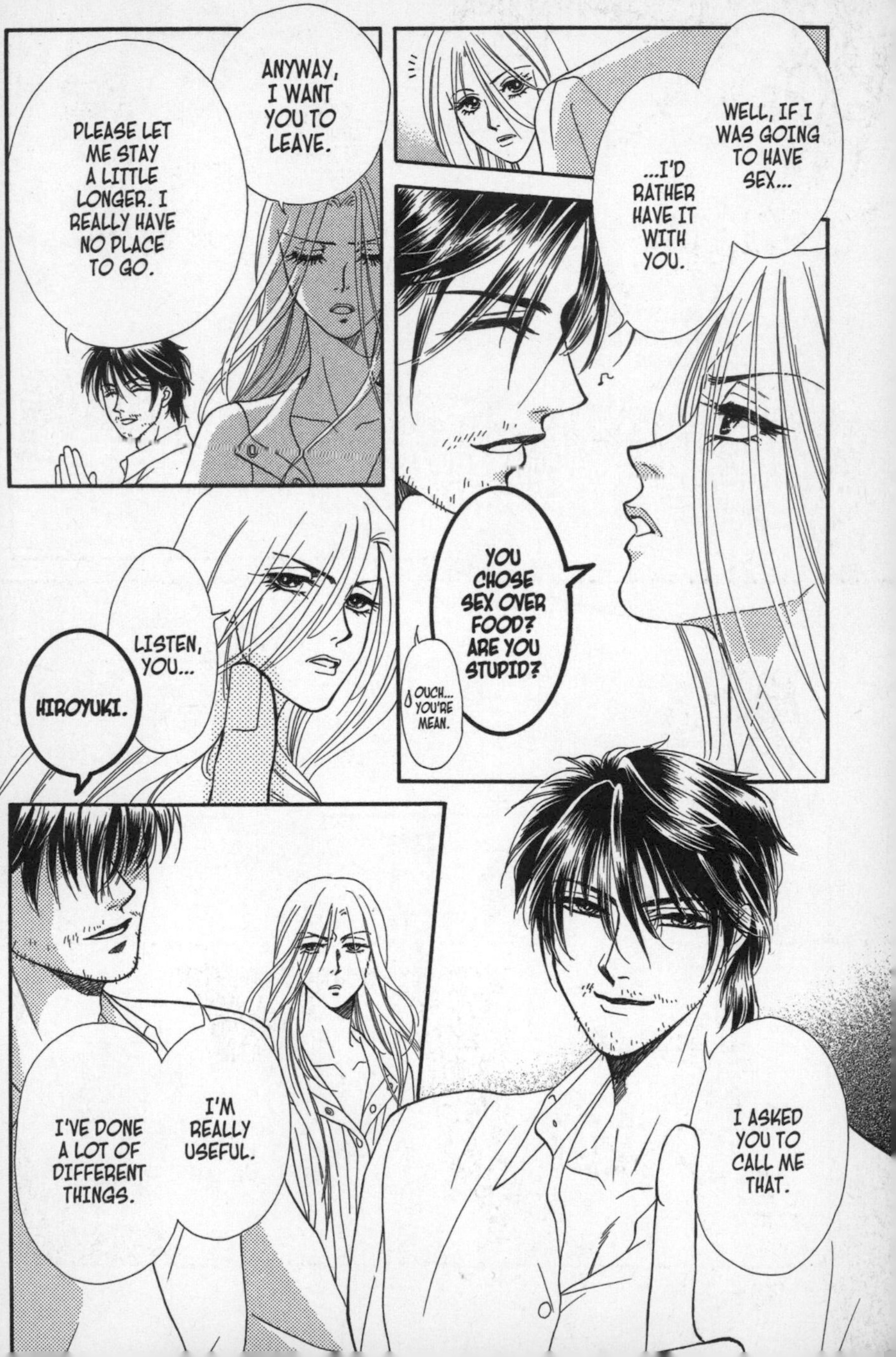

WELL, IF I WAS GOING TO HAVE SEX...
...I'D RATHER HAVE IT WITH YOU.
YOU CHOSE SEX OVER FOOD? ARE YOU STUPID?
OUCH... YOU'RE MEAN.
ANYWAY, I WANT YOU TO LEAVE.
PLEASE LET ME STAY A LITTLE LONGER. I REALLY HAVE NO PLACE TO GO.
LISTEN, YOU...
HIROYUKI.
I ASKED YOU TO CALL ME THAT.
I'M REALLY USEFUL.
I'VE DONE A LOT OF DIFFERENT THINGS.

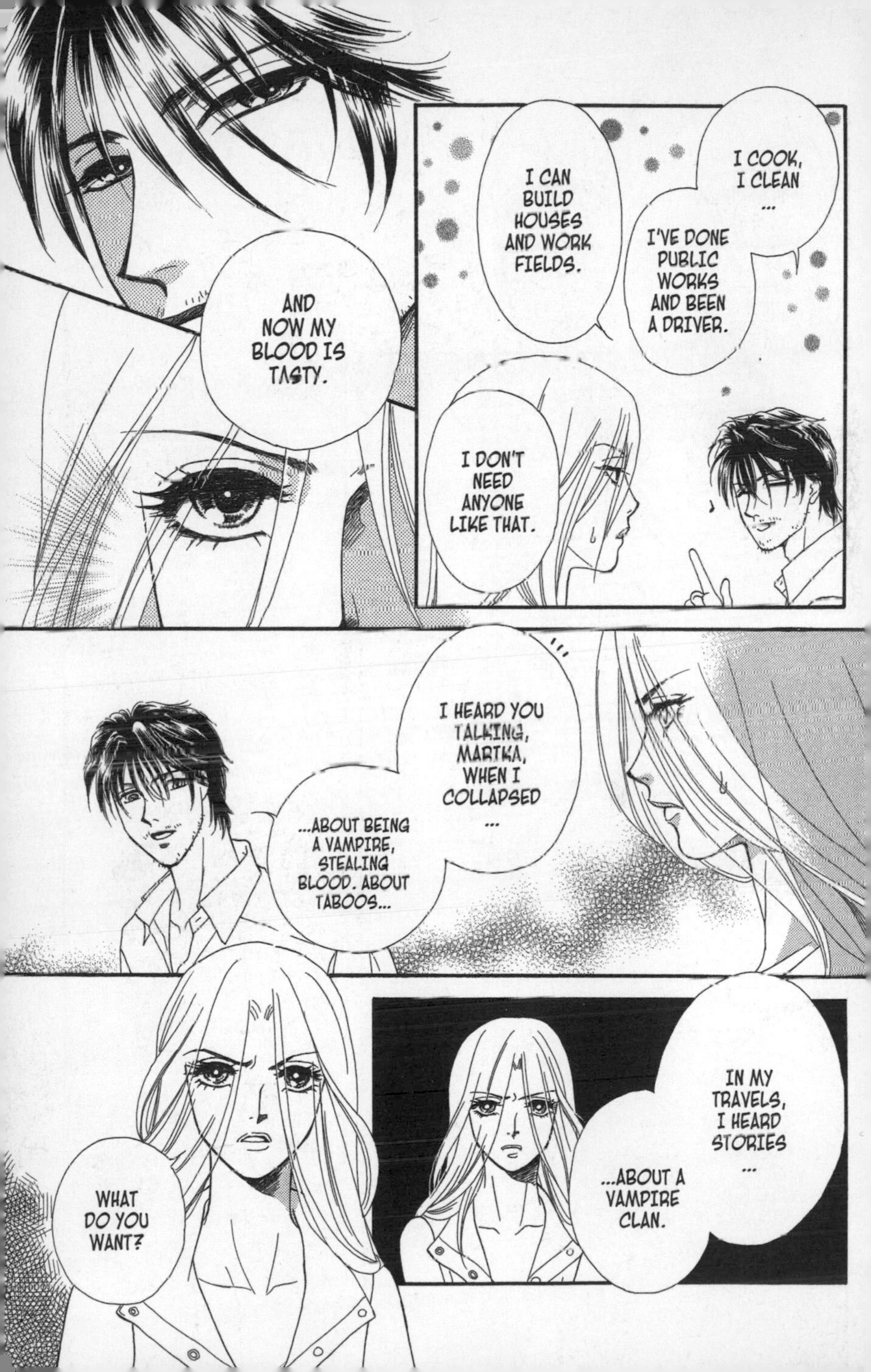
I COOK, I CLEAN ...
I'VE DONE PUBLIC WORKS AND BEEN A DRIVER.
I CAN BUILD HOUSES AND WORK FIELDS.
I DON'T NEED ANYONE LIKE THAT.
AND NOW MY BLOOD IS TASTY.
I HEARD YOU TALKING, MARTKA, WHEN I COLLAPSED ...
...ABOUT BEING A VAMPIRE, STEALING BLOOD. ABOUT TABOOS...
IN MY TRAVELS, I HEARD STORIES ...
...ABOUT A VAMPIRE CLAN.
WHAT DO YOU WANT?

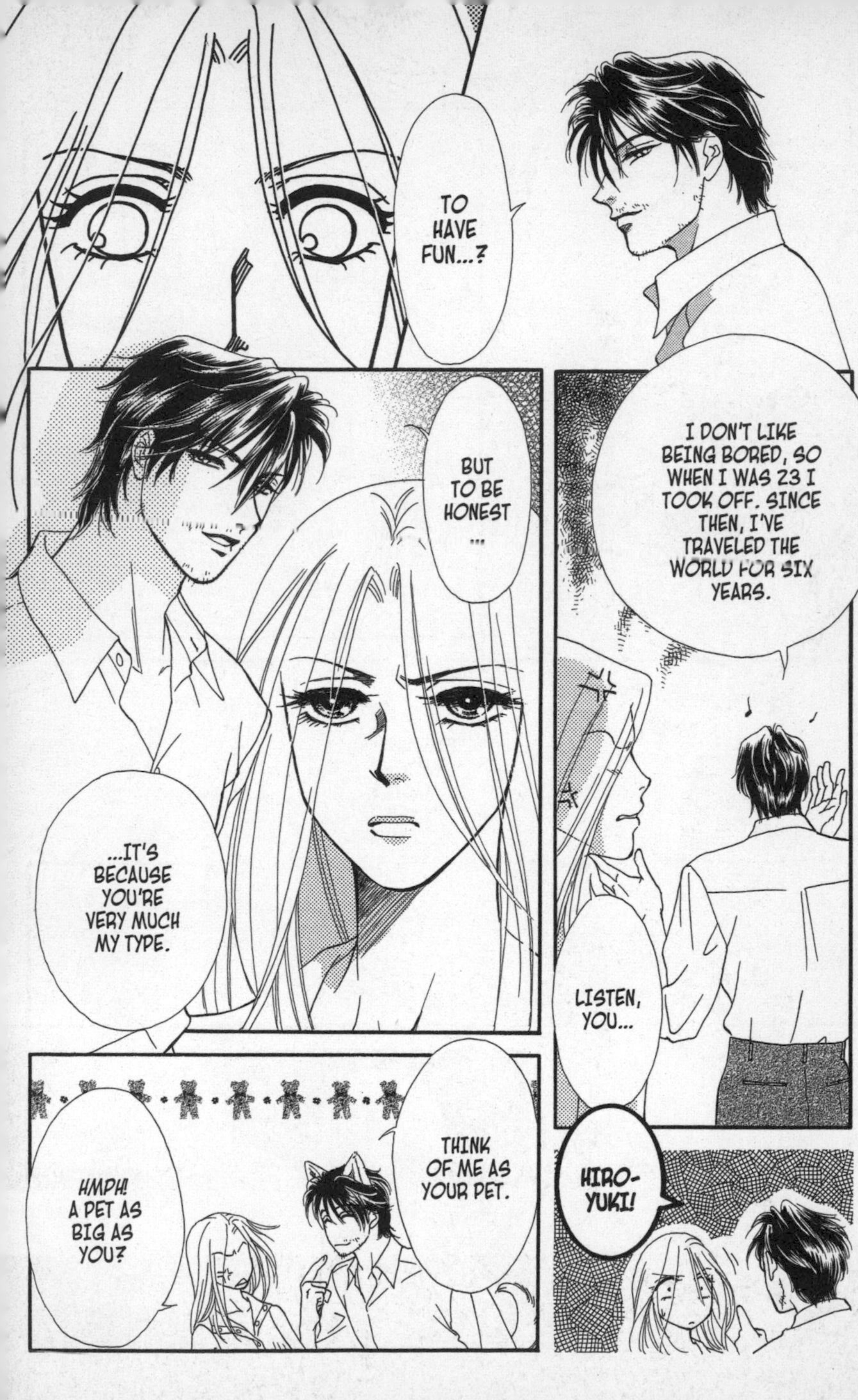
TO HAVE FUN...?
I DON'T LIKE BEING BORED, SO WHEN I WAS 23 I TOOK OFF. SINCE THEN, I'VE TRAVELED THE WORLD FOR SIX YEARS.
LISTEN, YOU...
BUT TO BE HONEST ...
...IT'S BECAUSE YOU'RE VERY MUCH MY TYPE.
THINK OF ME AS YOUR PET.
HMPH! A PET AS BIG AS YOU?
HIRO-YUKI!

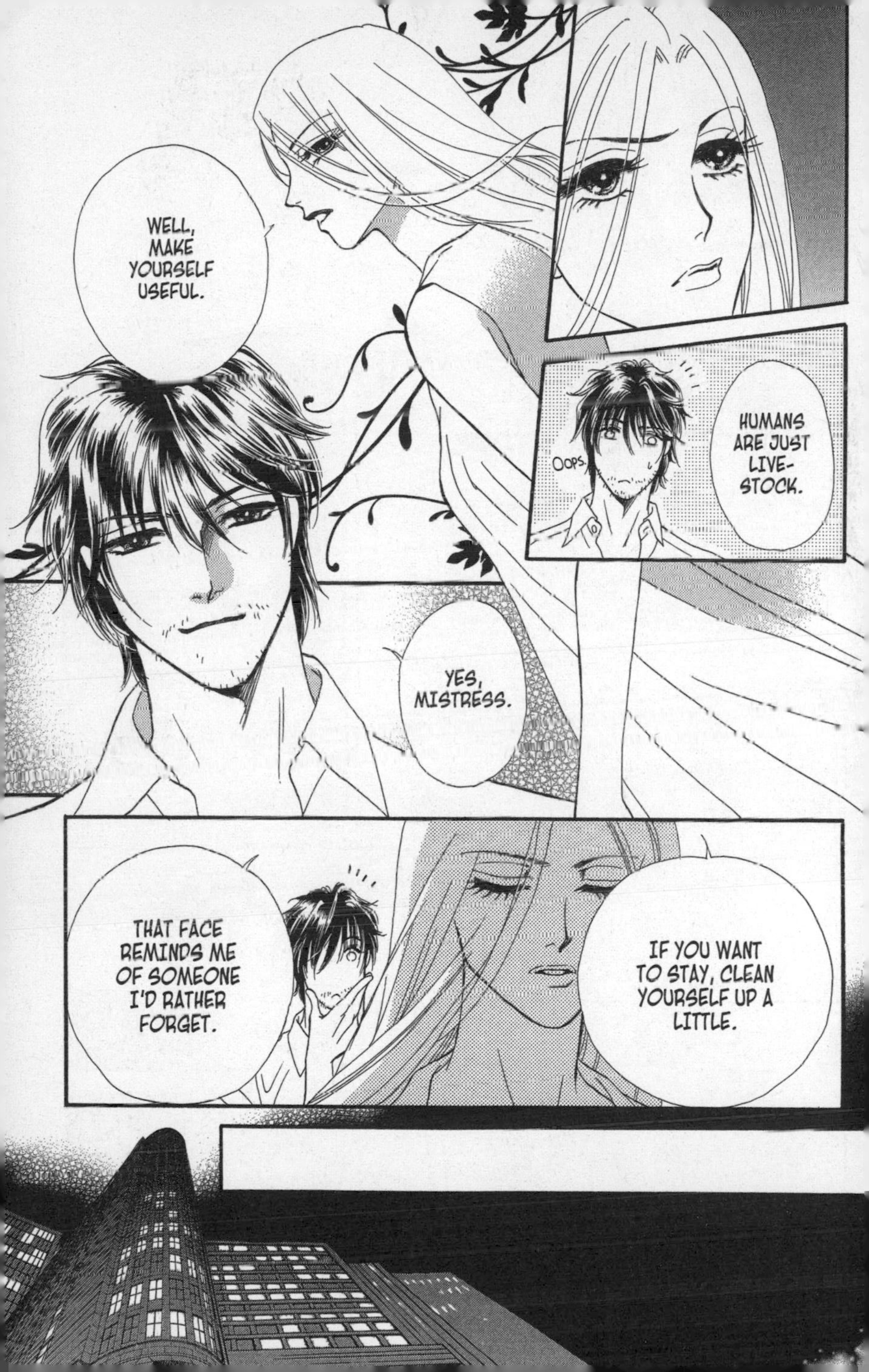
HUMANS ARE JUST LIVE-STOCK.
OOPS.
WELL, MAKE YOURSELF USEFUL.
YES, MISTRESS.
IF YOU WANT TO STAY, CLEAN YOURSELF UP A LITTLE.
THAT FACE REMINDS ME OF SOMEONE I'D RATHER FORGET.

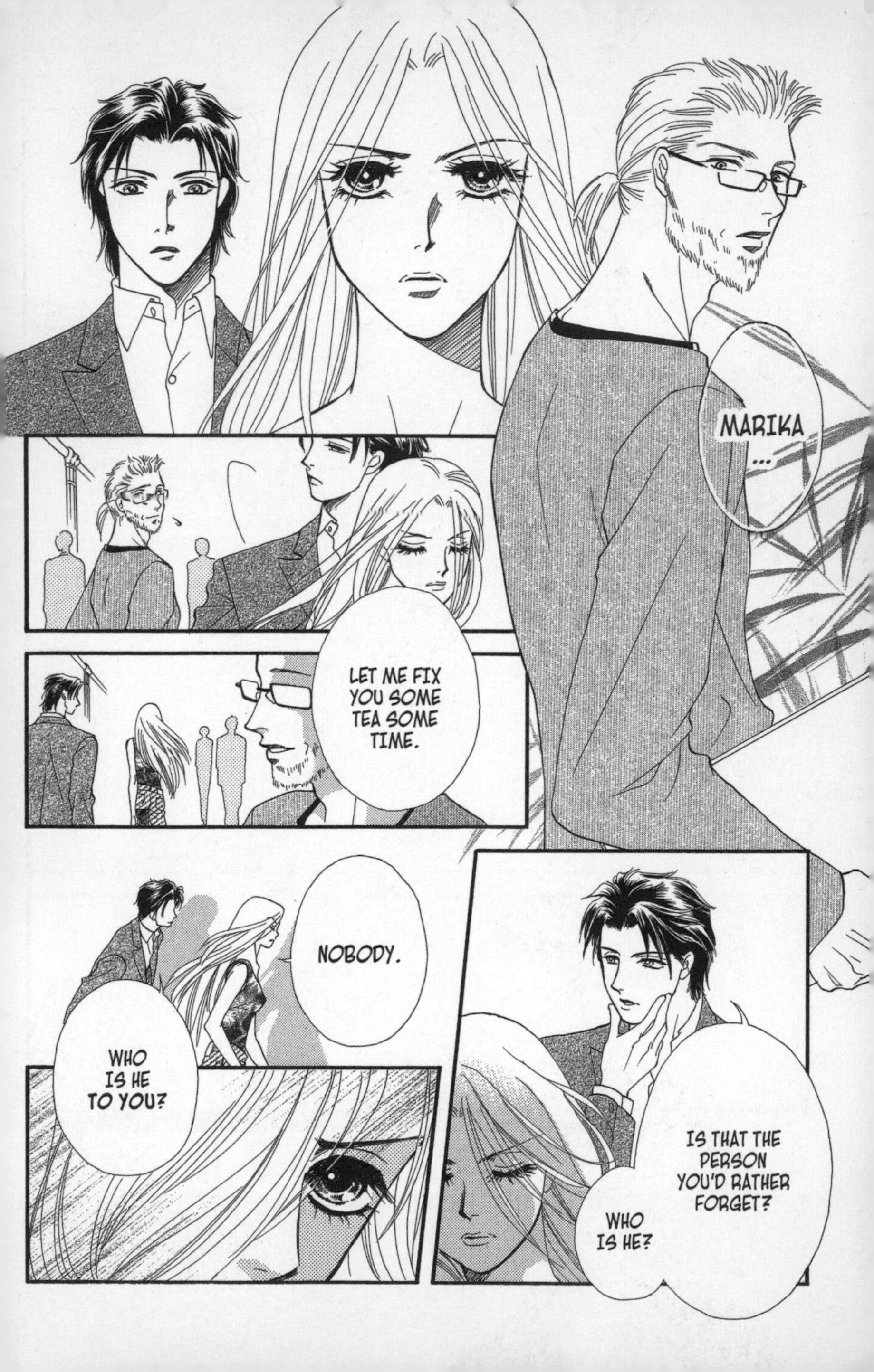
MARIKA ...
LET ME FIX YOU SOME TEA SOME TIME.
IS THAT THE PERSON YOU'D RATHER FORGET?
WHO IS HE?
NOBODY.
WHO IS HE TO YOU?

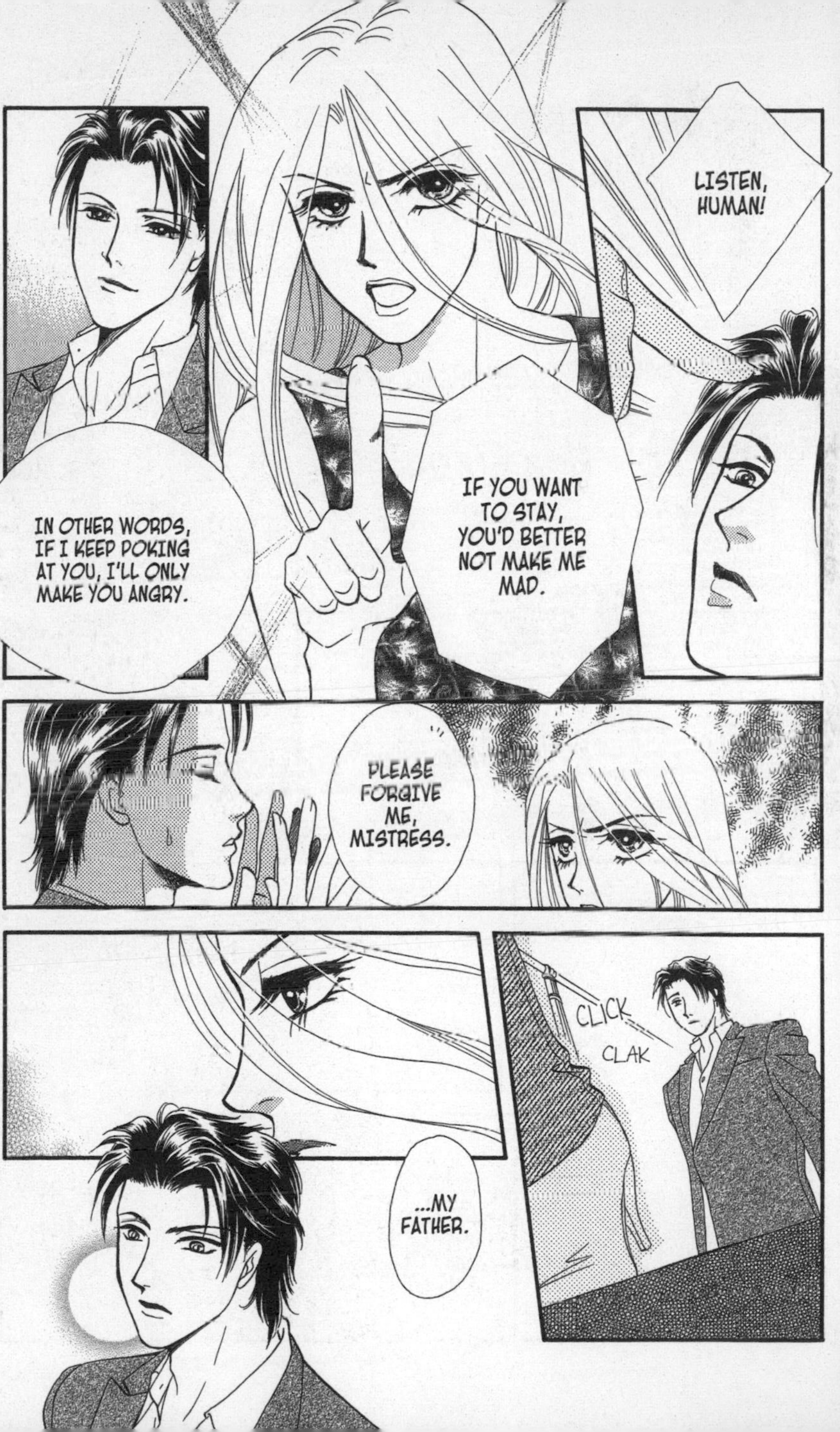
LISTEN, HUMAN!
IF YOU WANT TO STAY, YOU'D BETTER NOT MAKE ME MAD.
IN OTHER WORDS, IF I KEEP POKING AT YOU, I'LL ONLY MAKE YOU ANGRY.
PLEASE FORGIVE ME, MISTRESS.
CLICK
CLAK
...MY FATHER.

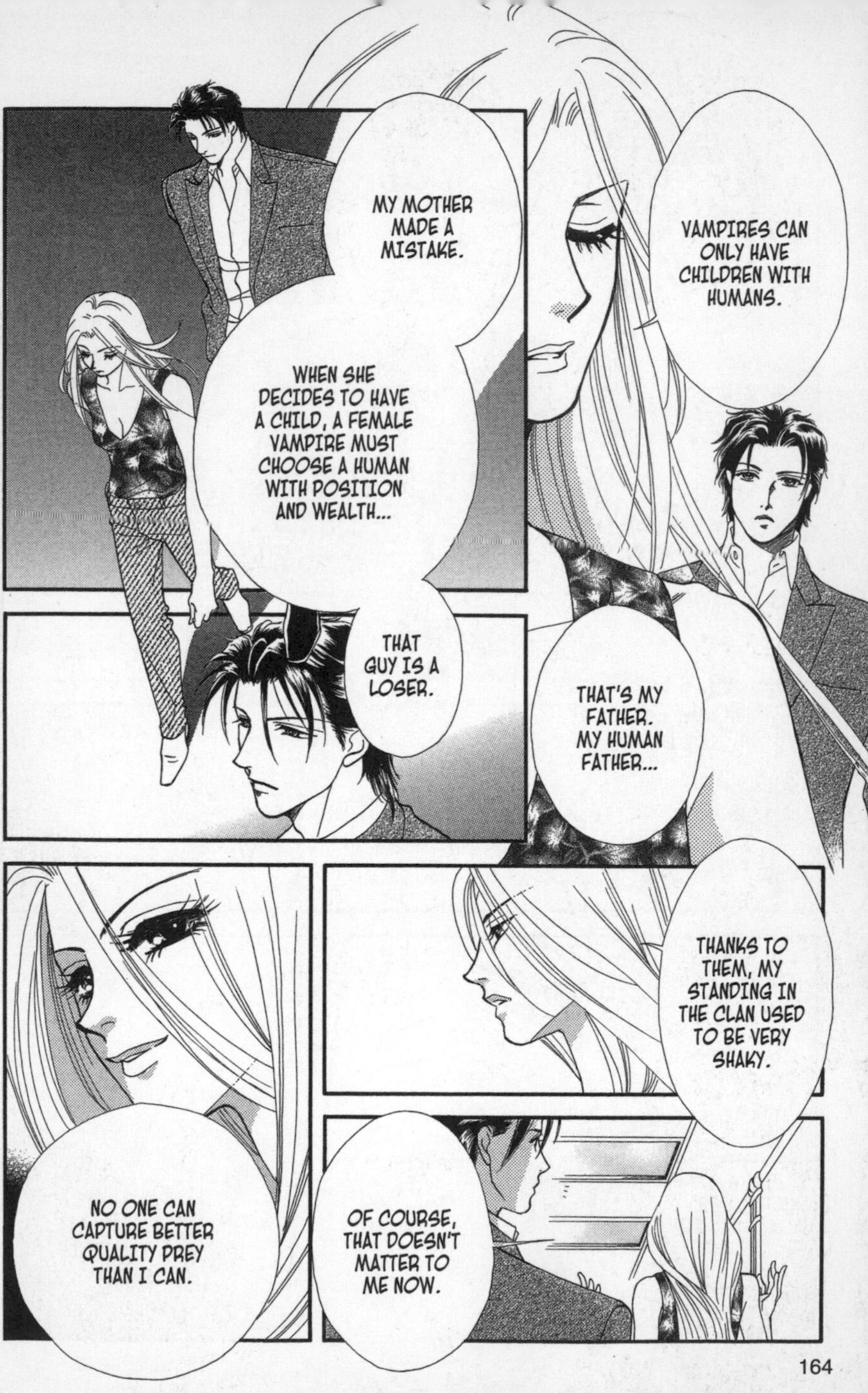
VAMPIRES CAN ONLY HAVE CHILDREN WITH HUMANS.
MY MOTHER MADE A MISTAKE.
WHEN SHE DECIDES TO HAVE A CHILD, A FEMALE VAMPIRE MUST CHOOSE A HUMAN WITH POSITION AND WEALTH...
THAT GUY IS A LOSER.
THAT'S MY FATHER. MY HUMAN FATHER...
THANKS TO THEM, MY STANDING IN THE CLAN USED TO BE VERY SHAKY.
OF COURSE, THAT DOESN'T MATTER TO ME NOW.
NO ONE CAN CAPTURE BETTER QUALITY PREY THAN I CAN.

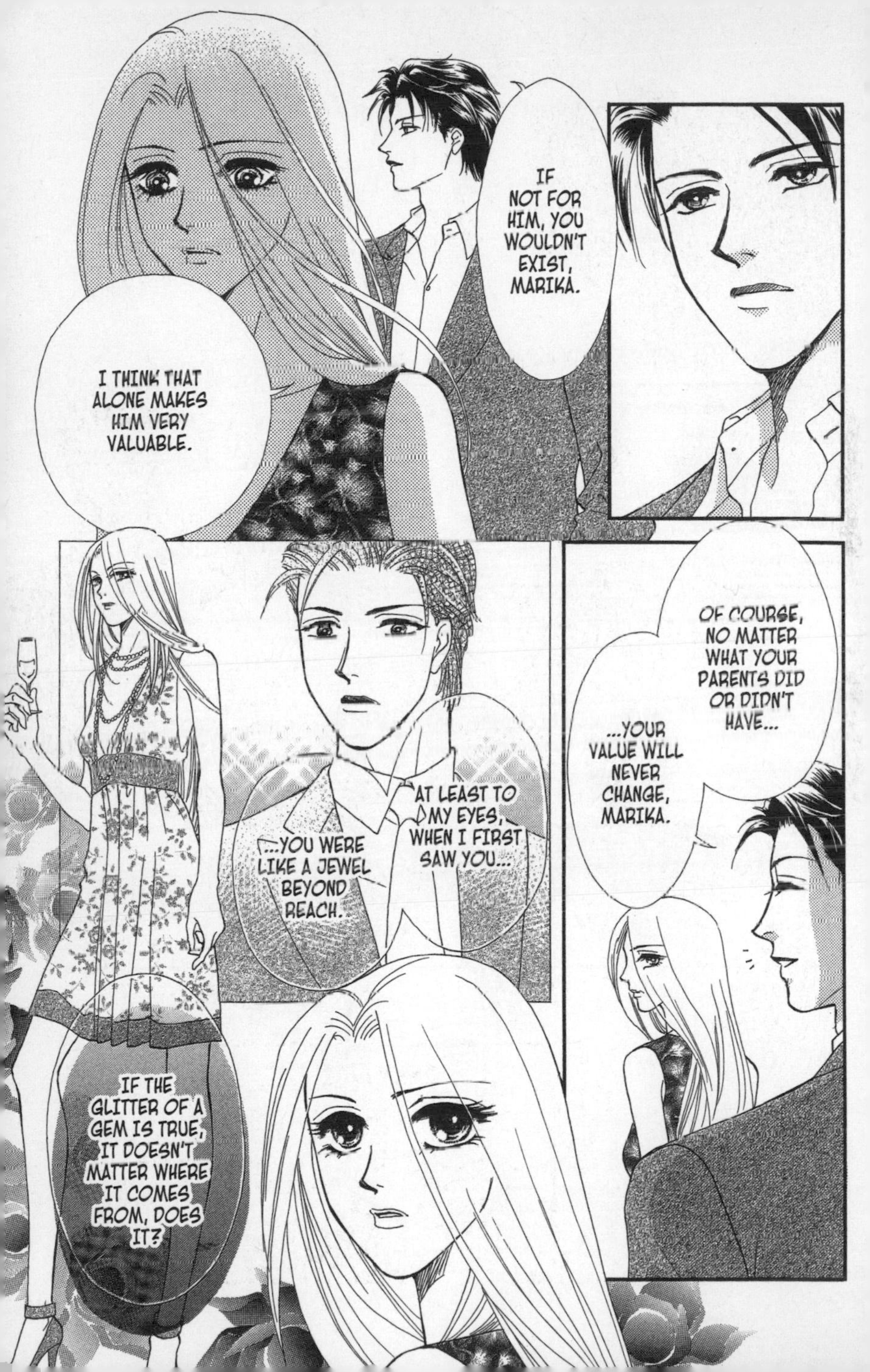
IF NOT FOR HIM, YOU WOULDN'T EXIST, MARIKA.
I THINK THAT ALONE MAKES HIM VERY VALUABLE.
OF COURSE, NO MATTER WHAT YOUR PARENTS DID OR DIDN'T HAVE...
...YOUR VALUE WILL NEVER CHANGE, MARIKA.
AT LEAST TO MY EYES, WHEN I FIRST SAW YOU...
...YOU WERE LIKE A JEWEL BEYOND REACH.
IF THE GLITTER OF A GEM IS TRUE, IT DOESN'T MATTER WHERE IT COMES FROM, DOES IT?

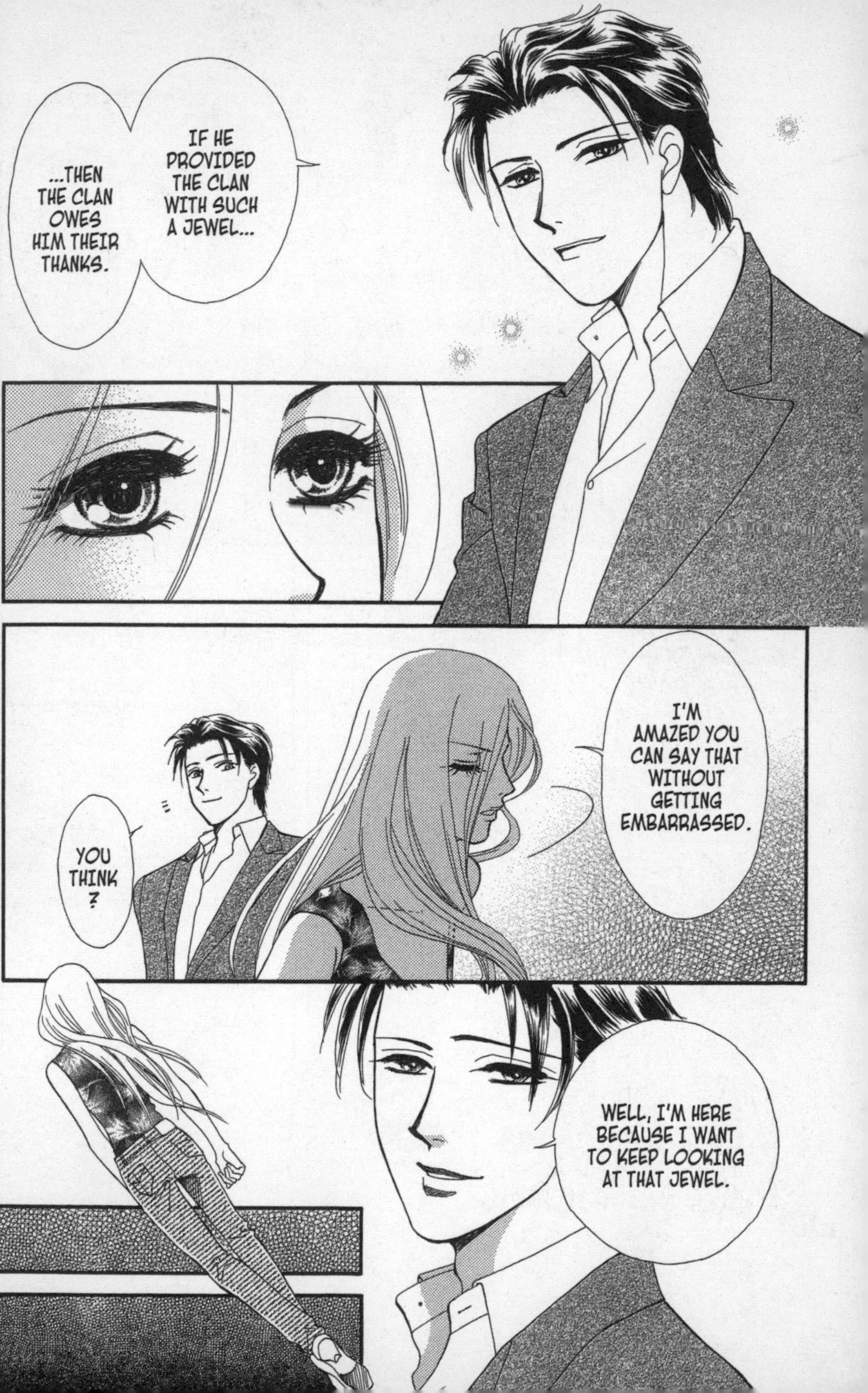
IF HE PROVIDED THE CLAN WITH SUCH A JEWEL...
...THEN THE CLAN OWES HIM THEIR THANKS.
I'M AMAZED YOU CAN SAY THAT WITHOUT GETTING EMBARRASSED.
YOU THINK?
WELL, I'M HERE BECAUSE I WANT TO KEEP LOOKING AT THAT JEWEL.

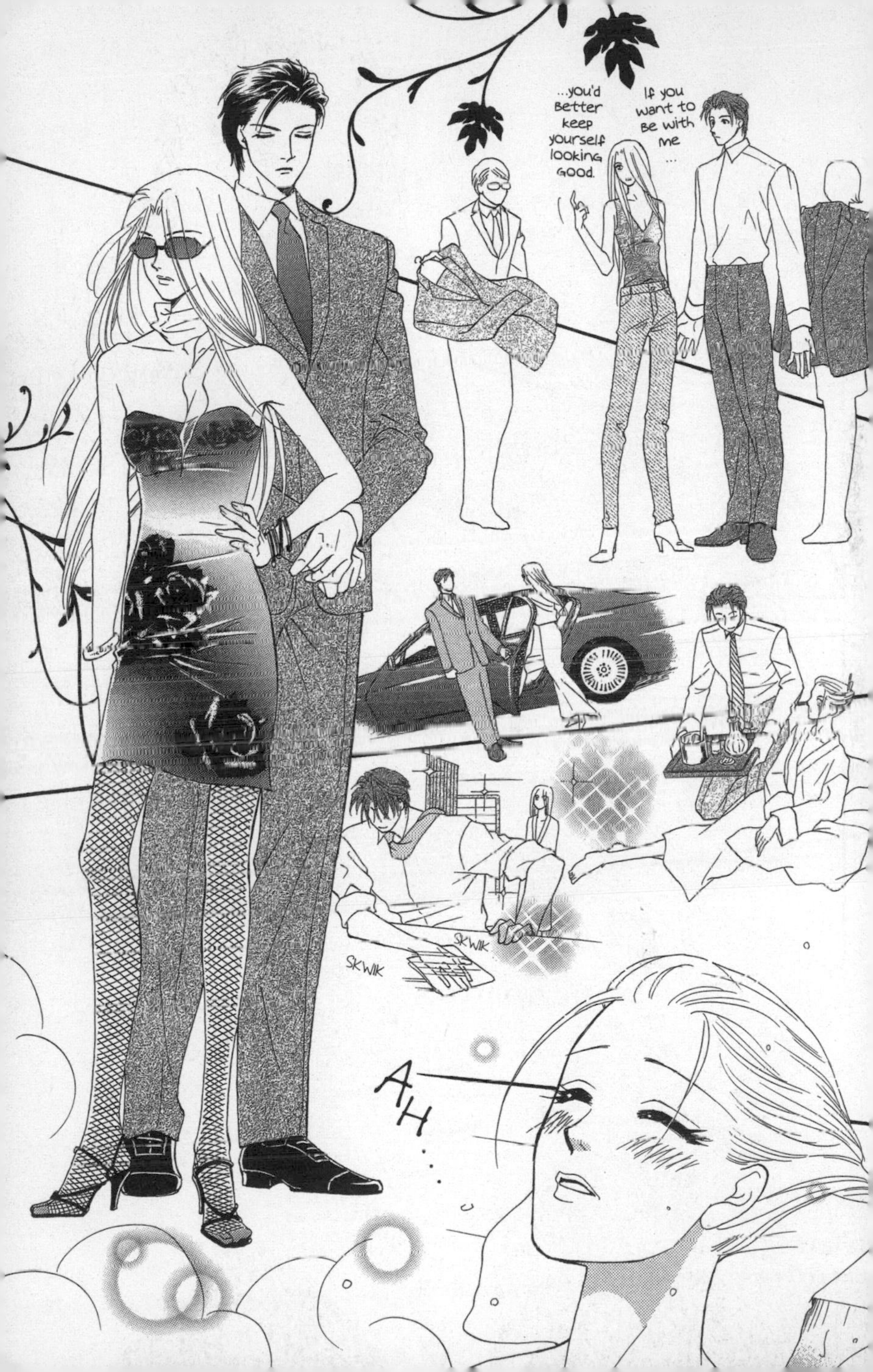
If you want to be with me ...
...you'd better keep yourself looking good.
SKWIK
SKWIK
AH...

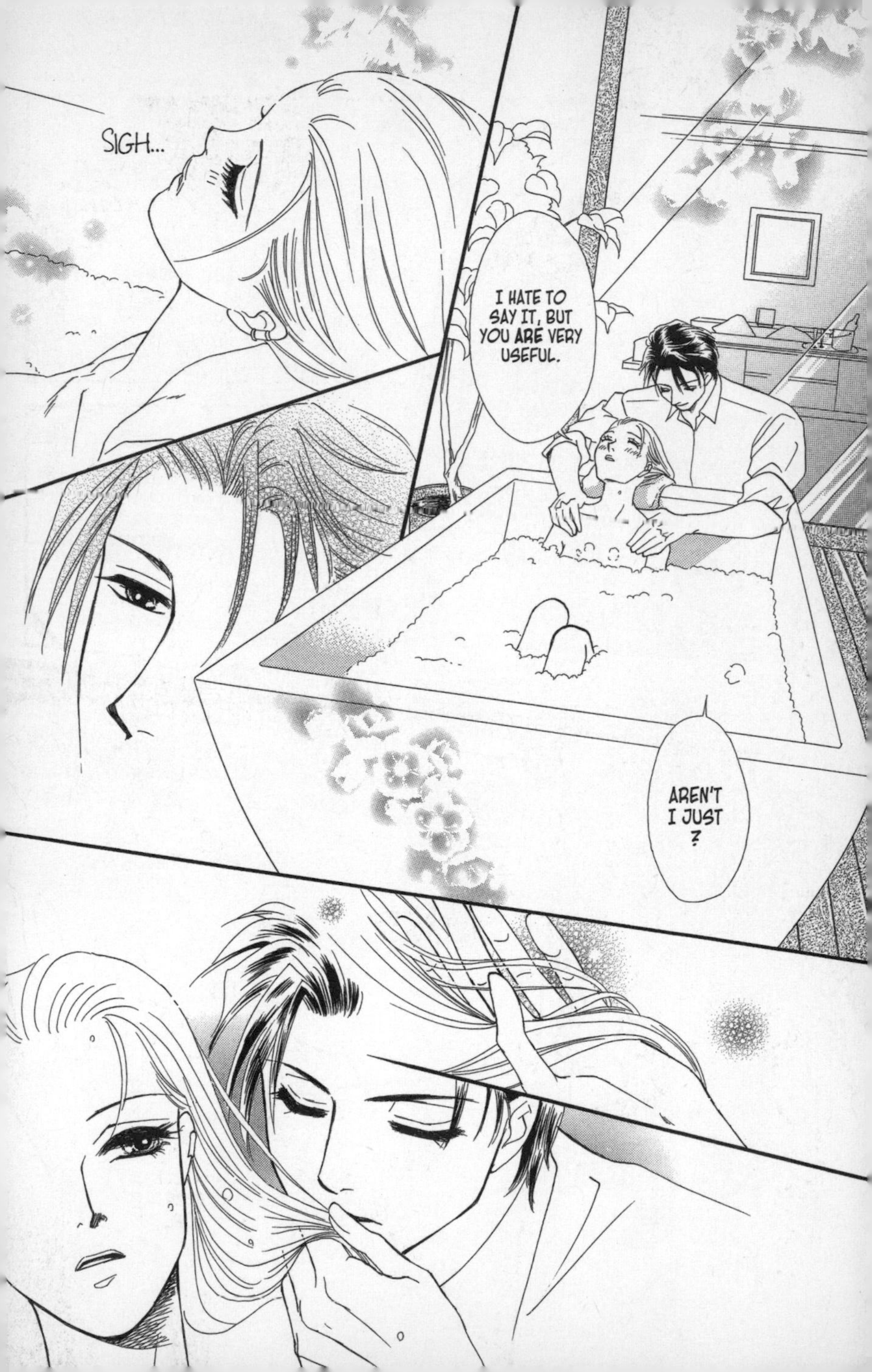
SIGH...
I HATE TO SAY IT, BUT YOU ARE VERY USEFUL.
AREN'T I JUST ?

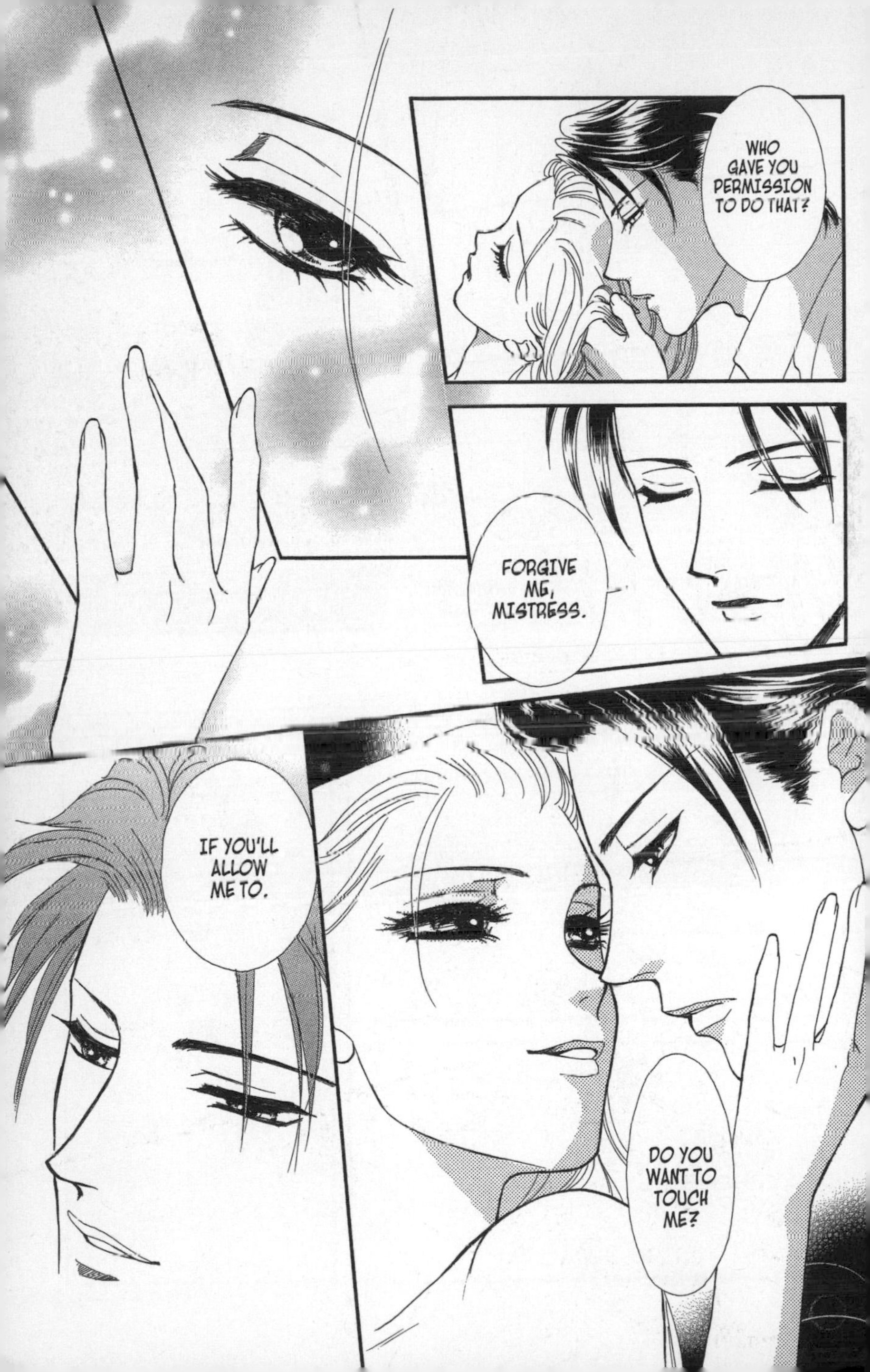
WHO GAVE YOU PERMISSION TO DO THAT?
FORGIVE ME, MISTRESS.
DO YOU WANT TO TOUCH ME?
IF YOU'LL ALLOW ME TO.

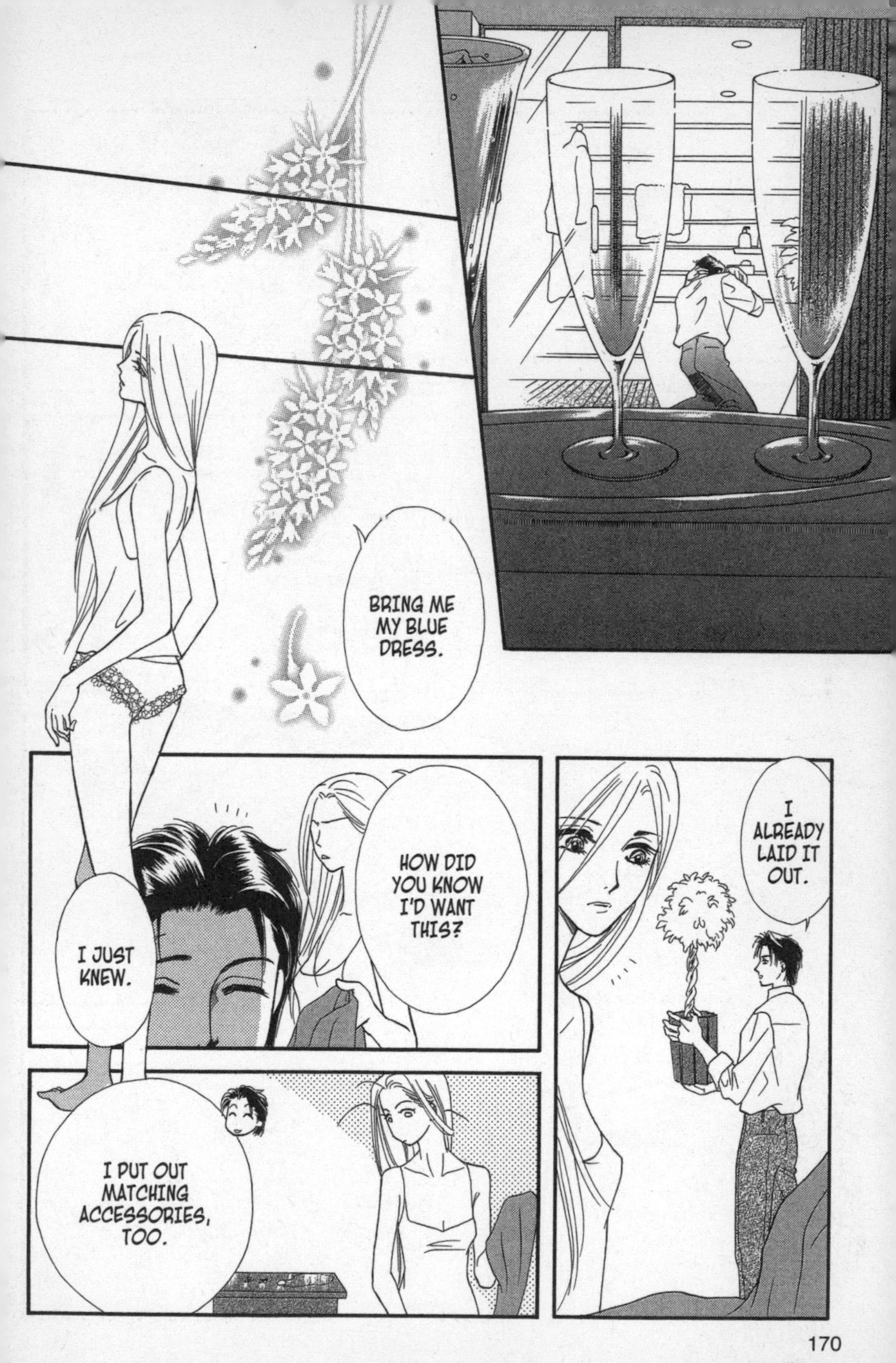
BRING ME MY BLUE DRESS.
I ALREADY LAID IT OUT.
HOW DID YOU KNOW I'D WANT THIS?
I JUST KNEW.
I PUT OUT MATCHING ACCESSORIES, TOO.

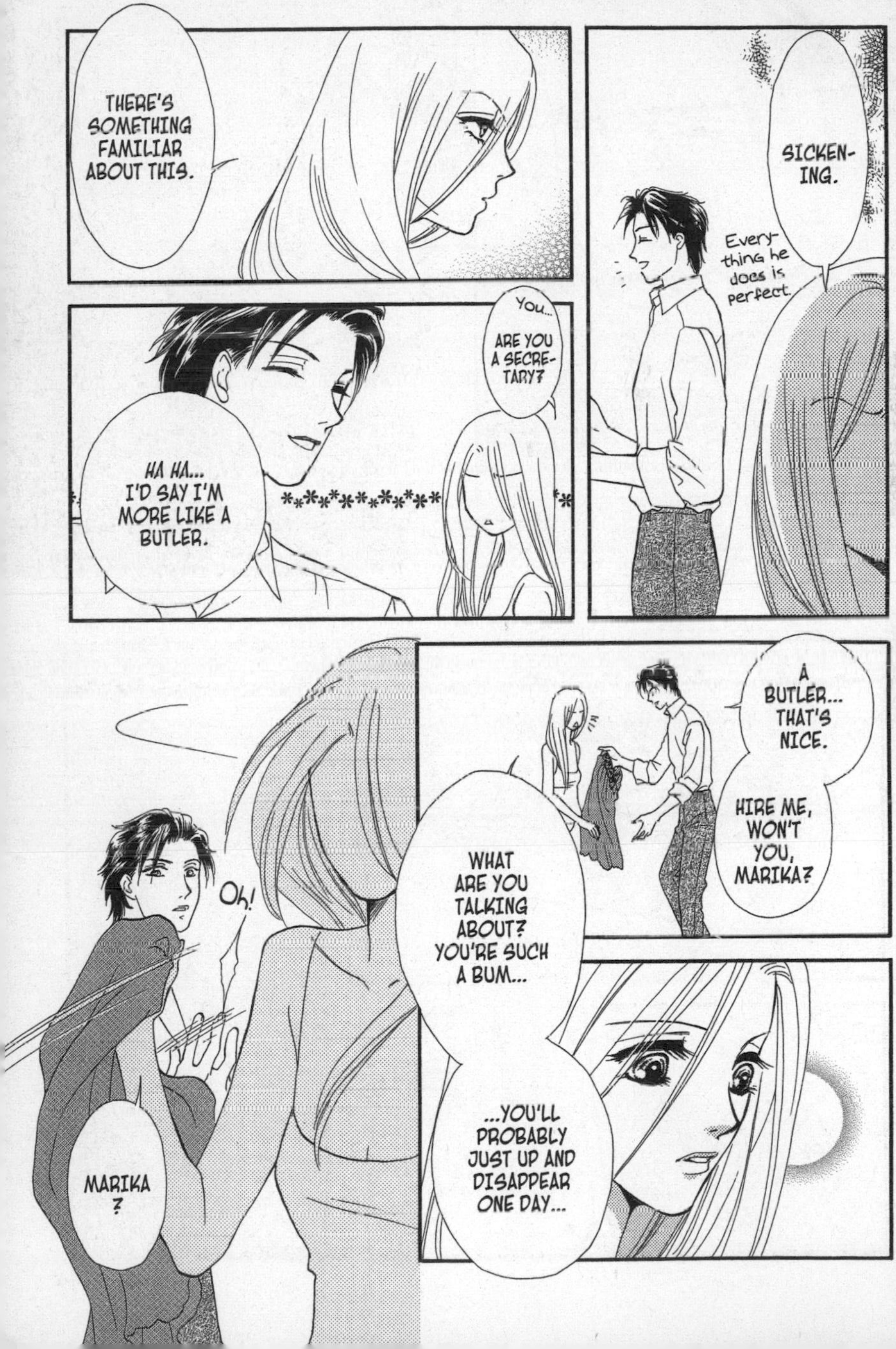
SICKEN-ING.
Every-thing he does is perfect.
THERE'S SOMETHING FAMILIAR ABOUT THIS.
You...
ARE YOU A SECRE-TARY?
HA HA... I'D SAY I'M MORE LIKE A BUTLER.
A BUTLER... THAT'S NICE.
HIRE ME, WON'T YOU, MARIKA?
WHAT ARE YOU TALKING ABOUT? YOU'RE SUCH A BUM...
...YOU'LL PROBABLY JUST UP AND DISAPPEAR ONE DAY...
Oh!
MARIKA?

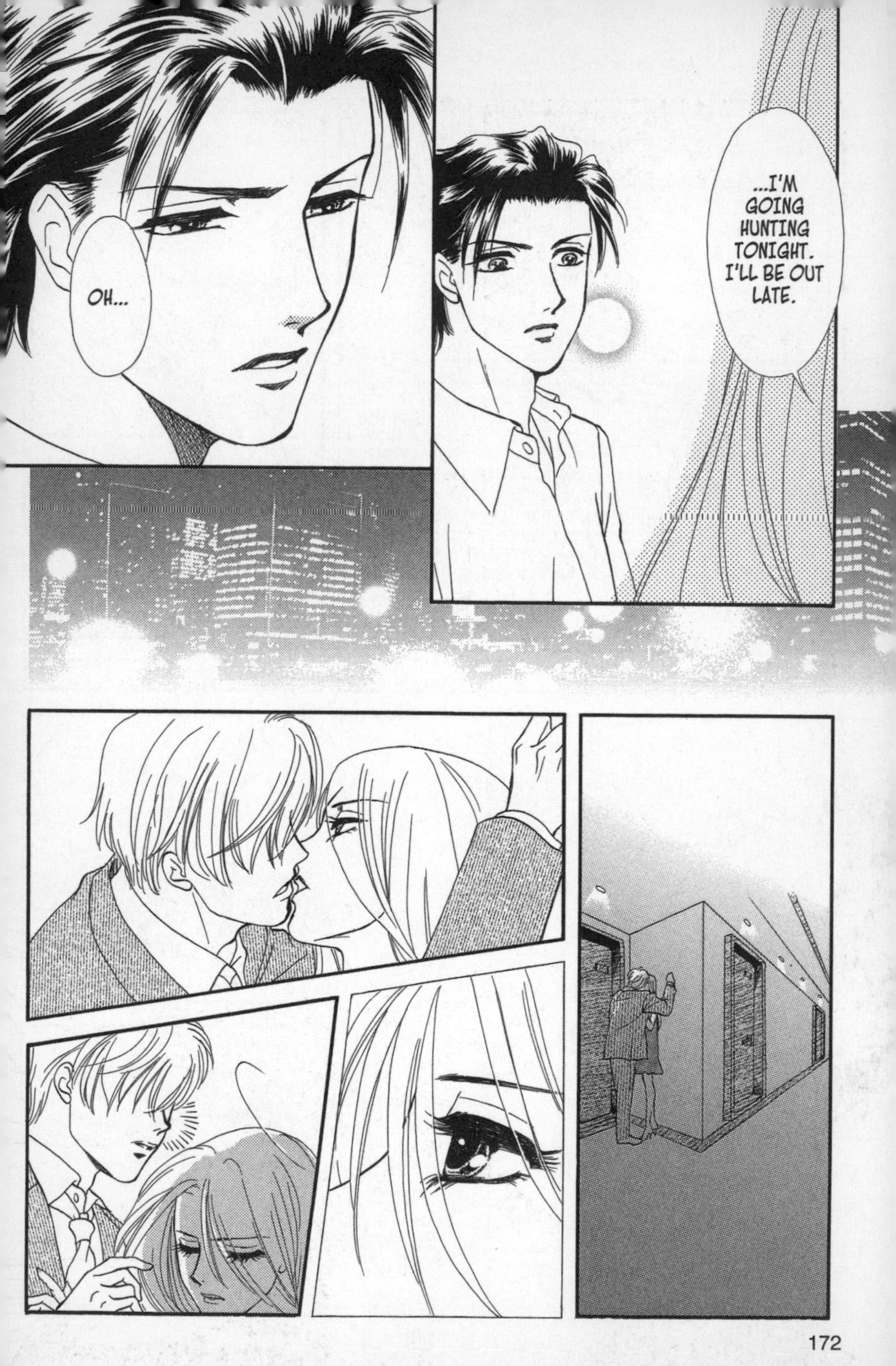
...I'M GOING HUNTING TONIGHT. I'LL BE OUT LATE.
OH...

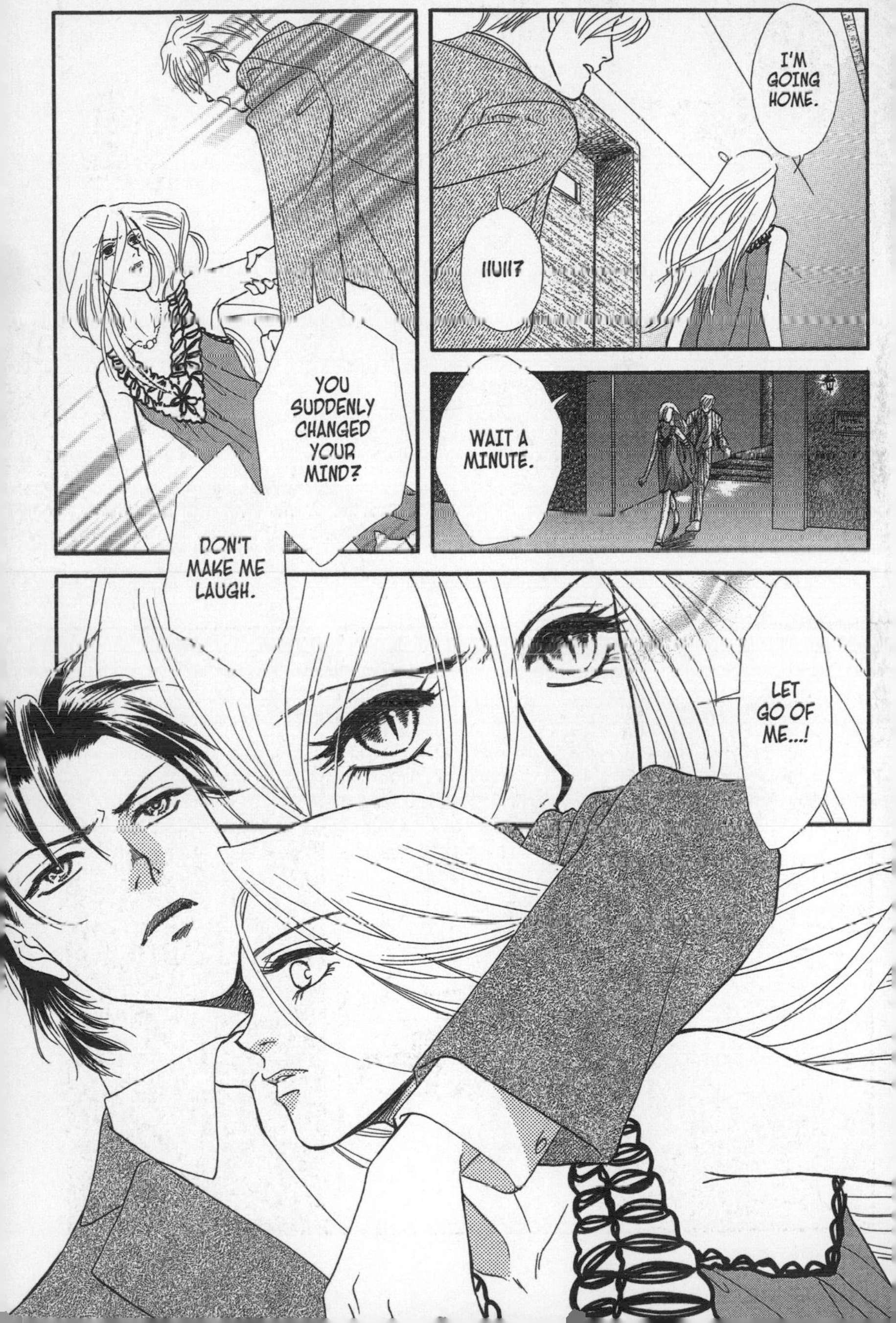
I'M GOING HOME.
HUH?
WAIT A MINUTE.
YOU SUDDENLY CHANGED YOUR MIND?
DON'T MAKE ME LAUGH.
LET GO OF ME...!

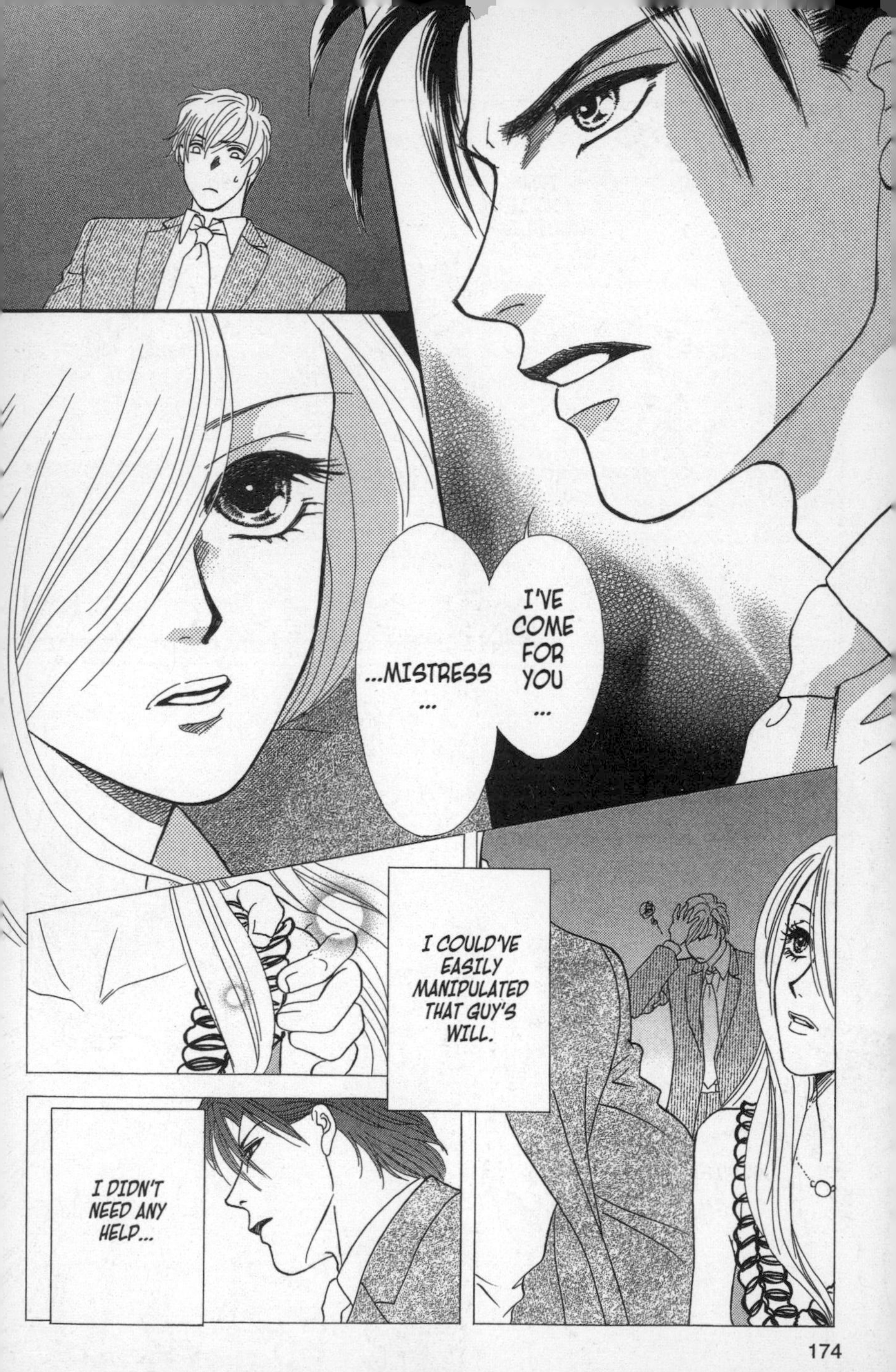
I'VE COME FOR YOU ...
...MISTRESS ...
I COULD'VE EASILY MANIPULATED THAT GUY'S WILL.
I DIDN'T NEED ANY HELP...

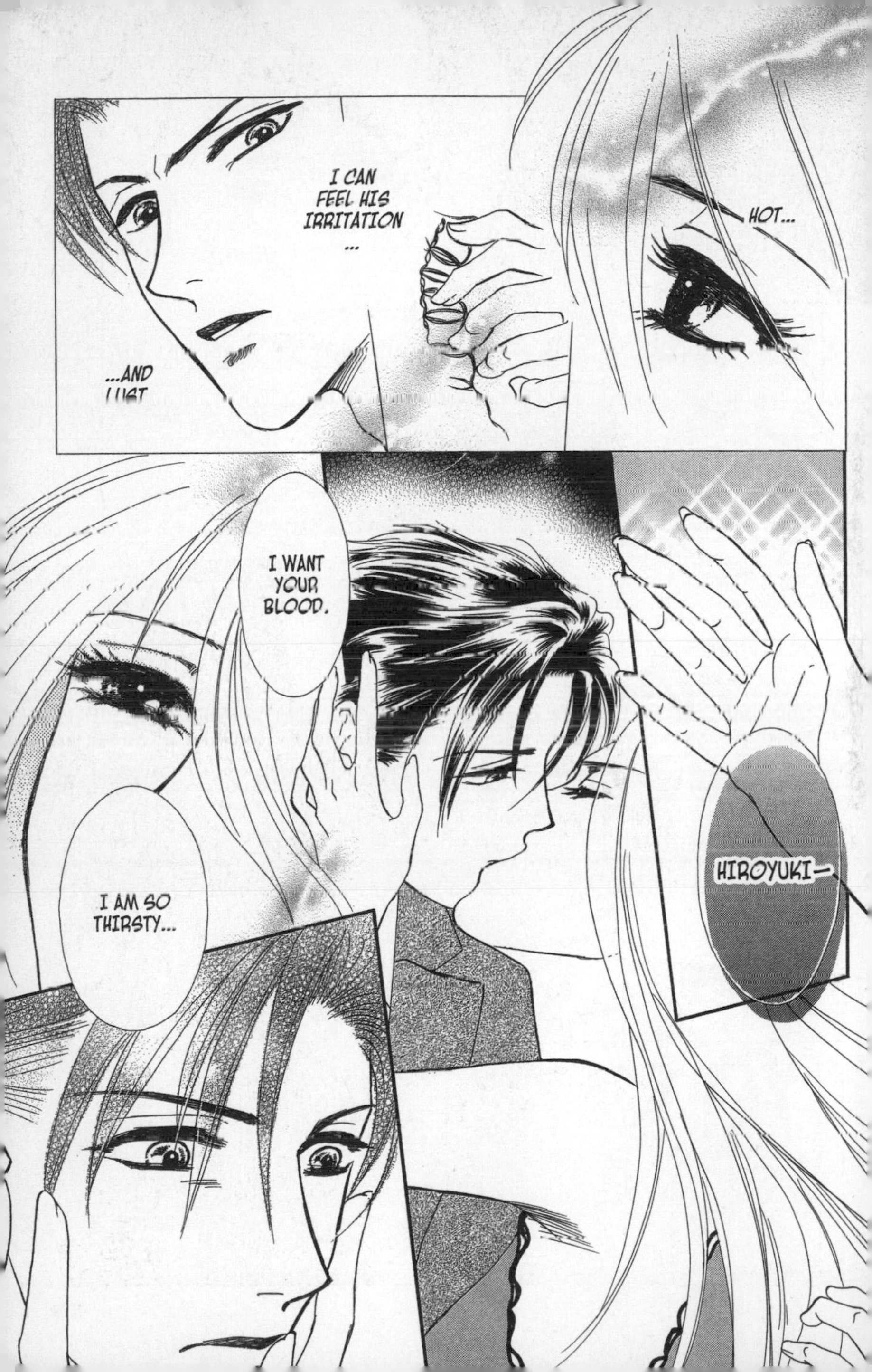
HOT...
I CAN FEEL HIS IRRITATION ...
...AND LUST
HIROYUKI—
I WANT YOUR BLOOD.
I AM SO THIRSTY...

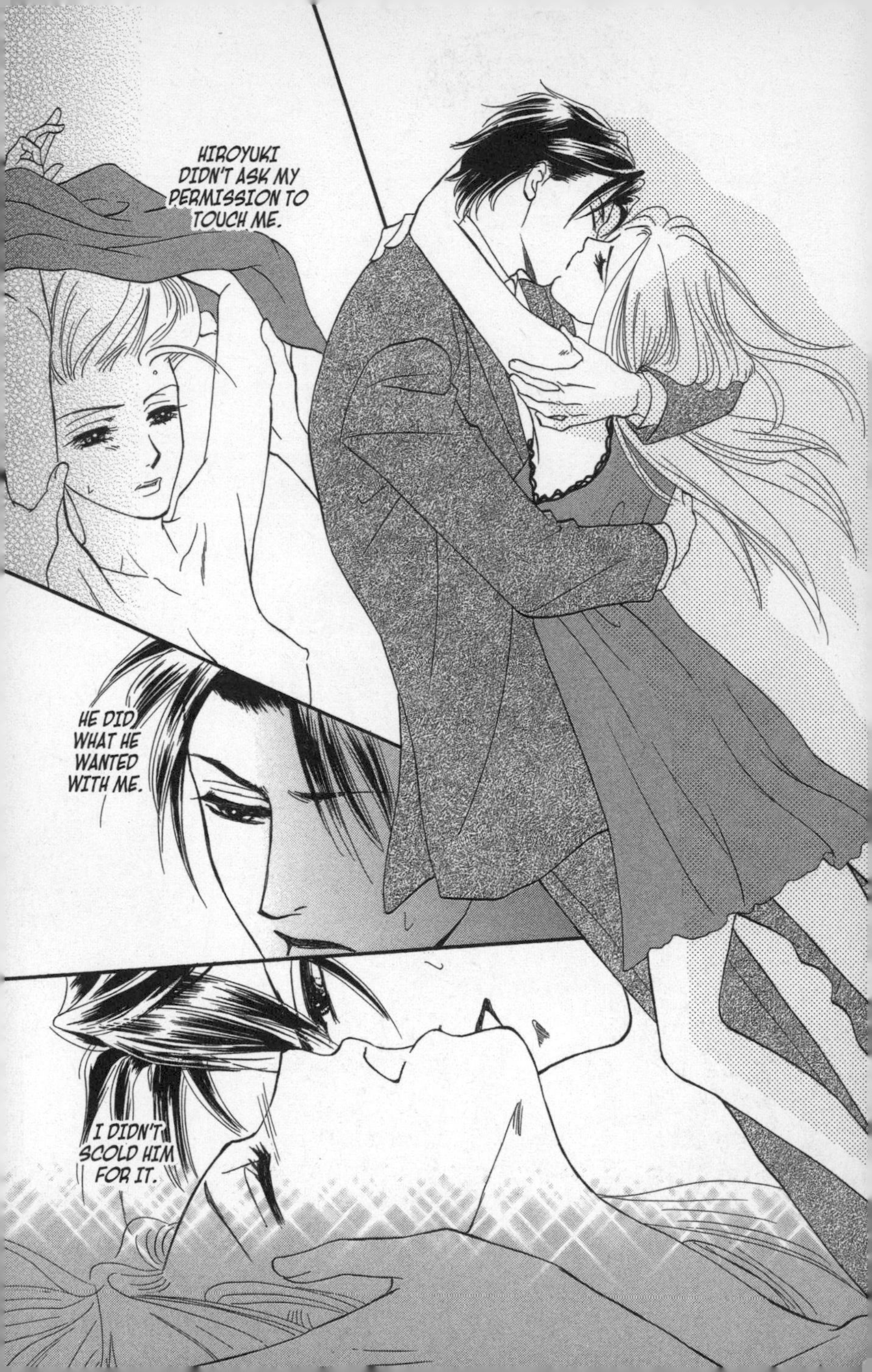
HIROYUKI DIDN'T ASK MY PERMISSION TO TOUCH ME.
HE DID WHAT HE WANTED WITH ME.
I DIDN'T SCOLD HIM FOR IT.

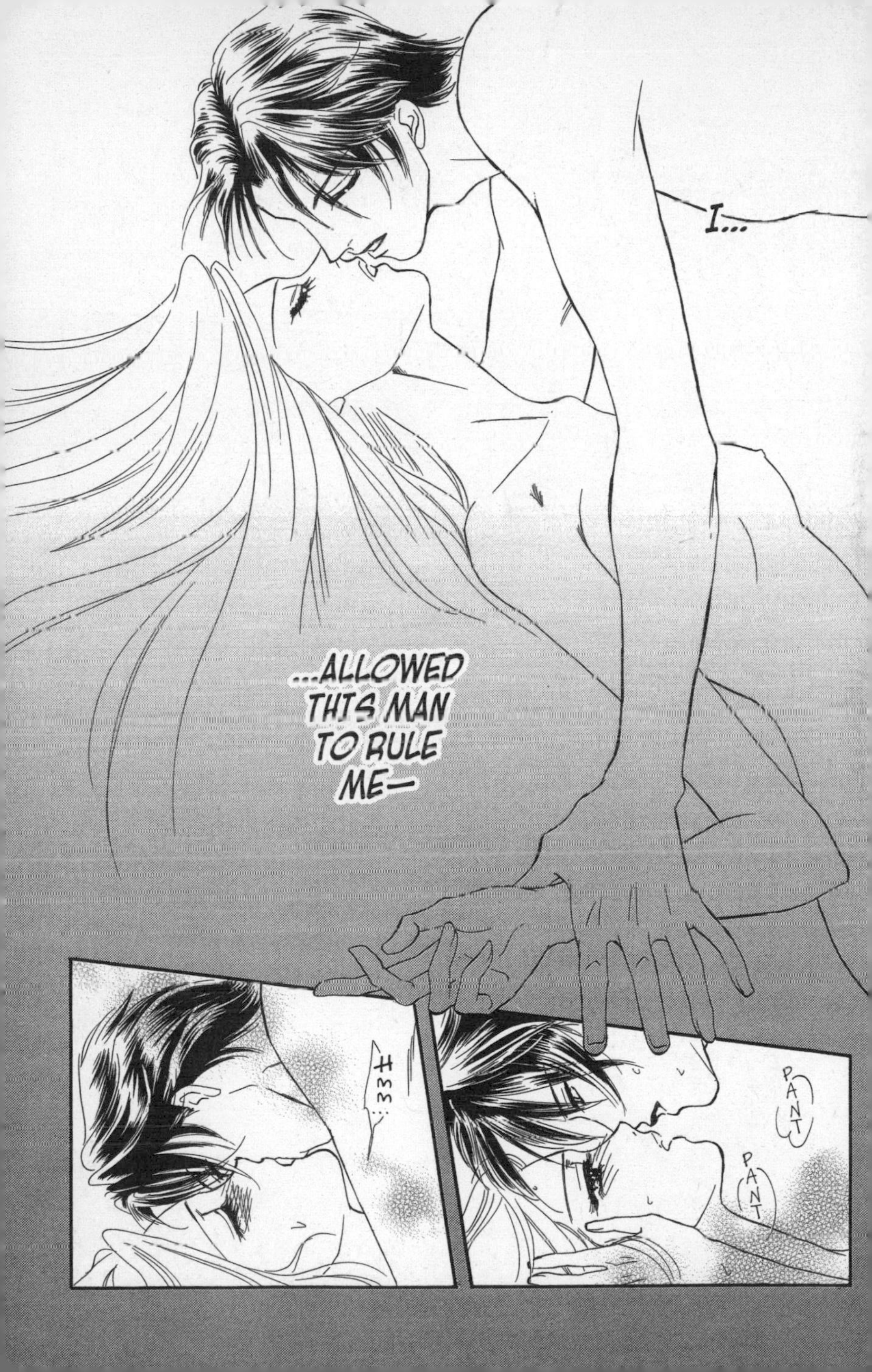
I...
...ALLOWED THIS MAN TO RULE ME—
PANT
PANT
Hmm...

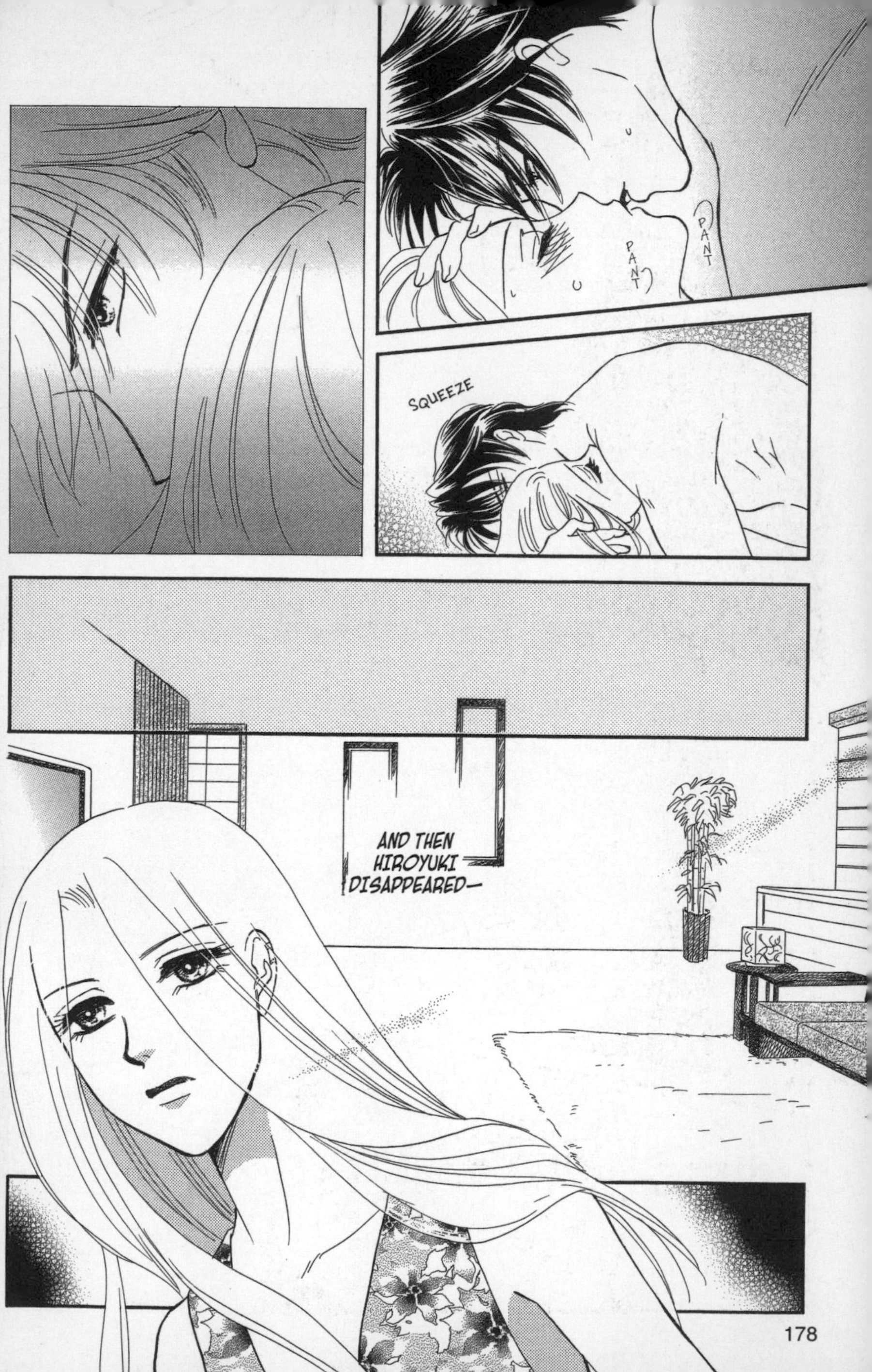
PANT
PANT
SQUEEZE
AND THEN HIROYUKI DISAPPEARED—

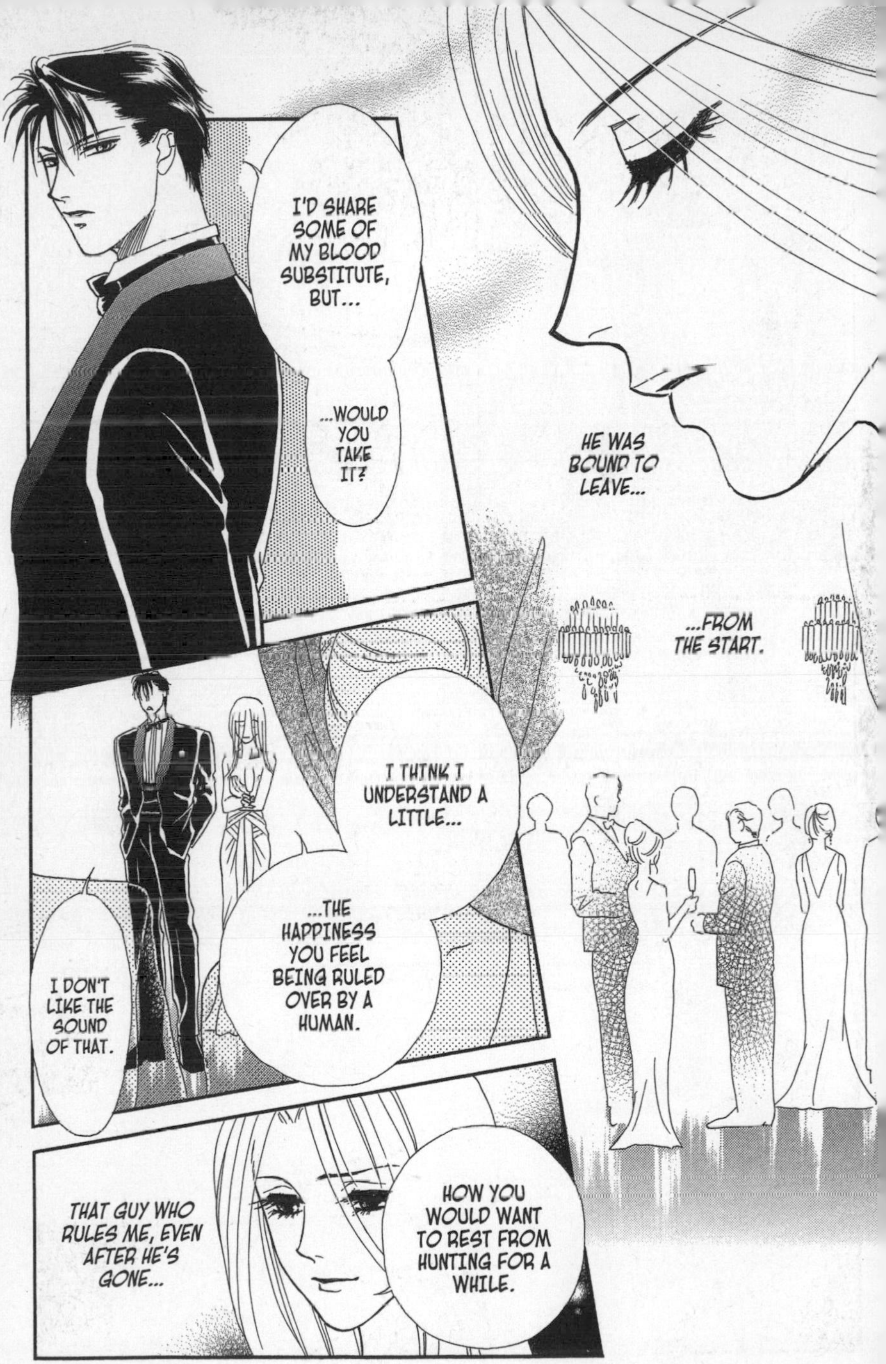
HE WAS BOUND TO LEAVE...
...FROM THE START.
I'D SHARE SOME OF MY BLOOD SUBSTITUTE, BUT...
...WOULD YOU TAKE IT?
I THINK I UNDERSTAND A LITTLE...
...THE HAPPINESS YOU FEEL BEING RULED OVER BY A HUMAN.
I DON'T LIKE THE SOUND OF THAT.
HOW YOU WOULD WANT TO REST FROM HUNTING FOR A WHILE.
THAT GUY WHO RULES ME, EVEN AFTER HE'S GONE...

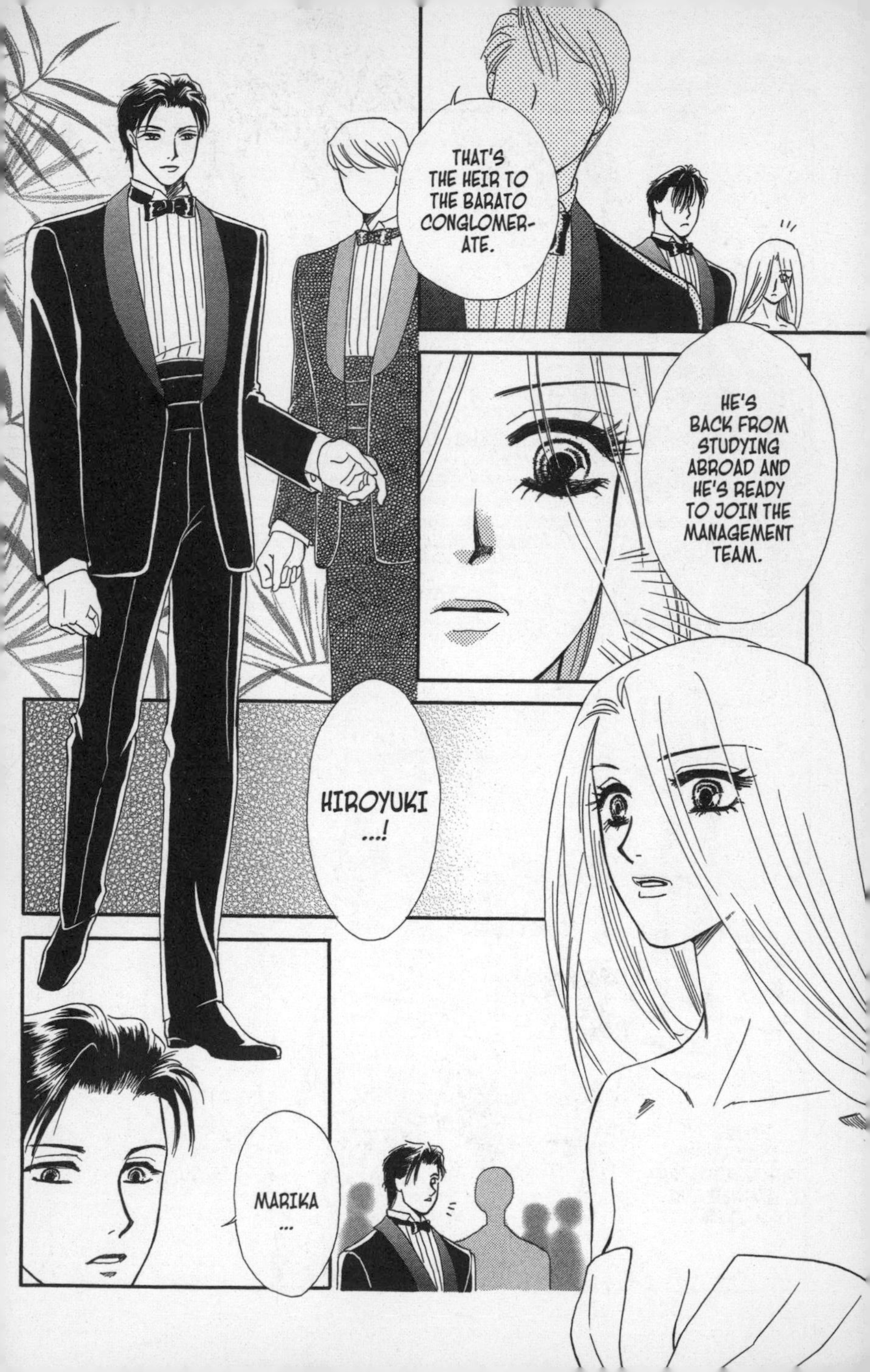
THAT'S THE HEIR TO THE BARATO CONGLOMER-ATE.
HE'S BACK FROM STUDYING ABROAD AND HE'S READY TO JOIN THE MANAGEMENT TEAM.
HIROYUKI ...!
MARIKA ...

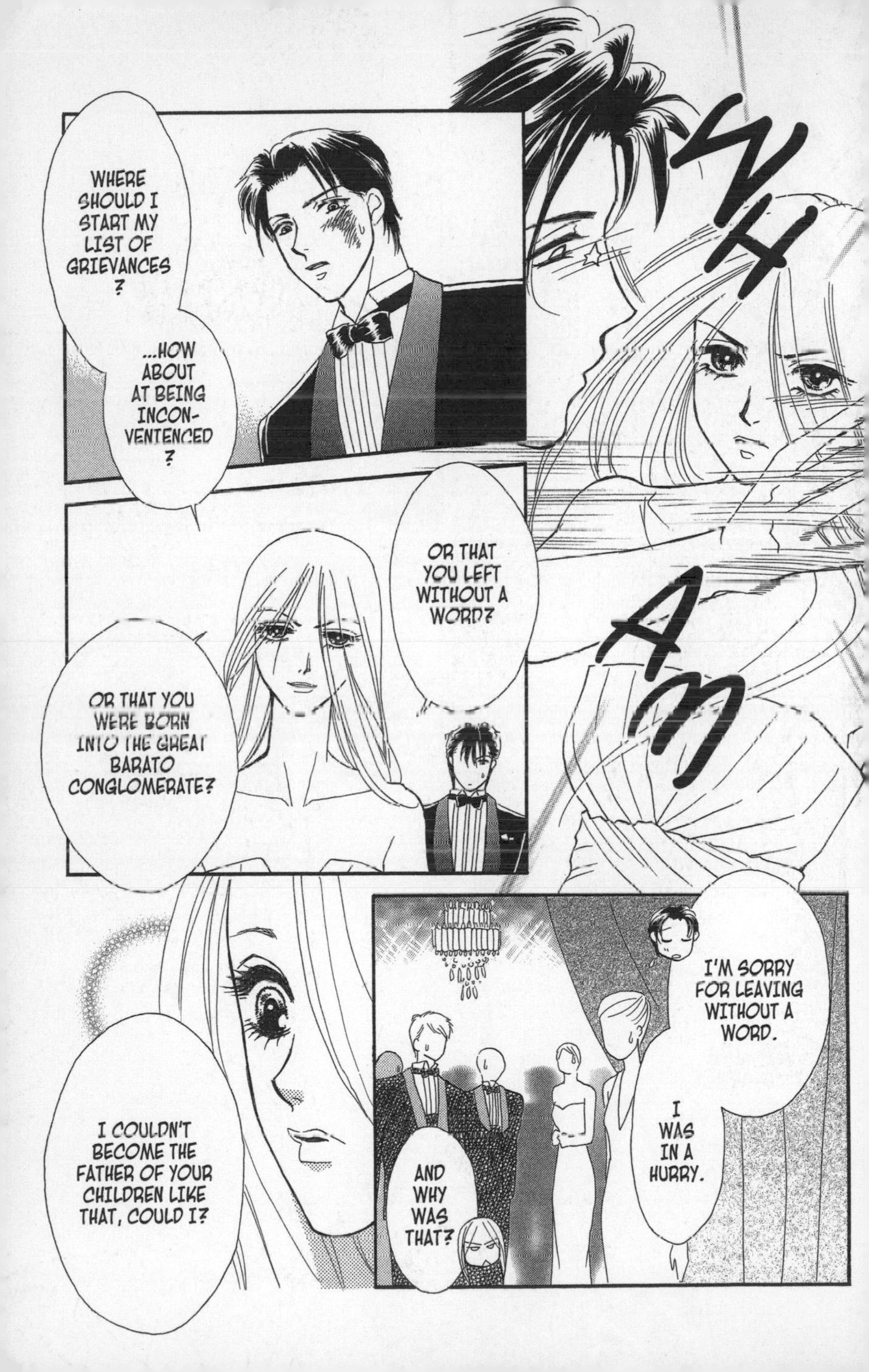
SWHAM
WHERE SHOULD I START MY LIST OF GRIEVANCES?
...HOW ABOUT AT BEING INCON-VENTENCED?
OR THAT YOU LEFT WITHOUT A WORD?
OR THAT YOU WERE BORN INTO THE GREAT BARATO CONGLOMERATE?
I'M SORRY FOR LEAVING WITHOUT A WORD.
I WAS IN A HURRY.
AND WHY WAS THAT?
I COULDN'T BECOME THE FATHER OF YOUR CHILDREN LIKE THAT, COULD I?

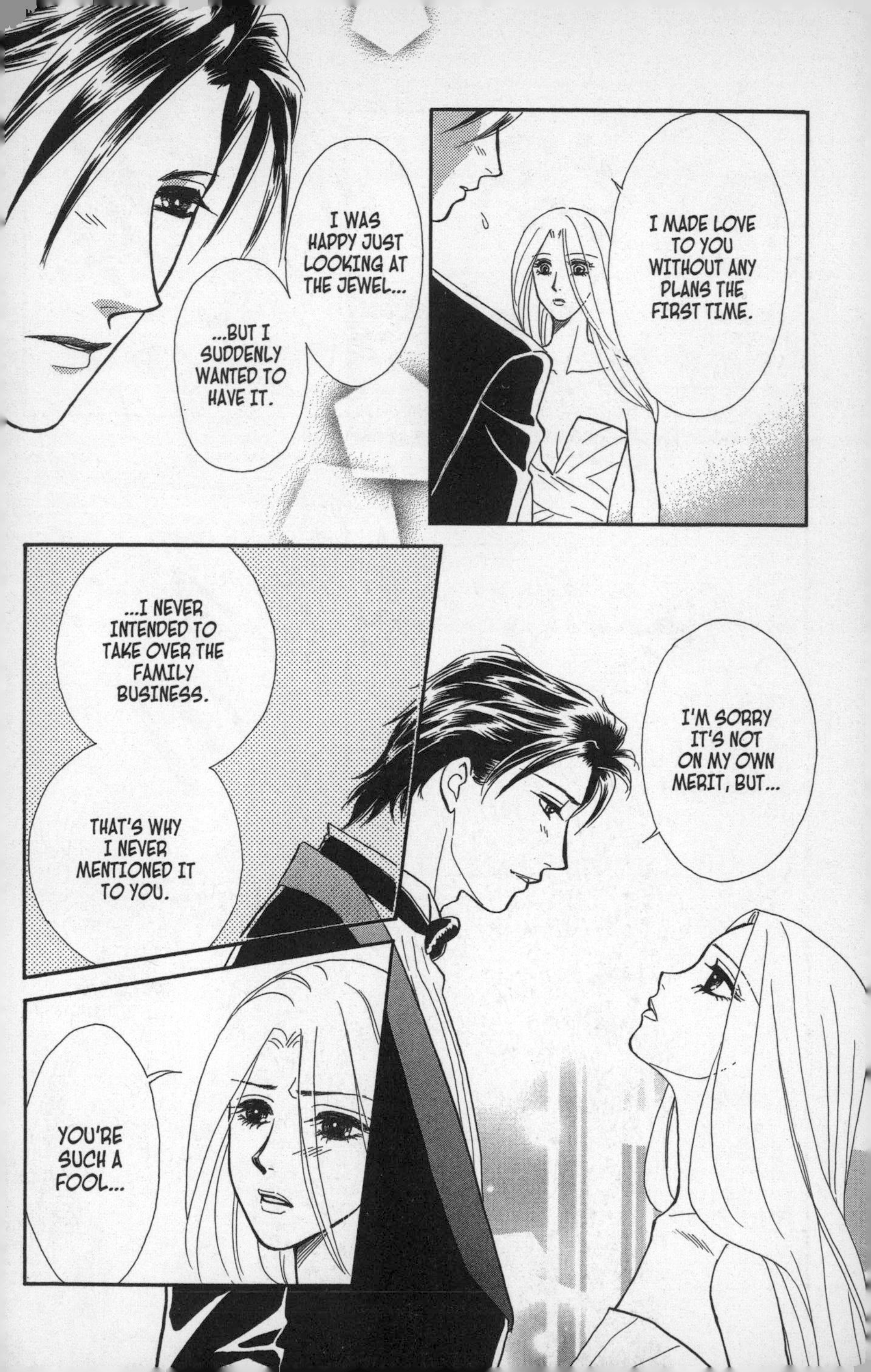
I MADE LOVE TO YOU WITHOUT ANY PLANS THE FIRST TIME.
I WAS HAPPY JUST LOOKING AT THE JEWEL...
...BUT I SUDDENLY WANTED TO HAVE IT.
I'M SORRY IT'S NOT ON MY OWN MERIT, BUT...
...I NEVER INTENDED TO TAKE OVER THE FAMILY BUSINESS.
THAT'S WHY I NEVER MENTIONED IT TO YOU.
YOU'RE SUCH A FOOL...

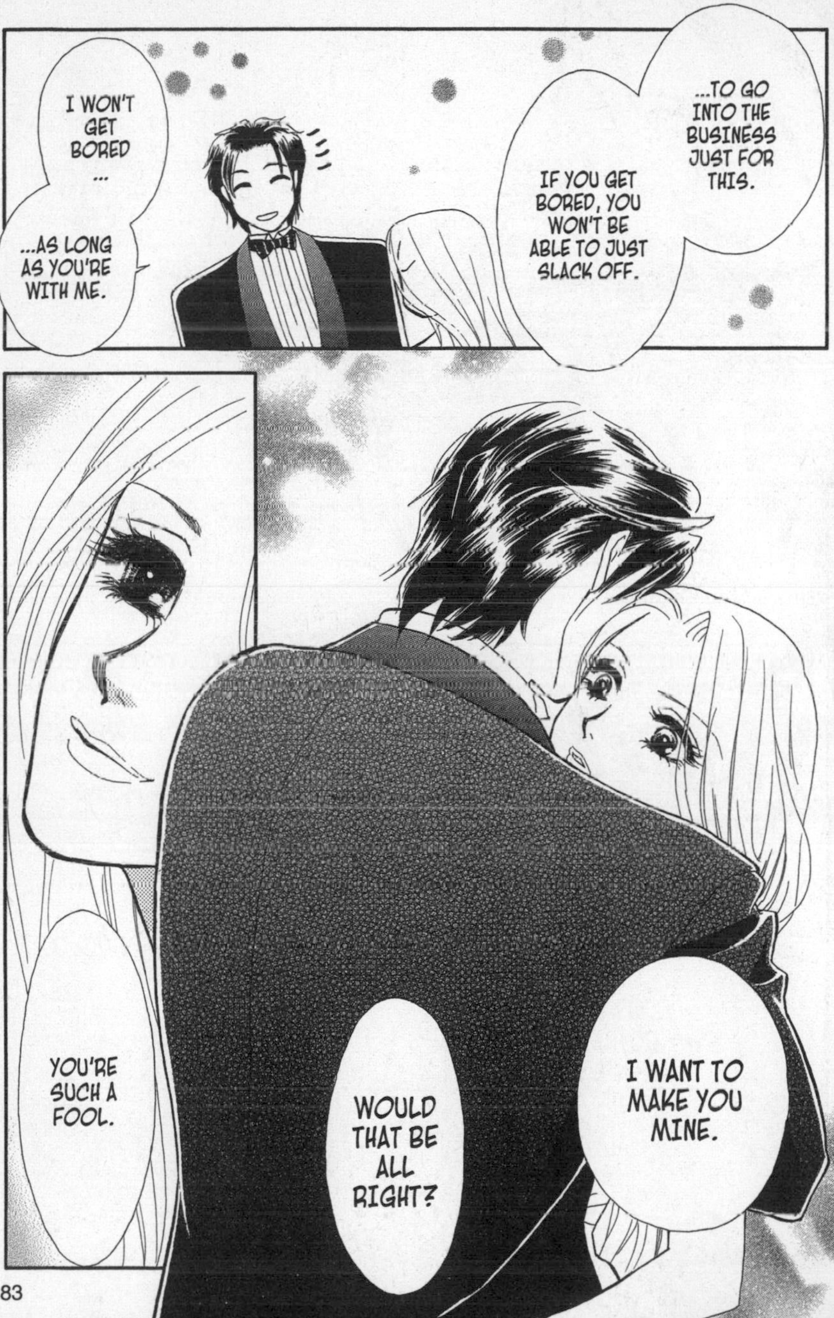
...TO GO INTO THE BUSINESS JUST FOR THIS.
IF YOU GET BORED, YOU WON'T BE ABLE TO JUST SLACK OFF.
I WON'T GET BORED ...
...AS LONG AS YOU'RE WITH ME.
I WANT TO MAKE YOU MINE.
WOULD THAT BE ALL RIGHT?
YOU'RE SUCH A FOOL.

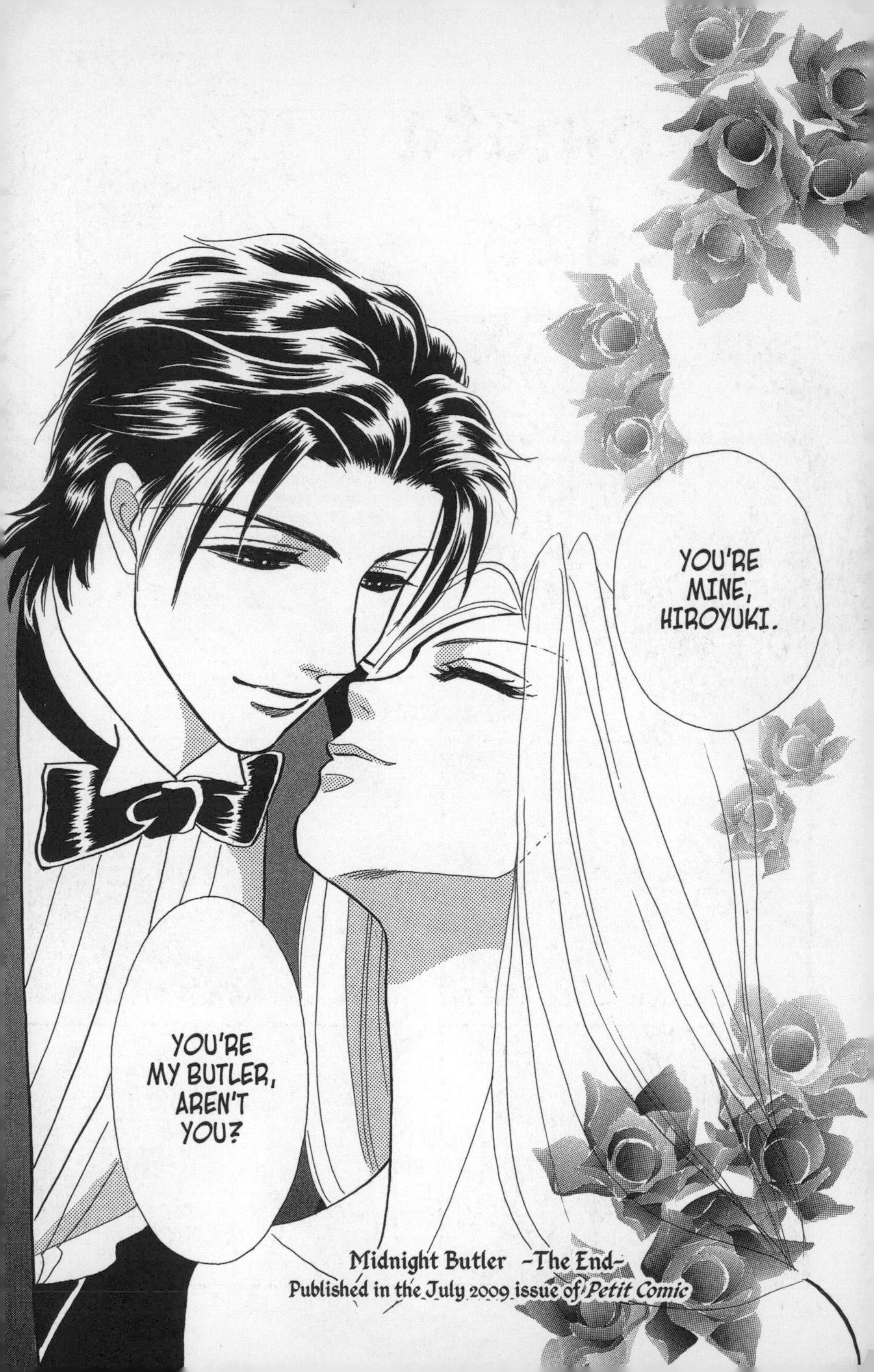
YOU'RE MINE, HIROYUKI.
YOU'RE MY BUTLER, AREN'T YOU?

Midnight Butler -The End-
Published in the July 2009 issue of *Petit Comic*

# Nekomata Today

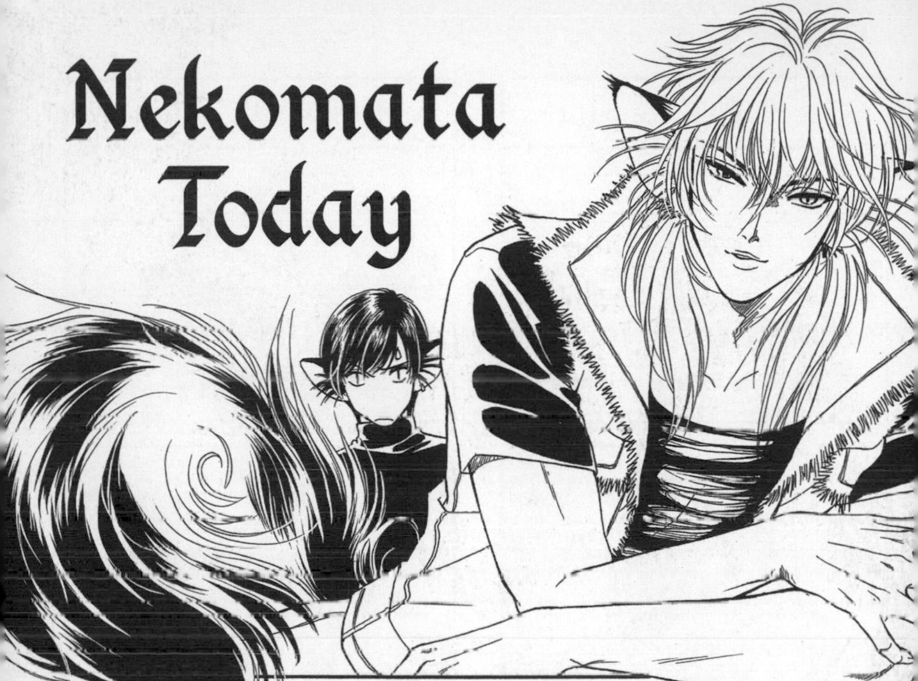

## International

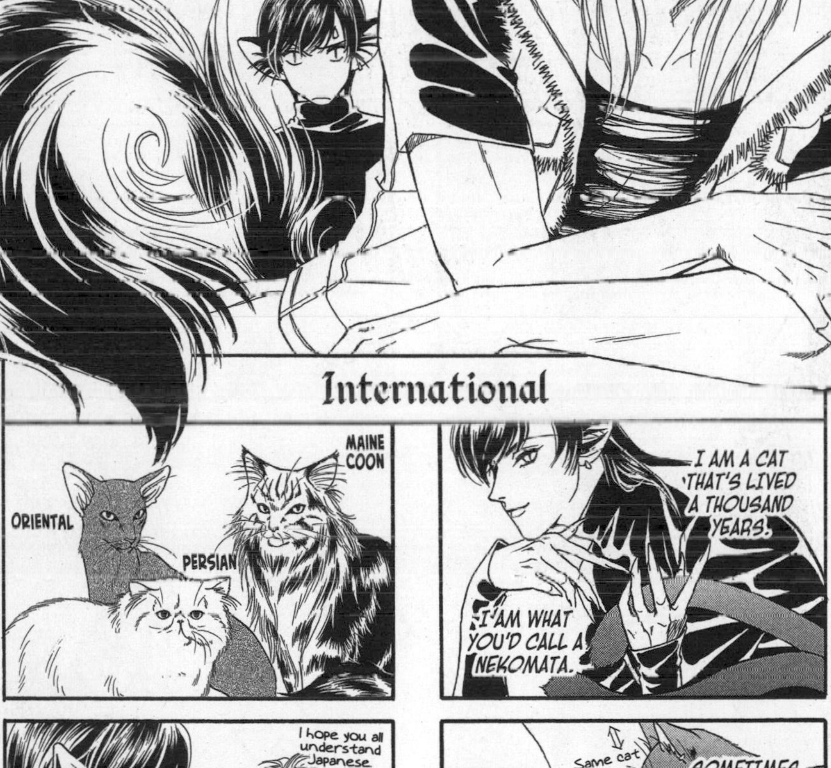
I AM A CAT THAT'S LIVED A THOUSAND YEARS.
I AM WHAT YOU'D CALL A NEKOMATA.
MAINE COON
ORIENTAL
PERSIAN
SOMETIMES YOUNG CATS COME TO ME TO TRAIN...
Same cat
YOU HAVE SOME NEW TRAINEES.
...TO BECOME NEKOMATA.
I hope you all understand Japanese
AFTER A THOUSAND YEARS, NEKOMATA HAVE BECOME VERY INTERNATIONAL.

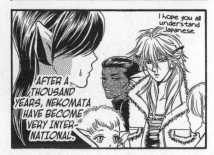

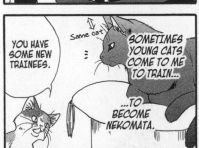

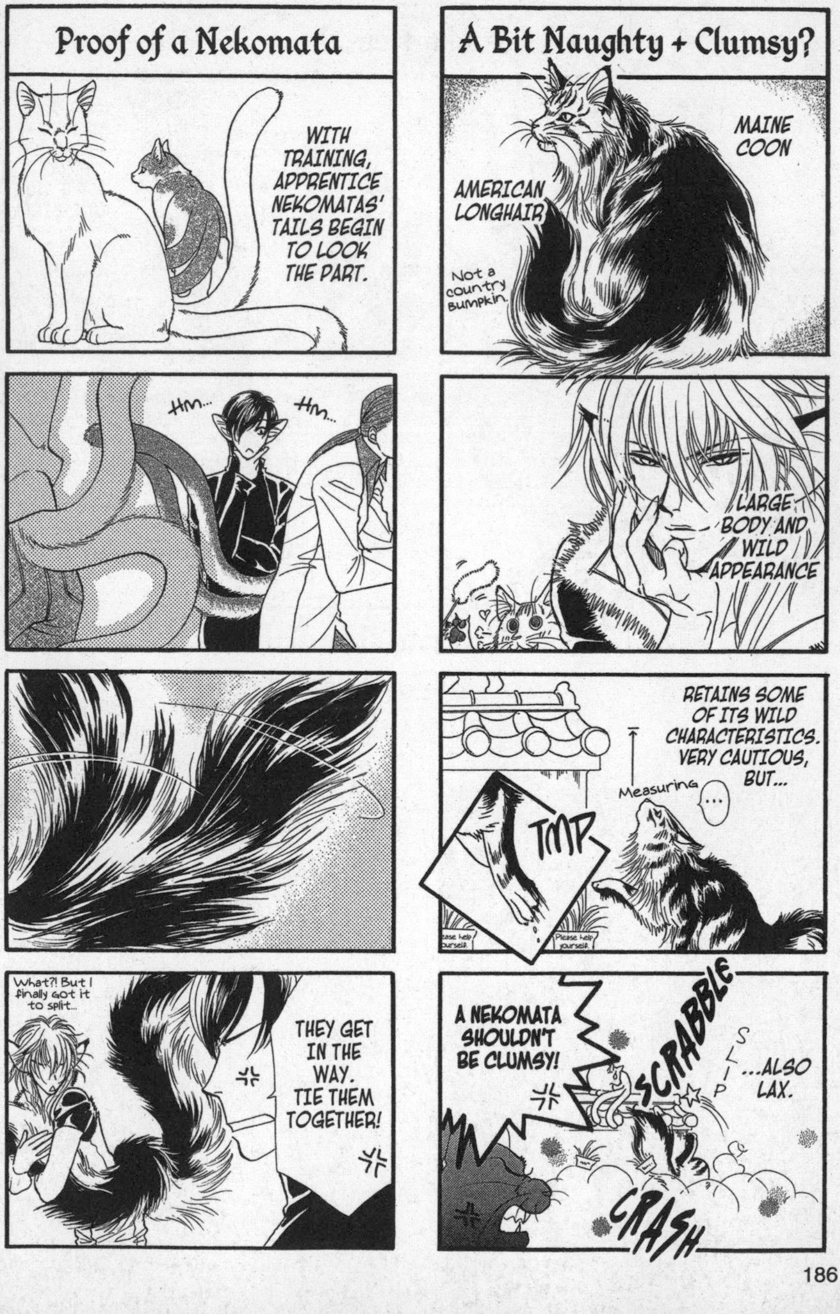
A Bit Naughty + Clumsy?
MAINE COON
AMERICAN LONGHAIR
Not a country bumpkin.
LARGE BODY AND WILD APPEARANCE
RETAINS SOME OF ITS WILD CHARACTERISTICS. VERY CAUTIOUS, BUT...
...
Measuring
TMP
Please help yourself.
Please help yourself.
...ALSO LAX.
SLIP
SCRABBLE
A NEKOMATA SHOULDN'T BE CLUMSY!
CRASH
Proof of a Nekomata
WITH TRAINING, APPRENTICE NEKOMATAS' TAILS BEGIN TO LOOK THE PART.
Hm...
Hm...
THEY GET IN THE WAY. TIE THEM TOGETHER!
What?! But I finally got it to split...

Graduation...?
WHAT ARE YOU GUYS PLANNING TO DO AFTER YOU GRADUATE?
I'm supposed to torment a certain man.
I'm going to haunt the house I lived in.
I-I'M GOING TO PROTECT THAT GIRL.
SHE CAN'T LIVE WITHOUT ME...
YOU'D BETTER HELP YOURSELF, FIRST.
That's right.
You're not ready to graduate yet.
SLIP
Ah!

Nekomata Today ~The End~

Published in the May 2007 *Special Petit Comic Supplement.*

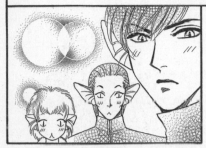

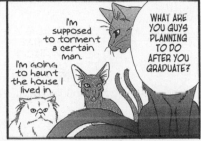

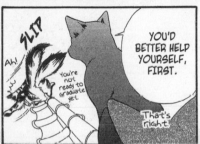

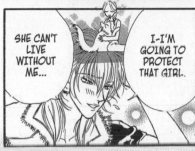

...in this story!

There are no Bats...

## ❦ Tomu Ohmi Profile ❧

Yay! ♥ It's my 22nd book! Thank you so much for choosing to read this! This is the final volume of *Midnight Secretary*. I hope you will keep Kaya and Kyohei in your hearts. A sincere "thank you" for reading this series from beginning to end!

-Tomu Ohmi

# Midnight Secretary
## Volume 7
### Shojo Beat Edition

STORY AND ART BY
## Tomu Ohmi

MIDNIGHT SECRETARY Vol. 7
by Tomu OHMI
© 2007 Tomu OHMI
All rights reserved.
Original Japanese edition published by SHOGAKUKAN.
English translation rights in the United States of America, Canada,
United Kingdom, Ireland, Australia and New Zealand arranged with
SHOGAKUKAN.

English Translation & Adaptation/JN Productions
Touch-up Art & Lettering/Joanna Estep
Design/Izumi Evers
Editor/Pancha Diaz

Printed in the U.S.A.

Published by VIZ Media, LLC
P.O. Box 77010
San Francisco, CA 94107

10 9 8 7 6 5 4 3 2 1
First printing, September 2014

www.viz.com    www.shojobeat.com

# *Happy Marriage?!*

Story & Art by **Maki Enjoji**

## *Can two strangers living together find their way to a happy marriage?!*

In order to help her father, Chiwa Takanashi agrees to an arranged marriage with the company president, Hokuto Mamiya—a man she doesn't know—at the request of Hokuto's grandfather. Chiwa believes the arrangement isn't binding, but her new partner seems to think otherwise...

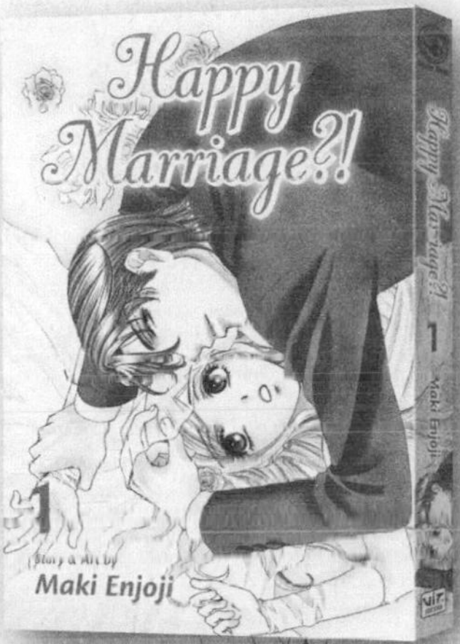
Happy Marriage?!
1
Story & Art by
Maki Enjoji
VIZ

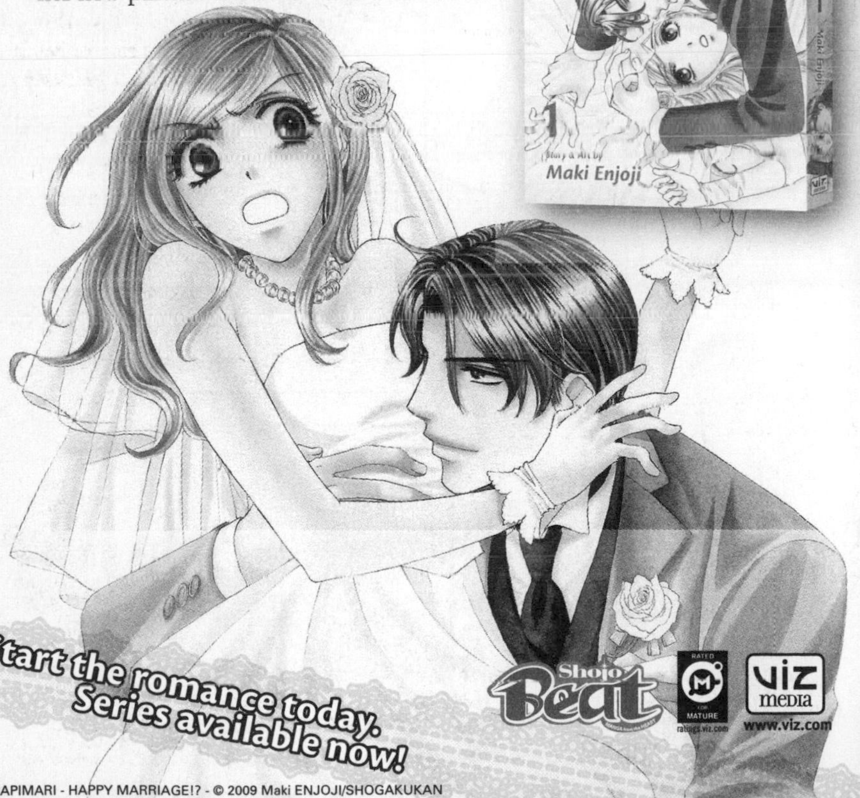
Start the romance today.
Series available now!
Shojo Beat
RATED M FOR MATURE
ratings.viz.com
VIZ media
www.viz.com

# This is the last page.

In keeping with the original Japanese comic format, this book reads from right to left—so action, sound effects, and word balloons are completely reversed. This preserves the orientation of the original artwork—plus, it's fun! Check out the diagram shown here to get the hang of things, and then turn to the other side of the book to get started!

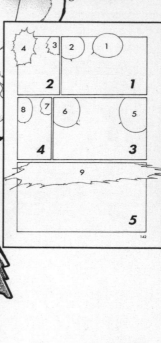